Holiday in
Victoria

CONTENTS

VICTORIA IS...

Barracking for your team at a footy match at the MCG / Watching penguins waddle

from the sea to their burrows on PHILLIP ISLAND / Taking a paddlesteamer ride on the

Murray River from ECHUCA / Panning for gold and enjoying traditional hard-boiled

lollies at SOVEREIGN HILL in Ballarat / Soaking in a mineral spa in DAYLESFORD

MOUNTAIN ASH TREES, YARRA RANGES NATIONAL PARK

or HEPBURN SPRINGS / Driving along the spectacular GREAT OCEAN ROAD to

see the TWELVE APOSTLES / Bushwalking in a timeless mountain landscape in

GRAMPIANS NATIONAL PARK / A daytrip to the DANDENONGS, stopping off at

some cellar doors in the YARRA VALLEY / Hitting the slopes at MOUNT BULLER

VICTORIA is possibly Australia's most diverse state. In a half-hour drive from Melbourne you could be taking in mist-laden mountain ranges and fern gullies. In an hour you could be lying on a sandy beach in a sheltered bay, or surfing in the rugged Southern Ocean. In around four hours you could be standing on the edge of the immense desert that stretches away into Australia's interior. In a country full of mind-numbing distances, nothing seems far away in Victoria.

More than five million people live in Victoria, with 3.8 million in Melbourne. The city was only founded in 1835, as a kind of afterthought to Sydney and Hobart, but by the 1850s Victoria was off to a racing start. A deluge of people from all corners of the world fanned out across the state in response to the madness that was gold. It brought prosperity to Victoria and it also brought the certain wildness treasured in the state's history – uprisings like the Eureka Rebellion and bushrangers like Ned Kelly.

Two centuries later, Victoria has also recognised the richness of its natural landscape. To the west of Melbourne, beyond Geelong, a tract of cool-temperate rainforest unravels on its way to the vivid green Cape Otway, where a lighthouse stands on the cliff-top. The Great Ocean Road winds past here, en route to the state's iconic limestone stacks, the Twelve Apostles.

On the other side of Melbourne, the land falls away into a series of peninsulas, islands and isthmuses. One leads to Wilsons Promontory, an untouched landscape of forested

fact file

Population 5 297 560
Total land area 227 010 square kilometres
People per square kilometre 22.1
Sheep per square kilometre 94
Length of coastline 1868 kilometres
Number of islands 184
Longest river Goulburn River (566 kilometres)
Largest lake Lake Corangamite (209 square kilometres)
Highest mountain Mount Bogong (1986 metres), Alpine National Park
Hottest place Mildura (77 days per year above 30°C)
Wettest place Weeaproinah (1900 millimetres per year), Otway Ranges
Oldest permanent settlement Portland (1834)

Most famous beach Bells Beach, Torquay
Tonnes of gold mined 2500 (2 per cent of world total)
Litres of milk produced on Victorian dairy farms per year 7 billion
Quirkiest festival Great Vanilla Slice Triumph, Ouyen
Famous people Germaine Greer, Barry Humphries, Kylie Minogue
Original name for the Twelve Apostles The Sow and Piglets
Best invention Bionic ear
First Ned Kelly film released *The Story of the Kelly Gang*, 1906 (also believed to be the world's first feature film)
Local beer Victoria Bitter

hills, tea-brown rivers and beaches strewn with enormous rust-red boulders.

The amber-hued Yarra Valley produces some of the country's finest cool-climate wines, and from here the landscape begins its gradual climb up into the High Country, which becomes a vista of snowfields in winter.

Perhaps Victoria's most cherished place is the Grampians, an offshoot of the Great Dividing Range. With a quarter of the state's flora and 80 per cent of its Aboriginal rock art, the Grampians is a living gallery and a superb place for bushwalking and camping.

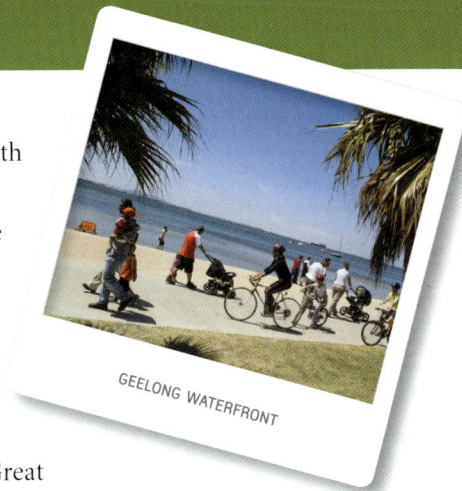

GEELONG WATERFRONT

gift ideas

Raspberry drops (Sovereign Hill, Ballarat) Delicious, old-fashioned lollies from the gold-rush days are still made and sold at Charles Spencer's Confectionery Shop in Main Street and at the Sovereign Hill Gift Shop. See Ballarat p. 64

Replica of Melbourne tram (Best of Souvenirs, Melbourne) Prince Christian of Denmark received a real tram on the occasion of his birth, but you can take home a smaller – and beautifully crafted – version of Melbourne's distinctive transportation. Melbourne Visitor Information Centre, Federation Sq, cnr Flinders and Swanston sts, Melbourne. See p. 8

Football souvenirs (National Sports Museum, Richmond) Scarves, beanies and jerseys with team colours and souvenirs from the home of Australian Rules Football. See MCG and National Sports Museum p. 23, 6 D3

Bread, pastries and provisions (Phillippa's, Armadale and Brighton, Melbourne) A small business that produces delicious baked goods. Highly recommended are the chocolate brownie and the caramel, date and walnut blondie. 1030 High St, Armadale; 608 Hampton St, Brighton. 7 E5

Beach boxes souvenirs (The Esplanade Market St Kilda, Melbourne) Victoria's famous beach boxes are represented on fridge magnets, key holders, coasters and prints. See Markets p. 26, 6 D5

Stefano's products (Mildura) Dine at the acclaimed Stefano's restaurant and then take home jams, chutneys, pasta and pasta sauces. See Mildura p. 120

Wine (Yarra Valley and Mornington Peninsula) Fantastic chardonnay, pinot noir and sparkling varieties from these two wine-producing regions. See Yarra & Dandenongs pp. 32–3, 281 E4 and Mornington Peninsula pp. 34–5, 282 B3

Red Hill muesli (Red Hill Market) This popular muesli comes in five different varieties including roast hazelnut, tropical and Wicked (with chocolate). See Flinders p. 94, 281 E4

Ned Kelly memorabilia (Glenrowan) Victoria's famous bushranger is remembered through everything from replicas of his head armour to belt buckles and T-shirts. See Glenrowan p. 96, 284 C2

Spa and skincare products (Hepburn Springs and Daylesford) The heart of Victoria's Spa Country offers a range of locally made beauty, spa and skincare products from shops and spa centres. See Spa & Garden Country pp. 38–9, p. 88

MELBOURNE is...

A footy match at the MCG / Admiring architecture and art in

FEDERATION SQUARE / Shopping for produce at the QUEEN VICTORIA

MARKET / A stroll along the ST KILDA foreshore / Taking a ferry

trip to WILLIAMSTOWN / Moonlight Cinema in the ROYAL BOTANIC

VISITOR INFORMATION
Melbourne Visitor Information Centre
→ Federation Sq, cnr Flinders and Swanston sts
→ (03) 9658 9658
www.visitmelbourne.com

YARRA RIVER FROM PRINCES BRIDGE

GARDENS during summer / Sweating it out in the crowd at the

AUSTRALIAN OPEN / Stopping for coffee in DEGRAVES STREET, one

of the city's laneways / Live music at a pub in BRUNSWICK STREET,

Fitzroy / Waterside dining at SOUTHGATE or NewQuay, DOCKLANDS

Grid: A B C D

Brunswick West
Brunswick
Brunswick East
Moonee Ponds
Ascot Vale
Flemington
Travancore
Parkville
Carlton North
Princes Hill
Footscray
Seddon
Yarraville
Kensington
North Melbourne
West Melbourne
Docklands
Melbourne
Spotswood
Newport
Port Melbourne
South Melbourne
Southbank
Albert Park
Middle Park
Williamstown
St Kilda
Elwood

CORDITE AV RALEIGH
Homemaker City Maribyrnong
Highpoint SC
Maribyrnong
Flemington Up Market
Flemington Racecourse
Melbourne Zoo
University of Melbourne
Ian Potter Museum of Art
La Mama Theatre
Royal Exhibition Building
Brunetti
Abla's
Carlton
Melbourne Museum
Mari
Claypots
Fire Service Museum
Fitzroy Gardens
Babk Bake Cafe
Footscray Market
Southern Star Observation Wheel
Wonderland Park
Harbour Town
Waterfront City
Cow Up A Tree
NewQuay
Etihad Stadium
Fox Classic Car Collection
Victoria Harbour
Blowhole
Webb Bridge
Carlton Gardens
SEE MELBOURNE PRECINCTS
Melbourne
DFO South Wharf
Sidney Myer Music Bowl
Kings Domain
Shrine of Remembrance
La Trobe's Cottage
South Melbourne Market
Melbourne Park
Olympic Park
Governor House
Children's Park
Royal Botanic Gardens
The Hatton
The Albany
Moonlig Cinem
France Soir
The Hotel Charsfield
Scienceworks & Melbourne Planetarium
Gasworks Art Park
Melbourne Sports & Aquatic Centre
Australian Grand Prix Circuit
Albert Park
ARHS Railway Museum
Fountain Terrace
Tolarno Hotel
The Prince & Il Fornaio
St Kilda Pier
The Palais
St Kilda Sea Baths
Stokehouse
Cafe Di Stasio
The Esplanade Hotel
The Esplanade Market St Kilda
Luna Park
Claypots
Jewish Museum Australi
To Brighton Beach

HOBSONS BAY
PORT PHILLIP BAY
Sandridge Beach
Princes Pier
Station Pier
Ferguson St Pier
Gem Pier
Gellibrand Pier
Breakwater Pier
Williamstown Beach
Shelley Beach
Point Gellibrand
Spirit of Tasmania ferries Melbourne to Devonport
Greenwich Bay
Coode Island
Swanson Dock
Appleton Dock
Victoria Dock
Webb Dock

MAP LEGEND
- ✪ Attraction
- ✪ Where to eat & Where to stay
- ℹ Tourist information
- Shopping precinct

NORMANBY RD
AV Thornbury
45 DAREBIN
CERES Market
ARTHURTON RD SEPARATION
ST GEORGES CK
ST Northcote
HIGH
29 VICTORIA
WESTGARTH
38 ST
Fitzroy North PDE
HEIDELBERG RD
To Heide Museum of Modern Art
46 Clifton Hill
Yarra Bend Park
XANDRA PDE
MERRI
M3 EASTERN FWY
JOHNSTON ST Abbotsford
Studley Park Boathouse
29
34
llingwood
Collingwood Children's Farm Farmers' Market
STUDLEY PARK RD
HODDLE
RIVER
VICTORIA Kew
PDE
32 ST
East lbourne
Victoria Gardens SC
MCG and National Sports Museum
BRIDGE
Richmond 30 RD
Corner Hotel Villa Donati
Dimmees SWAN
BURNLEY
Burnley ST
lbourne ctangular dium
BURNLEY TUNNEL
20
CITYLINK CHURCH
Herring Island
M1
Kanteen
uth rra M1
21
Como House
The Lyall Hotel
The Como
TOORAK
Jam Factory
Toorak RD
28 RD
ahran arket
CHAPEL
MALVERN Cotterville
The Cullen
Greville Records
Chapel Prahran
Street ST HIGH
Bazaar
Windsor Jacques Reymond
24
To Phillippa's ST
DANDENONG ORRONG
Astor Theatre
Armadale RD
ALMA
ALT 1
KERMAN 25 St Kilda East
ST INKERMAN RD
ST BALACLAVA
HOTHAM Caulfield RD
Balaclava
ORRONG KOOYONG RD
To Rippon Lea Estate

Melbourne is renowned as Australia's cultural capital. The city has a decidedly European feel, with neo-Gothic banks and cathedrals, much-loved department stores, art galleries and theatres around every corner. And hidden among these buildings is a string of vibrant laneways given over to cafe culture and boutique shopping. Yet Melbourne wouldn't be Melbourne without sport – seeing a footy match at the MCG is a must.

Melbourne was born in 1835, and quickly became a city. With the boom of Victoria's goldfields, unbelievable wealth was poured into public buildings and tramways, grand boulevards and High Victorian masterpieces.

Today Melbourne's population of around 3 806 000 still enjoys the good life, at the very centre of which is a love of good food and fine dining. You can find comfort food in a cosy corner pub or meals with a view and a waterfront setting – a trend in so many of the country's coastal cities. Southbank, the shopping and eating precinct on the Yarra River, has become an extension of the city centre, while Docklands is the city's latest waterside area.

You might come to Melbourne for the dining and the shopping; the gardens and the architecture; the arts and music; the football, cricket and tennis. The city has as much diversity as it has suburbs, and at last check these were marching right down the Mornington Peninsula.

CBD CENTRAL

Melbourne's central business district (CBD) lies on the north bank of the Yarra River. The train system runs a ring around the CBD and trams amble up and down most of its main streets. Melbourne's heart is bounded by Flinders, Elizabeth, Little Bourke and Russell streets. This central core takes in the eclectic corner of Swanston and Flinders streets, and further in there's a charming network of arcades and backstreets.

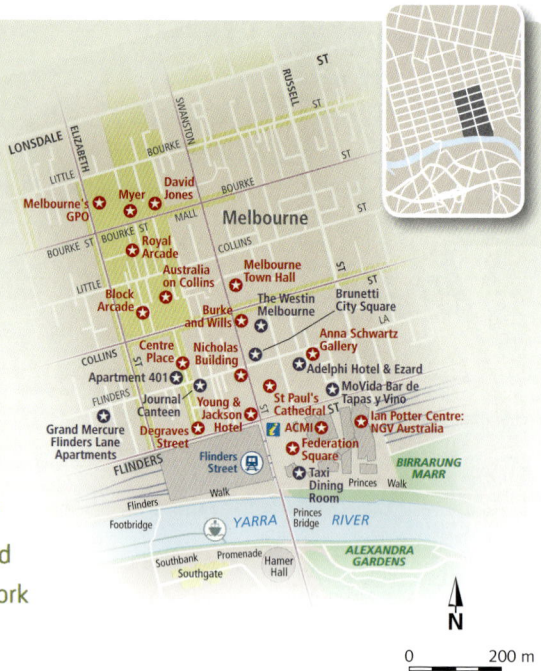

0   200 m

A station, a pub and a cathedral

As the major train station in the CBD, **Flinders Street Station** is the first port of call for many people travelling in from the suburbs.

On the three corners facing the station are three other landmarks: Federation Square *(see next entry)*, St Paul's Cathedral and the **Young and Jackson Hotel**. Across Swanston Street, the grandiose **St Paul's Cathedral** was built in 1891. Its mosaic interior is well worth a look.

Federation Square

Federation Square is the biggest building project to occur in Melbourne in decades – if not in actual size, then at least in terms of its public significance and architectural ambition. The central piazza is paved with 7500 square metres of coloured Kimberley sandstone. Surrounding it are bars, cafes, restaurants and shops, many of them with unique views over Flinders Street Station and the Yarra.

Fed Square's must-visit attractions are the Ian Potter Centre: NGV Australia *(see below)* and the Australian Centre for the Moving Image *(see p. 9)*. One-hour guided tours are available (Mon–Sat, departing at 2.30pm) if you're keen to learn more about the square. *(03) 9928 0096.*

Ian Potter Centre: NGV Australia

Australian art has finally found a home of its own at this gallery. On the ground floor is a large space dedicated to Indigenous art – from traditional sculptures and bark paintings to the bright and expressive works of modern Aboriginal artists. Also in the gallery are the best of the colonial artists, such as Tom Roberts and Arthur Streeton. *Federation Sq; (03) 8620 2222; open 10am–5pm Tues–Wed and Fri–Sun, 10am–9pm Thurs; general admission free. The National Gallery of Victoria's international collection can be found on St Kilda Rd (see p. 17).*

RED CENTRE SCULPTURE, FEDERATION SQUARE

Australian Centre for the Moving Image (ACMI)

ACMI is a museum of the 21st century and an Australian first, exploring all current guises of the moving image. Here you will find cinemas screening films and darkened galleries with screen-based art, as well as temporary exhibitions. Check the newspapers for details of films running or visit the website (www. acmi.net.au). *Federation Sq; (03) 8663 2200, bookings (03) 8663 2583; open 10am–6pm Fri– Wed, 10am–9pm Thurs; general admission free.*

Swanston Street

Your experience of Swanston Street can be totally different depending on which side of the road you walk on. One side of the street is a grand boulevard lined with trees, and dotted with significant buildings and quirky public sculptures. The other side (the west side) seems overcrowded with discount stores, souvenir shops and fast-food outlets. Swanston Street is closed to cars other than taxis.

On the corner of Swanston and Collins streets is the prominent **Melbourne Town Hall**, a venue for various public events including the Melbourne Comedy Festival. Opposite is a statue of **Burke and Wills**, the two explorers who set out on a doomed journey to find the fabled inland sea. On the corner of Bourke Street is the quirky sculpture *Three Businessmen Who Brought Their Own Lunch*. Swanston Street also boasts some fine historic buildings *(see Grand old buildings, p. 27)*, and further north is the State Library of Victoria *(see p. 14)*.

Collins Street

This is Melbourne's most dignified street. The top end near Spring Street has been dubbed the 'Paris end' with its European ambience and designer boutiques. Near Elizabeth Street is **Australia on Collins**, where you will find all the big names in Australian fashion as well as a ground-floor food court. Towards Spencer Street are impressive buildings, such as the Old ANZ Bank *(see Grand old buildings, p. 27)*.

Laneways and arcades

From Flinders Street Station to Bourke Street Mall, you can slip through a world of cafes, fashion boutiques and jewellers, many of them selling one-off items that you just won't find in malls and department stores. But it is also worth it for the walk alone – narrow, darkened and usually bustling, these laneways seem to be a completely separate world to the rest of the city.

The section of **Degraves Street** closest to Flinders Lane is closed to cars and is full of cafes spilling onto the paved street. Across from Degraves Street is **Centre Place**, with more cafes as well as bars and designer-fashion outlets. Towards Collins Street, Centre Place becomes a covered arcade.

Block Arcade runs between Collins and Little Collins streets. It boasts Italian mosaic floors, ornate glass ceilings, tearooms and exclusive clothing boutiques. Follow the arcade to Elizabeth Street, or to the laneway that joins it to Little Collins Street, where there are yet more cafes.

Over Little Collins Street is **Royal Arcade**, Australia's oldest surviving arcade. Above the Little Collins Street entrance stand two giants, **Gog and Magog**, of the ancient British legend. You can take Royal Arcade to either Bourke Street Mall or Elizabeth Street. (To get to the mall you can also take the adjacent, cafe-lined **Causeway**.)

Recent building works in the city, such as the GPO development in Bourke Street Mall *(see next entry)*, the renovation of Melbourne Central *(see p. 15)* and the QV site *(see p. 14)*,

have opened up more of the old laneways, restoring the original vision of Melbourne's designer, Robert Hoddle.

Bourke Street Mall

Bourke Street Mall is the heart of Melbourne's shopping district, with big department stores and brand-name fashion outlets. Between Elizabeth and Swanston streets the mall is closed to cars, making it the territory of trams and pedestrians.

The **Myer** and **David Jones** department stores both have entrances on the mall. Myer, in particular, is renowned for its fine window displays at Christmas. At the west end of the mall is **GPO Melbourne**, once the city's post office but now a smart shopping complex showcasing a who's who of fashion labels, cafes and bars. If you fancy a break from shopping, grab a seat along the mall and watch life wander by. More often than not there will be a busker performing for your entertainment.

Art spaces

Flinders Lane is home to a terrific array of art galleries *(see Flinders Lane galleries, p. 13)*, including the **Anna Schwartz Gallery**. With exhibitions that draw on a wide variety of art forms and often push the envelope, expect to be surprised and delighted, especially if you're into conceptual art. On the corner of Flinders Lane and Swanston Street, the **Nicholas Building** is an important address in the Melbourne arts scene, home to numerous small artist-run spaces. Keep an ear out for open studio days, when painters, jewellers, shoe makers, illustrators and the like open their doors to the public. *Anna Schwartz Gallery: 185 Flinders La; (03) 9654 6131; open 12–6pm Tues–Fri, 1–5pm Sat; admission free. Nicholas Building: 37 Swanston St; open studio inquiries (03) 9650 2590.*

CBD WEST

This part of Melbourne stretches from the Queen Victoria Market down to the Yarra River, taking in the city's legal district including the **Supreme Court of Victoria** on William Street. Bounded by Spencer Street to the west, the old Spencer Street train station was replaced in 2006 with the architecturally superb **Southern Cross Railway Station**. It is worth a visit even if you're not planning a train ride.

Hardware Lane

Sitting between Bourke and Lonsdale streets, west of Bourke Street Mall, Hardware Lane comes alive at lunchtime and in the evening when office workers and bar seekers crowd the outdoor tables. The cobblestone paving, the window boxes and the brightly painted facades of the old buildings add to the atmosphere.

Former Royal Mint

Two blocks north-west of the Supreme Court of Victoria, the Old Royal Mint was built in Renaissance Revival style, set off by a dazzling coat of arms. Originally constructed to mint the bounty from Victoria's goldfields, it operated until 1968 and is now home to the **Hellenic Museum**, which holds items from the Byzantine period and displays related to Greek migration to Australia. *Cnr William and Latrobe sts; (03) 8615 9016; open 10am–3pm Tues–Thurs.*

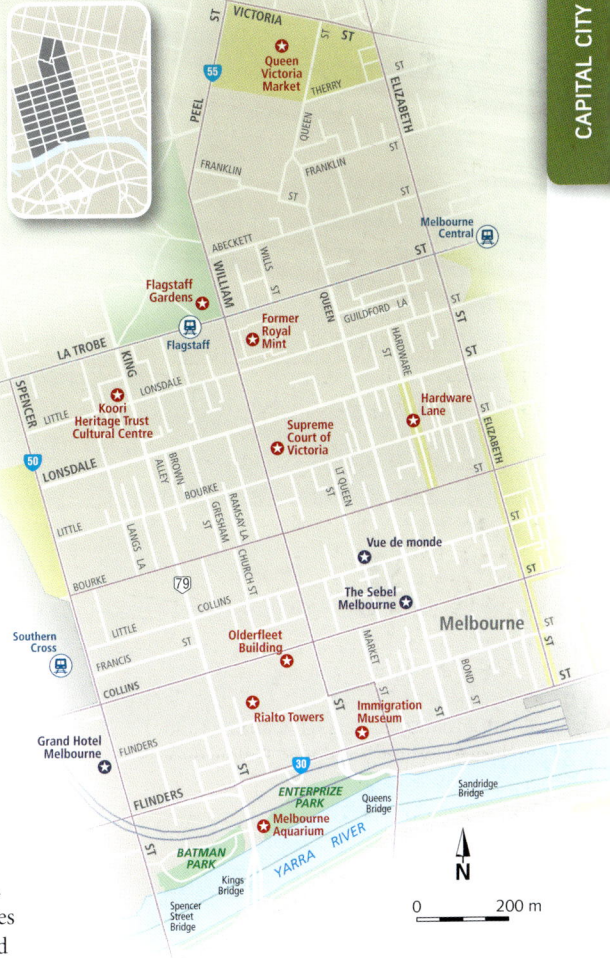

Melbourne Aquarium

Beside the Yarra River, take a journey into the depths of the ocean, past rockpool and mangrove habitats and a surreal display of jellyfish, then into a tunnel and the 'fishbowl' for a close-up encounter with sharks, stingrays and multitudes of fish. For kids there is the interactive 'Fishworks', and for those still yearning for the colours of the tropics, an impressive floor-to-ceiling coral atoll. The spectacular new **Antarctica**

FRUIT AND VEGETABLE SHED, QUEEN VICTORIA MARKET

exhibition, featuring King and Gentoo penguins among other Antarctic creatures, is a must-see. *Cnr King and Flinders sts; (03) 9923 5999; open 9.30am–6pm daily.*

Immigration Museum

At first glance this might seem like a specialist museum, but no subject could be more generally relevant in Australia, where migration has been constant since the first days of European settlement. The Immigration Museum is about journeys, tumultuous new beginnings, and people coming from all corners of the world and bringing their traditions with them. It also investigates Australia's changing government policies on immigration, and how they continue to shape the country. *400 Flinders St; (03) 9927 2700; open 10am–5pm daily.*

Koorie Heritage Trust Cultural Centre

As you walk through this centre you realise the drastic, violent and totally irreversible changes made to a culture over 40 000 years old. Displays take you through the local traditions and lifestyle, including food and crafts, as well as events that have occurred in the last two centuries. There are also changing exhibitions by local Aboriginal artists. *295 King St; (03) 8622 2600; open 10am–4pm Tues–Sun; entry by gold coin donation.*

Queen Victoria Market

This famous market is spread across 7 hectares under the shelter of a massive shed. The meat hall is at the Elizabeth Street end, while outside all manner of fruit, vegetable and herb stalls extend towards the horizon. On weekends, Saturdays in particular, the aisles are crammed with shoppers from all over Melbourne, and the wide range of clothing and souvenirs make this a hot spot for tourists as well. *Main entrance cnr Elizabeth and Victoria sts; (03) 9320 5822; open 6am–2pm Tues and Thurs, 6am–5pm Fri, 6am–3pm Sat, 9am–4pm Sun.*

On Wednesday evenings during summer, the 'Queen Vic' takes on a whole new character with the **Suzuki Night Market**. At these times it feels more like a festival than a market, with live music, international food and a healthy dose of alternative-clothing and craft stalls.

Flagstaff Gardens

Originally known as Burial Hill – many of Melbourne's early settlers ended up here – Flagstaff Gardens were Melbourne's first public gardens and once served as a signalling station for ships arriving from Britain. With open lawns, mature trees (including several lovely Moreton Bay fig trees and avenues of elms), a rose garden, public barbecues and tennis/netball/handball/volleyball courts, it is a lovely space in which to enjoy some time out from the city bustle. *Bounded by William, Latrobe, King and Dudley sts; sports bookings (03) 9663 5888.*

CBD EAST

This is Melbourne's most distinguished quarter, taking in some fine old buildings and the government district. The Parliament of Victoria occupies a suitably prominent position on Spring Street at the top of a hill. At the top end of Collins Street is the Melbourne Club, where Melbourne's male elite have been socialising and doing business since the city's earliest days.

0   200 m

N

Parliament of Victoria

The Parliament of Victoria is perched atop a grand run of steps, which are a popular spot for wedding photos. Built in stages between 1856 and 1929, the building remains incomplete – an ornate dome in the centre was originally supposed to be double its height. From 1901 to 1927 this was the seat of federal government before it moved to Canberra. Free tours of the building run on days when parliament is not sitting; sitting dates are published on the parliament's website (www.parliament.vic.gov.au). *Spring St, facing Bourke St; (03) 9651 8911.*

Flinders Lane galleries

This laneway boasts the highest concentration of commercial galleries in Australia, mainly in the section between Spring and Swanston streets. There is a strong focus on Indigenous and contemporary art, with standout galleries including **Flinders Lane Gallery**, exhibiting emerging and established Australian contemporary artists; **Gallery Gabrielle Pizzi**, with Aboriginal art from many of Australia's lesser known regions; and **Craft Victoria**, with an excellent gallery and retail space fostering creativity in craft and design. *Flinders Lane Gallery: 137 Flinders La; (03) 9654 3332; open 11am–6pm Tues–Fri, 11am–4pm Sat. Gallery Gabrielle Pizzi: Level 3, 75 Flinders La; (03) 9654 2944; open 10am–5.30pm Tues–Fri, 11am–5pm Sat. Craft Victoria: 31 Flinders La; (03) 9650 7775; open 10am–5pm Tues–Sat; admission free.*

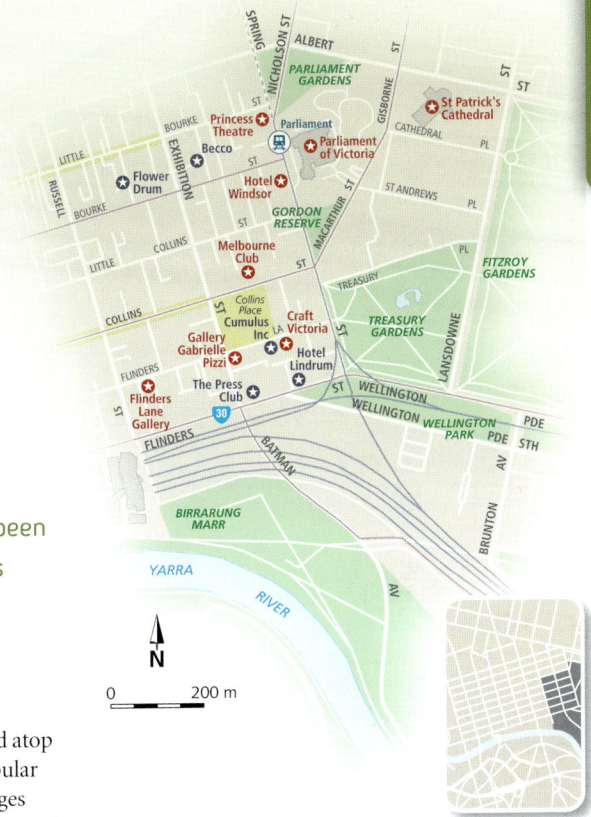

CBD NORTH

This part of town is occupied mainly by office buildings, but there are some interesting places among them, such as the Old Melbourne Gaol, the State Library of Victoria, Chinatown, and the QV shopping and food precinct.

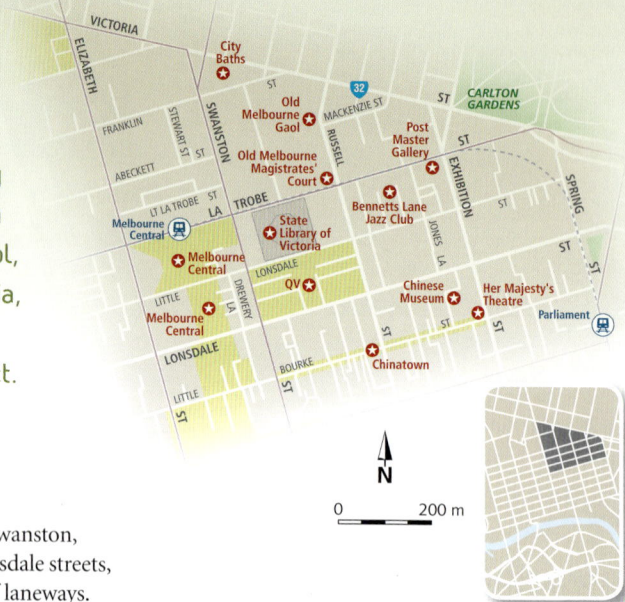

0   200 m

QV

Occupying the block between Swanston, Lonsdale, Russell and Little Lonsdale streets, QV is divided up into a series of laneways. You can weave through here at your leisure, maybe stopping in at one of the cafes, or go shopping with a purpose: high-end fashion stores line Albert Coates Lane, while Artemis Lane is a wonderland of homewares. You can also explore Red Cape and Jane Bell lanes. (The medical-themed lane names relate to the site's history – QV was once the site of the Queen Victoria Women's Hospital, a part of which still remains.) When you've finished shopping, step into one of QV's various eateries. *Open 10am–6pm Mon–Wed and Sat, 10am–7pm Thurs, 10am–9pm Fri, 10am–5pm Sun.*

State Library of Victoria

The State Library of Victoria's front steps and lawn make a great spot for soaking up the sun. In fact, pre–Fed Square, this was the city centre's biggest public space and the main meeting spot for demonstrations. On the third floor of the Roman-style building is an impressive five-storey octagonal reading room, recently restored to its original sky-lit splendour. The library also incorporates several art galleries and a cafe. *Cnr Lonsdale and Swanston sts; (03) 8664 7000; open 10am–9pm Mon–Thurs, 10am–6pm Fri–Sun.*

Old Melbourne Gaol

Melbourne Gaol was the setting for the execution of some of early Victoria's most notorious criminals. Discover the horrifying reality of death masks and the *Particulars of Execution*, a how-to book on this gruesome subject. If you are brave enough, join a candle-lit Hangman's Night Tour (conducted four times weekly at 8.30pm, 7.30pm in winter) or a ghost hunt (held monthly); contact Ticketek (13 2849) for bookings. *Russell St, between Victoria and Latrobe sts; (03) 8663 7228; open 9.30am–5pm daily; at 12.30pm and 2pm Sat the story of Ned Kelly, 'Such a Life', is performed (free with entry).*

ONE OF THE ARCHWAYS AT THE ENTRANCE TO MELBOURNE'S CHINATOWN

Chinatown

Chinatown has prospered and flourished since the first Chinese migrated to Victoria at the beginning of the gold rush. Decorated archways herald the entrance to the Little Bourke Street strip at the Swanston, Russell and Exhibition street ends. Like Chinatowns around the world, Melbourne's Chinatown is distinctive, with lanterns decorating the street at night and exotic aromas drifting out through the doorways of small restaurants.

The **Chinese Museum**, in Cohen Place off Little Bourke Street, tells the tale of the Chinese who migrated to Australia in search of the 'New Gold Mountain', and is also the resting place of Dai Loong (Big Dragon), which roams the streets during Chinese New Year. *22 Cohen Pl; (03) 9662 2888; open 10am– 5pm daily.*

Lonsdale Street

The section of Lonsdale Street between Russell and Swanston streets is the centre of Melbourne's Greek community. On the southern side are Greek bookshops, music stores and, of course, cafes and restaurants.

Melbourne Central

The Melbourne Central shopping complex has undergone a major facelift, with some serious thought given to the way Melburnians like to shop. The central shot tower and pointed glass ceiling remain, but the complex now offers less of a one-stop shopping experience and more of an adventure through a network of arcades and laneways, each with its own unique character. But this is not so much an innovation as a restoration of Melbourne as it was intended to be. An underground shopping concourse leads from the Lonsdale Street entrance to Melbourne Central Station. *Open 10am–6pm Mon–Thurs and Sat, 10am–9pm Fri, 10am–5pm Sun.*

SOUTHBANK

This inner-city suburb takes in some of Melbourne's best leisure and dining precincts, as well as a concentration of public arts institutions. Behind Flinders Street Station is Southgate, a stylish shopping and dining area on the Yarra River. On the riverbanks here are also some interesting public sculpture pieces.

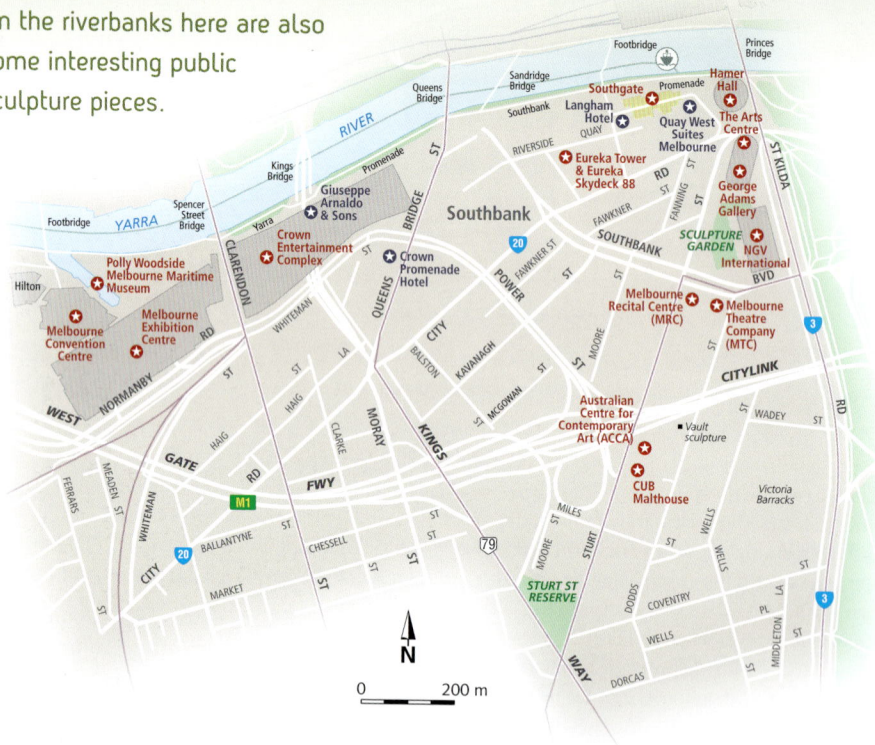

Map labels: Footbridge, Princes Bridge, Sandridge Bridge, Hamer Hall, Queens Bridge, Southgate, Promenade, Southbank, Langham Hotel, The Arts Centre, Quay West Suites Melbourne, RIVERSIDE, QUAY, Eureka Tower & Eureka Skydeck 88, RD, George Adams Gallery, Kings Bridge, Promenade, ST, RD, ST KILDA, Spencer Street Bridge, Giuseppe Arnaldo & Sons, FANNING, Footbridge, YARRA, Yarra, Southbank, FAWKNER, SCULPTURE GARDEN, NGV International, Crown Entertainment Complex, BRIDGE, SOUTHBANK, BVD, Polly Woodside Melbourne Maritime Museum, Crown Promenade Hotel, CLARENDON, QUEENS, POWER, ST, Melbourne Recital Centre (MRC), Melbourne Theatre Company (MTC), Hilton, WHITEMAN, CITY, BALSTON, KAVANAGH, MOORE, ST, CITYLINK, Melbourne Convention Centre, Melbourne Exhibition Centre, RD, NORMANBY, ST, LA, ST, MCGOWAN, Australian Centre for Contemporary Art (ACCA), Vault sculpture, WADEY, RD, WEST, HAAG, CLARKE, MORAY, KINGS, ST, CUB Malthouse, Victoria Barracks, GATE, HAIG, RD, FWY, STURT, WELLS, FERRARS, MEADEN, WHITEMAN, CITY, BALLANTYNE, CHESSELL, ST, MILES, MOORE ST, MARKET, ST, STURT ST RESERVE, DODDS, COVENTRY, PL, MIDDLETON, WELLS, WAY, DORCAS

0   200 m

N

Eureka Tower

Standing 300 metres and 92 storeys high, the Eureka Tower usurped the title of 'Melbourne's tallest building' from the Rialto (see p. 12) in 2006. This structure is a particularly prominent feature of Melbourne's city skyline due to the 24-carat, gold-plated glass across the top ten levels. On the 88th floor, **Eureka Skydeck 88** offers the ultimate 360-degree view of the city, bay and mountains. Viewfinders placed around the deck pinpoint major attractions. For a heart-stopping experience, step inside

The Edge, a 3-metre glass cube that projects out of the side of the building. On the ground floor is the Serendipity Table, with information on the history of Melbourne. *7 Riverside Quay, Southbank; (03) 9693 8888; open 10am–10pm daily.*

Southgate

Over 15 years ago, Southgate was just like Docklands (see p. 19) – an industrial site being slowly reinvented. Apartments, office blocks, shops, restaurants and a tree-lined promenade have been added to form what is today an essential part of Melbourne.

On the ground floor of the complex is a food court and shops. As you make your way to the top, the restaurants and bars become increasingly exclusive and the shops become boutiques selling glassware, art and jewellery. Some of Melbourne's finest restaurants are located on the top floors.

Crown Entertainment Complex

This huge complex begins just over Queensbridge Street. As well as a casino, Crown contains shops, a food court, nightclubs and cinemas. Restaurants include world-class dining such as Neil Perry's Rockpool Bar and Grill, Japanese restaurant Nobu and Silks for Chinese banquets. The big names in fashion such as Versace and Armani reside here too, and items regularly top the $1000 mark.

Melbourne Convention and Exhibition Centre and Polly Woodside

Over Clarendon Street from Crown is the **Melbourne Convention and Exhibition Centre**, with its striking entrance angled upwards over the water. This is the venue for most of Melbourne's major expos, from car shows to wedding exhibitions. *2 Clarendon St, Southbank; (03) 9235 8000.*

Next to the centre is the **Polly Woodside Melbourne Maritime Museum**, which allows the 1885 tall ship *Polly Woodside* to shine in all her glory. Visitors can walk around the deck and experience some maritime history. A glamorous new riverfront promenade links Southbank and Docklands, with new cafes, retail outlets, apartments and offices. *South Wharf, Southbank; (03) 9656 9800.*

The Arts Centre

The Arts Centre, on St Kilda Road over Princes Bridge from Flinders Street Station, consists of two main buildings – **Hamer Hall** and the **Theatres Building**, with its distinctive lattice spire intended to resemble a ballerina's tutu.

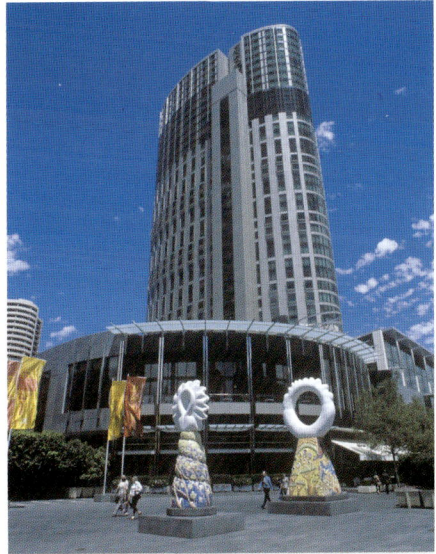

SCULPTURES OUTSIDE CROWN CASINO

The Theatres Building plunges six levels below St Kilda Road and includes three theatres: the State Theatre, with seating for 2000 and a venue for opera, ballets and musicals; the Playhouse, for drama; and the George Fairfax Studio, a smaller drama venue.

If you are not heading to a concert or a theatre show, you can still visit the **George Adams Gallery**, also under the spire. This is the main exhibition space for the **Performing Arts Museum**, which preserves a variety of Australian performing-arts memorabilia. *100 St Kilda Rd; (03) 9281 8000; open 8am–end of last performance daily; admission free.*

NGV International

The large grey building next to the Arts Centre has been the home of the National Gallery of Victoria since 1968. After recent renovations, it now houses the gallery's highly regarded international component, including permanent and touring exhibitions. There are more than 30 galleries, a water curtain at the entrance that has become a Melbourne icon, and a magnificent stained-glass roof by Leonard French towards the back of the building. *180 St Kilda Rd; (03) 8620 2222; open 10am–5pm Wed–Mon; general admission free. NGV Australia can be found at Federation Square (see p. 8).*

Sturt Street arts

Behind St Kilda Road is Sturt Street, home to four arts institutions – the CUB Malthouse, the Australian Centre for Contemporary Art (ACCA) and the new Melbourne Recital Centre (MRC)/Melbourne Theatre Company (MTC) complex.

Once a malt factory, the **CUB Malthouse** has four theatres and is home to the Malthouse Theatre company, dedicated to contemporary theatre. Next door, the **ACCA** is housed in a rusted-steel building that is intended to resemble the colour of Uluru against a blue sky. Inside the stark structural forms are changing contemporary Australian and international exhibitions, quite often confronting and interactive. *CUB Malthouse: 113 Sturt St; bookings (03) 9685 5111. ACCA: 111 Sturt St; (03) 9697 9999; open 10am–5pm Tues–Fri, 11am–6pm Sat–Sun and public holidays; admission free.*

Resembling a giant beehive in parts, the stunning new **Melbourne Recital Centre** gives ACCA a run for its money in the architectural stakes. Comprising the 1001-seat Elisabeth Murdoch Hall for chamber music, the 150-seat Salon for more intimate performances and public spaces including a cafe-bar, it's an exciting addition to Melbourne's arts precinct. The adjacent new home of the **Melbourne Theatre Company** is an equally fascinating, cutting-edge structure. *Cnr Sturt St and Southbank Blvd, Southbank; MRC bookings (03) 9699 3333, MTC bookings 1300 723 038.*

CBD SOUTH-EAST

Sidney Myer Music Bowl 6 D3

Set in the Kings Domain gardens, the iconic Sidney Myer Music Bowl is a massive grassy

amphitheatre leading down to a stage, above which floats a soaring, tent-like roof. Much-loved by Melburnians for its annual Christmas extravaganza, Carols by Candlelight, it also hosts numerous other summertime events, including free concerts by the Melbourne Symphony Orchestra. Just fabulous for a champagne picnic on a starry summer's eve. *Linlithgow Ave, Kings Domain; (03) 9281 8000.*

Gardens 6 D3, 6 D4

Bordered by the curve of the Yarra and the bitumen of St Kilda Road is a series of public gardens, including Kings Domain and the Royal Botanic Gardens. In **Kings Domain** is the Sidney Myer Music Bowl *(see previous entry)* and the imposing **Shrine of Remembrance**. Deep within the shrine stands a statue of two soldiers, representing the generations of Australians who have fought in various wars around the world. You access the shrine from the chambers below, through the visitor centre. From the balcony at the top there are views straight down St Kilda Road. The shrine is the centre for Anzac Day commemorations. *Birdwood Ave, South Yarra; (03) 9661 8100; open 10am–5pm daily; admission free.*

To the east of the shrine is **La Trobe's Cottage**, a prefabricated house built in England and brought to Australia for the residence of Victoria's first lieutenant governor. Tours of this structure and magnificent **Government House**, located nearby but hidden behind a tangle of vegetation, run from here on Mondays and Wednesdays. *Tour bookings (03) 8663 7260.*

Directly opposite the shrine, across Birdwood Avenue, is Observatory Gate, behind which are the renowned **Royal Botanic Gardens**. Inside the gate is a cafe and the Old Melbourne Observatory. The visitor centre here has information on walks and activities in the gardens, including night tours at the observatory and the Aboriginal Heritage Walk *(see Walks and tours, p. 29).* The **Children's Garden**, open from Wednesday to Sunday (daily during school holidays), was created as a fun and interactive space for kids, with a program of hands-on activities. In summer the botanic gardens also host **Moonlight Cinema**; programs are available around town, and the films on offer range from new releases to the classics.

If you are after a riverfront picnic spot, look just outside the botanic gardens across Alexandra Avenue. Free gas barbecues dot the Yarra bank from Swan Street Bridge to Anderson Street.

Melbourne and Olympic parks 6 D3

Between the city and the suburbs of Richmond and Abbotsford are Melbourne's biggest sporting venues, scattered on either side of the rail yards like giant resting UFOs. The two major ones are the **MCG** (p. 23) and **Melbourne Park**, incorporating the **Rod Laver** and **Hisense** arenas, and home of the Australian Open and big-ticket concerts. Heading towards Richmond, the soon-to-be-open **Melbourne Rectangular Stadium** in

the **Olympic Park** precinct will be the home of Storm (rugby) and Melbourne Victory (soccer). *Olympic Blvd; (03) 9286 1600.*

DOCKLANDS

Melbourne's CBD is once again on the move, this time west across Spencer Street and the rail yards to Docklands. Until the 1960s this was a busy shipping port; now it is being transformed into a residential, business, entertainment and retail precinct, with seven mini neighbourhoods including NewQuay, Waterfront City and Victoria Harbour.

NewQuay and Waterfront City 6 C3

At the northern end of Docklands, the adjacent waterfront neighbourhoods of NewQuay and

ETERNAL FLAME, SHRINE OF REMEMBRANCE

Waterfront City comprise high-rise apartments, offices, retail outlets, galleries, marinas and the bulk of Docklands' bars and restaurants. Entertainment options also abound, including **Movies on the Waterfront**, free outdoor movies screened between September and December (Thursdays and Fridays from 7.30pm); **Wonderland Park**, with a host of rides for kids and an ice-skating rink; and Waterfront City's exciting **Southern Star Observation Wheel**. The new **Harbour Town** shopping centre is home to a large range of brand outlets and fashion stores, while trash-and-treasure lovers will want to check out the weekly **Collector's Sunday Market** (10am–4pm).

Etihad Stadium 6 C3

A major venue for Australian Football League (AFL) games, A-League soccer matches and concerts, Etihad Stadium is a Colosseum-like stadium with a retractable roof (very handy for when the weather is inclement). You can go on a 'Behind the Scenes' tour to inspect, among other things, the AFL players' change rooms and the coaches' box. The one-hour tours leave at 11am, 1pm and 3pm Monday to Friday from the Customer Service Centre opposite Gates 2 and 3. *Bounded by Bourke and Latrobe sts, Wurundjeri Way and Harbour Esplanade; tour bookings (03) 8625 7277.*

Art Journey 6 C3

A self-guided urban art tour, the Art Journey takes you past 29 superb, large-scale public artworks, including the whimsical wind-powered **Blowhole**, the sublimely sculptural **Webb Bridge** for pedestrians and cyclists, and the amusing **Cow Up A Tree** (which is exactly that). You can also make use of the facilities along the way, including barbecues, recreation areas and a terrific children's playground. Pick up a copy of the Art Journey brochure from the Melbourne Visitor Information Centre, or download one from the Melbourne Docklands website (www.docklands.com.au).

Fox Classic Car Collection 6 C3

With its incredible collection of vintage cars, including Bentley, Jaguar, Rolls Royce and some ultra-cool Porsche and Mercedes Benz makes, the Fox Classic Car Collection has up to 80 vehicles on display at any given time. Located in the historic Queen's Warehouse building (originally built as a customs house). *Cnr Batman's Hill Dr and Collins St; (03) 9620 4086; open 10am–2pm Tues Feb–Nov.*

INNER SOUTH-EAST

Beyond the gardens south-east of the CBD are some of the city's most exclusive suburbs: South Yarra, Toorak, Malvern and Armadale. South Yarra and Toorak centre on Toorak Road, where exclusive clothing and footwear stores, as well as cafes and food shops, line the street. Chapel Street runs in the other direction, from South Yarra into St Kilda, and is virtually non-stop shops for three major blocks, from Toorak Road to Dandenong Road.

Chapel and Greville streets 7 E4

The northern end of Chapel Street, between Toorak and Commercial roads, is the place to come for the latest in fashion. About halfway down this stretch is the **Jam Factory**, a shopping complex and food court inside the old premises of the Australian Jam Company. Inside is a cinema complex that screens most of the new releases as well as some arthouse titles.

Just around the corner from Chapel Street on Commercial Road is the **Prahran Market**, Australia's oldest continually running market. *163 Commercial Rd, South Yarra; (03) 8290 8220; open dawn–5pm Tues, Thurs and Sat, dawn–6pm Fri, 10am–3pm Sun.*

A little further up Chapel Street, Greville Street runs off to the west. The narrow strip is lined with cafes, bars, hip clothing shops and original occupants such as Greville Records.

If the northern end of Chapel Street is the fashion darling, the Prahran/Windsor end, south of Commercial Road, is its more down-to-earth, homely sibling. Lined with dozens of interesting cafes, restaurants and shops, it is a fantastic stretch to browse and graze.

Como House and Herring Island 7 E4

Como House is a National Trust–listed mansion at the end of Williams Road. Stroll around the gardens and take a tour of the house, complete with the original furnishings of the Armytage family. You can visit the gorgeous cafe (open Wednesday to Sunday) without paying admission. Nearby is Como Landing, where you can take a punt across to Herring Island in the middle of the Yarra. This artificial island boasts a sculpture park and picnic/barbecue facilities. *Como House: Cnr Williams Rd and Lechlade Ave, South Yarra; (03) 9827 2500; open 10am–5pm daily. Herring Island punt: 12–5pm Sat–Sun during daylight saving.*

INNER NORTH

Carlton and Fitzroy are two lively inner suburbs to the north and north-east of the city. Carlton is the heart of Victorian terrace territory, while Fitzroy is where many young Melburnians would choose to live if they could afford it. Smith Street, a major street to the east, is blossoming with cafes, health-food shops and independent fashion designers.

Lygon Street, Carlton 6 D2

This is Carlton's main artery and the centre of Melbourne's Italian population, with many restaurants, cafes, bookstores, clothing shops and the excellent **Cinema Nova**. Stop for authentic pasta, pizza, gelato and good coffee at places such as **Brunetti**, on Faraday Street, an institution that is always crowded with Italian pastry lovers. You can also head to **Rathdowne Street**, parallel to Lygon Street, which has more cafes, restaurants and food stores.

Brunswick Street, Fitzroy 6 D2

Brunswick Street offers an eclectic mix of cafes, pubs and shops. Anything goes in Brunswick Street – young professionals come here for leisurely weekend breakfasts at cafes such as **Babka Bakery/Cafe** and **Mario's**. This is also the centre of Melbourne's live-music scene *(see Entertainment, p. 28).*

Royal Exhibition Building 6 D2

The Royal Exhibition Building is Melbourne's most significant historic building – and arguably the country's now that it has become Australia's first man-made structure to achieve World Heritage status. The building and the adjacent Carlton Gardens were admitted to the list in 2004, joining the likes of Uluru and the Great Barrier Reef.

A vast hall topped with a central dome, it is considered an enduring monument to the international exhibition movement that began in the mid-19th century. No comparable 'great halls' survive from other international exhibitions held elsewhere in the world.

At dusk each night the building is illuminated, creating a vista that harks back to the heady days of 1880s Melbourne. Tours to view its interior run from the adjacent Melbourne Museum *(see next entry)* at 2pm daily whenever the building is not in use (bookings 13 1102). The area comes alive during the Melbourne International Flower & Garden Show (March–April). *11 Nicholson St, Carlton.*

Melbourne Museum 6 D2

Melbourne Museum is housed in the spaceship-like structure of metal and glass next to the Royal Exhibition Building. It is

ST KILDA PIER AT SUNSET

the home of Phar Lap, Australia's champion racing horse, standing proud and tall in a dimly lit room. Bunjilaka is an Aboriginal cultural centre telling the Koorie story from the Koorie perspective. Other features of the museum include dinosaur skeletons, a living rainforest and impressive displays on science, the mind and the body. Located in the same building is the **IMAX Theatre**, screening films in 2D and 3D. *Melbourne Museum: Nicholson St, Carlton; 13 1102; open 10am–5pm daily.*

Melbourne Zoo 6 C1

This is Australia's oldest zoo, and the single iron-barred enclosure that remains is a testimony to the days when animals were kept in minuscule cages. Today things are rather different – take the Trail of the Elephants, for instance, where elephants live in a re-creation of an Asian rainforest, complete with an elephant-sized plunge pool (and Asian hawker stalls for visitors). Another perennial favourite here is the Butterfly House, where butterflies are quite happy to land on you as you pass through. From mid-January to mid-March the zoo runs a popular program of open-air, evening jazz sessions called Zoo Twilights. *Elliott Ave, Parkville; (03) 9285 9300; open 9am–5pm daily, to 9.30pm for Zoo Twilights.*

INNER EAST

Richmond and Abbotsford lie to the east of the city, and for both food and clothing the combination of quality and price here is hard to beat. Further out is a stretch of parkland that follows the winding path of the Yarra River.

Bridge Road, Richmond 7 E3

Bridge Road is Richmond's main artery, and between Hoddle and Church streets it is a shopper's heaven. Many a tour bus pulls up here, with shoppers pouring into the designer-clothing stores and factory outlets. In the next block, between Church and Burnley streets, is a strip of reasonably priced restaurants offering various cuisines.

Swan Street, Richmond 7 E3

Swan Street, south of Bridge Road, is another good spot for wining and dining, and features the Corner Hotel, staging local bands. The original Dimmeys store is on Swan Street too, with its distinctive domed clock tower. This has been a great place for a bargain since 1853.

Victoria Street, Abbotsford 7 E3

Victoria Street, north of Bridge Road, is a living, breathing piece of Vietnam. From Hoddle Street to Church Street it overflows with Asian grocery stores and Vietnamese restaurants, where the focus is on authentic food, fast.

Melbourne Cricket Ground (MCG) and National Sports Museum 6 D3

A footy or cricket match at the MCG (or the 'G' as it is locally called) would have to be one of Melbourne's top experiences. But if you visit in the off-season or simply can't get enough sport in your system, then you can take a tour on non-event days, 10am–3pm, from Gate 3 in the Olympic Stand. Tour prices can include entry to the MCG's interactive National Sports Museum. Impressive artefacts include swimmer Ian Thorpe's swimsuit, the inaugural Brownlow Medal and legendary cricketer Sir Don Bradman's baggy green cap. Visitors can also try out their own sporting skills in the 'Game On' room. *Brunton Ave, Richmond; (03) 9657 8888.*

Fitzroy Gardens 6 D3

Fitzroy Gardens, bounded by Albert, Clarendon and Lansdowne streets and Wellington Parade, are one of a handful of public gardens surrounding the CBD, but the only one that can boast **Cooks' Cottage**, a fairy tree and a model Tudor village. *Cottage: (03) 9419 4677; open 9am–5pm daily.*

Yarra Bend Park 7 E2

Yarra Bend Park is a bushland sanctuary that feels far, far away from the city even though it is, in fact, just a few minutes' drive from it. It features walking tracks and a golf course, and boat-hire facilities at the historic **Studley Park Boathouse**. Go boating on the river, then dock for a spot of Devonshire tea.

BAYSIDE

Melbourne's eastern bayside suburbs sprawl down towards the Mornington Peninsula. At the top of the bay is **Port Melbourne**, once the entry point for many thousands of migrants and now the docking point for Spirit of Tasmania ferries. Port Melbourne's Bay Street has a range of pubs, shops and cafes, as does Clarendon Street in **South Melbourne**. On Coventry Street is the South Melbourne Market and south of here is **Albert Park**, the venue for the Australian Formula One Grand Prix each March as well as a spot for jogging and boating. Various other sports are also on offer in Albert Park's Melbourne Sports and Aquatic Centre. Further south again is St Kilda.

St Kilda 6 D5

St Kilda began life as a seaside holiday destination, so separate from the city that on the sandy track that was then St Kilda Road, travellers ran the risk of a run-in with a bushranger.

Fitzroy Street is a long line of shoulder-to-shoulder cafes, restaurants, bars and pubs. Straight ahead is the palm-lined foreshore and the beach, and around the corner is the much-loved **St Kilda Pier** with its historic kiosk that offers great views and quality food.

The path along the foreshore goes from Port Melbourne in the north to beyond Brighton in the south and is almost always busy with cyclists, rollerbladers and walkers. **The Esplanade Hotel** is an integral part of Melbourne's live-music scene, and **The Palais**, a grand, French-style theatre, is the venue for big-billed concerts. Luna Park *(see next entry)* is next door to The Palais, and there is an art and craft market on The Esplanade every Sunday *(see Markets, p. 26)*.

Just around the corner from The Esplanade are the continental cake shops that have made **Acland Street** famous.

South from St Kilda is a string of swimming beaches, including **Brighton Beach** with its trademark colourful bathing boxes and views of the city. **Rippon Lea Estate**, on Hotham Street in Elsternwick, is a grand Romanesque mansion set in beautiful gardens and open daily.

Luna Park 6 D5

While it is now appropriately modernised, Luna Park still feels like a chunk of the early 20th century, when a ride on the Scenic Railway rollercoaster was a big night out. Since it opened in 1912, many things about the park have lived on, including the huge and famous (and much-renovated) face that forms its entrance. Among the traditional rides such as the carousel, Ferris wheel and rollercoaster are the more modern Shock Drop, Enterprise and G Force. *Lower Esplanade, St Kilda; (03) 9525 5033; open 7–11pm Fri, 11am–11pm Sat, 11am–6pm Sun summer, 11am–6pm Sat–Sun outside summer, open daily during school holidays.*

WESTERN BAYSIDE

Williamstown 6 A5

Travel over the West Gate Bridge and you'll find a landscape of factories and new suburbs. But south of the bridge, on the western arm of Hobsons Bay, is Williamstown – one of Melbourne's true gems. Along Nelson Place are restaurants, bars and cafes in old maritime buildings. Williamstown's main beach is around the other side of the bay. For those after an alternative to driving, there is a ferry service to Williamstown from St Kilda and Southgate, with an optional stop at Scienceworks *(see next entry). For information on the ferry, see Walks and tours, p. 29.*

Scienceworks 6 A3

This is the place to come to 'push it, pull it, spin it, bang it', and inadvertently get a grasp on science. It is a great place to bring the kids, with interactive exhibitions and the **Melbourne Planetarium**, featuring simulated night skies and 3D adventures through space. A historic pumping station is located on-site, and tours are available. *2 Booker St, Spotswood; (03) 9392 4800; open 10am–4.30pm daily.*

NORTH-EAST

Heide Museum of Modern Art 279 E2

Surrounded by beautiful parklands and intriguing sculptures, this complex was formerly home to museum founders John and Sunday Reed. The Reeds emerged as patrons of the arts in the 1930s and '40s, and today the support for modern art continues in the museum, which has changing exhibitions in its three galleries. The excellent Cafe Vue, operated by renowned chef Shannon Bennett, serves breakfast and lunch daily. *7 Templestowe Rd, Bulleen; (03) 9850 1500; open 10am–5pm Tues–Fri, 12–5pm Sat–Sun and public holidays; admission free to gardens and sculpture park.*

CITY ESSENTIALS
MELBOURNE

☀ Climate

'Four seasons in one day' is a familiar phrase to all Melburnians. It might reach 38°C in the morning then drop to 20°C in the afternoon – and the weather the next day is anyone's guess. Generally though, winter is cold – daytime temperatures of 11–12°C are not unusual – and spring is wet. January and February are hot, with temperatures anywhere between the mid-20s and high 30s. The favourite season of many locals is autumn, when the weather is usually dry and stable.

	MAX °C	MIN °C	RAIN MM	RAINDAYS
JANUARY	25	14	48	5
FEBRUARY	25	14	47	5
MARCH	23	13	50	6
APRIL	20	10	57	8
MAY	16	8	56	9
JUNE	14	6	49	9
JULY	13	5	47	9
AUGUST	14	6	50	10
SEPTEMBER	17	7	58	10
OCTOBER	19	9	66	10
NOVEMBER	21	11	59	8
DECEMBER	24	12	59	7

🚃 Getting around

Melbourne's trams are an icon, but also a very good way of getting around the city. The City Circle tram is free and extends to Docklands. Trams depart every 12 minutes between 10am and 6pm from Sunday to Wednesday, and till 9pm from Thursday to Saturday. Other (paid) services head out into the suburbs, with especially good coverage of the eastern, south-eastern and northern suburbs. A map of the different services can be found inside most trams.

Trains are generally a faster option if there is a service that goes to your destination. Details of services can be found at each of the five stations in the CBD (see map on p. 134).

Buses tend to cover the areas that trains and trams don't service. The free Melbourne City Tourist Shuttle is a hop-on, hop-off bus service stopping at 11 key city destinations. The service runs every 15 to 20 minutes between 9.30am and 4.30pm daily and includes an informative on-board commentary. Details of routes and stops can be found at www.thatsmelbourne.com.au, or pick up a brochure from the Melbourne Visitor Information Centre at Federation Square.

All modes of public transport are covered by the one ticket, a Metcard. The price of the ticket depends on which of the two 'zones' you need to travel to, and different kinds of Metcards are available, such as two-hour and one-day tickets. Metcards are available at train stations, on trams (for coin purchases only), on buses and at shops – usually newsagents – displaying a Metcard flag.

For drivers, the much-talked-about feature of Melbourne's roads is the hook-turn, a process of moving to the left of the road in order to turn right, and therefore getting out of the way of trams. If you wish to use the tollways CityLink or the new EastLink, either an e-TAG or a day pass is required (there are no tollbooths, but day passes can be purchased over the phone either before or after making a journey).

Public transport Tram, train and bus information line 13 1638

Airport shuttle bus Skybus (03) 9335 2811

Tollways CityLink 13 2629; EastLink 13 5465

Motoring organisation RACV 13 7228, roadside assistance 13 1111

Car rental Avis 13 6333; Budget 1300 362 848; Hertz 13 3039; Thrifty 1300 367 227

Taxis 13CABS 13 2227; Silver Top 13 1008; West Suburban (03) 9689 1144

Water taxi Melbourne Water Taxis 0416 068 655

Tourist bus Melbourne on the Move 1300 558 686

Bicycle hire Rentabike @ Federation Square 0417 339 203; Bike Now (South Melbourne) (03) 9696 8588; St Kilda Cycles (03) 9534 3074

Top events

Australian Open One of the world's four major tennis Grand Slams. JANUARY.

Australian Grand Prix The first round of the FIA World Championships. MARCH.

Melbourne Food and Wine Festival Eat your way through Melbourne and regional Victoria. MARCH–APRIL.

Melbourne International Comedy Festival Just as many laughs as in Edinburgh and Montreal. APRIL.

Melbourne International Film Festival Features, shorts and experimental pieces from around the world. JULY–AUGUST.

AFL Grand Final The whole city goes footy-mad. SEPTEMBER.

Melbourne International Arts Festival Visual arts, theatre, dance and music in indoor and outdoor venues. The alternative Melbourne Fringe Festival is held around the same time. OCTOBER.

Melbourne Cup The pinnacle of the Spring Racing Carnival. NOVEMBER.

Boxing Day Test Boxing Day in Melbourne wouldn't be the same without this cricket match. DECEMBER.

Shopping

Bourke Street Mall, City With department stores Myer and David Jones as well as the swish GPO Melbourne. See p. 8

Collins Street, City Glamorous shopping strip with the big names in high-end fashion. Check out the boutique-style shopping on adjacent Flinders Lane and Little Collins Street too. See p. 8

Melbourne Central and QV, City These two nearby precincts are a shopper's paradise. See p. 14

Chapel Street, South Yarra Where shopping is an event to dress up for. 7 E4

DFO, South Wharf, Southbank Shopping mall of factory outlets for bargain hunters. 6 C3

Southgate, Southbank A classy range of clothing, art and gifts. See p. 16

Bridge Road, Richmond Back-to-back factory outlets and designer warehouses. 7 E3

Brunswick Street, Fitzroy Unique fashion boutiques and giftshops. 6 D2

Markets

Sunday Market, Southbank Crafts galore, leading from the Arts Centre. See p. 16

The Esplanade Market St Kilda Melbourne's oldest art and craft market, with over 200 artisans. Sun. 6 D5

Collingwood Children's Farm – Farmers' Market Victorian produce, from free-range eggs to fresh fruit and vegetables, in a lovely setting on the Yarra. 2nd Sat each month. 7 E2

South Melbourne Market Produce, deli items, clothing and homewares. Wed and Fri–Sun. 6 C4

Flemington Up Market Held at the Flemington Racecourse, with art, craft and regional produce. 4th Sun each month. 6 B2

CERES Market Old-style breads and organic produce on a community-run property in Brunswick East. While you're there, visit the bushfoods nursery and the ecohouse. Wed and Sat. 7 E1

Camberwell Market Melbourne's best trash-and-treasure event. Sun. 279 E3

St Andrews Market Laid-back market with alternative crafts, foods, music and clothing, an hour's drive from the city. Sat. 279 F2

See also Queen Victoria Market, p. 12, and Prahran Market, p. 20

Grand old buildings

Old ANZ Bank Known as the Gothic Bank, with an incredible, gold-leafed interior. 380 Collins St.

Manchester Unity Building Chicago-style building with stark vertical lines, once the city's tallest skyscraper. Cnr Collins and Swanston sts.

Capitol Theatre Designed by the architects of Canberra with a ceiling that will amaze you. 109–117 Swanston St.

St Patrick's Cathedral Victoria's largest church building, built with tonnes of Footscray bluestone. Cnr Gisborne St and Cathedral Pl, East Melbourne.

Princess Theatre The dramatic exterior culminates in three domes with cast-iron tiaras. 163 Spring St.

Forum Theatre Moorish domes, and a starry night sky on the inner ceiling. Cnr Russell and Flinders sts.

St Paul's Cathedral Gothic cathedral made of sandstone. Cnr Flinders and Swanston sts.

Old Melbourne Magistrates' Court The rough sandstone exterior and deeply set archways make for a grim atmosphere. Cnr Russell and Latrobe sts.

Olderfleet Building An intricate Gotham City facade. Nearby is InterContinental Melbourne The Rialto, designed by the same architect. 477 Collins St.

Regent Theatre Melbourne's most glamorous theatre, with an interior of Spanish-style lattice and red carpet. 191 Collins St.

St James' Old Cathedral A humble relic of Melbourne's founding years. 419–435 King St.

University of Melbourne More historic buildings than you can count. Parkville.

Hotel Windsor Layered like a wedding cake and fit for a queen. 111 Spring St.

City Baths A feast of domes on the skyline, this building dates back to the days when bathrooms were a luxury few could afford. Cnr Swanston and Victoria sts.

See also Royal Exhibition Building, p. 21

Museums

Jewish Museum of Australia A record of the experiences of Australia's many Jewish migrants. 26 Alma Rd, St Kilda; (03) 8534 3600; open 10am–4pm Tues–Thurs, 11am–5pm Sun.

Montsalvat An artists' colony that began in 1934, with magnificent French provincial buildings and artworks for view in the gallery. 7 Hillcrest Ave, Eltham; (03) 9439 7712; open 9am–5pm daily.

Champions: Australian Racing Museum Celebrating Australia's horses, jockeys, trainers and owners. Federation Sq; 1300 139 407; open 10am–6pm daily.

ANZ Banking Museum Old money boxes, staff uniforms, historic displays and an interactive ATM exhibit in the glorious Gothic setting of the Old ANZ Bank. 380 Collins St; open 10am–3pm Mon–Fri; admission free.

Post Master Gallery For the stamp enthusiast, but also for those interested in art and design. 321 Exhibition St (enter from Latrobe St); (03) 9204 5021; open 10am–5pm Mon–Fri, 12–5pm Sat; admission free.

Ian Potter Museum of Art An extensive art collection, including cultural artefacts and contemporary artworks. University of Melbourne, Swanston St, between Faraday and Elgin sts, Parkville; (03) 8344 5148; open 10am–5pm Tues–Fri, 12–5pm Sat–Sun; admission free.

Victoria Police Museum Victoria's life of crime revealed, from the capture of Ned Kelly to the Hoddle Street shootings. Lower Concourse Level,

World Trade Centre, 637 Flinders St; (03) 9247 5213; open 10am–4pm Mon–Fri; admission free.

Fire Services Museum   Huge collection of fire brigade memorabilia, including vintage vehicles and historic photos. 39 Gisborne St, East Melbourne; (03) 9662 2907; open 9am–3pm Thurs–Fri, 10am–4pm Sun.

ARHS Railway Museum   Open-air museum with historic locomotives. Champion Rd, North Williamstown; (03) 9397 7412; 12–5pm Sat, Sun and public holidays.

See also Melbourne Museum, p. 21, City Museum at Old Treasury, p. 13, Immigration Museum, p. 12, Koorie Heritage Trust Cultural Centre, p. 12, ACCA, p. 18, Heide Museum of Modern Art, p. 24, Ian Potter Centre: NGV Australia, p. 8, NGV International, p. 17, Australian Centre for the Moving Image, p. 9, Chinese Museum, p. 15, Flinders Lane galleries, p. 13

Entertainment

Cinema   The major cinemas in the city are Hoyts in Melbourne Central's On3 entertainment floor and Greater Union in Russell Street. For arthouse films, try Kino Cinemas in Collins Place. Standout cinemas in the inner-city area include: Cinema Nova in Carlton for a great range of popular and arthouse films; Village Jam Factory in South Yarra or Village in the Crown Entertainment Complex for a Hollywood-style experience; the Rivoli in Camberwell for an old-world cinema experience; and the Astor in St Kilda East, where they play re-runs of the classics and recent releases. See daily newspapers for details.

Live music   Melbourne is renowned for its live-music scene. Fitzroy is one of the major centres of original music, with venues like Bar Open, the Laundry and the Evelyn hosting bands most nights. On the south side of town is The Esplanade Hotel in St Kilda, one of Melbourne's best original rock venues, and in Richmond there's the Corner Hotel, showing many local acts. For jazz, try Bennetts Lane Jazz Club, off Little Lonsdale Street, or Manchester Lane, off Flinders Lane. For a boogie to anything from reggae to funk, try the relaxed and lamplit Night Cat in Johnston Street, Fitzroy. Bigger local and international acts play at other venues around town. Pick up one of the free street publications, *Beat* or *Inpress*, or get the 'EG' lift-out from *The Age* on Fridays.

Classical music and performing arts   The Arts Centre is Melbourne's premier venue for theatre, opera and ballet, and Hamer Hall, next door, is the venue for classical music concerts. The new Melbourne Recital Centre is a world-class chamber music venue. Popular musicals and theatrical productions are held at the Regent, Her Majesty's, the Princess and the Athenaeum theatres. The Malthouse Theatre company and the Melbourne Theatre Company (MTC) host plays, and La Mama in Carlton is the venue for more experimental works. Check out the arts section of *The Age* for details. Most performances are booked through Ticketmaster and Ticketek.

Parks and gardens

Birrarung Marr   Melbourne's newest park, with sculptural displays and a bike track leading up to Federation Square. City. See p. 8

Albert Park   A great spot for exercising around the lake, and the site for the Australian Formula One Grand Prix. Albert Park. 6 D4

Gasworks Arts Park   Sculptures, native gardens, barbecues, a cafe and artist studios in the former South Melbourne Gasworks. Albert Park. 6 C4

Yarra Bend Park   Closest bushland to the city, with boats for hire, a golf course, great views and a strong Aboriginal heritage. Kew/Fairfield. 7 E2

Eltham Lower Park   Featuring the Diamond Valley Miniature Railway, which offers rides for kids on Sunday 11am–5pm. Eltham. 279 F2

Brimbank Park   With wetlands, a children's farm, a visitor centre with a cafe and walking trails along the Maribyrnong River. Keilor. 279 E2

Jells Park   A haven for waterbirds and a great place for a stroll through the bush. Wheelers Hill. 279 F3

Wattle Park Native bush and birds, a nine-hole golf course and accessible by tram. Surrey Hills. 279 E3

Westerfolds Park On the Yarra and popular for canoeing and cycling, with the Mia Mia Aboriginal Art Gallery on top of the hill. Templestowe. 279 E2

See also Royal Botanic Gardens, p. 18, Fitzroy Gardens, p. 23

Walks and tours

Golden Mile Heritage Trail Walk with a guide or navigate this trail on your own. It leads from the Immigration Museum to Melbourne Museum, taking in historic buildings and heritage attractions (walkers gain discounted entry to various places). Bookings on 1300 780 045, or get a self-guide brochure from the Melbourne Visitor Information Centre at Federation Square. 10am daily.

Aboriginal Heritage Walk With an Aboriginal guide and a gum leaf for a ticket, stroll through the Royal Botanic Gardens and learn about the bushfoods, medicines and traditional lore of the Boonerwrung and Woiwurrung people, whose traditional lands meet here. Bookings (03) 9252 2429; 11am–12.30pm Thurs–Fri, 11am–12pm alternate Sun.

Hidden Secrets Tours Various tours focusing on the city's innovative fashion, design and gourmet food culture. Bookings (03) 9329 9665.

Haunted Melbourne Ghost Tours Traipse down dark alleys and enter city buildings that the ghosts of early Melbourne are known to haunt. Bookings (03) 9670 2585; 8.30pm Sat.

Chocoholic Tours A range of tours to get you drooling, taking in Melbourne's best chocolatiers, candy-makers, ice-creameries and cafes. Bookings (03) 9686 4655.

Harley-Davidson Tours Take the Introduction to Melbourne Tour, exploring the bay and over the West Gate Bridge with the wind whistling through your hair. Bookings on 1800 182 282; tours daily.

Foodies' Tours Get tips on picking the best fresh produce, meet the specialist traders and taste samples from the deli at Queen Victoria Market. Bookings (03) 9320 5835; 10am Tues and Thurs–Sat.

Carlton & United Brewery Tours Free tastings of CUB draught beers are preceded by a tour around Abbotsford Brewery, the home of Fosters. Bookings (03) 9420 6800. 10am and 2pm Mon–Fri.

River Cruises A trip down the Yarra or the Maribyrnong will give you new views of Melbourne. Melbourne River Cruises (03) 8610 2600, City River Cruises (03) 9650 2214, Williamstown Bay and River Cruises (03) 9397 2255, Maribyrnong River Cruises (03) 9689 6431.

Sport

Melbourne is possibly Australia's most sporting city, with hardly a gap in the calendar. **AFL** (Australian Football League) is indisputably at the top of the list. The season begins at the end of March and as it nears the finals in September, footy madness eclipses the city. Victoria has ten teams in the league, and the blockbuster matches are played at the **MCG** and **Etihad Stadium**.

After the football comes the **Spring Racing Carnival**, as much a social event as a horseracing one. October and November are packed with events across the state, with the city events held at Caulfield, Moonee Valley, Sandown and Flemington racetracks. The Melbourne Cup, 'the race that stops the nation', is held at Flemington on the first Tuesday in November, and is a local public holiday.

Cricket takes Melbourne through the heat of summer. One Day International and Test matches are usually played at the MCG, and the popular Boxing Day Test gives Christmas in Melbourne a sporting twist.

In January Melbourne hosts the Australian Open, one of the world's four major **tennis** Grand Slams. The venue is Melbourne Park, home to the Rod Laver Arena and the Hisense Arena.

Come March, and the **Australian Formula One Grand Prix** comes to town, attracting a large international crowd. The cars race around Albert Park Lake.

Other suburbs

Brunswick Sydney Road is the place to come to for cheap fabrics, authentic Turkish bread and a healthy dose of Middle Eastern culture. 6 D1

Footscray A mini-Saigon that is the lesser-known version of Victoria Street, Abbotsford, now with a growing African flavour. Jam-packed with cheap eateries and one of Melbourne's best produce markets. 6 A2

Camberwell and Canterbury Melbourne's eastern money belt, with fashion outlets lining Camberwell's Burke Road, and the elegant Maling Road shopping precinct in Canterbury. 279 E3

Yarraville A gem tucked away in a largely industrial sweep of suburbs, with cafes and a superb Art Deco cinema. 6 A3

Hawthorn With a strong student culture from the nearby university, and a strip of shops on Glenferrie Road offering everything from Asian groceries to smart fashion. 279 E3

Balaclava Kosher butchers and an emerging cafe culture. Here and neighbouring Elwood are affordable alternatives to St Kilda. 7 E5

Black Rock One of many bayside suburbs shifting from a sleepy village into sought-after real estate, fronting two of Melbourne's best beaches. 279 E3

Dandenong The base for Melbourne's Indian community – with food stores galore and also one of Melbourne's oldest markets. 279 F3

Eltham All native trees and mud-brick architecture, this suburb feels like a piece of the country only 30 minutes from the city. 279 F2

Day tours

The Dandenongs These scenic hills at the edge of Melbourne's eastern suburbs are a popular daytrip. Native rainforests of mountain ash and giant ferns, cool-climate gardens, the popular steam train Puffing Billy, and galleries, craft shops and cafes, many serving Devonshire tea, are among the many attractions. *For more details see pp. 32–3*

Yarra Valley and Healesville High-quality pinot noir and sparkling wines are produced across one of Australia's best-known wine areas. Pick up a brochure from the information centre in Healesville and map out your wine-tasting tour. Worthy of its own daytrip is Healesville Sanctuary, featuring around 200 species of native animals in a bushland setting. *For more details see pp. 32–3*

Mornington Peninsula This holiday centre features fine-food producers, around 40 cool-climate vineyards, historic holiday villages, quiet coastal national parks, 18 golf courses and many attractions for children. *For more details see pp. 34–5*

Phillip Island The nightly Penguin Parade on Phillip Island is one of Victoria's signature attractions. For the avid wildlife-watcher, seals and koalas are the other stars of the show, though the island also boasts magnificent coastal scenery and great surf breaks. *For more details see pp. 36–7*

Sovereign Hill Ballarat's award-winning re-creation of a 19th-century goldmining village conjures up the detail and drama of life during one of the nation's most exciting periods of history. You can even stay the night at a new accommodation complex within the village, with full period costume thrown in! *For more details see Ballarat, p. 64*

Bellarine Peninsula The Bellarine Peninsula separates the waters of Port Phillip from the famously rugged coastline of Victoria's south-west. Beyond the historic buildings, streets and Geelong's waterfront are quaint coastal villages, excellent beaches, golf courses and wineries. *For more details see p. 40–1*

Mount Macedon and Hanging Rock Country mansions and superb 19th- and 20th-century European-style gardens sit comfortably in the native bushland. Here you'll find wineries, cafes, nurseries, galleries and the mysteriously beautiful Hanging Rock. *For more details see pp. 38–9*

Spa country For a few hours of health-giving indulgence, visit the historic spa complex at Hepburn Springs. Explore Daylesford, enjoy a meal at one of the region's excellent eateries, or take a peaceful forest drive. *For more details see pp. 38–9*

OTWAY FLY, SOUTH-WEST COAST

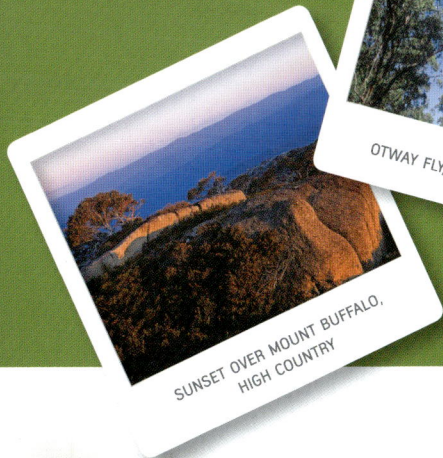
SUNSET OVER MOUNT BUFFALO, HIGH COUNTRY

REGIONS
victoria

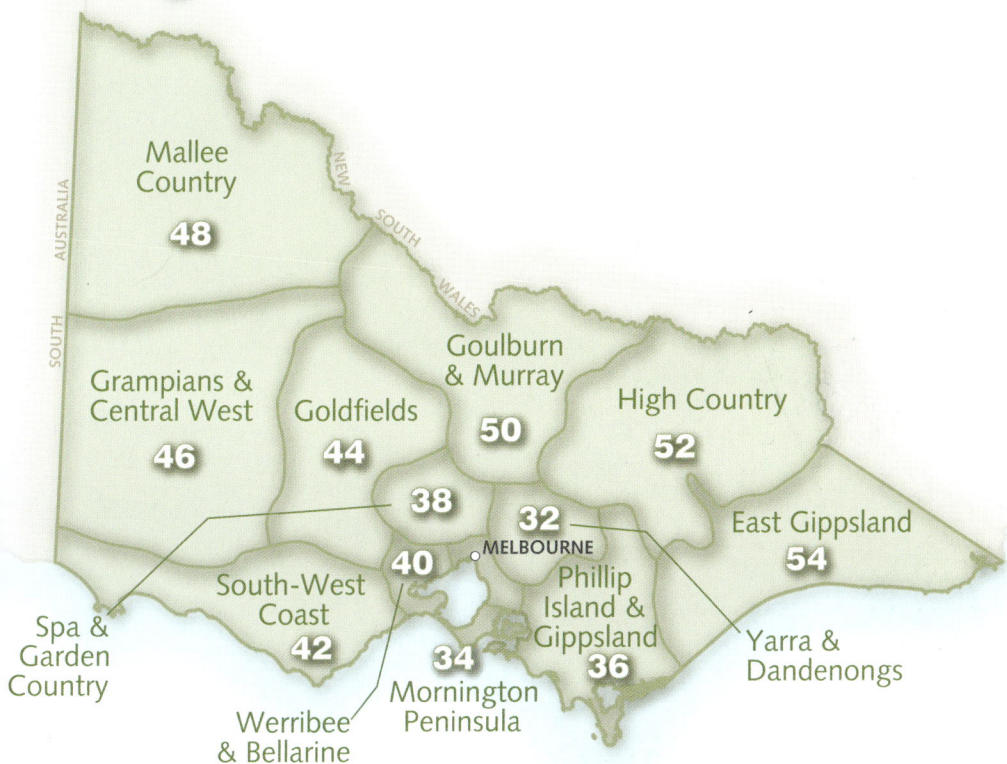

NEW SOUTH WALES

SOUTH AUSTRALIA

Mallee Country
48

Grampians & Central West
46

Goldfields
44

Goulburn & Murray
50

High Country
52

38

32

MELBOURNE

East Gippsland
54

40

South-West Coast
42

Spa & Garden Country

Phillip Island & Gippsland
36

Yarra & Dandenongs

34

Mornington Peninsula

Werribee & Bellarine

YARRA & DANDENONGS

A daytrip to the Dandenongs, stopping off at cellar doors in the Yarra Valley, combines native forest landscapes with indulgent wining and dining on Melbourne's doorstep.

CLIMATE	HEALESVILLE											
MONTH	JAN	FEB	MAR	APR	MAY	JUN	JUL	AUG	SEP	OCT	NOV	DEC
MAXIMUM °C	26	26	24	19	16	12	12	14	16	19	22	24
MINIMUM °C	11	12	11	9	7	4	4	5	6	8	9	11
RAIN MM	58	68	64	91	96	82	87	98	94	106	93	86
RAINDAYS	7	7	8	11	14	14	16	17	15	14	12	10

→   For more detail see maps 279, 282, 287 & 289. For descriptions of 🇹 towns see Towns A–Z (p. 56).

1 **Healesville Sanctuary** Spread across 32 hectares of bushland, this world-renowned native animal sanctuary has over 200 species, most roaming in natural settings. Special features include talks by keepers, a nocturnal viewing area, the bird-of-prey displays and the platypus exhibit.

2 **Marysville and Lake Mountain** For 100 years, the beautiful subalpine village of Marysville was a much-frequented holiday destination for Melburnians. Providing access to the magnificent 84-metre Steavenson Falls nearby, the town charmed visitors with its cafes, galleries and popular guesthouses. In February 2009, Marysville was destroyed by bushfire, and many people lost their lives. The surviving residents have vowed to rebuild their much-loved town. Nearby Lake Mountain also suffered in the bushfires but it remains a popular tobogganing and cross-country skiing resort in winter, and a great bushwalking destination in summer.

3 **Puffing Billy Steam Train** This magical little steam train takes you on a 25-kilometre journey through lush forest and tree ferns from Belgrave to Gembrook and back again. Kids love the two-hour round trip, dangling their legs out the windows. You can alight at Emerald Lake along the way, a lovely tranquil spot ideal for picnics, paddleboating and walks, then return on the train in the late afternoon.

4 **Gardens of the Dandenongs** Mountain ash forests and fern gullies frame one of Australia's best-known gardening regions. Many of the private gardens are open daily. Public gardens include the National Rhododendron Gardens and the R. J. Hamer Forest Arboretum (both near Olinda), the William Ricketts Sanctuary (Mount Dandenong) and the Alfred Nicholas Memorial Gardens (Sherbrooke).

5 **Yarra Valley wineries** The 50 or so wineries of this district produce high-quality chardonnay, cabernet sauvignon and pinot noir. While touring the region for wines, follow the Yarra Valley Regional Food Trail, a self-guide tour taking in the many gourmet food outlets in the region.

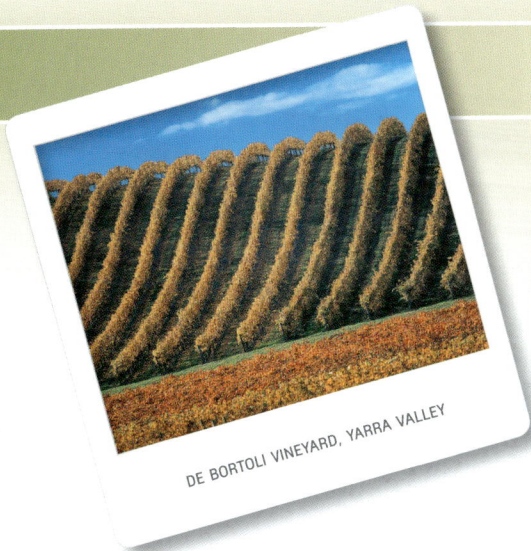

DE BORTOLI VINEYARD, YARRA VALLEY

TOP EVENTS

FEB	Grape Grazing Festival (throughout Yarra Valley wine region)
MAY	Great Train Race (Emerald)
JULY	Winterfest (Warburton)
AUG–NOV	Rhododendron and Daffodil Festivals (Olinda)
SEPT–OCT	Tesselaar's Tulip Festival (Silvan, near Olinda)

TOURS OF THE FOREST

This area has some of the state's best forest scenery. Bushwalkers, horseriders and cyclists can travel the 38-kilometre Warburton Rail Trail, starting in Lilydale. The Beeches, an area of rainforest near Marysville, has a 5-kilometre stroll through forests of ancient beech and mountain ash. The less energetic can take a forest drive, choosing from the Black Spur Drive (between Healesville and Marysville), Acheron Way (from Warburton to Marysville) and the Lady Talbot Forest Drive (a shorter drive in the Marysville region). For something special, visit Mount Donna Buang Rainforest Gallery (near Warburton), which includes a viewing platform and a raised walkway through the rainforest.

MORNINGTON PENINSULA

This region's well-serviced seaside towns are popular during summer, while in winter wineries in the beautiful hinterland have welcoming cellar doors.

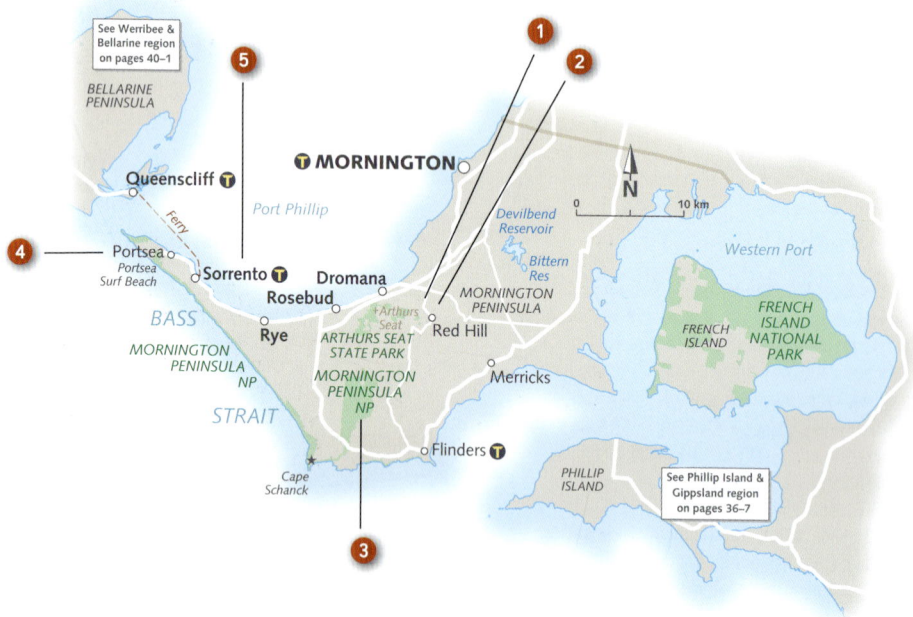

CLIMATE   MORNINGTON

MONTH	JAN	FEB	MAR	APR	MAY	JUN	JUL	AUG	SEP	OCT	NOV	DEC
MAXIMUM °C	25	25	23	19	16	14	13	14	16	18	20	23
MINIMUM °C	13	14	13	11	9	7	7	7	8	10	11	12
RAIN MM	45	42	50	63	70	71	69	71	72	71	59	54
RAINDAYS	7	7	8	11	14	15	15	16	14	13	10	8

→ For more detail see maps 278–9, 280–1, 287 & 289. For descriptions of ⓣ towns see Towns A–Z (p. 56).

1 Arthurs Seat   Just inland from Dromana, Arthurs Seat offers superb views across Melbourne and the bay. The 300-metre summit is reached by foot or vehicle – at the top are picnic facilities and a restaurant. Nearby is Arthurs Seat Maze with a series of themed gardens and mazes, where the large Maize Maze Festival is held each autumn.

2 Red Hill Market   The small town of Red Hill, in the scenic undulating landscape of the Mornington Peninsula, is famous for its market held on the first Saturday of each month (from September to May). Affectionately known as the 'grand dame' of Victoria's craft market scene, the market has featured exceptional local produce, clothing and crafts for over 30 years. A visit to this much-lauded community event is a real treat.

3 Mornington Peninsula National Park   This park extends along the south-west coast of the peninsula, where the Bass Strait surf pounds windswept beaches and headlands. A 32-kilometre walking track runs from Portsea Surf Beach right down to Cape Schanck, with its historic 1858 lighthouse (offering accommodation).

4 Portsea   Near the north-west tip of the peninsula, this village has long been favoured by Melbourne's wealthy. It has large houses (some with private boathouses), elegant hotels, B&Bs, good restaurants and a legendary pub. Further west, don't miss Fort Nepean, once an important defence site, and London Bridge, a rock formation off Portsea Surf Beach.

5 Sorrento sojourns   The Queenscliff–Sorrento car ferry crosses Port Phillip several times a day, offering visitors a tour of the two peninsulas – Bellarine and Mornington – without a long drive by land. Dolphin cruises, some including a swim with Port Phillip's bottlenose dolphins, operate in summer.

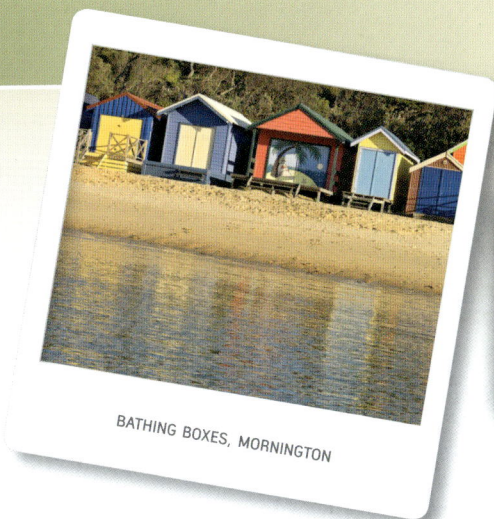

BATHING BOXES, MORNINGTON

TOP EVENTS

JAN	Portsea Swim Classic
FEB	Rye Beach Sand Sculpting Championship
FEB–APR	Maize Maze Festival (Arthurs Seat)
MAR	Colour the Sky Kite Festival (Rosebud)
OCT	Pinot Week (throughout wine region)
OCT	Mornington Food and Wine Festival (throughout wine region)

WINERIES

The grape came relatively late to the peninsula: the oldest vineyard, Elgee Park, north of Merricks, was established early in the 1970s. Viticulture exploded during the 1980s and '90s; now there are nearly 40 wineries in this cool-climate region, most clustered around Red Hill and many set in postcard-perfect landscapes. The vineyards tend to be small and concentrate on the classic varieties of pinot noir and chardonnay. Stonier, Tucks Ridge and Main Ridge Estate are a few of the names to look out for.

PHILLIP ISLAND & GIPPSLAND

This diverse area features historic towns, snowfields, the remote beauty of Wilsons Promontory and the famous Phillip Island penguins.

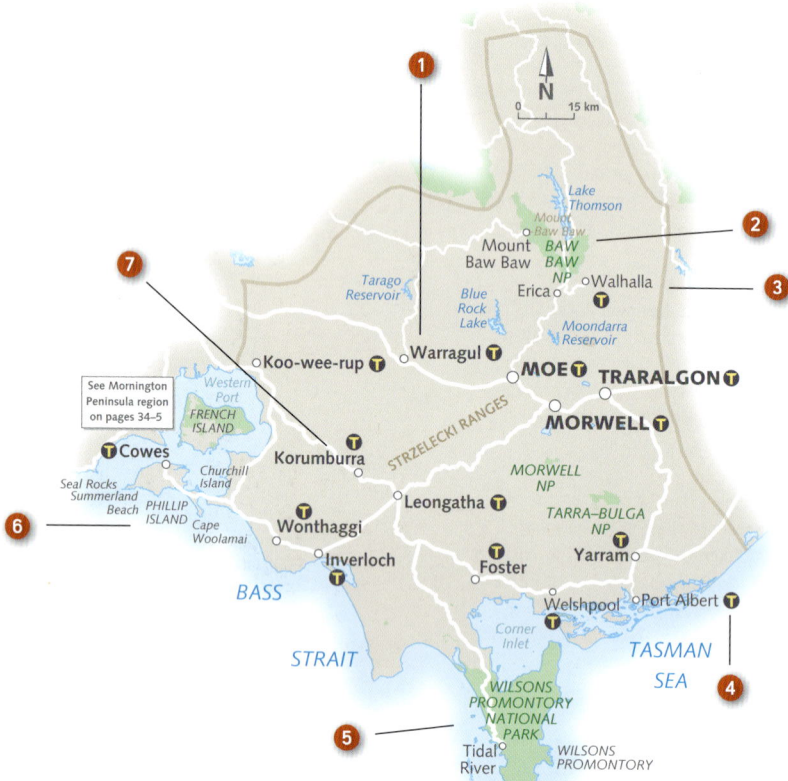

CLIMATE   WARRAGUL

MONTH	JAN	FEB	MAR	APR	MAY	JUN	JUL	AUG	SEP	OCT	NOV	DEC
MAXIMUM °C	26	26	24	20	16	13	13	14	16	19	21	23
MINIMUM °C	13	13	12	9	7	5	4	5	6	8	9	11
RAIN MM	62	52	69	84	94	93	91	103	104	109	89	80
RAINDAYS	8	7	10	13	15	16	16	17	16	15	13	11

→ For more detail see maps 279, 281, 287 & 289. For descriptions of ⊤ towns see Towns A–Z (p. 56).

WILSONS PROMONTORY COASTLINE

1 **Gourmet Deli Trail**   Central Gippsland is home to producers of trout, venison, cheese, berries, potatoes, herbs and wine. The trail covers the area north and south of Warragul, and annotated maps are available from visitor centres.

2 **Baw Baw National Park**   The highest part of the park, Mount Baw Baw (via Moe), has ski facilities and, unlike many other slopes, is seldom crowded. The eastern section (via Erica and Walhalla) is popular in summer with bushwalkers, wildflower enthusiasts and campers.

3 **Walhalla**   The perfectly preserved former goldmining town of Walhalla is set in a steep valley. Take the signposted town walk or a 45-minute ride on the Walhalla Goldfields Railway, or inspect the Long Tunnel Mine.

4 **Port Albert**   Today Port Albert is a quaint fishing village, but as the state's first official port, it was once the gateway to Gippsland and Victoria. About 40 old buildings survive. Plentiful snapper, whiting, flathead, bream and trevally are found in the protected waters offshore.

5 **Wilsons Promontory**   The Prom is a remote and beautiful landscape supporting diverse native flora and fauna in a near-wilderness. Around 150 kilometres of walking tracks along bays and through bush begin at Tidal River and other points along the access road.

6 **Phillip Island**   Phillip Island is best known for its little penguins, but visitors can also walk around Cape Woolamai, drive across the bridge to Churchill Island to see a historic homestead, or immerse themselves in motor-racing history at the Phillip Island Grand Prix Circuit Visitor Centre.

7 **Korumburra's Coal Creek Heritage Village**
A delightful re-creation of a 19th-century coalmining village on the site of the original Coal Creek mine (1890s), this heritage village has over 30 historic buildings. Visitors can take a guided tour through a coalmine, go on a carriage ride or board a small locomotive for a meander through tranquil bushland.

TOP EVENTS

FEB–MAR	World Superbike Championships (Phillip Island)
MAR	Jazz Festival (Inverloch)
MAR	Blue Rock Classic (multi-sport race, Moe)
MAR	Fishing Contest (Port Albert)
EASTER	Tarra Festival (Yarram)
OCT	Australian Motorcycle Grand Prix (Phillip Island)

PHILLIP ISLAND WILDLIFE

The Penguin Parade on Summerland Beach is a major international tourist attraction. Just after sunset, the world's smallest penguins, at 33 centimetres tall, come home to their burrows in the sand dunes after a day in the sea. To protect the penguins, visitors are restricted to designated viewing areas and cameras are prohibited. Bookings are essential during peak holiday periods. The visitor centre also offers a simulated underwater tour showing the penguins foraging for food and avoiding predators. On the island's western tip you can walk along a cliff-top boardwalk for views across to Seal Rocks, 2 kilometres offshore, where thousands of Australian fur seals live. For an up-close view of the frolicking animals, take a cruise from Cowes or watch them on cameras that you control yourself at the Nobbies Centre. Also visit the Koala Conservation Centre near Cowes, where you can see the delightful marsupials snoozing in the treetops.

SPA & GARDEN COUNTRY

Grand European-style gardens and historic spa towns feature in this district, which retains the air of a 19th-century hill retreat.

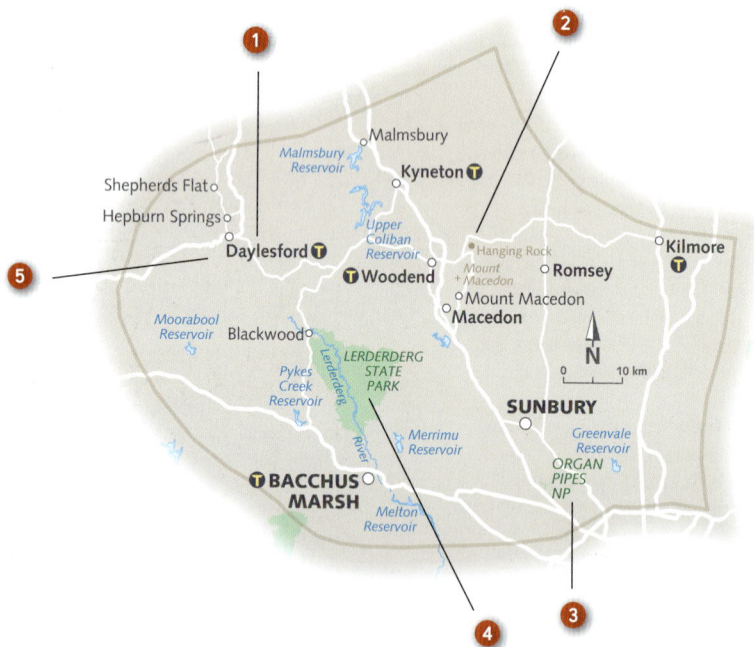

CLIMATE   KYNETON

MONTH	JAN	FEB	MAR	APR	MAY	JUN	JUL	AUG	SEP	OCT	NOV	DEC
MAXIMUM °C	27	27	24	18	14	11	10	12	15	18	22	25
MINIMUM °C	10	10	8	6	4	2	2	2	3	5	7	9
RAIN MM	37	39	47	54	75	90	82	84	74	69	52	50
RAINDAYS	5	5	6	9	12	15	16	16	13	11	9	7

→ For more detail see maps 278, 283, 287 & 288–9. For descriptions of ⓣ towns see Towns A–Z (p. 56).

1 Daylesford and Hepburn Springs The spa complex at Hepburn Springs offers heated mineral spas, flotation tanks, saunas and massages. The adjacent town of Daylesford is an attractive weekend destination with galleries, antique shops, heritage buildings, B&Bs and fantastic restaurants and cafes. The Convent Gallery, a 19th-century former convent, houses local artwork, sculpture and jewellery.

2 Hanging Rock This impressive rock formation north-east of Woodend was created by the erosion of solidified lava. The spot was the inspiration for Joan Lindsay's novel *Picnic at Hanging Rock*, and a setting for the subsequent film. Walking tracks lead up to a superb view, with glimpses of koalas along the way, and the Discovery Centre tells the story of the site.

PARMA VILLA, HEPBURN SPRINGS

3 Organ Pipes National Park Lava flows have created a 20-metre wall of basalt columns in this small park near Sunbury. The 'organ pipes', within a gorge, can be seen close-up via an easy walking trail. A regeneration program is gradually bringing this formerly denuded area back to its native state.

4 Lerderderg State Park The Lerderderg River has cut a deep gorge through sandstone and slate in this 14 250-hectare park. Rugged ridges enclose much of the river, and there are also some interesting relics of old goldmining days. Explore on foot, or take a scenic drive via O'Briens Road (turn off south of Blackwood).

5 Lake House Daylesford's beloved Lake House is regarded as one of regional Victoria's best restaurants, if not the best. Opened in 1984, it is partly responsible for the town's transformation into a gourmet destination. The white, light-filled restaurant overlooks picturesque Lake Daylesford, and the menu might feature local yabbies, free-range pork and dishes that tip their hat to the owner's Russian heritage. Luxury accommodation is also available, as is pampering at the on-site Salus Day Spa.

TOP EVENTS

JAN	New Year's Day and Australia Day races (Hanging Rock, near Woodend)
APR–MAY	Hepburn Springs Swiss–Italian Festival (Hepburn Springs)
JUNE	Winter Arts Festival (Woodend)
SEPT	Daffodil and Arts Festival (Kyneton)
OCT	Macedon Ranges Budburst Food and Wine Festival (throughout wine region)
DEC	Highland Gathering (Daylesford)

COUNTRY GARDENS

Gardens flourish in the volcanic soil and cool, moist climate of the spa country. There are botanic gardens in Daylesford and Malmsbury. Around the beautiful village of Mount Macedon, classic mountain-side gardens surround large houses; check with a visitor centre for their spring and autumn open days. Cope-Williams Winery at Romsey is well known for its English-style garden and cricket green, while at Blackwood the beautiful Garden of St Erth offers 2 hectares of exotic and native species (closed Wednesday and Thursday). For something special, visit the Lavandula Swiss Italian Farm at Shepherds Flat, where lavender sits beside other cottage-style plants.

WERRIBEE & BELLARINE

Beyond the regional centre of Geelong, diverse attractions beckon: watersports, wineries, Victorian-era hotels and even an African-style safari park.

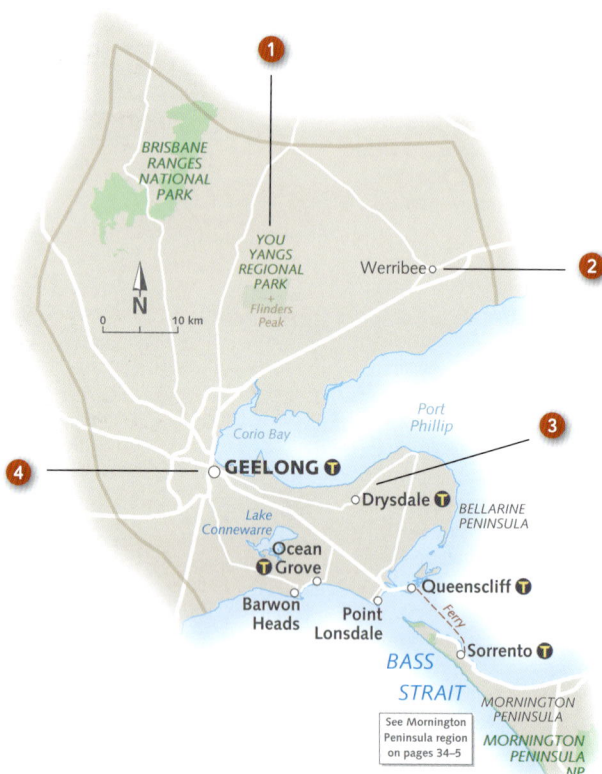

BRISBANE
RANGES
NATIONAL
PARK

YOU
YANGS
REGIONAL
PARK

*Flinders
Peak*

0   10 km

N

Werribee

Port
Phillip

Corio Bay

GEELONG 🇹

Lake
Connewarre

Drysdale 🇹

BELLARINE
PENINSULA

Ocean
🇹 Grove

Barwon
Heads

Point
Lonsdale

Queenscliff 🇹

Ferry

BASS

STRAIT

Sorrento 🇹

MORNINGTON
PENINSULA

See Mornington
Peninsula region
on pages 34–5

MORNINGTON
PENINSULA
NP

CLIMATE	GEELONG											
MONTH	JAN	FEB	MAR	APR	MAY	JUN	JUL	AUG	SEP	OCT	NOV	DEC
MAXIMUM °C	25	26	24	20	17	14	14	15	17	19	21	24
MINIMUM °C	14	14	13	10	8	6	5	6	7	8	10	12
RAIN MM	44	38	35	39	47	43	42	47	53	63	52	48
RAINDAYS	8	6	9	12	14	16	16	17	16	15	13	10

→ For more detail see maps 278, 280, 286–7, 288–9. For descriptions of 🇹 towns see Towns A–Z (p. 56).

1 **The You Yangs** These granite tors rise abruptly from the Werribee Plains. There is a fairly easy walk (3.2 kilometres return) from the carpark to the top of Flinders Peak. On a clear day the view extends to Mount Macedon, Geelong and the skyscrapers of Melbourne.

2 **Werribee Park** Built in Italianate style during the 1870s, Werribee Mansion is now preserved in all its splendour, grandly furnished to re-create the lifestyle of a wealthy family in Victoria's boom years. Take a tour through the house, then visit the Victoria State Rose Garden before heading off on a safari at the Werribee Open Range Zoo.

3 **Geelong wine region** Vines were first planted around Geelong in the 1850s, but were uprooted during the 1870s phylloxera outbreak. Today's industry was established in the 1960s and there are now around 20 wineries, including eight on the Bellarine Peninsula. Scotchmans Hill, near Drysdale, has views to the coast and a growing reputation for pinot noir and chardonnay.

4 **Geelong** Victoria's second largest city is a bustling port that grew with the state's wool industry. The redeveloped Eastern Beach Waterfront district features cafes, restaurants and colourful sculptures, with the historic Cunningham Pier as a centrepiece. Take a stroll along the promenade or cool off in the restored 1930s sea baths.

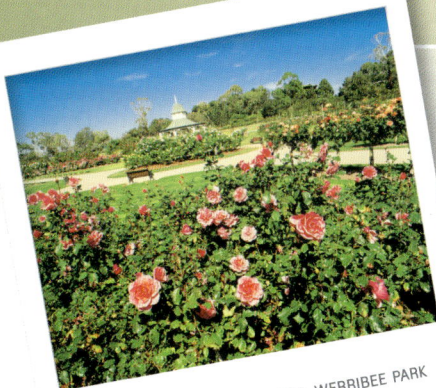

VICTORIA STATE ROSE GARDEN, WERRIBEE PARK

TOP EVENTS

JAN	Skandia Geelong Week
FEB–MAR	Spray Farm Estate summer concert series (Bellarine)
MAR	Highland Gathering (Geelong)
JUNE	National Celtic Folk Festival (Geelong)
OCT	Geelong Cup (horseracing)
NOV	Queenscliff Music Festival

HOLIDAY HAVENS

Just an hour or so from Melbourne, this district is enormously popular for weekend getaways. Queenscliff offers luxurious accommodation and fine dining, and the Maritime Centre and Museum in town displays the region's historic relationship with the sea. The tiny historic town of Point Lonsdale has great views of the turbulent entrance to Port Phillip. Ocean Grove, the peninsula's biggest town, is popular with retirees, surfers and scubadivers. A bridge across the estuary leads to Barwon Heads, which was the setting for the television series *SeaChange*. This is a small town with an excellent surfing beach and good accommodation and restaurants.

SOUTH-WEST COAST

The breathtaking coastal landscape and charming holiday towns of the Great Ocean Road are world renowned, while inland lies a volcanic landscape.

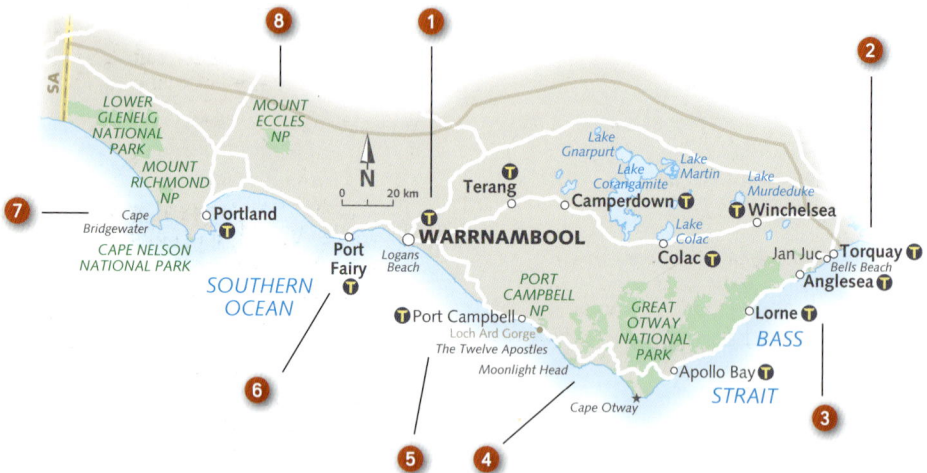

CLIMATE   WARRNAMBOOL

MONTH	JAN	FEB	MAR	APR	MAY	JUN	JUL	AUG	SEP	OCT	NOV	DEC
MAXIMUM °C	23	24	22	19	16	14	13	14	15	17	19	21
MINIMUM °C	11	12	11	9	7	6	5	6	7	7	9	10
RAIN MM	49	35	53	69	75	101	96	107	109	82	66	63
RAINDAYS	11	9	12	15	17	20	20	20	19	16	15	13

→ For more detail see maps 286–7 & 288. For descriptions of ⊤ towns see Towns A–Z (p. 56).

THE TWELVE APOSTLES, PORT CAMPBELL NATIONAL PARK

1 Warrnambool's southern right whales
Each year from June to September, southern right whales can be spotted from Warrnambool's Logans Beach. There's a purpose-built viewing platform at the beach (binoculars or a telescope are recommended).

2 Surf coast Torquay is Victoria's premier surfing town. Factory outlets offer great bargains on surf gear and the local Surfworld Australia museum celebrates the wonders of the wave. Bells and Jan Juc beaches are just around the corner.

3 Lorne This popular resort village has excellent cafes and restaurants and a lively summertime crowd. Nearby, in Great Otway National Park, beautiful forests and waterfalls provide time-out for bushwalkers and nature lovers.

4 The Otways In the north of Great Otway National Park, the Otway Fly takes visitors on a suspended walkway to a treetop lookout; in the south, at Cape Otway, a lighthouse offers views over the sea. Another highlight is Melba Gully, where, at dusk, visitors can witness a show of twinkling lights from glow worms.

5 The Twelve Apostles These spectacular limestone stacks were part of the cliffs until wind and water left them stranded in wild surf off the shore. Preserved in Port Campbell National Park, they are one of Australia's most photographed sights.

6 Port Fairy This superbly preserved whaling port boasts historic bluestone buildings. In summer it offers lazy beachside holidays, and in winter, a refuge from the cold in one of the many cosy restaurants and B&Bs.

7 Cape Bridgewater A two-hour walk leads to a viewing platform overlooking one of the country's largest Australian fur seal colonies; take a boat trip into the mouth of a cave for a closer look at these charming creatures.

8 Mount Eccles National Park This park is at the far edge of the 20 000-year-old volcanic landscape that extends west from Melbourne. There are excellent walking trails, and camping is available.

TOP EVENTS

JAN	Pier to Pub Swim and Mountain to Surf Foot Race (Lorne)
FEB	Go Country Music Festival and Truck Show (Colac)
FEB	Wunta Fiesta (Warrnambool)
MAR	Port Fairy Folk Festival
EASTER	Rip Curl Pro (Bells Beach, near Torquay)
DEC–JAN	Falls Festival (Great Otway National Park)

SHIPWRECKS

There are about 80 wrecks along the south-west-coast shipping route. Victoria's Historic Shipwreck Trail, between Moonlight Head (in Port Campbell National Park) and Port Fairy, marks 25 sites with plaques telling the history of each wreck. Not to be missed is the evocative *Loch Ard* site, near Port Campbell. On a direct route from London to Melbourne, the *Loch Ard* ran into trouble while negotiating the entrance to the Bass Strait; fog and haze prevented the captain from seeing nearby cliffs. In the struggle to change direction the ship hit the cliffs and soon sank — only two people managed to swim ashore to the now well-known Loch Ard Gorge. At Flagstaff Hill Maritime Village in Warrnambool you can see a magnificent statue of a peacock, which was being transported on the *Loch Ard* for display in Melbourne's International Exhibition of 1880 and was washed ashore after the wreck. You can also watch the sound-and-laser spectacular 'Shipwrecked', which brings the tale of the *Loch Ard* to life.

GOLDFIELDS

This region is a historic jewel of rural Australia with an intense concentration of Victorian architecture in grand public buildings and parks.

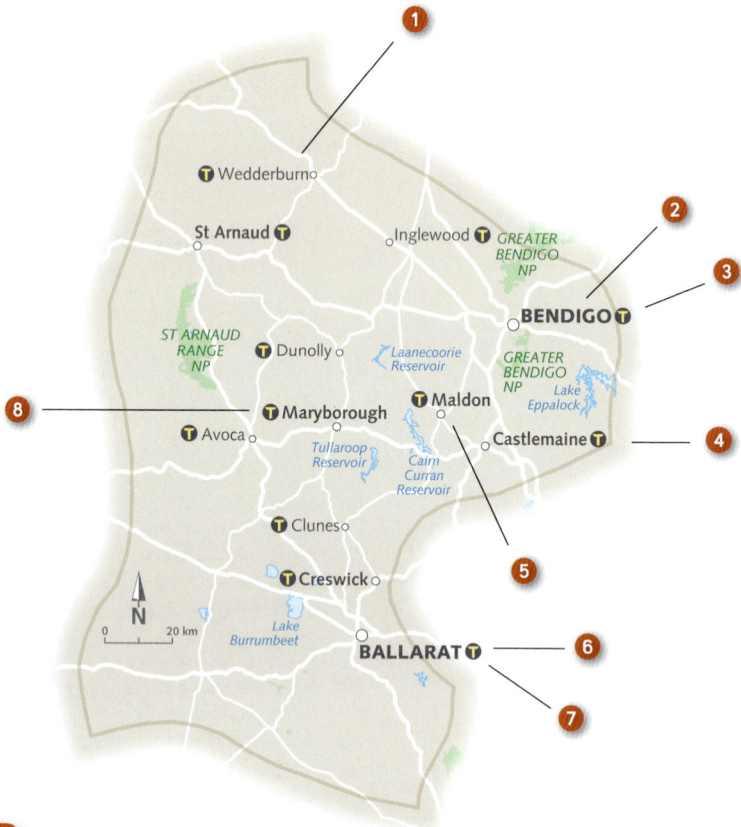

Wedderburn

St Arnaud

Inglewood   GREATER BENDIGO NP

BENDIGO

ST ARNAUD RANGE NP

Dunolly   Laanecoorie Reservoir

GREATER BENDIGO NP   Lake Eppalock

Maryborough   Maldon

Avoca   Castlemaine

Tullaroop Reservoir   Cairn Curran Reservoir

Clunes

Creswick

N
0   20 km

Lake Burrumbeet

BALLARAT

CLIMATE	BENDIGO											
MONTH	JAN	FEB	MAR	APR	MAY	JUN	JUL	AUG	SEP	OCT	NOV	DEC
MAXIMUM °C	29	29	26	21	16	13	12	14	16	20	24	26
MINIMUM °C	14	15	13	9	7	4	3	5	6	8	11	13
RAIN MM	33	32	36	41	55	61	56	59	54	52	37	33
RAINDAYS	5	4	5	7	10	12	13	13	11	10	7	6

→   For more detail see maps 283, 287, 288 & 291. For descriptions of ⓣ towns see Towns A–Z (p. 56).

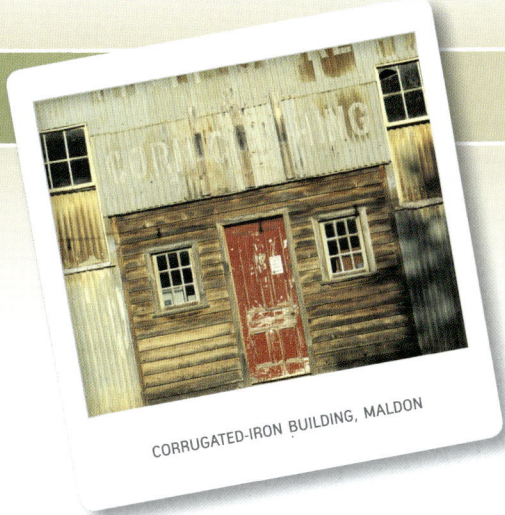

CORRUGATED-IRON BUILDING, MALDON

1 **Backblocks of the goldfields** In the town of Dunolly, 126 nuggets were found – see replicas of some of the most impressive finds at the Goldfields Historical and Arts Society. St Arnaud boasts the beautiful Queen Mary Gardens and a number of old pubs and verandah-fronted shops. There are eucalyptus distilleries at Inglewood and Wedderburn.

2 **Bendigo's Chinese sites** The restored Joss House and the Golden Dragon Museum in Bridge Street are reminders of the substantial presence of Chinese immigrants on the goldfields. A ceremonial archway leads from the museum to the Garden of Joy.

3 **Pall Mall** The tree-lined, French-style boulevard of Pall Mall in Bendigo is probably country Australia's most impressive street, with many of its buildings dating back to the gold rush. To complete the picture, Bendigo's vintage trams rattle up and down the street.

4 **Castlemaine** This historic goldmining town's original market building, with its classical Roman facade, now houses visitor information and a gold-diggings interpretive centre. Visit the 1860s Buda Historic Home and the Castlemaine Art Gallery.

5 **Maldon** The 1860s streets of Maldon are shaded by European trees and lined with old buildings of local stone. Declared a Notable Town by the National Trust, Maldon has historic B&Bs and a tourist steam train.

6 **Ballarat Begonia Festival** Every year in early March, Ballarat's 40-hectare Botanic Gardens are awash with colour. The 20 000-plus people who come to the festival enjoy gardening forums, street parades, fireworks, art shows, kids' activities and much more.

7 **Sovereign Hill** Ballarat's Sovereign Hill is a living museum. Blacksmiths, bakers and storekeepers in period dress ply their trades amid the tents, while miners pan for gold.

8 **Maryborough Old Railway Station** The former railway station now houses a tourist complex that includes an antique emporium, a woodworking shop and a restaurant and cafe.

TOP EVENTS

JAN	Organs of the Ballarat Goldfields (Ballarat)
MAR	Country Food and Wine Race Meeting (Avoca)
MAR	Ballarat Begonia Festival
EASTER	Easter Festival (Bendigo)
OCT–NOV	Folk Festival (Maldon)
NOV	Festival of Gardens (Castlemaine)

GOLD-RUSH HISTORY

Sovereign Hill in Ballarat offers a complete re-creation of life on the 1850s goldfields. The nearby Gold Museum, part of the Sovereign Hill complex, features displays of gold nuggets and coins, and changing exhibits on the history of gold. The Eureka Stockade Centre offers interpretive displays on Australia's only armed insurrection, which took place in 1854. See the original Eureka Flag at the Ballarat Fine Art Gallery, which also houses an excellent collection of work by artists such as Tom Roberts, Sidney Nolan and Russell Drysdale. In Eureka Street is the tiny Montrose Cottage (1856), an ex-miner's house furnished in the style of the period; here a museum display movingly recalls the lives and contribution of women in the gold-rush era. In Bendigo, the Central Deborah Gold Mine offers tours 80 metres down a reef mine, and excellent displays on goldmining techniques.

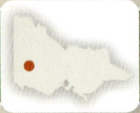

GRAMPIANS & CENTRAL WEST

Ancient mountains, semi-arid plains and farming landscapes typify this area, while Aboriginal rock-art sites are remnants of life before white settlement.

1

7

Jeparit T

Warracknabeal T   Lake Buloke

T Nhill o

Wycheproof T

WIMMERA

T Dimboola o

Donald o

LITTLE DESERT NATIONAL PARK

Mount Arapiles

O HORSHAM T

MOUNT ARAPILES–TOOAN STATE PARK

Natimuk T

AUSTRALIA

Laharumo

2

Edenhope T

Toolondo Reservoir

Wartook Reservoir

Lake Lonsdale

T Stawell T

Great Western

3

Halls Gap T

SOUTH

Rocklands Reservoir

GRAMPIANS NATIONAL PARK

T Ararat o

6

N

0   20 km

T Casterton o

T Coleraine o

THE GRAMPIANS

Lake Muirhead

Dunkeld T

Lake Bolac

T Hamilton o

MOUNT NAPIER STATE PARK

5

4

CLIMATE   STAWELL

MONTH	JAN	FEB	MAR	APR	MAY	JUN	JUL	AUG	SEP	OCT	NOV	DEC
MAXIMUM °C	27	28	25	20	16	13	12	14	16	19	22	26
MINIMUM °C	13	13	12	9	7	5	4	5	6	8	9	11
RAIN MM	36	28	33	41	57	60	67	67	64	58	36	29
RAINDAYS	6	5	7	9	12	16	18	18	14	12	9	7

→ For more detail see maps 288 & 291. For descriptions of T towns see Towns A–Z (p. 56).

VIEW FROM MOUNT ARAPILES

1 **The olive groves of Laharum**   Mount Zero Olives at Laharum is the largest olive plantation in the Southern Hemisphere, with 55 000 trees on 730 hectares. The first trees were planted in 1943, after World War II stopped olive oil imports. You can buy oil, vinegar and lentils, and stay overnight.

2 **Grampians day drive and balloon flights**
From Halls Gap, drive to Boroka Lookout, Reed Lookout and MacKenzie Falls. Break for lunch at Zumsteins, home to a large kangaroo population. Dawn hot-air balloon flights over the Grampians leave from Stawell.

3 **Wines of Great Western**   Grapevines were first planted at Seppelt's Great Western vineyards in 1865. Today the winery is best known for its red and white sparkling wines. Other wineries in the area include Best's and Garden Gully.

4 **Byaduk Caves**   These caves, located in Mount Napier State Park, are part of a giant, 24-kilometre lava flow stretching to Mt Eccles in the south-west, evidence of the volcanic activity that shaped the region's landscape. The caves, one of which is open, are a wonderland of ropey lava, columns, stalactites and stalagmites.

5 **Hamilton**   Hamilton is the commercial hub of the wool-rich Western District. Gracious houses and churches on its tree-lined streets testify to over a century of prosperity. Close to town are historic homesteads in magnificent gardens.

6 **Mount Arapiles**   Mount Arapiles is regarded as Australia's best rock-climbing venue, attracting interstate and international enthusiasts with its 2000 rock-climbing routes marked out across 365 metres of sandstone cliffs.

7 **Little Desert National Park**   During spring, more than 600 varieties of wildflowers and over 40 types of ground orchids flourish in this 132 647-hectare park. With nearly 600 kilometres of tracks, it is ideal for four-wheel driving, but perhaps the best way to appreciate the colourful spring display is on foot: for keen hikers, there is the 84-kilometre Desert Discovery Walk.

TOP EVENTS

JAN	Picnic Races (Great Western)
FEB	Grampians Jazz Festival (Halls Gap)
MAR	Jailhouse Rock Festival (Ararat)
EASTER	Stawell Easter Gift (professional footrace)
MAY	Grampians Grape Escape (Halls Gap)
JUNE–JULY	Australian Kelpie Muster and Kelpie Working Dog Auction (Casterton)

ABORIGINAL CULTURE

The Djab Wurrung and Jardwadjali people shared the territory they called Gariwerd for at least 5000 years before European settlement, although some evidence suggests up to 30 000 years of habitation. Brambuk – The National Park and Cultural Centre near Halls Gap, run by five Koorie communities, is an excellent first stop for information about the region's Indigenous heritage. The region contains 100 recorded rock-art sites, representing more than 80 per cent of all sites in Victoria. A Brambuk-guided tour of some of the sites (most are in Grampians National Park) is probably the most rewarding way to experience the meaning and nature of the art. Notable sites include Gulgurn Manja, featuring over 190 kangaroo, emu and handprint motifs, and Ngamadidj, a site decorated with 16 figures painted in white clay. Bunjil's Shelter is just outside the park near Stawell, and is the only site in the area where more than one colour is used and a known figure is represented. Bunjil was a creator spirit from the Dreaming.

MALLEE COUNTRY

The Murray River is the lifeblood of this region, allowing the cultivation of fruit crops and the development of various riverside settlements.

CLIMATE	MILDURA											
MONTH	JAN	FEB	MAR	APR	MAY	JUN	JUL	AUG	SEP	OCT	NOV	DEC
MAXIMUM °C	32	32	28	23	19	16	15	17	20	24	27	30
MINIMUM °C	17	16	14	10	8	5	4	5	7	10	12	15
RAIN MM	21	22	19	19	27	23	26	28	29	31	24	23
RAINDAYS	4	3	4	4	7	8	9	9	8	7	6	4

→ For more detail see map 291. For descriptions of ⊤ towns see Towns A–Z (p. 56).

1 Mildura With its museums and galleries, excellent dining and surrounding wineries and orchards, Mildura is like a colourful Mediterranean oasis. Go to the zoo, visit the Mildura Arts Complex and the Rio Vista museum (once the home of William Chaffey), or book a day tour with Indigenous guides to Mungo National Park in New South Wales.

2 River district wines The wine-producing areas of Mildura and Swan Hill are an unrecognised heartland of the Australian wine industry, producing 37 per cent of the total output – most for the bulk market, although prestige production is rising. The dozen or so wineries include the large Lindemans Karadoc estate, with cellar-door tastings and sales.

3 Swan Hill Pioneer Settlement This 7-hectare park offers a lively experience of river-port life in early Australia. Wander through the 19th-century-style streets, complete with staff in period dress. Ride on a paddlesteamer or book for the popular Sound and Light Tour. Also in the park is an Aboriginal canoe tree.

4 Wyperfeld National Park A park of brilliant sunsets, huge open spaces and spring wildflowers, Wyperfeld is explored via walks from Wonga Campground and Information Centre, 50 kilometres west of Hopetoun. The park is home to the endangered mallee fowl, a turkey-size bird that makes nesting mounds up to 5 metres across.

5 Stefano's The star of Mildura is Stefano's, the kind of place you dine at one night and love so much you go again the next. This may have something to do with the restaurant's beautiful setting in a historic hotel cellar – and celebrity chef Stefano de Pieri's food. The menu is degustation, with five different courses nightly, each focusing on the best local and seasonal produce; you can expect handmade pastas and dishes featuring the finest quality beef, pork and lamb.

EMU AND CHICKS, HATTAH–KULKYNE NATIONAL PARK

TOP EVENTS

MAR	Arts Festival (Mildura)
AUG–SEPT	Great Australian Vanilla Slice Triumph (Ouyen)
SEPT	Vintage Tractor Pull (Mildura)
SEPT–OCT	Country Music Festival (Mildura)

MURRAY AND MALLEE WILDLIFE

This landscape of rivers and plains is home to abundant wildlife. Most notable is the birdlife: spoonbills, herons, eagles, mallee fowl, harriers and kites are to be found in the parks and on the roadsides and riverbanks. Hattah–Kulkyne National Park protects around 200 bird species as well as the red kangaroo. Murray–Sunset National Park – true desert country in parts – includes riverine plains. It supports an array of native fauna, including mallee fowl and the rare black-eared miner. To see the kangaroos and birdlife of Wyperfeld National Park, follow the Brambruk Nature Trail.

GOULBURN & MURRAY

The Goulburn Valley contains Victoria's richest farm land, while the Murray has historical attractions, particulary the paddlesteamers of Echuca.

CLIMATE   ECHUCA

MONTH	JAN	FEB	MAR	APR	MAY	JUN	JUL	AUG	SEP	OCT	NOV	DEC
MAXIMUM °C	31	31	27	22	18	14	13	15	18	22	26	29
MINIMUM °C	15	15	13	9	7	5	4	5	6	9	11	14
RAIN MM	27	27	31	33	42	43	41	43	40	43	32	28
RAINDAYS	4	4	5	6	9	10	11	11	10	9	6	5

→   For more detail see maps 287 & 288–9. For descriptions of ⊕ towns see Towns A–Z (p. 56).

1 **Barmah State Park and State Forest** These neighbouring areas form the state's biggest river red gum forest. This is a popular area for bushwalking, canoeing and camping. Walking trails take in various Aboriginal sites, and the Dharnya Centre interprets the culture of the local Yorta Yorta people.

2 **Cobram** This lovely fruit-growing town is surrounded by peach, nectarine, pear and orange orchards. It also offers access to a number of wide, sandy beaches on the Murray, perfect for swimming, fishing, picnicking and watersports. Camping facilities are available, and across the river in New South Wales is the renowned 36-hole Cobram Barooga golf course.

3 **Seymour's Royal Hotel** Dating from 1848, this classic old pub on Emily Street in Seymour is a great spot to stop for a beer and counter meal. If the hotel looks vaguely familiar, it is because you might have seen it before in the famous, haunting painting *The Cricketers* (1948), by one of Australia's most notable artists, Russell Drysdale.

4 **Tahbilk winery** Tahbilk was established in 1860 on the sandy loam of the Goulburn River north of Nagambie. One of Australia's most beautiful wine properties, it has a National Trust–classified cellar, which – along with other buildings – is a timepiece of the early Australian wine industry. Tahbilk wines have won over 1000 awards.

5 **Echuca** The historic port of Echuca, with its impressive red-gum wharf, recalls the late 19th century, when the Murray carried wool and other goods from farms and stations. A number of beautifully restored paddlesteamers are moored here, including some offering cruises up the river.

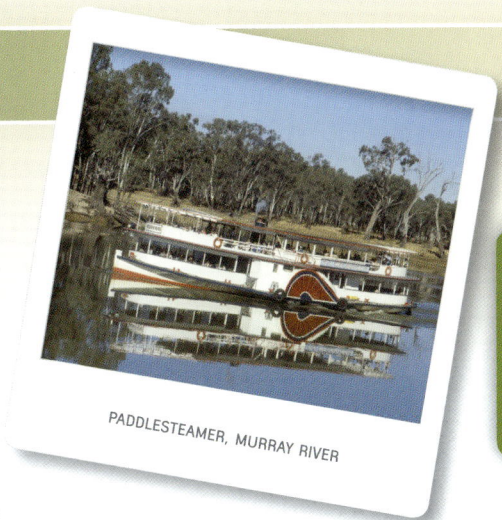

PADDLESTEAMER, MURRAY RIVER

TOP EVENTS

JAN	Peaches and Cream Festival (Cobram, odd-numbered years)
FEB	Southern 80 Ski Race (Torrumbarry Weir to Echuca)
FEB	Riverboats, Jazz, Food and Wine Festival (Echuca)
MAR	Bridge to Bridge Swim (Cohuna)
APR	Barmah Muster (Barmah State Forest)
JUNE	Steam, Horse and Vintage Rally (Echuca)

FOOD AND WINE

Irrigation has transformed the once-dusty Goulburn Valley into the fruit bowl of Victoria. Orchards, market gardens and farms supply the canneries in Shepparton, which are among the largest in the Southern Hemisphere. The valley is dotted with outlets for venison, poultry, smoked trout, berries, organic vegetables, honey, jams, preserves, fruit juices, mustards, pickles, vinegar and liquored truffles. The region's nine wineries make reliable reds and distinctive whites. Near Nagambie, Mitchelton Wines is known for shiraz and rieslings grown on sandy, riverine soils. At nearby Avenel, Plunkett Fowles Wines makes long-finishing chardonnay from grapes grown high in the Strathbogie Ranges.

HIGH COUNTRY

The Victorian Alps offer challenging skiing; beyond
the foothills lie charming old gold towns and
Rutherglen wineries.

CLIMATE MOUNT BULLER

MONTH	JAN	FEB	MAR	APR	MAY	JUN	JUL	AUG	SEP	OCT	NOV	DEC
MAXIMUM °C	16	17	14	10	7	3	2	2	5	8	12	14
MINIMUM °C	8	8	6	4	1	−1	−3	−2	−1	1	4	6
RAIN MM	83	66	79	136	161	160	190	185	156	185	155	124
RAINDAYS	7	5	8	12	14	14	15	16	14	16	13	11

→ For more detail see maps 279, 282, 284–5, 289 & 290. For descriptions of ⊤ towns see Towns A–Z (p. 56).

ALPINE LAKE, BOGONG HIGH PLAINS

1 Mount Buffalo National Park This 31 000-hectare national park is the state's oldest, declared in 1898. The Horn is the park's highest point and a great place for views at sunrise. Walking tracks are set among streams, waterfalls, wildflowers, and snow gum and mountain ash forest. There is summer camping, swimming and canoeing at Lake Catani. In winter, the Mount Buffalo ski area is popular with families.

2 Horseback riding Jack Riley, believed to be the original Man from Snowy River, is buried in Corryong's pretty hillside cemetery. Each year, at an annual festival honouring his memory, horseriding competitions are held to find his modern-day equivalent. A gentle trail ride through this stunning countryside is a great way to appreciate this High Country legend.

3 Lake Eildon Created by damming the Goulburn River in the 1950s, this lake is popular with watersports enthusiasts, anglers and houseboat holiday-makers. The surrounding Lake Eildon National Park offers bushwalking, camping and four-wheel-drive tracks through the foothills of the Victorian Alps.

4 Historic Beechworth The National Trust has classified over 30 buildings in what is now one of Australia's best-preserved gold-rush towns. Dine in a stately former bank, visit the powder magazine, wander through a cemetery for Chinese goldminers, and sample the goods from Beechworth Bakery.

5 Kelly country A giant effigy of Ned Kelly greets visitors to Glenrowan. After killing three local policemen in 1878, the Kelly Gang hid for two years in the Warby Range, raiding nearby towns. Visit the Ned Kelly Memorial Museum and Homestead in Gladstone Street.

6 Wines of Rutherglen The vines on the alluvial flats in a shallow loop of the Murray produce some of the world's great fortified wines. The region is known for tokays and muscats, big reds and – more recently – lighter reds such as gamay. There are over a dozen wineries near Rutherglen; look out for All Saints, Pfeiffer, Chambers, Gehrig Estate and Campbells.

TOP EVENTS

MAR	The High Country Autumn Festival (Mansfield)
MAR	Tastes of Rutherglen (district wineries)
APR	The Man from Snowy River Bush Festival (Corryong)
APR–MAY	Autumn Festival (Bright)
OCT–NOV	Festival of Jazz (Wangaratta)
NOV	Celtic Festival (Beechworth)

SKI COUNTRY

Victoria's ski resorts are within easy reach of Melbourne. They include, in order of their distance from the city: Mount Buller (via Mansfield), Mount Buffalo (via Myrtleford), Mount Hotham (via Bright) and Falls Creek (via Mount Beauty). All resorts offer a range of skiing, from protected runs for beginners to cross-country ski trails. Mount Hotham, known as the 'powder snow capital' of Australia, has the most challenging runs for experienced downhill skiers and snowboarders. After the snow melts a range of summer activities come in to play. The adventurous can try mountain-bike riding, tandem paragliding, abseiling or caving. Mountain lakes and streams offer trout fishing, swimming, sailing and canoeing. Trails across the mountains, ablaze with wildflowers in summer, can be explored on horseback or on foot. The less energetic can just breathe the crystalline air and gaze across the hazy blue ridges.

EAST GIPPSLAND

Natural wonders and outdoor activities abound in this region, which is blessed with some magnificent national parks and inland waterways.

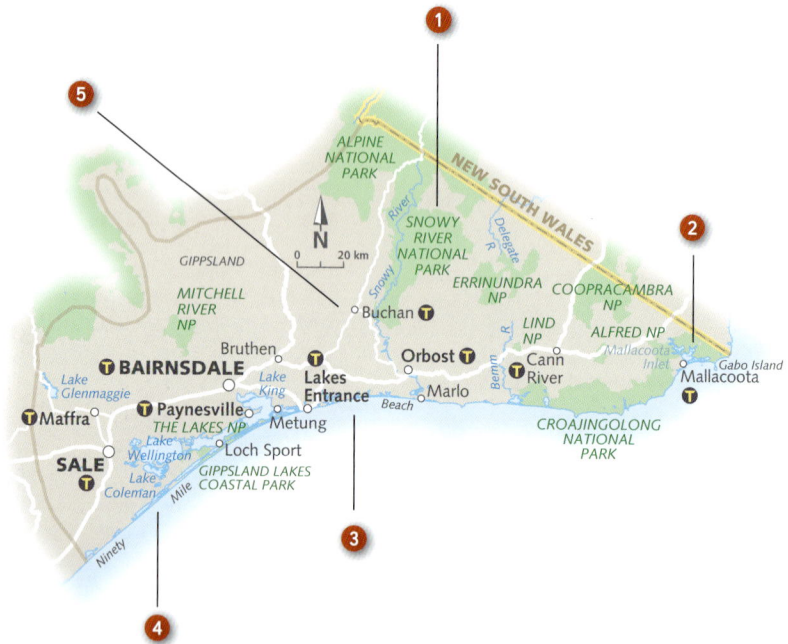

CLIMATE   LAKES ENTRANCE

MONTH	JAN	FEB	MAR	APR	MAY	JUN	JUL	AUG	SEP	OCT	NOV	DEC
MAXIMUM °C	24	24	22	20	17	15	15	16	17	19	20	22
MINIMUM °C	15	15	13	11	9	7	6	6	8	9	11	13
RAIN MM	56	41	56	63	67	65	54	51	59	64	71	70
RAINDAYS	9	7	10	10	11	13	12	14	13	13	12	11

→ For more detail see maps 289 & 290. For descriptions of ⓣ towns see Towns A–Z (p. 56).

1 Snowy River National Park The much-celebrated Snowy River begins as a trickle near Mount Kosciuszko and passes through wild limestone gorges and forest country before reaching a coastal lagoon. McKillops Bridge (via Buchan) is a beautiful area with camping and barbecue facilities, swimming spots and some good short walks.

2 Mallacoota Surrounded by the remote ocean beaches, estuarine waterways and unspoiled bush of Croajingolong National Park, this old-fashioned resort offers one of the best nature-based holidays in the state, with excellent fishing, walking, boating and swimming. Hire a boat in town and explore Mallacoota Inlet.

3 Lakes Entrance Lakes Entrance, at the head of the lakes, is a great base for fishing and boating, and offers accommodation to suit all budgets. For a holiday afloat, book a self-drive cruiser from nearby Metung. There are several wineries in the area – Wyanga Park Winery offers a lakes cruise from town to its cellar door and restaurant.

4 Large lakes and a long beach The Gippsland Lakes are fed by five major rivers and contained on the coastal side by Ninety Mile Beach. At the system's centre, The Lakes National Park offers birdwatching, walking, swimming and camping. Access is via boat from Paynesville or road and foot from Loch Sport.

5 Buchan Caves Reserve This spectacular limestone cave system comprises more than 350 caves, of which the Royal and Fairy caves are the most accessible. Fairy Cave is over 400 metres long, with impressive and elaborate stalactites and stalagmites, while Royal Cave impresses with pretty calcite-rimmed pools. Tours of both caves are run daily. After exploring the caves, you can cool off in a spring-fed swimming pool.

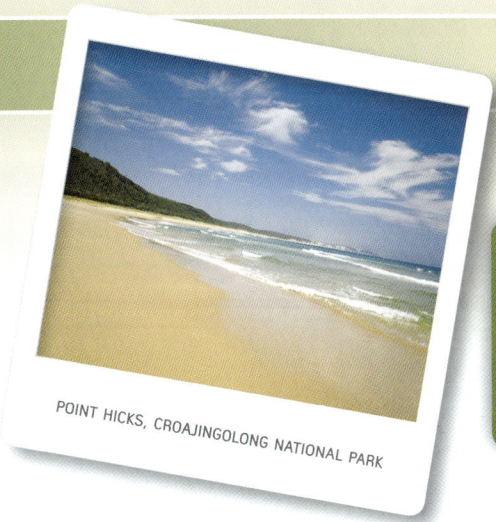

POINT HICKS, CROAJINGOLONG NATIONAL PARK

TOP EVENTS

JAN	Foothills Festival (Buchan)
FEB	Jazz Festival (Paynesville)
FEB	Blues and Arts Festival (Bruthen)
MAR	Marlay Point–Paynesville Overnight Yacht Race (from Marlay Point, near Sale)
MAR	Line Dancing Championships (Bairnsdale)
EASTER	Rodeo (Buchan)

FISHING

Fishing is a huge drawcard in East Gippsland. Fish for trout in the mountain streams and rivers – such as the Delegate River – or head for the coast. The lakes, rivers and inlets around Paynesville, Marlo, Bemm River and Mallacoota are great for bream, trevally and flathead. Boat angling is the best choice here, although land-based angling also yields results. Ninety Mile Beach and the remote beaches of The Lakes National Park provide some of the best surf-fishing in Victoria, with salmon, tailor and flathead among the prospects.

TOWNS A-Z
victoria

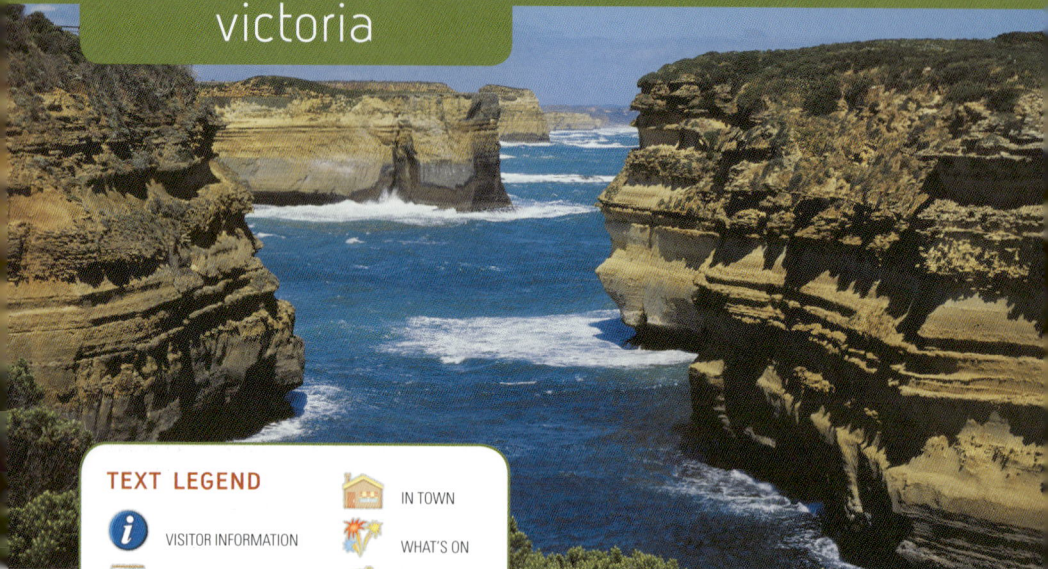

COAST NEAR LOCH ARD GORGE, PORT CAMPBELL NATIONAL PARK

TEXT LEGEND

(i) VISITOR INFORMATION

(radio) RADIO STATION

(house) IN TOWN

(whats on) WHAT'S ON

(compass) NEARBY

MAP LEGEND

══20══	Highway, sealed, with national route marker
══M1══	Main road, sealed, with state route marker
──────	Other road, sealed and unsealed
─ ─ ─ ─	Vehicle track
··········	Walking track
··········	Rail trail
🚉	Railway with station
GEELONG	Town / suburb

✪ Attraction	✚ Hospital	National park
◉ Where to eat / where to stay	Police station	Other reserve
✈ Airport	✉ Post office	Swamp / salt / flood
★ Lighthouse	S School	Sand
▲ Hill, peak, mountain	C College	Mine area
⚒ Mine site	U University	Reef
✟ Church		

Accredited Information	Fishing	Rail trail
Adventure	Golf course	Shopping
Barbecue	Lookout	Surfing
Bowling club	National Park	Toilets
Caravan park	Parking	Walking
Cycling	Picnic area	Wildlife

Alexandra

279 G1 | 282 C1 | 284 A5 | 287 D2 | 289 F3

(i) 36 Grant St; (03) 5772 1100 or 1800 652 298; www.alexandratourism.com

(radio) 102.9 FM ABC Local Radio, 106.9 UGFM Upper Goulburn Community Radio

Alexandra was apparently named after Alexandra, Princess of Wales, although, coincidentally, three men named Alexander discovered gold here in 1866. Situated in the foothills of the Great Dividing Range, Alexandra is supported primarily by agriculture. Nearby, the Goulburn River is an important trout fishery.

(house) ***Alexandra Timber Tramways:*** museum housed in the original railway station that offers an insight into the timber industry

around Alexandra; open 2nd Sun each month; Station St. *Art and craft galleries:* many outlets around town displaying and selling local art, pottery and glassware.

Bush market: Perkins St; 3rd Sat each month (excluding winter). *Picnic Races:* Jan, Mar, Oct and Nov. *Truck, Ute and Rod Show:* June. *Open Gardens Weekend:* Oct. *Rose Festival:* Nov.

McKenzie Nature Reserve: established in virgin bushland, with orchids and wildflowers during winter and spring; on the southern edge of town. *Self-guide tourist drives:* the Skyline Rd from Alexandra to Eildon features a number of lookouts along the way; information from visitor centre. *Taggerty:* home to the Willowbank Gallery and a bush market; open 4th Sat each month; 18 km s. *Trout fishing:* in the Goulburn, Acheron and Rubicon rivers. *Lake Eildon National Park:* excellent walking trails in the north-west section of the park, to the east of town; *for more details see Eildon.* *Bonnie Doon:* a good base for exploring the lake region. Activities include trail-riding, bushwalking, watersports and scenic drives; 37 km NE near Lake Eildon.

See also HIGH COUNTRY, pp. 52–3

Anglesea

278 C4 | 286 C2 | 287 A5 | 288 D4

Off Great Ocean Rd; or ring Torquay Information Centre, (03) 5261 4219 or 1300 614 219; www.visitsurfcoast.com

94.7 The Pulse FM, 774 AM ABC Local Radio

A pretty and sheltered part of the surf coast, Anglesea is one of the smaller holiday hamlets along the Great Ocean Road. The main beaches are patrolled from Christmas through to Easter, making it a favourite destination for both swimmers and beginner surfers.

Coogoorah Reserve Set on the Anglesea River, the name of this park means 'swampy reed creek'. Coogoorah was established after the 1983 Ash Wednesday fires and now features a network of boardwalks weaving through the distinctive wetland vegetation. Keep an eye out for fascinating local birdlife, including the peregrine falcon.

Anglesea Golf Course: golf enthusiasts share the green with kangaroos; Golf Links Rd. *Melaleuca Gallery:* open daily 11am–5.30pm; Great Ocean Rd. *Viewing platform:* overlooks open-cut brown-coal mine and power station; behind town in Coalmine Rd. *Paddleboats:* for hire on the banks of the Anglesea River.

Markets: local crafts and produce, held over summer, Easter and Melbourne Cup weekend; by the Anglesea River. *Rock to Ramp Swim:* Jan. *Anglesea Art Show:* June. *ANGAIR Wildflower and Art Show:* Sept.

Aireys Inlet This pretty little town is overlooked by a lighthouse built to guide passing ships along this treacherous coastline. Painkalac Creek flows out to the ocean here, creating the inlet of the town's name and a safe swimming spot. Horseriding and fishing are favourite activities along the sheltered beaches. South of town is the Great Ocean Road Memorial Arch, built in 1939. 11 km SW.

J. E. Loveridge Lookout: 1 km w. *Pt Roadknight Beach:* a shallow, protected beach, popular with families; 2 km SW. *Ironbark Basin Reserve:* features ocean views, local birdlife and good bushwalking. The Pt Addis Koorie Cultural Walk leads through the park, highlighting sites of Indigenous significance; 7 km NW, off Pt Addis Rd. *Great Otway National Park:* the park begins near Anglesea and stretches to the south and west. The section near Anglesea features unique heathland flora and good walking trails; access via Aireys Inlet, 11 km SW. *For more details see Apollo Bay.* *Surf Coast Walk:* 30 km from Torquay to Moggs Creek

TOWNS

(south of Aireys Inlet). The track passes through Anglesea. *Surf schools:* learn to surf on one of the beginner courses available at nearby beaches; details from visitor centre.

See also South-West Coast, pp. 42–3

Apollo Bay

278 A5 | 286 B3 | 288 D5

ℹ️ **Great Ocean Road Visitor Information Centre, 100 Great Ocean Rd; 1300 689 297; www.visitgreatoceanroad.org.au**

📻 89.5 FM ABC Local Radio, 104.7 Otway FM

Named after a local schooner, Apollo Bay has become the resting place of many shipwrecks, yet it maintains an appeal for all lovers of the ocean. The town is situated near Otway National Park with a wonderful contrast between rugged coastline and tranquil green hills. The seaside town is popular with fishing enthusiasts and, like many other towns along this stretch of coast, its population swells significantly over summer as visitors flock here for the holidays.

🏠 *Old Cable Station Museum:* features artefacts from Australia's telecommunications history and informative displays exploring the history of the region; open 2–5pm weekends and school and public holidays; Great Ocean Rd. *Bass Strait Shell Museum:* holds an impressive array of shells and provides many facts about the marine life along the Victorian south-west coast; Noel St. *Great Ocean Walk:* enjoy stunning views on this 91 km walk between Apollo Bay and Glenample Homestead, near the Twelve Apostles. Walkers must register to use campgrounds en route. Further information available at www. greatoceanwalk.com.au

🎆 *Foreshore Market:* each Sat. *Apollo Bay Music Festival:* Apr.

🛡️ **Great Otway National Park** Formerly named Otway National Park, this section of the 103 000 ha park includes some of the most rugged coastline in Victoria, particularly around Cape Otway and the stretch of coast towards Princetown. It is an ideal location for a bushwalking adventure taking in sights through the park to the sea, from the scenic Elliot River down to adjacent Shelly Beach. Many species of wildlife inhabit the park, including koalas and the rare tiger quoll. Also look out for the historic Cape Otway Lighthouse, built in 1848. The Great Ocean Rd, west of Apollo Bay, passes through the park. Contact Parks Victoria on 13 1963; 13 km sw.

Otway Fly The consistently popular Otway Fly is a steel-trussed walkway perched high among the temperate rainforest treetops of the Otway Ranges. The 'Fly' is 25 m high and stretches for 600 m. It is accessible to all ages and levels of mobility. Get a bird's-eye view of ancient myrtle beech, blackwood and mountain ash while looking out for a variety of wildlife, including pygmy possums and the raucous yellow-tailed black cockatoo. A springboard bridge takes you over Youngs Creek, where you might spot a shy platypus. Inquiries on 1800 300 477; 62 km nw via Lavers Hill.

Marriners Lookout: with views across Skenes Creek and Apollo Bay; 1.5 km nw. *Barham Paradise Scenic Reserve:* in the Barham River Valley, it is home to a variety of distinctive moisture-loving trees and ferns; 7 km nw. *Tanybryn Gallery:* displays and sells art and craft work in the magnificent surrounds of the Otway Ranges; Skenes Creek Rd; 20 km ne. *Forests and Waterfall Drive:* 109 km loop drive featuring spectacular Otway Ranges scenery. Waterfalls include Beauchamp, Triplet and Houptoun falls. Drive starts at Apollo Bay, travels west to Lavers Hill and around to Skenes Creek. Map from visitor centre. *Charter flights:* views of the Twelve Apostles, the Bay of Islands and the 'Shipwreck Coast'; details from visitor centre.

See also South-West Coast, pp. 42–3

Ararat

288 C3

ℹ️ Railway Station Complex, 91 High St; (03) 5355 0281 or 1800 657 158; www.visitararat.com.au

📻 99.9 VoiceFM, 107.9 FM ABC Local Radio

Ararat is a city with a vibrant history. Once inhabited by the Tjapwurong Aboriginal people, the promising lands soon saw squatters move in, and the area really started to boom when gold was discovered in 1854. Thousands of prospectors arrived, and Ararat finally came into existence when Chinese immigrants rested on the town's site in 1857, after walking from South Australian ports in order to avoid Victorian poll taxes. One member of the party discovered alluvial gold, and Ararat was born. Today Ararat is a service centre to its agricultural surrounds.

🏠 **J Ward** The town's original gaol, 'J Ward' served as an asylum for the criminally insane for many years and offers an eerie glimpse into the history of criminal confinement. Now guided tours reveal in chilling detail what life was like for the inmates. Girdlestone St; daily tours (03) 5352 3357.

Gum San Chinese Heritage Centre Gum San means 'hill of gold', a fitting name for this impressive centre built in traditional Southern Chinese style and incorporating the principles of feng shui. The centre celebrates the contribution of the Chinese community both to Ararat, which is said to be the only goldfields town founded by Chinese prospectors, and to the surrounding Goldfields region. The experience is brought to life with interactive displays and an original Canton lead-mining tunnel, uncovered during the building of the centre. Western Hwy; (03) 5352 1078.

Alexandra Park and Botanical Gardens: an attractive formal garden featuring ornamental lakes, fountains and an orchid glasshouse;

Vincent St. *Historical self-guide tours (walking or driving):* of particular note are the bluestone buildings in Barkly St, including the post office, town hall, civic square and war memorial; details from visitor centre. *Ararat Art Gallery:* a regional gallery specialising in wool and fibre pieces by local artists; Barkly St. *Langi Morgala Museum:* displays Aboriginal artefacts; Queen St.

🎆 *Jailhouse Rock Festival:* Mar. *Australian Orchid Festival:* Sept. *Golden Gateway Festival:* held over 10 days; Oct.

🧭 **Mt Buangor State Park** The park features the Fern Tree Waterfalls and the 3 impressive peaks of Mt Buangor, Mt Sugarloaf and Cave Hill. Its diverse terrain with many varieties of eucalypts offers great sightseeing, bushwalking and picnicking. There are more than 130 species of birds, as well as eastern grey kangaroos, wallabies and echidnas. Contact Parks Victoria on 13 1963. Access to the southern section is via Ferntree Rd off the Western Hwy; 30 km E. Mt Buangor and Cave Hill can be accessed from the main Mt Cole Rd in the Mt Cole State Forest.

Garden Gully Winery: hosts a scarecrow competition each Apr, with ingenious entries from across the state scattered through the vineyard; 17 km N on Western Hwy. Many more of the region's wineries can be accessed on the Great Grape Rd, a circuit through Ballarat and St Arnaud. This region is famous for sparkling whites and traditional old shiraz varieties; brochure and map from visitor centre. *Green Hill Lake:* great for fishing and water activities; 4 km E. *McDonald Park Wildflower Reserve:* an extensive display of flora indigenous to the area, including wattles and banksias, particularly impressive during the spring months; 5 km N on Western Hwy. *One Tree Hill Lookout:* 360-degree views across the region; 5 km NW. *Langi Ghiran State Park:* Mt Langi Ghiran and Mt Gorrin form the key features of this park. A popular walk starts at the picnic area along Easter Creek, then goes to the Old Langi Ghiran Reservoir and along the stone water race to a scenic lookout; access via Western Hwy, Kartuk Rd; 14 km E. *Mt Cole State Forest:* adjoins Mt Buangor State Park, with bushwalking, horseriding, four-wheel driving and trail-bike riding. The Ben Nevis Fire Tower offers spectacular views; 35 km E.

See also GRAMPIANS & CENTRAL WEST, pp. 46–7

Avoca

283 A3 | 288 C3

ⓘ **122 High St; (03) 5465 1000 or 1800 206 622; www.pyreneestourism.com.au**

📻 91.1 FM ABC Local Radio, 96.5 Radio KLFM

Avoca was built during the gold boom of the 19th century and is renowned for its wide main street, divided by a stretch of park complete with trees and a war memorial. Avoca is set in the picturesque Pyrenees Ranges, with the Avoca River flowing by the town.

🏠 **Historic walk:** takes in the original courthouse, one of the oldest surviving courts in Victoria, as well as the powder magazine and Lalor's, one of the state's earliest pharmacies; map from visitor centre. *Cemetery:* Chinese burial ground from the goldmining period; on outskirts of town.

🎆 **Avoca Fine Wine, Arts and Craft Market:** 3rd Sun each month. *Blue Pyrenees Pink Lamb and Purple Shiraz Race Meeting:* country race meeting; Mar. *Petanque Tournaments (French Bowls):* Mar and Dec. *Mt Avoca Anzac Day Races:* Apr. *Taltarni Cup Races:* Oct.

🏅 **Pyrenees Ranges State Forest** Covering an extensive stretch of bushland, these ranges are great for bushwalking and are popular for picnics and camping. Visitors can see a variety of wildlife, including koalas, wallabies,

kangaroos and goannas. Orchids and lilies can be found growing around the base of the ranges in season. An 18 km walking track starts at The Waterfall camping area and finishes at Warrenmang–Glenlofty Rd. Access via Sunraysia or Pyrenees hwys. For further information contact the Department of Sustainability and Environment Customer Sevice Centre on 13 1186.

Blue Pyrenees Estate: with underground cellar, petanque piste and gourmet lunches on weekends; 7 km W. *Mt Lonarch Arts:* displays and sells fine bone china made on the premises; Mt Lonarch; 10 km S. *Warrenmang Vineyard Resort:* with cottage-style accommodation and a restaurant specialising in regional produce. The vineyard is also the venue for A Sparkling Affair each Nov, an event celebrating the release of sparkling wines; 22 km NW. *Wine-tasting tours:* including self-guide Great Grape Rd; details from visitor centre.

See also GOLDFIELDS, pp. 44–5

Bacchus Marsh

278 D2 | 283 D5 | 287 B3 | 288 D3

ⓘ **156 Main St; (03) 5367 7488; www.discoverbacchusmarsh.org**

📻 98.5 3APL Apple FM, 774 AM ABC Local Radio

Bacchus Marsh shares part of its name with the Roman god of wine, but is actually better known for the apples that grow so well in the fertile valley region between the Werribee and Lerderderg rivers. Although it is now considered a satellite town within commuting distance of Melbourne, Bacchus Marsh retains a certain charm with stunning heritage buildings and a rural atmosphere.

🏠 **Avenue of Honour** Visitors to the town are greeted by the sight of the renowned Avenue of Honour, an elm-lined stretch of road built in honour of the Australian soldiers who fought in WW I. Eastern approach to town.

Big Apple Tourist Orchard: fresh produce market; Avenue of Honour. *Historic buildings:* include The Manor, the original home of the town's founder, Captain Bacchus (now privately owned), and Border Inn, built in 1850, thought to be the state's first service stop for Cobb & Co coaches travelling to the goldfields; details from visitor centre. *Local history museum:* connected to the blacksmith cottage and forge; open Sat–Sun; Main St. *Naturipe Fruits, Strawberry, Peach and Nectarine Farm:* pick-your-own fruits and roadside sales; Avenue of Honour.

🎆 *Rotary Art Show:* June.

🧭 **Lerderderg State Park** Featuring the imposing Lerderderg Gorge, the park is a great venue for picnics, bushwalking and swimming, while the Lerderderg River is ideal for trout fishing. The area was mined during the gold rush, and remnants from the water races used for washing gold can still be found upstream from O'Brien's Crossing. Late winter and spring are good times to see wildflowers and blossoming shrubs. Look out for koalas nestled in giant manna gums and for the magnificent sulphur-crested cockatoo and the wedge-tailed eagle. Contact Parks Victoria on 13 1963. Access via Western Fwy to Bacchus Marsh–Gisborne and Lerderderg Gorge rds; 10 km N.

Werribee Gorge State Park Over time the Werribee River has carved through ancient seabed sediment and lava flows to form a spectacular gorge. The name 'Werribee' comes from the Aboriginal word 'Wearibi', meaning 'swimming place' or 'backbone', perhaps in reference to the snake-like path of the river. Rock climbing is permitted at Falcons Lookout and a popular walk follows the Werribee River from the Meikles Pt picnic area, providing views of the river and the gorge cliff-faces. Contact Parks Victoria on 13 1963. Access via

Western Fwy and Pentland Hills Rd to Myers Rd, or via Ironbark Rd (the Ballan–Ingliston Rd) from the Bacchus Marsh–Anakie Rd; 10 km W.

Long Forest Flora Reserve: a great example of the distinctive mallee scrub that once covered the region; 2 km NE. *St Anne's Vineyard:* with a bluestone cellar built from the remains of the old Ballarat Gaol; Western Fwy; 6 km W. *Merrimu Reservoir:* attractive park area with picnic facilities; about 10 km NE. *Melton:* now virtually a satellite suburb of Melbourne, this town has a long and rich history of horse breeding and training. Visit the Willow Homestead to see exhibits detailing the life of early settlers (open Wed, Fri and Sun), picnic on the Werribee River at Melton Reservoir, or taste the fine wines in the nearby Sunbury Wine Region; 14 km E. *Brisbane Ranges National Park:* with good walking tracks, wildflowers during spring and the imposing, steep-sided Anakie Gorge; 16 km SW. *Ballan:* try the refreshing mineral-spring water at Bostock Reservoir, or join in the festivities at the Vintage Machinery and Vehicle Rally in Feb, and an Autumn Festival held each Mar; 20 km NW. *Blackwood:* places to visit include the Mineral Springs Reserve and Garden of St Erth (closed Wed and Thurs). Blackwood is also the start of the 53 km return scenic drive through the Wombat State Forest; 31 km NW.

See also Spa & Garden Country, pp. 38–9

Bairnsdale

289 H4 | 290 A4

ℹ️ **240 Main St; (03) 5152 3444 or 1800 637 060; www.lakesandwilderness.com.au**

📻 100.7 FM ABC Local Radio, 105.5 3REG Radio East Gippsland FM

An attractive rural centre situated on the Mitchell River Flats and considered to be the

TOWNS

western gateway to the lakes and wilderness region of East Gippsland. The area has a rich Koorie history brought to life through local landmarks, especially in Mitchell River National Park, where a fascinating piece of Aboriginal folklore is based around the Den of Nargun.

Aboriginal culture The Krowathunkoolong Keeping Place, on Dalmahoy St, details the cultural history of the region's Kurnai Aboriginal people and provides an insight into the impact of white settlement. To explore local Aboriginal history further, visit Howitt Park, Princes Hwy – a tree here has a 4 m scar where bark has been removed to make a canoe. The Bataluk Cultural Trail from Sale to Cann River takes in these and other Indigenous sites of East Gippsland. Details of the trail from Krowathunkoolong.

Historical Museum: built in 1891, contains relics from Bairnsdale's past; Macarthur St. *Jolly Jumbuck Country Craft Centre:* wool spinning and knitting mills, plus woollen products for sale; edge of town. *Self-guide heritage walks:* take in St Mary's Church, with wall and ceiling murals by Italian artist Francesco Floreani, and the Court House, a magnificent, castle-like construction; details from visitor centre.

Howitt Park Market: 4th Sun each month. *Line Dancing Championships:* Mar. *East Gippsland Agricultural Field Days:* popular event with family entertainment; Apr. *Bairnsdale Easter Races:* Easter. *Bairnsdale Cup:* Sept.

Mitchell River National Park Set in the remnants of temperate rainforest, this park has its own piece of mythology. According to Koorie history, Nargun was a beast made all of stone except for his hands, arms and breast. The fierce creature would drag unwary travellers to his den, a shallow cave beneath a waterfall on the Woolshed Creek. This Den of Nargun can be found within the park, as can giant kanooka trees, wildflowers and over 150 species of birds. There is a circuit walk to Bluff Lookout and

Mitchell River, and Billy Goat Bend is a good spot for picnics. Contact Parks Victoria on 13 1963; Princes Hwy; 15 km w near Lindenow.

McLeods Morass Wildlife Reserve: a boardwalk extends over the freshwater marshland, allowing a close-up view of the many species of waterbirds found here; southern outskirts of town, access via Macarthur St; 2 km s. *Wineries:* include Nicholson River Winery, for tastings and sales; 10 km E. *Bruthen:* hosts a Blues Bash each Feb; 24 km NW. *Dargo:* historic township in Dargo River valley and major producer of walnuts. Dargo Valley Winery has accommodation and cellar-door sales. The road beyond Dargo offers a scenic drive through high plains to Hotham Heights, stunning in spring when wattles bloom (unsealed road, check conditions); 93 km NW.

See also EAST GIPPSLAND, pp. 54–5

Ballarat

see inset box on page 64

Beechworth

284 D2 | 289 G2

i Ford St; (03) 5728 3233 or 1300 366 321; www.beechworth.com

101.3 Oak FM, 106.5 FM ABC Local Radio

Set in the picturesque surrounds of the Australian Alps, Beechworth is one of the state's best preserved 19th-century gold towns, with over 30 buildings listed by the National Trust. The grandeur of Beechworth's buildings can be explained by the fact that during the 1850s over four million ounces of gold were mined here. There is a delightful tale about Beechworth's heyday: the story goes that Daniel Cameron, a political candidate vying for support from the Ovens Valley community, rode at the head of a procession through the town on a horse shod with golden shoes. Sceptics claim they were merely gilded, but the tale offers a glimpse into the wealth of Beechworth during the gold rush.

Historic and cultural precinct This fantastic precinct provides a snapshot of 19th-century Beechworth. Featuring fine, honey-coloured granite buildings, the area incorporates the telegraph station, gold office, Chinese prospectors' office, town hall and powder magazine. Of particular interest is the courthouse, site of many infamous trials including Ned Kelly's, and where Sir Isaac Isaacs began his legal career. Also in the precinct is the Robert O'Hara Burke Memorial Museum, with the interesting 'Strand of Time' exhibition where 19th-century Beechworth shops are brought to life.

Beechworth Gaol Built in 1859, the original wooden gates of this gaol were replaced with iron ones when it was feared prisoners would break out in sympathy with Ned Kelly during his trial. The gaol is located in William St but not presently open to the public.

Walking tours: Ned Kelly and Gold Rush walking tours operate daily, and Ghost Tours are available at the former Mayday Hills Asylum; bookings at visitor centre. *Carriage Museum and Australian Light Horse Exhibition:* National Trust horse-drawn carriage display and Australian Light Horse Exhibition housed at the historic Murray Breweries, which also offers turn-of-the-century gourmet cordial made to time-honoured recipes; 29 Last St. *Beechworth Honey Experience:* interpretive display on the history of honey; includes a glass-fronted live bee display. A wide range of premium Australian honey is on offer in the concept shop; Cnr Ford and Church sts. *Harry Power's Cell:* under the shire offices, where the 'gentleman bushranger' was once briefly held; Albert Rd. *The Beechworth Pantry:* gourmet cafe and centre for produce of the north-east; Ford St. *Beechworth Bakery:* famous for its pastries and cakes; Camp St.

Country Craft Market: Queen Victoria Park, 4 times a year; details from visitor centre. *Golden Horseshoes Festival:* a celebration of the town's past, with street parades and a variety of market stalls; Easter. *Beechworth Harvest Celebration:* May; details from visitor centre. *Drive Back in Time:* vintage car rally; May. *Celtic Festival:* music festival; Nov.

Beechworth Cemetery This cemetery is a fascinating piece of goldfields history. More than 2000 Chinese goldminers are buried here. Twin ceremonial Chinese burning towers stand as a monument to those who died seeking their fortune far from home. Northern outskirts of town.

Beechworth Historic Park: surrounds the town and includes Woolshed Falls Historical Walk through former alluvial goldmining sites. *Gorge Scenic Drive (5 km):* starts north of town. *Beechworth Forest Drive:* takes in Fletcher Dam; 3 km SE towards Stanley. *Kellys Lookout:* at Woolshed Creek; about 4 km N. *Mt Pilot Lookout:* views of Murray Valley, plus signposted Aboriginal cave paintings nearby; 5 km N. *Stanley:* a historic goldmining settlement with fantastic views of the alps from the summit of Mt Stanley; 10 km SE. *Wineries:* 5 cellar doors in and around Beechworth for tastings and sales; map from visitor centre.

See also HIGH COUNTRY, pp. 52–3

Benalla

284 B2 | 289 F2

14 Mair St; (03) 5762 1749; www.benallaonline.com.au

97.7 FM ABC Local Radio, 101.3 Oak FM

Motorists from Melbourne entering Benalla will notice the Rose Gardens positioned beside the highway a short distance before Lake Benalla – gardens for which the city has

TOWNS

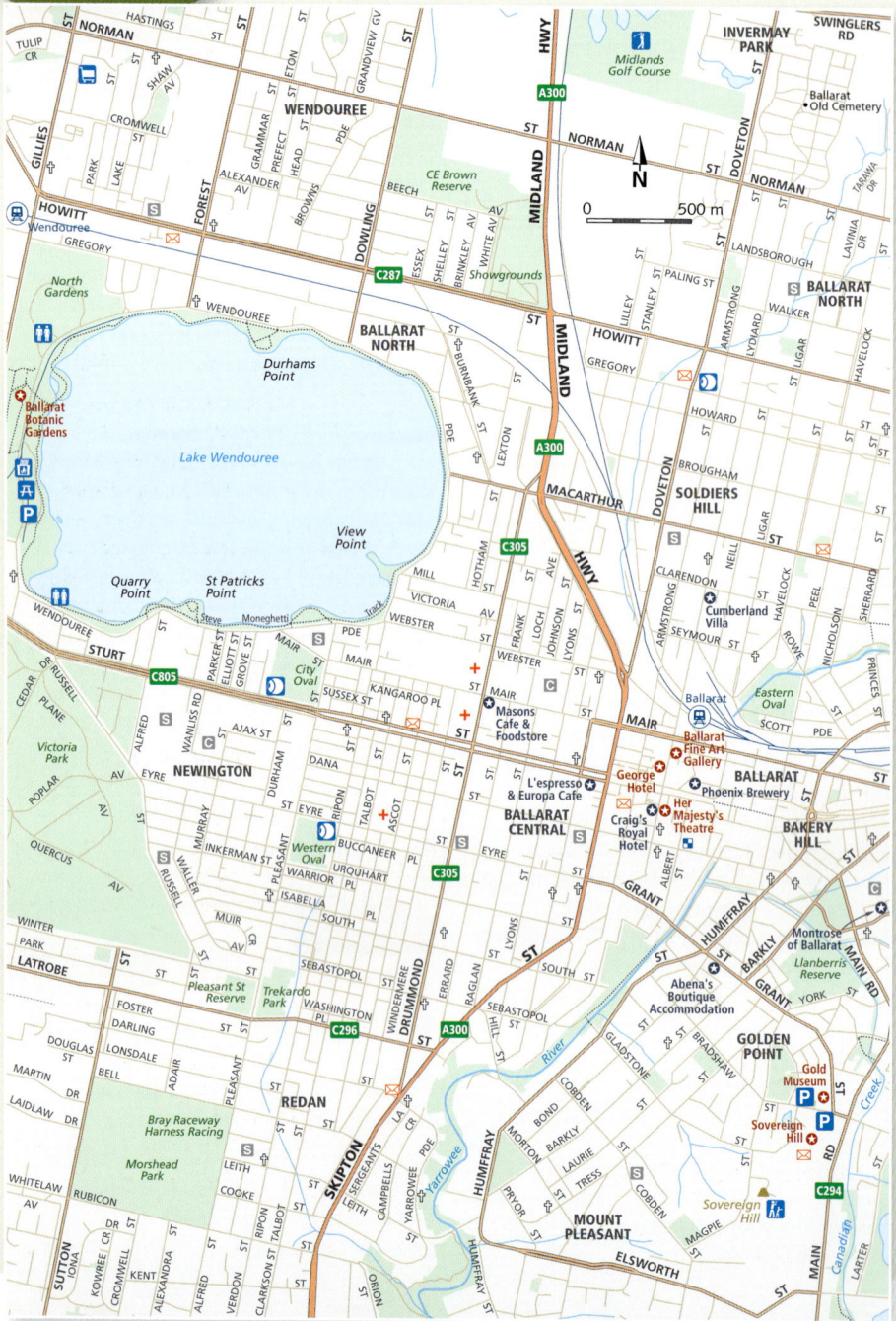

BALLARAT

Midlands Golf Course

Ballarat Old Cemetery

INVERMAY PARK

SWINGLERS RD

A300

NORMAN

WENDOUREE

CE Brown Reserve

Showgrounds

C287

HOWITT

Wendouree

GREGORY

North Gardens

BALLARAT NORTH

WENDOUREE

BALLARAT NORTH

LANDSBOROUGH

Durhams Point

Ballarat Botanic Gardens

Lake Wendouree

HOWITT

GREGORY

View Point

MACARTHUR

SOLDIERS HILL

BROUGHAM

Quarry Point

St Patricks Point

Steve Moneghetti Track

VICTORIA

WEBSTER

HOWARD

CLARENDON

Cumberland Villa

SEYMOUR

WENDOUREE

STURT

C805

City Oval

KANGAROO PL

MILL

PDE

MAIR

WEBSTER

MAIR

Ballarat

Eastern Oval

SCOTT

PDE

AJAX ST

SUSSEX ST

Victoria Park

NEWINGTON

DANA

MAIR

Ballarat Fine Art Gallery

L'espresso & Europa Cafe

George Hotel

Phoenix Brewery

BALLARAT

Western Oval

C305

Masons Cafe & Foodstore

BALLARAT CENTRAL

Craig's Royal Hotel

Her Majesty's Theatre

BAKERY HILL

WINTER PARK

LATROBE

Pleasant St Reserve

Trekardo Park

SOUTH

SEBASTOPOL

WASHINGTON

C296

WINDERMERE

DRUMMOND

A300

SEBASTOPOL

GRANT

HUMFFRAY

BARKLY

GRANT

Montrose of Ballarat

Llanberris Reserve

YORK

Abena's Boutique Accommodation

GOLDEN POINT

FOSTER

DARLING

LONSDALE

BELL

REDAN

Bray Raceway Harness Racing

Morshead Park

SKIPTON

Gold Museum

Sovereign Hill

Sovereign Hill

MOUNT PLEASANT

ELSWORTH

C294

Yarrowee River

Canadian Creek

0 — 500 m

N

278 B2 | 283 B5 | 287 A3 | 288 D3

ℹ The Eureka Centre, cnr Rodier and Eureka sts; 1800 446 633; www.ballarat.com

📻 99.9 VoiceFM, 107.9 FM ABC Local Radio

Ballarat is Victoria's largest inland city and features grand old buildings and wide streets that create an air of splendour. Built on the wealth of the region's goldfields, Ballarat offers activities ranging from fine dining in the many restaurants to real-life experiences of the area's goldmining past. Although dry in recent years, Lake Wendouree provides a beautiful backdrop for picnics and the many festivals that take place during the year. Ballarat was the site of the infamous Eureka Rebellion of 3 December 1854. When goldfields police attempted to quell the miners' anger over strict mining-licence laws, a bloody massacre eventuated. The Eureka Rebellion is viewed by many as a symbol of the Australian workers' struggle for equity and a 'fair go'. The best place to get a feel for this historic event is at Sovereign Hill.

🏠 **Sovereign Hill** This is the main destination for visitors to Ballarat and a good place to get a taste for what life was like on the Victorian goldfields. Spread over 60 ha, Sovereign Hill is a replica goldmining town, complete with authentically dressed townspeople. Panning for gold is a popular activity, while in the evening the 'Blood on the Southern Cross' show re-enacts the Eureka Rebellion. Bradshaw St; (03) 5337 1100.

Eureka Stockade Centre: a uniquely designed building, with information about the infamous battle; Eureka St. *Ballarat Botanic Gardens:* an impressive collection of native and exotic plants; Prime Minister Ave features busts of all of Australia's prime ministers. *Ballarat Wildlife Park:* houses native Australian animals such as koalas, kangaroos, quokkas and crocodiles; Cnr Fussel and York sts.

Ballarat Fine Art Gallery: holds a significant collection of Australian art. The original Eureka Rebellion flag is also on display; 40 Lydiard St. *Gold Museum:* details the rich goldmining history of the area; opposite Sovereign Hill. *Historic buildings:* include Her Majesty's Theatre, built in 1875 and Australia's oldest intact, purpose-built theatre, and Craig's Royal and the George hotels, with classic old-world surroundings; Lydiard St. *Vintage Tramway:* via Wendouree Pde; rides weekends, and public and school holidays. *Avenue of Honour and Arch of Victory:* honours those who fought in WW I; western edge of city.

🎆 *Pleasant St Market:* 4th Sun each month. *Ballarat Lakeside Farmers Market:* Lake Wendouree foreshore; 2nd Sat each month. *Organs of the Ballarat Goldfields:* music festival held in historic venues; Jan. *Begonia Festival:* popular event for garden lovers; Mar. *Royal South Street Eisteddfod:* music festival; Sept–Nov. *Ballarat Cup:* Nov.

🧭 **Enfield State Park** Great for bushwalking or horseriding, the park is home to many species of orchids and numerous animals including echidnas, koalas, bats and frogs. There is a pretty picnic ground at Remote Long Gully, and numerous walking tracks. Also featured are the remnants of early goldmining settlements, including the Berringa Mines Historic Reserve. Contact Parks Victoria on 13 1963; access via Incolls and Misery Creek rds; 16 km s.

Buninyong Buninyong features many fine art and craft galleries. Ballarat Bird World, home to many species of parrots, has raised walkways through the aviaries. Visit in Mar for the Gold King Festival, which celebrates the early history of the town, and in May for the Buninyong Film Festival. The Mt Buninyong Lookout east of town offers great views. 13 km SE.

continued overleaf

TOWNS

📻 RADIO STATION   🏠 IN TOWN   🎆 WHAT'S ON   🧭 NEARBY

BALLARAT continued

Kirks and Gong Gong reserves: ideal for picnics and bushwalking, these parks include many unique, indigenous plants; on opposite sides of Daylesford Rd; 5 km NE. *Kryal Castle:* replica of a medieval castle, with daily tours and family entertainment; 9 km E. *Yuulong Lavender Estate:* set in scenic landscaped gardens, the estate produces and sells lavender products; 15 km SE at Yendon. *Lal Lal Falls:* plunge 30 m into the Moorabool River; 18 km SE. *Lal Lal Blast Furnace:* fascinating 19th-century archaeological remains; 18 km SE. *Lake Burrumbeet:* this 2100 ha lake is a popular fishing spot, especially for redfin in spring and summer. Watersports and family activities are available on the lake; various boat ramps provide access. Caravan parks are set on the lakeside and are popular with holiday-makers; 22 km NW. *Skipton:* in town is an eel factory selling smoked eel and other products; 51 km SW. South of town are the Mt Widderin Caves – one has been named the Ballroom, as it was once a venue for dances and concerts. The caves are on private property; tours by appt (03) 5340 2081. *Beaufort:* a small town on the shores of Lake Beaufort, an artificial lake surrounded by gardens, providing a picturesque location for picnics and leisurely walks; 54 km W. South of town is Lake Goldsmith, home of a major rally of steam-driven machinery and vehicles each May and Nov. *Mooramong Homestead:* built in the 1870s and then altered during the 1930s by its ex-Hollywood owners. It is surrounded by beautiful gardens and a flora and fauna reserve, and is open for tours 3rd Sun each month; 56 km NW via Skipton. *Great Grape Rd:* circuit through Avoca, St Arnaud and Stawell, visiting local wineries.

See also GOLDFIELDS, pp. 44–5

PANNING FOR GOLD, SOVEREIGN HILL

become known as the 'Rose City'. The town is Sir Edward 'Weary' Dunlop's birthplace and proudly advertises the fact with a museum display and a statue in his honour at the Benalla Botanical Gardens.

Benalla Art Gallery Set by picturesque Lake Benalla, the gallery features an impressive collection including contemporary Australian art, works by Sidney Nolan, Arthur Streeton, Tom Roberts and Arthur Boyd, and a substantial collection of Indigenous art. Built in 1975, the gallery is a striking work of modern architecture. There is a permanent exhibition featuring the works of Laurie Ledger, a local resident, and examples of the Heidelberg School and early colonial art. Bridge St; (03) 5762 3027.

Benalla Ceramic Art Mural: a Gaudi-inspired community construction, this fascinating 3D mural is opposite the art gallery on Lake Benalla. *The Creators Gallery:* paintings, pottery and craft; at the information centre. *Benalla Costume and Pioneer Museum:* has period costumes, a Ned Kelly exhibit (including Kelly's cummerbund) and a feature display of Benalla's 'famous sons', in particular, Sir Edward 'Weary' Dunlop; Mair St. *Lake Benalla:* created in Broken River, it has good recreation and picnic facilities and is a haven for waterbirds. Take the self-guide walk around the lake. *Botanical Gardens:* features a splendid collection of roses and memorial statue of Sir Edward 'Weary' Dunlop; Bridge St. *Aeropark:* centre for the Gliding Club of Victoria, offering hot-air ballooning and glider flights; northern outskirts of town; bookings (03) 5762 1058.

Lakeside Craft and Farmers Market: near the Civic Centre; 3rd Sat each month. *Benalla Festival:* Feb/Mar.

Reef Hills State Park The forest here features grey box, river red gum, wildflowers in spring and wattle blossom in winter. The park is popular for scenic drives, bushwalks, picnics and horseriding. There are more than 100 species of birds, including gang-gang cockatoos and crimson rosellas, plus animals such as eastern grey kangaroos, sugar gliders, brush-tailed possums, echidnas and bats. Contact Parks Victoria on 13 1963; 4 km sw, western side of the Midland Hwy.

Lake Mokoan: depending on water levels, great for fishing, boating and waterskiing; 10 km NE. *1950s-style cinema:* showing classic films at Swanpool; 23 km s.

See also HIGH COUNTRY, pp. 52–3

Bendigo

see inset box on page 70

Bright

see inset box on page 76

Buchan

290 B3

ℹ️ General Store, Main St; (03) 5155 9202 or 1800 637 060; www.lakesandwilderness.com.au

📻 90.7 FM 3REG Radio East Gippsland, 828 AM ABC Local Radio

Situated in East Gippsland, Buchan is primarily an agricultural town renowned for offering some of the best caving in Victoria. Although the origin of the town's name is disputed, it is said to be derived from the Aboriginal term for either 'smoke-signal expert' or 'place of the grass bag'.

Foothills Festival: Jan. *Canni Creek Races:* Jan. *Rodeo:* Easter. *Flower Show:* Nov.

Buchan Caves Reserve The reserve features more than 350 limestone caves, of which the Royal and Fairy caves are the most accessible – the Fairy Cave alone is over 400 m long, with impressive stalactites. Europeans did not discover the caves until 1907, but from then on they became a popular tourist destination. Now visitors can cool off in the spring-fed swimming pool after exploring the caves. Tours of the Royal and Fairy caves run daily. Off Buchan Rd, north of town; (03) 5162 1900.

Snowy River Scenic Drive The drive takes in the Buchan and Snowy rivers junction and runs along the edge of Snowy River National Park to Gelantipy. Beyond Gelantipy is Little River Gorge, Victoria's deepest gorge. A short walking track leads to a cliff-top lookout. Near the gorge is McKillops Bridge, a safe swimming spot, a good site to launch canoes, and the starting point for 2 walking tracks. Care is required on the road beyond Gelantipy; 4WD is recommended. Details from visitor centre.

Suggan Buggan: this historic townsite, surrounded by Alpine National Park, features an 1865 schoolhouse and the Eagle Loft Gallery for local art and craft; 64 km N.

See also EAST GIPPSLAND, pp. 54–5

Camperdown

286 D4 | 288 C4

ⓘ Old Courthouse, Manifold St; (03) 5593 3390; www.greatoceanrd.org

104.7 Otway FM, 594 AM ABC Local Radio

Located at the foot of Mount Leura, a volcanic cone, Camperdown is more famous for its natural attractions than for the town itself, being situated on the world's third largest volcanic plain. But that should not detract from Camperdown – National Trust–listed Finlay Avenue features 2 kilometres of regal

elm trees, while in the town centre the Gothic-style Manifold Clock Tower proudly stands as a tribute to the region's first European pioneers.

Manifold Clock Tower: an imposing structure built in 1896; open 1st Sun each month; Cnr Manifold and Pike sts. *Historical Society Museum:* displays Aboriginal artefacts, local historical photographs, and household and farming implements; Manifold St. *Courthouse:* built in 1886–87, described as one of the most distinctive courthouses in Australia; Manifold St. *Buggy Museum:* collection of 30 restored horse-drawn buggies; Ower St.

Craft market: Finlay Ave or Theatre Royal; 1st Sun each month. *Heritage Festival:* Nov.

Crater lakes Surrounding Camperdown are spectacular crater lakes that provide an interesting history of volcanic activity over the past 20 000 years, as well as opportunities for watersports and excellent fishing. Travelling west of town, take the scenic drive around the rims of lakes Bullen Merri and Gnotuk, and join in the watersports and swimming at South Beach. The lakes are regularly stocked with Chinook salmon and redfin. For a scenic picnic spot, and some of the best fishing, visit Lake Purrumbete; 15 km SE. By far one of the most impressive lakes is Lake Corangamite, the Southern Hemisphere's largest permanent salt lake. This lake lies 25 km E, but the best viewing spot is Red Rock Lookout; *see Colac.*

Derrinallum and Mt Elephant Mt Elephant rises to almost 200 m behind the small township of Derrinallum – it doesn't sound like a lot, but across the plains of the Western District you can see it from up to 60 km away. A gash in the elephant's western side is the result of decades of quarrying. The mountain is actually the scoria cone of an extinct volcano, and inside is a 90 m deep crater. Now owned by the community, there is a walking trail to the top, and the Music on the Mount festival is held here in Nov. Lake Tooliorook on the other side of town offers good fishing for trout and redfin, and watersports. 40 km N.

Camperdown–Timboon Rail Trail: walking or riding track through bush, following historic railway line. **Mt Leura:** extinct volcano close to the perfect cone of Mt Sugarloaf. A lookout offers excellent views over crater lakes and volcanoes, and north across the plains to the Grampians; 1 km S. **Camperdown Botanic Gardens:** feature rare examples of Himalayan oak and a lookout over lakes Bullen Merri and Gnotuk; 3 km W. **Cobden Miniature Trains:** operates 3rd Sun each month; Cobden; 13 km S.

See also SOUTH-WEST COAST, pp. 42–3

Cann River

290 C4

ⓘ Parks Victoria Cann River office, (03) 5158 6351; or East Gippsland Visitor Information Centre, 1800 637 060; www.lakesandwilderness.com.au

📻 101.7 FM 3MGB Wilderness Radio, 106.1 FM ABC Local Radio

Cann River is situated at the junction of the Princes and Cann Valley highways, and is notable for its proximity to several spectacular national parks. The area boasts excellent fishing, bushwalking and camping in the rugged hinterland, with nearby Point Hicks notable for being the first land on the east coast of Australia to be sighted by Europeans.

🧭 **Lind National Park** The park includes the Euchre Valley Nature Drive through temperate rainforest gullies. It also supports open eucalypt forests with grey gum, messmate and silvertop ash. Watch for wildlife such as the pretty masked owl and the elusive long-footed potoroo. Has picnic facilities. 15 km W.

Coopracambra National Park In one of the most remote sections of Victoria, the park remains largely undisturbed. Ancient fossil footprints have been found in the red sandstone gorge of the Genoa River, and the surrounding granite peaks create a spectacular scene. The 35 000 ha area protects unique ecosystems and rare flora and fauna. Only experienced and well-equipped hikers should undertake walks in the rugged and remote parts of this park. A 'trip intentions' form needs to be lodged at the Cann River or Mallacoota office of Parks Victoria prior to departure, and parks staff must be notified upon return. 30 km N near NSW border.

Croajingolong National Park: the road travelling south of Cann River leads to Pt Hicks and its historic 1890 lighthouse (daily tours offered); *for further details on the park see Mallacoota.*

See also EAST GIPPSLAND, pp. 54–5

Casterton

288 A3

ⓘ Shiels Tce; (03) 5581 2070; www.castertonnow.org.au

📻 94.1 FM ABC Local Radio, 99.3 Coastal FM

Casterton is a Roman name meaning 'walled city', given to the town because of the natural wall of lush hills surrounding the valley where it lies. These hills, combined with the Glenelg River that flows through town, create an idyllic rural atmosphere. The region is colloquially known as 'Kelpie Country' as it is the birthplace of this world-famous breed of working dog. In the mid-1800s a prized Scottish collie female pup from nearby Warrock Homestead was sold to a stockman named Jack Gleeson, who named her 'Kelpie' – she was bred out with various 'black and tan'

TOWNS

BENDIGO

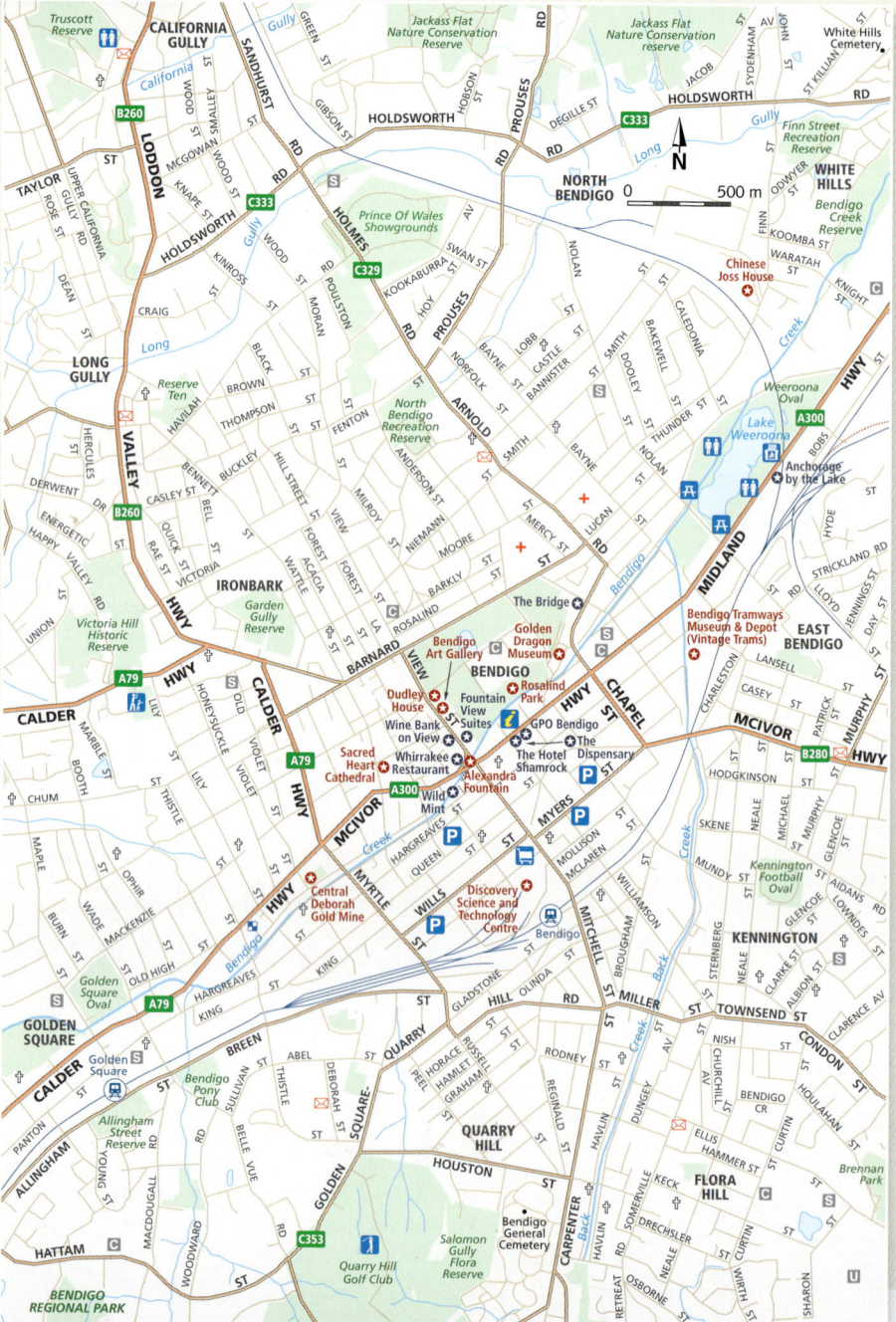

283 C1 | 287 B1 | 288 D2 | 291 D5

🛈 Post Office, 51–67 Pall Mall;
(03) 5434 6060 or 1800 813 153;
www.bendigotourism.com

📻 89.5 The Fresh FM, 91.1 FM ABC Local
Radio, 96.5 Radio KLFM

A bold beginning continues to shape
contemporary Bendigo. It was the place of
one of the world's most exciting gold rushes,
with more gold found here between 1850
and 1900 than anywhere else in the world.
Elaborate buildings and monuments from
the golden past line the main streets, offering
an ever-present reminder of the riches from
the goldfields. Today modern life weaves
itself around this legacy with a vibrant pace.
The town's new wealth can be seen in many
areas including art, culture, dining, wine
and shopping.

Golden Dragon Museum The museum
commemorates the contribution of the
Chinese community to life on the goldfields.
On display are exhibitions depicting the daily
life and hardships of Chinese immigrants
and an impressive collection of Chinese
memorabilia and processional regalia,
including what is said to be the world's
oldest imperial dragon, 'Loong' (which first
appeared at the Bendigo Easter Fair in 1892),
and the world's longest imperial dragon,
'Sun Loong'. Adjacent to the museum is the
Classical Chinese Garden of Joy. Bridge St;
(03) 5441 5044.

Central Deborah Gold Mine Perhaps the best
way to get a feel for life in a goldmining town
is to take a trip down this mine, where you
can still see traces of gold in the quartz reef
20 storeys below the ground. The Central
Deborah Gold Mine was the last commercial
goldmine to operate in Bendigo. From 1939
to 1954 around a tonne of gold was excavated.
Violet St; tour details (03) 5443 8322.

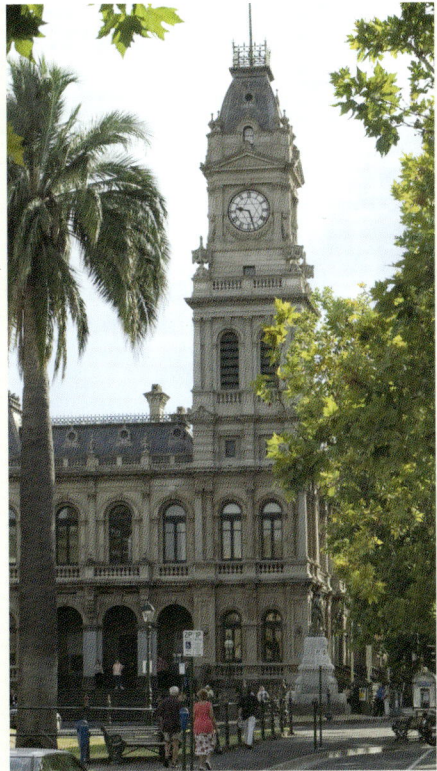

THE HISTORIC BENDIGO POST OFFICE, NOW HOME
TO THE BENDIGO VISITOR INFORMATION AND
INTERPRETIVE CENTRE

Bendigo Art Gallery: well regarded for
contemporary exhibitions plus an extensive
permanent collection with a focus on
Australian artists, including Arthur Boyd,
Tom Roberts and Arthur Streeton. Guided
tours daily; View St; (03) 5434 6088. *Self-
guide heritage walk:* takes in landmarks
including The Hotel Shamrock, built in 1897,
cnr Pall Mall and Williamson St; Sacred Heart
Cathedral, the largest outside Melbourne,
Wattle St; Alexandra Fountain, built in 1881,
one of the largest and most ornate fountains
in regional Victoria, at Charing Cross; and

continued overleaf

RADIO STATION   IN TOWN   WHAT'S ON   NEARBY

BENDIGO continued

the Renaissance-style post office and law courts at Pall Mall; details from visitor centre. **Bendigo Pottery:** Australia's oldest working pottery, with potters at work, a cafe and sales; Midland Hwy, Epsom. **Dudley House:** National Trust–classified building; View St. **Vintage Trams:** run from Central Deborah Gold Mine on 8 km city trip, including a stop at the Tram Depot Museum; taped commentary provided. **Chinese Joss House:** National Trust–classified temple built by Chinese miners; included on the vintage tram trip; Finn St, North Bendigo. **Rosalind Park:** majestic parklands that sit beautifully in the centre of Bendigo, offering stately gardens for leisure and relaxation; includes a lookout tower, Cascades water feature and Conservatory Gardens; Pall Mall. **Discovery Science and Technology Centre:** features more than 100 hands-on displays; Railway Pl. **Making of a Nation Exhibition:** permanent interpretive display providing details about Bendigo's role in Federation; at the visitor centre, Pall Mall.

Bridge Street Market: Bendigo's newest market features local produce and handmade arts and crafts; Bridge St near Golden Dragon Museum; 8am–2pm 3rd Sat each month. **Large undercover market:** Prince of Wales Showgrounds, Holmes St; 8.30am–3pm each Sun. **Bendigo Summer Fiesta:** a full summer program of arts and entertainment in Bendigo's most stunning locations. **Bendigo International Madison:** major cycling event; Mar long weekend. **Bendigo Easter Festival:** first held in 1871, the festival spans 4 days and is a major event on the town's calendar, with free music and entertainment, craft markets, art exhibits, food, wine and the famous procession

featuring 'Sun Loong'. **Australian Sheep and Wool Show:** showcases everything from farming to fashion; July. **Bendigo Heritage Uncorked:** wine event in the historic streets; 2nd weekend Oct. **National Swap Meet:** Australia's largest meet for vintage cars and bikes; Bendigo Showgrounds; Nov. **Bendigo Cup:** horseracing; Nov.

Greater Bendigo National Park The park, which extends to the north and south of town, protects some high-quality box-ironbark forest and is popular for scenic driving, cycling, walking and camping. Relics of the region's goldmining and eucalyptus-oil industries can be found within. Fauna includes over 170 species of birds including the grey shrike-thrush, a pretty songbird. In the early morning and later in the evening, look out for eastern grey kangaroos, black wallabies and echidnas. Detailed maps of the park are available at the visitor centre. Contact Parks Victoria on 13 1963; access via Loddon Valley Hwy through Eaglehawk; 8 km N.

One Tree Hill observation tower: panoramic views; 4 km s. **Eaglehawk:** site of the gold rush in 1852, it features remnants of goldmining days and fine examples of 19th-century architecture; details of self-guide heritage tour from visitor centre; 6.5 km NW. **Mandurang:** features historic wineries and is the exact centre of Victoria; 8 km SE. **Bendigo Wine Region:** more than 30 wineries are located around Bendigo, producing award-winning wines and offering welcoming cellar-door experiences with tastings and sales; wine booklet with map available from visitor centre.

See also GOLDFIELDS, pp. 44–5

dogs, and so began the long line of the working man's best friend.

Historical Museum: housed in the old railway station, the museum displays local artefacts; open by appt; Cnr Jackson and Clarke sts. *Alma and Judith Zaadstra Fine Art Gallery:* Henty St. *Mickle Lookout:* a great view across the town; Moodie St, off Robertson St on the eastern edge of town.

Vintage Car Rally: Mar. *Polocrosse Championships:* Mar. *Casterton Cup:* June. *Australian Kelpie Muster and Kelpie Working Dog Auction:* June/July.

Dergholm State Park The park features a great diversity of vegetation, including woodlands, open forests, heaths and swamps. In this tranquil setting an abundance of wildlife thrives, including echidnas, koalas, kangaroos, reptiles and the endangered red-tailed black cockatoo. A key attraction is Baileys Rocks, unique giant green-coloured granite boulders. Contact Parks Victoria on 13 1963; 50 km N.

Long Lead Swamp: waterbirds, kangaroos, emus and a trail-bike track; Penola Rd; 11 km w. *Geological formations:* in particular, The Hummocks, 12 km NE, and The Bluff, viewable from Dartmoor Rd, 20 km sw. Both rock formations are around 150 million years old. *Warrock Homestead:* a unique collection of 33 buildings erected by its founder, George Robertson. The homestead was built in 1843 and is National Trust–classified; open day on Easter Sun; 26 km N. *Bilston's Tree:* 50 m high and arguably the world's largest red gum; Glenmia Rd; 30 km N.

See also Grampians & Central West, pp. 46–7

Castlemaine

283 C3 | 287 A2 | 288 D3

Castlemaine Market Building, 44 Mostyn St; (03) 5471 1795 or 1800 171 888; www.maldoncastlemaine.com

91.1 FM ABC Local Radio, 106.3 Radio KLFM

Castlemaine is a classic goldmining town known for its grand old buildings and sprawling botanical gardens. This area was the site of the greatest alluvial gold rush that the world has ever seen. Now the town relies largely on agriculture and the manufacturing sectors, as well as being home to a thriving artistic community that takes inspiration from the area's red hills.

Castlemaine Art Gallery Housed in an elegant Art Deco building, the gallery was designed in 1931 by Peter Meldrum and is renowned for its collection of Australian art. Along with the permanent collection, many exhibitions appear here. Works by Rembrandt, Francisco Goya and Andy Warhol have all been displayed at this delightful gallery. 14 Lyttleton St; (03) 5472 2292.

Buda Historic Home and Garden Buda is considered to have one of the most significant examples of 19th-century gardens in Victoria. The house itself is furnished with period pieces and art and craft created by the Leviny family, who lived here for 118 years. Ernest Leviny was a silversmith and jeweller. Five of his 6 daughters never married, but remained at Buda and pursued woodwork, photography and embroidery. Open 12–5pm Wed–Sat, 10am–5pm Sun; 42 Hunter St; (03) 5472 1032.

Victorian Goldfields Railway This historic railway runs from Castlemaine to Maldon. The steam train journeys through box-ironbark

RADIO STATION IN TOWN WHAT'S ON NEARBY

forest in a region that saw some of the richest goldmining in the country. As well as the regular timetable, it also hosts special events throughout the year. Castlemaine Railway Station, Kennedy St; recorded information (03) 5475 2966, inquiries (03) 5470 6658.

Diggings Interpretive Centre: housed in the restored 19th-century Castlemaine Market building, the centre features interactive displays about the area's many goldmines as well as various exhibitions; Mostyn St. *Theatre Royal:* hosts live shows and films and also offers luxurious backstage accommodation; Hargraves St. *Castlemaine Botanic Gardens:* one of Victoria's oldest and most impressive 19th-century gardens; Cnr Walker and Downes rds. *Old Castlemaine Gaol:* restored gaol now offers tours; Bowden St. *Food and wine producers:* dotted throughout the area; food and wine trail brochures from visitor centre.

Castlemaine Farmers Market: 1st Sun each month. *Wesley Hill Market:* each Sat; 2.5 km E. *Castlemaine State Festival:* odd-numbered years, Apr. *Festival of Gardens:* Nov.

Castlemaine Diggings National Heritage Park The wealth on Castlemaine's streets springs from the huge hauls of gold found on the Mt Alexander Diggings, east and south of town. Thousands of miners worked the fields. Towns such as Fryerstown, Vaughan and Glenluce, now almost ghost towns, supported breweries, schools, churches and hotels. Today visitors can explore Chinese cemeteries, mineral springs, waterwheels and old townsites. Fossicking is popular. Details of self-guide walks and drives from visitor centre. 4 km s.

Chewton: historic buildings line the streets of this former gold town; 4 km E. *Harcourt:* this town is known for its many wineries, including Harcourt Valley Vineyard and Blackjack Vineyards, with tastings and cellar-door sales. Also at Harcourt is the Skydancers Orchid and Butterfly Gardens. The town hosts the Apple Festival in Mar and spring, and the Orchid

Festival in Oct; 9 km NE. *Big Tree:* a giant red gum over 500 years old; Guildford; 14 km SW. *Koala Reserve:* Mt Alexander; 19 km NE.

See also GOLDFIELDS, pp. 44–5

Chiltern

284 D1 | 289 G2

ℹ 30 Main St; (03) 5726 1611; www.chilternvic.com

📻 101.3 Oak FM, 106.5 FM ABC Local Radio

Now surrounded by rich pastoral farmland, Chiltern was once at the centre of a goldmining boom and had as many as 14 suburbs. After the Indigo gold discovery in the 1850s, there was a major influx of miners and settlers. Although the gold boom was brief, farming was soon prominent in the town's economy. Today the rich heritage of the 19th century can be seen in the well-preserved streetscapes, a vision not lost on Australian filmmakers keen for that 'authentic' 1800s scene.

Athenaeum Museum: historic building with heritage display; Conness St. *Dow's Pharmacy:* old chemist shop with original features; Conness St. *Star Theatre and Grapevine Museum:* the quaint theatre still operates and the museum, formerly the Grapevine Hotel, boasts the largest grapevine in Australia, planted in 1867 and recorded in the *Guinness World Records*; Main St. *Federal Standard newspaper office:* open by appt for groups; Main St. *Lakeview House:* former home of author Henry Handel Richardson; open afternoons on weekends and public and school holidays; Victoria St. *Lake Anderson:* picnic and barbecue facilities; access via Main St.

Antique Fair: Aug. *Ironbark Festival:* heritage fair with woodchopping, live music and markets; Oct.

Chiltern–Mt Pilot National Park This park stretches from around Chiltern south to Beechworth and protects remnant box-ironbark forest, which once covered much of this part of Victoria. Also featured are significant goldmining relics, including the impressive Magenta Goldmine (around 2 km E). Of the park's 21 000 ha, 7000 were exposed to bushfire in Jan 2003. But its regeneration is evidence of the hardiness of the forest, and there are now upgraded visitor facilities. An introduction to the forest scenery and goldmining history is on the 25 km scenic drive signposted from Chiltern. Other activities include canoeing and rafting, fishing, and cycling and walking trips along the many marked trails. Contact Parks Victoria on 13 1963; access via Hume Hwy and the road south to Beechworth.

Koendidda Historic Homestead: wonderfully landscaped gardens and B&B; near Barnawartha; 10 km NE.

See also HIGH COUNTRY, pp. 52–3

Clunes

278 B1 | 283 B3 | 287 A2 | 288 D3

i Old School Complex, 70 Bailey St; (03) 5345 3896; www.visitclunes.com.au

99.9 VoiceFM, 107.9 FM ABC Local Radio

The first registered gold strike in the state was made at Clunes on 7 July 1851. The town, north of Ballarat, is said to be one of the most intact gold towns in Victoria, featuring historic buildings throughout, including the imposing town hall and courthouse. Surrounding the town are a number of extinct volcanoes. A view of these can be obtained 3 kilometres to the south, on the road to Ballarat. The town was used as a location for the film *Ned Kelly*, starring Heath Ledger.

Clunes Museum: local history museum featuring displays on the gold-rush era; open weekends and school and public holidays; Fraser St. *Bottle Museum:* in former South Clunes State School; open Wed–Sun; Bailey St. *Queens Park:* on the banks of Creswick Creek, the park was created over 100 years ago.

Market: Fraser St; 2nd Sun each month. *Booktown:* large-scale book fair; May. *Words in Winter Celebration:* Aug.

Talbot This delightful, historic town has many 1860–70 buildings, particularly in Camp St and Scandinavian Cres. Attractions include the Arts and Historical Museum in the former Methodist Church; the Bull and Mouth Restaurant in an old bluestone building, formerly a hotel; and a market (holds the honour of being the first farmers market in the region) selling local produce, 3rd Sun each month. 18 km NW.

Mt Beckworth Scenic Reserve: popular picnic and horseriding reserve with panoramic views from the mountain's summit; 8 km W.

See also GOLDFIELDS, pp. 44–5

Cobram

289 F1

i Cnr Station St and Punt Rd; (03) 5872 2132 or 1800 607 607

101.3 Oak FM, 106.5 FM ABC Local Radio

At Cobram and nearby Barooga (across the New South Wales border) the Murray River is bordered by sandy beaches, making it a great spot for fishing, watersports and picnics. The stretch of land between the township and the river features river red gum forests and lush wetlands, with tracks leading to various beaches, the most accessible of which is Thompsons Beach, located near the bridge

TOWNS

BRIGHT

285 E3 | 289 G2 | 290 A2

119 Gavan St; 1300 551 117;
www.brightescapes.com.au

89.7 FM ABC Local Radio, 101.3 Oak FM

Bright is situated in the Ovens Valley in the foothills of the Victorian Alps. A particularly striking element of the town is the avenues of deciduous trees, at their peak during the autumn months. The Bright Autumn Festival is held annually in celebration of the spectacular seasonal changes. The Ovens River flows through the town, providing a delightful location for picnics or camping. The town also offers off-the-mountain accommodation for nearby Mount Hotham and Mount Buffalo.

Old Tobacco Sheds You could easily spend half a day here – wandering through the sheds filled with antiques and bric-a-brac and through the makeshift museums, which give an insight into the local tobacco industry and the gold rush. Also on-site is a historic hut, and the Sharefarmers Cafe serves Devonshire tea. Great Alpine Rd.

Gallery 90: local art and craft; at the visitor centre. *Centenary Park:* with a deep weir, children's playground and picnic facilities; Gavan St. *Bright Art Gallery and Cultural Centre:* community-owned gallery, displays and sells fine art and handicrafts; Mountbatten Ave. *Bright Brewery:* enjoy award-winning beers or brew your own; 121 Great Alpine Rd. *Bright and District Historical Museum:* in the old railway station building, with artefacts and photographs from the town's past; open by appt (contact visitor centre); Cnr Gavan and Anderson sts. *Walking tracks:* well-marked tracks around the area include Canyon Walk along the Ovens River, where remains of gold-workings can be seen; details from visitor centre. *Murray to the Mountains Rail Trail:* Bright sits at one end of this 94 km track suitable for cycling and walking; links several townships.

Craft market: Burke St; 3rd Sat each month. *Autumn Festival:* activities include craft markets and entertainment; Apr/May. *Alpine Spring Festival:*

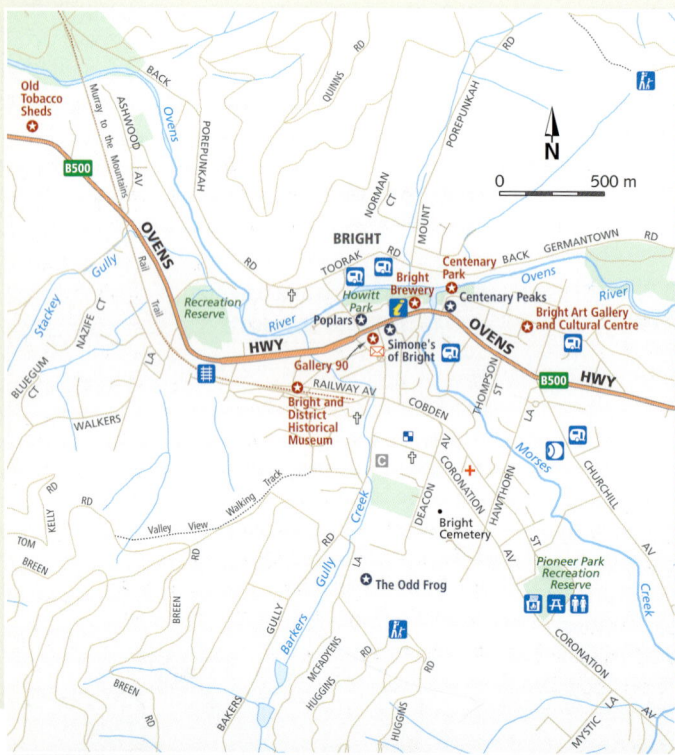

THE COLOURS OF AUTUMN CREATE A PICTURESQUE SETTING

TOWNS

free entertainment, displays and open gardens, celebrating the beauty of Bright in spring; Oct.

Wandiligong A National Trust–classified hamlet, the area contains well-preserved historic buildings from the town's goldmining days. The tiny village is set in a rich green valley, with an enormous hedge maze as the dominant feature and over 2 km of walkways surrounded by lush gardens. The maze is well signposted. Open 10am–5pm Wed–Sun; 6 km s.

Mt Buffalo National Park This is not a large park, but it is one of Victoria's favourites. In winter it is a haven for skiers. In summer bushwalkers and campers descend on the park, taking in the superb views from the granite peaks, the gushing waterfalls and the display of alpine wildflowers. Lake Catani is a popular spot for canoeists, and rock climbing and hang-gliding are also popular. Contact Parks Victoria on 13 1963; 10 km NW.

Tower Hill Lookout: 4 km NW. *Boyntons/Feathertop Winery:* open for sales and tastings; at junction of Ovens and Buckland rivers, Porepunkah; 6 km NW. *The Red Stag Deer and Emu Farm:* Hughes La, Eurobin; 16 km NW. *Harrietville:* a former goldmining village located just outside the Alpine National Park. Attractions include Pioneer Park, an open-air museum and picnic area; Tavare Park, with a swing bridge and picnic and barbecue facilities; and a lavender farm, with sales of lavender products; 20 km SE. *Alpine National Park: see Mount Beauty;* to the south-east of town.

See also HIGH COUNTRY, pp. 52–3

RADIO STATION   IN TOWN   WHAT'S ON   NEARBY

off Boorin Street. The town is supported by orchards and dairies, earning it the nickname 'peaches and cream country'. A biennial festival is held in honour of these industries.

🏠 **Historic log cabin:** built in Yarrawonga in 1875, then moved piece by piece to its current location; opposite the information centre on Station St. **Station Gallery:** at the railway station, displays a collection of art by local artists.

🎆 **Market:** Punt Rd; 1st Sat each month. **Peaches and Cream Festival:** free peaches and cream, a rodeo, fishing competitions and other activities; odd-numbered years, Jan. **Rotary Art Show:** May. **Antique Fair:** June. **Open Gardens Display:** Oct.

🧭 **Quinn Island Flora and Fauna Reserve:** home to abundant birdlife and Aboriginal artefacts, including scar trees, flint tools and middens, the island can be explored on a self-guide walk; on the Murray River, accessed via a pedestrian bridge off River Rd. **Binghi Boomerang Factory:** large manufacturer and exporter of boomerangs. Free throwing demonstrations are offered with purchases; Tocumwal Rd, Barooga, across the river. **Scenic Drive Strawberry Farm:** strawberry-picking during warmer months; Torgannah Rd, Koonoomoo; 11 km NW. **Cactus Country:** Australia's largest cacti gardens; Strathmerton; 16 km W. **Ulupna Island:** part of Barmah State Park; turn-off after Strathmerton; *see Echuca for details.* **Murray River Horse Trails:** a fantastic way to explore the Murray River beaches; (03) 5868 2221.

See also GOULBURN & MURRAY, pp. 50–1

Cohuna

288 D1 | 291 D4

ℹ️ Gannawarra Shire Council, 49 Victoria St, Kerang; (03) 5450 9333; www.gannawarra.vic.gov.au

📻 99.1 Smart FM, 594 AM ABC Local Radio

A peaceful, small service centre located on the Murray River. Cohuna's claim to fame is that its casein factory developed produce that became part of the diet of the astronauts flying the Apollo space missions. East of town is Gunbower Island, at the junction of the Murray River and Gunbower Creek. The island is home to abundant wildlife, including kangaroos and emus, plus breeding rookeries for birdlife during flood years.

🏠 **Cohuna Historical Museum:** housed in the former Scots Church, the museum features memorabilia relating to explorer Major Mitchell; Sampson St.

🎆 **Murray River International Music Festival:** Feb. **Bridge to Bridge Swim:** Mar. **Austoberfest:** Oct.

🧭 **Gunbower Island** This island, surrounded by Gunbower Creek and the Murray River, is an internationally recognised wetland, with a great variety of waterbirds and stands of river red gum forest. A 5 km canoe trail flows through Safes Lagoon and bushwalking is another highlight.

Grove Patchwork Cottage and Tearooms: for local art and craft; Murray Valley Hwy; 4 km SE. **Mathers Waterwheel Museum:** features waterwheel memorabilia and an outdoors aviary; Brays Rd; 9 km W. **Murray Goulburn Factory:** cheese factory; Leitchville; 16 km SE. **Kow Swamp:** bird sanctuary with picnic spots and fishing at Box Bridge; 23 km S. **Section of Major Mitchell Trail:** 1700 km trail that retraces this explorer's footsteps from Mildura to Wodonga via Portland. From Cohuna, follow the signposted trail along Gunbower Creek down to Mt Hope; 28 km S. **Torrumbarry Weir:** during winter the entire weir structure is removed, while in summer waterskiing is popular; 40 km SE.

See also GOULBURN & MURRAY, pp. 50–1

Colac

278 A4 | 286 A1 | 288 C4

ℹ️ **Cnr Murray and Queen sts (Princes Hwy); (03) 5231 3730; www.visitotways.com**

📻 104.7 Otway FM, 594 AM 3WV ABC Local Radio

Colac was built by the shores of Lake Colac on the volcanic plain that covers much of Victoria's Western District. The lake was once the largest freshwater body in Victoria, but harsh drought has seen it almost depleted. Still, the town acts as the gateway to the Otways. The area was once described by novelist Rolf Boldrewood as 'a scene of surpassing beauty and rural loveliness … this Colac country was the finest, the richest as to soil and pasture that I had up to that time ever looked on'.

🏠 **Colac Heritage Walk:** self-guide tour of the history and architectural wonders of Colac; details from visitor centre. **Performing Arts and Cultural Centre:** incorporates the Colac Cinema, open daily; and the Historical Centre, open 2–4pm Thurs, Fri and Sun; Cnr Gellibrand and Ray sts. **Botanic Gardens:** unusual in that visitors are allowed to drive through the gardens. Picnic, barbecue and playground facilities are provided; by Lake Colac. **Barongarook Creek:** prolific birdlife, and a walking track leading from Princes Hwy to Lake Colac; on the northern outskirts of town.

🎆 **Lions Club Market:** Memorial Sq, Murray St; 3rd Sun each month. **Go Country Music Festival and Truck Show:** Feb. **Colac Cup:** Feb. **Kana Festival:** community festival with family entertainment, music and displays; Mar. **Garden Expo:** Colac Showgrounds; Oct.

🧭 **Red Rock Lookout** The lookout features a reserve with picnic and barbecue facilities, plus spectacular views across 30 volcanic lakes, including Lake Corangamite, Victoria's largest saltwater lake. At the base of the lookout is the Red Rock Winery. Near Alvie; 22 km N. The Volcano Discovery Trail goes from Colac to Millicent in SA, and follows the history of volcanic activity in the region; details from visitor centre.

Old Beechy Rail Trail: 45 km trail that follows one of the state's former narrow-gauge railway lines from Colac to Beech Forest, suitable for walkers and cyclists. The trail starts at Colac railway station; details from visitor centre. **Art and craft galleries:** at Barongarook (12 km SE); details from visitor centre. **Burtons Lookout:** features Otway Estate Winery and Brewery with its well-known Prickly Moses ale range, views of the Otways; 13 km S. **Tarndwarncoort Homestead:** wool displays and sales; off Warncoort Cemetery Rd; 15 km E. **Birregurra:** township located at the foot of the Otway Ranges and the edge of volcanic plains; 20 km E. **Forrest:** old timber and logging town in the Otway Ranges; 32 km SE. Popular attractions nearby include fishing, walking and picnics at the West Barwon Reservoir (2 km S), or spotting a platypus at Lake Elizabeth, formed by a landslide in 1952 (5 km SE).

See also SOUTH-WEST COAST, pp. 42–3

Coleraine

288 A3

ℹ️ **Lonsdale St, Hamilton; 1800 807 056; www.sthgrampians.vic.gov.au**

📻 94.1 FM ABC Local Radio, 99.3 Coastal FM

Situated in Victoria's Western District, Coleraine is a small, picturesque town supported by wool and beef industries. A chocolate factory, the ultimate native garden and vintage cars are just a few of the intriguing prospects that await in Coleraine.

TOWNS

Peter Francis Points Arboretum Two thousand species of native flora are found here, including 500 species of eucalyptus. 'The Points' sprawls up the hillside behind the town, with great views from the top, on Portland–Coleraine Rd. In town is the Eucalyptus Discovery Centre, designed to complement the arboretum and give an insight into the natural history and commercial applications of eucalypts. Whyte St.

Glenelg Fine Confectionery: immerse yourself in the rich aroma of German-style continental chocolates; tastings available; Whyte St. *Historic Railway Station:* also site of the visitor centre, it displays and sells local arts and crafts; Pilleau St. *Coleraine Classic Cars:* open by appt; Whyte St.

Tour of Southern Grampians Cycling: Apr. *Coleraine Cup:* Sept.

Bochara Wines: wine-tasting available Fri–Sun; Glenelg Hwy. *Glacier Ridge Redgum:* gallery of wooden products for sale; open by appt. *Balmoral:* historic township west of the Grampians; 49 km N. Nearby features include the Glendinning Homestead, just east of town, with gardens and a wildlife sanctuary. The town is also the gateway to Rocklands Reservoir, for watersports and fishing, and Black Range State Park, popular for bushwalking. It also holds the Balmoral Annual Show in Mar.

See also Grampians & Central West, pp. 46–7

Corryong

285 H2 | 289 H2 | 290 B2

ℹ 50 Hanson St; (02) 6076 2277; www.pureuppermurrayvalleys.com

📻 88.7 FM Radio Upper Murray, 99.7 FM ABC Local Radio

Welcome to authentic 'Man from Snowy River' country. This district offers superb mountain scenery and excellent trout fishing in the Murray River and its tributaries, with the town being known as the home and final resting place of Jack Riley, the original 'Man from Snowy River'. A life-size statue depicting 'that terrible descent' made famous by Banjo Paterson's poem sits in the town. An annual festival honours Riley's memory with a feature event called the 'Challenge' to find his modern-day equivalent. Corryong is also the Victorian gateway to Kosciuszko National Park across the New South Wales border.

The Man from Snowy River Folk Museum Banjo Paterson's poem brought to life the struggles and triumphs of the settlers of the High Country. This charming museum proudly does the same, with local exhibits, memorabilia and photos depicting the hardships of local life, as well as a unique collection of historic skis. Hanson St.

Jack Riley's grave: Corryong cemetery. *Man from Snowy River Statue:* Hanson St. *Large wooden galleon:* Murray Valley Hwy. *Playle's Hill Lookout:* for a great view of the township; Donaldson St.

Towong Cup: Sat long weekend in Mar. *The Man from Snowy River Bush Festival:* music, art and horsemanship challenges; Apr. *Upper Murray Challenge:* 1st Sat in Oct. *Corryong Pro Rodeo:* New Year's Eve.

Burrowa–Pine Mountain National Park Pine Mountain is one of Australia's largest monoliths. Mt Burrowa is home to wet-forest plants and unique wildlife, including wombats and gliders. Both mountains provide excellent and diverse opportunities for bushwalkers, campers, climbers and birdwatchers. The Cudgewa Bluff Falls offer fabulous scenery and bushwalking. Contact Parks Victoria on 13 1963; main access is from the Cudgewa–Tintaldra Rd, which runs off Murray Valley Hwy; 27 km w.

Khancoban This NSW town was built by the Snowy Hydro for workers on the hydro-electric scheme. Its willow- and poplar-lined streets, historic rose garden and mountain surrounds give the town a European feel. Huge trout are caught in Khancoban Pondage. Nearby, Murray 1 Power Station Visitor Centre reveals the workings of this 10-turbine station. South, along Alpine Way through Kosciuszko National Park, is the spectacular Scammell's Spur Lookout and historic Geehi Hut. 32 km E.

Nariel: Nariel Creek is a good spot for trout fishing. The town hosts the Nariel Creek Folk Music Festival each Dec; 8 km SW. **Towong:** historic Towong Racecourse is where scenes from *Phar Lap* were filmed. Gangster Squizzy Taylor also once stole the takings; 12 km E. **Lookouts:** lookout with views over Kosciuszko National Park at Towong, 12 km NE; Embery's Lookout over Mt Mittamatite, 16 km N. **Walwa:** hire canoes and mountain bikes from Upper Murray Holiday Resort and Winery; 47 km NW. **Touring routes:** Murray River Rd, Lakeside Loop, Mitta Valley Loop; details from visitor centre.

See also HIGH COUNTRY, pp. 52–3

Cowes

see inset box on next page

Creswick

278 B1 | 283 B4 | 287 A3 | 288 D3

i 1 Raglan St; (03) 5345 1114; www.creswick.net

99.9 VoiceFM, 107.9 FM ABC Local Radio

Creswick is an attractive and historic town, a symbol of the rich and heady life of the gold-rush days of the 1850s. Unfortunately, the goldmining also meant that the surrounding forests were decimated. Today the town is surrounded by pine plantations over 100 years old; they exist thanks to the initiative and foresight of local pioneer John La Gerche and – while they are no replacement for the Australian bush – they have given Creswick the title of 'the home of forestry'. Creswick was the birthplace of renowned Australian artist Norman Lindsay, many of whose paintings can be seen in the local historical museum.

Historic walk: self-guide tour, map from visitor centre. **Giant Mullock Heaps:** indicate how deep mines went; Ullina Rd. **Creswick Museum:** photos and memorabilia from the town's goldmining past as well as an exhibition of Lindsay paintings; open Sun, public holidays or by appt; Albert St. **Gold Battery:** est. 1897; Battery Cres. **Creswick Woollen Mills:** last coloured woollen mill of its type in Australia; offers product sales, regular demonstrations and exhibitions; Railway Pde.

Creswick Makers Market: 1st Sun each month. **Creswick CALCAN Market:** 3rd Sat each month. **Forestry Fiesta:** Oct.

Creswick Regional Park After La Gerche set about replanting the denuded hills around Creswick in the 1890s, the state established a nursery and it continues to operate today. Further natural history can be explored on the various walking trails, including the 30 min Landcare Trail or the longer La Gerche Forest Walk. Visit St Georges Lake, once a mining dam and now popular for picnics and watersports, and Koala Park, an old breeding ground for koalas that was highly unsuccessful (they escaped over the fences). Slaty Creek is great for gold panning or picnics, with abundant birdlife. The park stretches east and south-east of town. Contact Parks Victoria on 13 1963 or the Creswick Landcare Centre, located within the park, on (03) 5345 2200.

Tangled Maze: a maze formed by climbing plants; 5 km E. **Smeaton:** pretty little town with attractions including the historic Smeaton House, the Tuki Trout Farm and Anderson's Mill; 16 km NE.

See also GOLDFIELDS, pp. 44–5

COWES

279 F5 | 281 F4 | 287 C5 | 289 E4

ℹ️ 895 Phillip Island Tourist Rd, Newhaven; (03) 5956 7447 or 1300 366 422; www.visitphillipisland.com

📻 89.1 3MFM South Gippsland, 774 AM ABC Local Radio

Situated on the north side of Phillip Island, Cowes is the island's major town. It is linked to the Mornington Peninsula by a ferry service to Stony Point and by road to Melbourne via the San Remo bridge. The Cowes foreshore offers fantastic coastal walks and safe swimming beaches, with the focal point being the town's jetty. It is a popular fishing spot, as well as a departure point for several ferries. Seal-watching cruises to Seal Rocks operate from the jetty and are the best way to see the fascinating fur seals close-up. A major drawcard for the island is the International Motorcycle Grand Prix, which has been held since 1928. There is an abundance of other activities and events that attract 3.5 million visitors to Phillip Island each year. All are within easy reach of Cowes.

🏠 *Seal-watching cruises:* depart from the jetty to Seal Rocks; bookings on 1300 763 739.

🎆 *Market:* crafts and second-hand goods; Settlement Rd; each Sun. *Farmers market:* Churchill Island; 4th Sat each month. *World Superbike Championships:* Grand Prix Circuit; Mar/Apr. *Churchill Island Working Horse Festival:* farm show; Easter. *Australian Motorcycle Grand Prix:* Grand Prix Circuit; Oct. *V8 Supercars:* Grand Prix Circuit; Nov/Dec.

🧭 **Penguin Parade** The nightly penguin parade is Phillip Island's most popular attraction. During this world-famous event, little penguins emerge from the sea after a tiring fishing expedition and cross Summerland Beach to their little homes in the dunes. Tours run at sunset each night, and the penguins can be spotted from the boardwalks and viewing platforms. The site also has an interactive visitor centre with fascinating details about these adorable creatures. Note that no cameras are allowed beyond the visitor centre. Inquiries and bookings (03) 5951 2800; 12 km sw.

The Nobbies Centre and Seal Rocks An interactive centre gives visitors an insight into local marine life, including Australia's largest colony of Australian fur seals via cameras that you can control yourself. Outside, the island features a cliff-side boardwalk with views of the fantastic natural landmark The Nobbies and out to Seal Rocks. Walk around to the Blowhole to hear the thunderous noise of huge waves and look out for the nesting sites of vast colonies of seagulls and short-tailed shearwaters that migrate to the island annually. Informative displays explain each natural attraction. Ventnor Rd; 15 km sw.

Phillip Island Wildlife Park: features native fauna, with visitors able to handfeed kangaroos and wallabies; 3 km s. *Koala Conservation Centre:* view these lovely creatures in their natural habitat. An elevated boardwalk runs through the park. The centre also has an informative display giving interesting facts and figures; Phillip Island Rd; 5 km se. *Grand Prix Circuit:* the circuit is steeped in both old and recent history, which is detailed thoroughly in the visitor centre. You can also go go-karting on a replica of the Grand Prix track; Back Beach Rd; 6 km s. *A Maze 'N Things:* family fun park featuring a large timber maze, optical-illusion rooms and 'maxigolf'; Phillip Island Rd; 6 km se. *Rhyll:* a small town on the eastern side of the island. The nearby Rhyll Inlet has wetlands of international significance, with the marshes and mangroves providing an important breeding ground for wading birds that migrate annually to breed here. There are various loop walks, as well as an excellent view from the Conservation Hill Observation

continued overleaf

📻 RADIO STATION   🏠 IN TOWN   🎆 WHAT'S ON   🧭 NEARBY

COWES   continued

Tower; 7 km E. *Wineries:* Philip Island Vineyard and Winery offers tastings, sales and casual dining; Berrys Beach Rd; 7 km SW. Purple Hen Wines also offers tastings and light meals; McFees Rd, Rhyll; 9 km SE. *Churchill Island:* a road bridge provides access to this protected parkland, which features a historic homestead, a walking track and abundant birdlife; 16 km SE. *National Vietnam Veterans Museum:* details the history of Australian involvement in the Vietnam War, displaying around 6000 artefacts; 25 Veterans Dr, Newhaven; 16 km SE. *Phillip Island Chocolate Factory:* visit Panny's Amazing World of Chocolate with information on the chocolate-making process and a model of Dame Edna made from 12 000 chocolate pieces; visitors can also see chocolate-making in action and even make their own chocolate; Newhaven; 16 km SE. *Pelicans:* see these unusual birds up close, with feeding time daily at 12pm; San Remo Pier (opposite the Fishing Co-op); 17 km SE. *Cape Woolamai:* the beach here is renowned Australia-wide for its fierce and exciting surf (patrolled in season). From the beach there are a number of 2–4 hr loop walks, many to the southern end of the cape and passing the Pinnacles rock formations on the way. South of Cape Woolamai township; 18 km SE. *Wildlife Wonderland:* this place is easy to spot on the road in to Phillip Island; just look out for the giant earthworm. The centre includes an Earthworm Museum and Wombat World; 31 km E.

See also PHILLIP ISLAND & GIPPSLAND, pp. 36–7

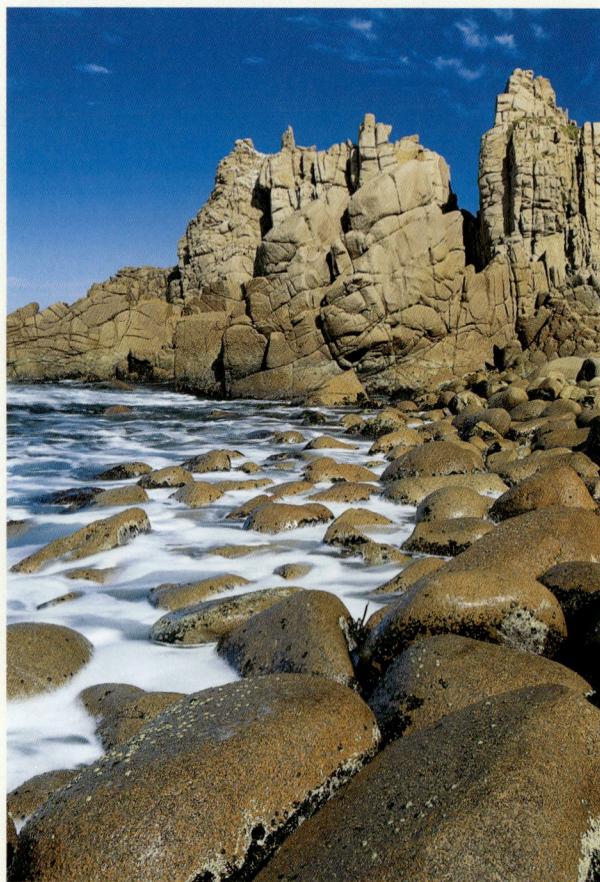

CAPE WOOLAMAI COASTLINE

Daylesford

see inset box on page 88

Dimboola

288 B2 | 291 B5

ℹ️ Dim E-Shop, 109–111 Lloyd St;
(03) 5389 1588; www.dimboola.com.au

📻 96.5 Triple H FM, 594 AM ABC
Local Radio

Dimboola, on the Wimmera River, is a key access point to the Little Desert National Park. The area was home to the Wotjobaluk Aboriginal people until the first European settlers arrived. The district was known as 'Nine Creeks' because of the many little streams that appear when the river recedes after floods. Many of the early white settlers were German.

🏠 *Historic buildings:* include the mechanics institute in Lloyd St and the Victoria Hotel, a grand 2-storey structure with grapevines hanging from the verandahs (cnr Wimmera and Victoria sts). *Walking track:* follows a scenic stretch of the Wimmera River. The track can be followed all the way to the Horseshoe Bend camping ground in the Little Desert National Park 7 km away; details of walks from visitor centre.

🧭 **Little Desert National Park** This park covers 132 647 ha. The eastern block (the section nearest to Dimboola) has picnic and camping facilities and good walking tracks. The park does not resemble the typical desert – it contains extensive heathlands and, during spring, more than 600 varieties of wildflowers and over 40 types of ground orchids. The park is home to the distinctive mallee fowl, and the large ground-nests built by the male birds can be seen during breeding season. Kangaroos, possums and bearded dragons are just some of the other wildlife that inhabit the park. 6 km SW. *See also Nhill.*

Pink Lake: a salt lake that reflects a deep pinkish colour, particularly impressive at sunset, but has dried up in recent years; 9 km NW. *Ebenezer Mission Station:* founded in 1859 in an attempt to bring Christianity to the local Aboriginal people. The site contains fascinating ruins of the original buildings, a cemetery and a restored limestone church; off the Dimboola–Jeparit Rd; 15 km N. *Kiata Lowan Sanctuary:* the first part of Little Desert National Park to be reserved, in 1955. Home to the mallee fowl; Kiata; 26 km W.

See also GRAMPIANS & CENTRAL WEST, pp. 46–7

Donald

288 C2 | 291 C5

ℹ️ Council Offices, cnr Houston and McCulloch sts; (03) 5497 1300.

📻 96.5 Triple H FM, 99.1 FM ABC
Local Radio

Donald is on the scenic Richardson River and referred to by locals as 'Home of the Duck', owing to the many waterbirds that live in the region. The town also features Bullocks Head, a tree on the riverbank with a growth that looks like its namesake. The 'bull' is the emblem for the local primary school and is also used as a flood gauge – according to how high the waters are, the 'bull' is either dipping his feet, having a drink or, when the water is really high, going for a swim.

🏠 *Bullocks Head Lookout:* beside Richardson River; Byrne St. *Steam Train Park:* a restored steam locomotive, an adventure playground and barbecue facilities; Cnr Hammill and Walker sts. *Historic Police Station:* dates back to 1865; Wood St. *Shepherds hut:* built by early settlers; Wood St.

TOWNS

📻 RADIO STATION 🏠 IN TOWN 🎆 WHAT'S ON 🧭 NEARBY

Agricultural Museum: an impressive collection of agricultural machinery; Hammill St. *Scilleys Island:* reserve on the Richardson River featuring wildlife, walking tracks and picnic facilities; access by footbridge from Sunraysia Hwy. *Kooka's Country Cookies:* tours and sales; Sunraysia Hwy.

Scottish Dancing Country Weekend: June. *Donald Cup:* Nov.

Lake Buloke The lake is filled by the floodwaters of the Richardson River, so its size varies greatly with the seasons. This extensive wetland area is home to a variety of birdlife and is a popular venue for fishing, picnicking and bushwalking. The end of the park closest to town is a protected bird sanctuary. 10 km N.

Fishing There is good fishing for redfin and trout in the many waterways close to town. Good spots include Lake Cope Cope, 10 km S; Lake Batyo Catyo and Richardson River Weir, both 20 km S; Watchem Lake, 35 km N; and the Avoca River, which runs through Charlton, 43 km NE.

Mt Jeffcott: flora, kangaroos and views over Lake Buloke; 20 km NE.

See also GRAMPIANS & CENTRAL WEST, pp. 46–7

Drysdale

278 D4 | 280 B2 | 287 B4 | 289 E4

ℹ️ **Queenscliff Visitor Information Centre,** 55 Hesse St, Queenscliff; (03) 5258 4843; www.visitgreatoceanroad.org.au

94.7 The Pulse FM, 774 AM ABC Local Radio

Drysdale, situated on the Bellarine Peninsula, is primarily a service centre for the local farming community. The town is close to the beaches of Port Phillip Bay and there are a number of wineries in the area, including the delightful Spray Farm Winery. Drysdale is now considered a satellite town of Geelong, yet retains a charming, holiday-resort atmosphere.

Old Courthouse: home of the Bellarine Historical Society; High St. *Drysdale Community Crafts:* High St.

Celtic Festival: June. *Community Market:* at the reserve on Duke St; 3rd Sun each month Sept–Apr.

Wineries For over 150 years vines have been grown on the Bellarine Peninsula, and most vineyards here today remain family owned and operated. Owing to the peninsula's varying soil conditions, a range of white and red wines are produced. Many wineries in the area offer cellar-door tastings and sales. These include the historic Spray Farm Winery, which runs the summer concert series each Feb and Mar, known as A Day on the Green, in a natural amphitheatre. Great views to the sea can be had from Scotchmans Hill Winery. Winery map from visitor centre.

Bellarine Peninsula Railway: steam-train rides from Queenscliff to Drysdale and return; *see Queenscliff. Lake Lorne picnic area:* 1 km SW. *Portarlington:* a popular seaside resort. Attractions include a restored flour mill with displays of agricultural history, a safe bay for children to swim in and fresh mussels for sale near the pier. There is a market at Parks Hall, last Sun each month; 10 km NE. *St Leonards:* a small beach resort, which includes Edwards Point Wildlife Reserve, a memorial commemorating the landing of Matthew Flinders in 1802 and of John Batman in 1835; 14 km E.

See also WERRIBEE & BELLARINE, pp. 40–1

Dunkeld

288 B3

ℹ️ **Lonsdale St, Hamilton; 1800 807 056;** www.sthgrampians.vic.gov.au

94.1 FM ABC Local Radio, 99.3 Coastal FM

Dunkeld is considered the southern gateway to the Grampians, and its natural beauty has long been recognised since the explorer Major Thomas Mitchell camped here in 1836. It was originally named Mount Sturgeon after the mountain that towers over the town. Both Mount Sturgeon and Mount Abrupt (to the north of town) have been renamed to recognise the ancient Aboriginal heritage of the landscape; they are now known as Mount Wuragarri and Mount Murdadjoog respectively.

Dunkeld Arboretum Exotic species from all over the world have been planted. Ideal for walking, cycling, fishing and picnics. Old Ararat Rd.

Historical Museum Housed in an old church, the museum features displays on the history of the local Aboriginal people, the wool industry and the journeys of explorer Major Mitchell. It also offers dining and accommodation. Open weekends or by appt; Templeton St.

Wineries: Corea Wines; open by appt. Varrenti Wines; open 12–5pm; Blackwood Rd. *Sandra Kranz Art Studio:* Glass St. *Waiting Room Art Gallery:* Parker St. *Bushwalking:* southern walking trails include Mt Abrupt, Mt Sturgeon and the Piccaninny Walk.

Dunkeld Cup: Nov. *Dunkeld Arts Festival:* biennial, Nov.

Grampians National Park The southern section of the park includes Victoria Valley Rd, a scenic drive that stops at Freshwater Lake Reserve (8 km N), popular for picnics. Also near Dunkeld are various hiking destinations and the Chimney Pots, a formation popular for rock climbing; access via Henty Hwy. *For further details on the park see Halls Gap.*

Grampians Pure Sheep Dairy: sample some of the sheep milk, yoghurts and cheeses while also watching how they are made; Glenelg Hwy.

See also GRAMPIANS & CENTRAL WEST, pp. 46–7

Dunolly

283 B2 | 287 A1 | 288 D2 | 291 D5

i 109 Broadway; (03) 5468 1205.

91.1 FM ABC Local Radio, 99.1 Goldfields FM

The towns of Dunolly, Wedderburn and Inglewood formed the rich goldfield region colloquially known in the 1850s as the 'Golden Triangle'. The district has produced more gold nuggets than any other goldfield in Australia, with 126 unearthed in Dunolly itself. The 'Welcome Stranger', considered to be the largest nugget ever discovered, was found 15 kilometres north-west of Dunolly, at Moliagul.

Restored courthouse: offers a display relating to gold discoveries in the area; open Sat afternoons; Market St. *Original lock-up and stables:* viewable from street only; Market St. *Gold-themed tours of the region:* include gold panning in local creeks; details from visitor centre.

Market: with local produce, crafts and second-hand goods; Market St; 3rd Sat each month. *Community Street Market:* Broadway; 4th Sat each month.

Moliagul: the Welcome Stranger Discovery Walk leads to a monument marking the spot where the Welcome Stranger nugget was found in 1869. Moliagul is also the birthplace of Rev. John Flynn, founder of the Royal Flying Doctor Service; 15 km NW. *Laanecoorie Reservoir:* a great spot for swimming, boating and waterskiing, water levels permitting, with camping and picnic facilities available; 16 km E. *Tarnagulla:* a small mining town with splendid Victorian architecture and a flora reserve nearby; 16 km NE. *Bealiba:* hosts a market 2nd Sun each month; 21 km NW.

See also GOLDFIELDS, pp. 44–5

TOWNS

RADIO STATION   IN TOWN   WHAT'S ON   NEARBY

DAYLESFORD

278 C1 | 283 C4 | 287 A2 | 288 D3

i 98 Vincent St; (03) 5321 6123;
www.visitdaylesford.com

99.9 VoiceFM, 107.9 FM ABC
Local Radio

Daylesford is at the centre of Victoria's spa
country. The area developed with the discovery
of gold, which lured many Swiss-Italian
settlers, but it was the discovery of natural
mineral springs that proved a more lasting
attraction. Of the 72 documented springs in
the area, the most famous are nearby Hepburn
Springs. The water is rich with minerals that
dissolve into it as it flows from the crest of the
Great Dividing Range through underground
rocks, and it is known for its rejuvenating and
healing qualities. Daylesford has grown as a
destination in itself, complete with beautiful
gardens, interesting shopping, great eating and
a huge range of accommodation. The streets
are lined with trees that blaze with colour in
autumn, and inside the attractive old buildings
are restaurants, cafes, galleries, bookshops,
bakeries and chocolate shops. Overlooking the
lake is one of regional Victoria's most highly
regarded restaurants, the Lake House.

Convent Gallery A magnificent building
surrounded by delightful cottage gardens,
this former convent and girls school has been
restored and features an impressive collection of
artwork, sculptures and jewellery. A cafe serves
local produce and Devonshire tea. Daly St.

Historical Museum: features a collection
of photographs from the region's past and
artefacts from the local Djadja Wurrung
people; open weekends and public and school
holidays; Vincent St. *Lake Daylesford:* a
lovely spot for picnics, with paddleboats and
rowboats for hire in the warmer months. The
Tipperary walking track starts here and ends at
the Mineral Springs Reserve; access to the lake
is from Bleakly Rd. *Wombat Hill Botanical
Gardens:* est. 1861, these lovely gardens
are situated on the hill overlooking town.
Daylesford Spa Country Train: leaves railway
station for Bullarto (11 km SE) each Sun.

continued overleaf

LAKE HOUSE RESTAURANT

TOWNS

RADIO STATION   IN TOWN   WHAT'S ON   NEARBY

DAYLESFORD continued

Market: for arts, crafts and local produce; near railway station; each Sun morning. **Silver Streak Champagne Train:** train journey with gourmet food; 1st Sat each month. **Hepburn Swiss–Italian Festival:** Apr/May. **Highland Gathering:** Dec.

Hepburn Springs spas The Hepburn Spa and Bathhouse Wellness Retreat offers pure mineral water spas and hydrotherapy, massage therapies and an extensive range of relaxation, health and beauty treatments. Mineral Springs Cres, Hepburn Springs; (03) 5348 8888. Dating back to 1894, the recently renovated Hepburn Bathhouse has state-of-the-art communal and private mineral bathing, spas and therapies utilising the renowned local mineral springs, plus a day spa for massage, facials and indulgent beauty treatments. Mineral Springs Reserve Rd, Hepburn Springs; (03) 5321 6000; 4 km N.

Lavandula Swiss Italian Farm A sprawling estate featuring fields of lavender, cottage gardens and sales of lavender-based products. The Lavandula Harvest Festival is a popular event with a variety of family entertainment, held in Jan. Open daily, winter months weekends only; Shepherds Flat; (03) 5476 4393; 10 km N.

Hepburn Regional Park: located around Daylesford and Hepburn Springs, this park features old goldmining relics, mineral springs and the impressive Mt Franklin, an extinct volcano, with panoramic views from the summit and picnic, barbecue and camping facilities around the base. There are good walking tracks throughout the park. **Waterfalls:** several in area, including Sailors Falls, 5 km S; Loddon Falls, 10 km NE; Trentham Falls, 21 km SE. **Breakneck Gorge:** early goldmining site; 5 km N. **Glenlyon:** small town that hosts the popular Glenlyon Sports Day on New Year's Day, and the Fine Food and Wine Fayre in July; 8 km NE. **Lyonville Mineral Springs:** picnic and barbecue facilities; 15 km SE. **Yandoit:** historic Swiss-Italian settlement; 18 km NW.

See also SPA & GARDEN COUNTRY, pp. 38–9

Echuca

289 E1

2 Heygarth St; (03) 5480 7555 or 1800 804 446; www.echucamoama.com

91.1 FM ABC Local Radio, 104.7 Radio EMFM

Visitors to this delightful town are transported back in time by the sight of beautiful old paddleboats cruising down the Murray River. The town is at the junction of the Murray, Campaspe and Goulburn rivers. Once Australia's largest inland port, its name comes from an Aboriginal word meaning 'meeting of the waters'. A historic iron bridge joins Echuca to Moama, over the river in New South Wales.

Port of Echuca The massive red-gum wharf has been restored to the grandeur of its heyday, with huge paddlesteamers anchored here. Cruises are available on many boats, including the paddlesteamer *Pevensey*, renamed *Philadelphia* for the TV miniseries *All the Rivers Run*; the D26 logging barge; PS *Alexander Arbuthnot*; and PS *Adelaide*. Cruises are also available on PS *Canberra*, *Pride of the Murray* and PS *Emmylou*. The MV *Mary Ann* also features a fine restaurant.

Historic buildings: many along Murray Espl include the Star Hotel, with an underground bar and escape tunnel, and the Bridge Hotel, built by Henry Hopwood, the founder of Echuca, who ran the original punt service. **Red Gum Works:** wood-turning demonstrations;

Murray Espl. *Sharp's Magic Movie House and Penny Arcade:* award-winning attractions; Murray Espl. *Echuca Historical Society Museum:* housed in former police station; open 11am–3pm daily; High St. *Billabong Carriages:* Murray Espl. *National Holden Museum:* Warren St.

Southern 80 Ski Race: from Torrumbarry Weir to Echuca; Feb. *Riverboats, Jazz, Food and Wine Festival:* Feb. *Steam, Horse and Vintage Rally:* June. *Winter Blues Festival:* July. *Port of Echuca Steam Heritage Festival:* Oct.

Barmah State Park This park combines with Barmah State Forest to contain the largest river red gum forest in Victoria. Nearby are Barmah Lakes, a good location for fishing and swimming. Canoes and barbecue pontoons are available for hire. Ulupna Island, in the eastern section of the park (near Strathmerton), has river beaches, camping and a large population of koalas. Barmah Muster, a cattle muster, is held in the state forest in Apr. Contact Parks Victoria on 13 1963; 39 km NE.

Moama: attractions include the Silverstone Go-Kart Track and the Horseshoe Lagoon nature reserve; 2 km N. *Mathoura:* set among the mighty red gums, Mathoura is a charming Murray town over the NSW border. Fishing is popular, with sites including Gulpa Creek and the Edward and Murray rivers. To see the forest in its splendour, take the Moira Forest Walkway or, for that authentic Murray River experience, visit nearby Picnic Pt, popular for camping, picnics, waterskiing and fishing; 40 km N. *Nathalia:* a town on Broken Creek with many historic buildings. Walking tracks along the creek take in fishing spots, old homesteads and a lookout; 57 km E.

See also GOULBURN & MURRAY, pp. 50–1

Edenhope

288 A2 | 291 A5

🛈 96 Elizabeth St; (03) 5585 1509; www.westwimmera.vic.gov.au

📻 94.1 FM ABC Local Radio, 96.5 Triple H FM

Just 30 kilometres from the South Australian border, Edenhope is set on the shores of Lake Wallace, a haven for waterbirds. The town is renowned as the site where, in 1868, Australia's first all-Aboriginal cricket team trained – their coach was T. W. Wills, who went on to establish Australian Rules football. A cairn in Lake Street honours the achievements of this early cricket team.

Edenhope Antiques: offers an extensive variety of antique wares; Elizabeth St. *Bennetts Bakery:* Elizabeth St. *Lake Wallace:* walking tracks and birdwatching hides; Wimmera Hwy.

Henley-on-Lake Wallace Festival: with market and family entertainment; Feb. *Races:* Mar long weekend.

Harrow One of Victoria's oldest inland towns, Harrow has many historic buildings in Main St, including the Hermitage Hotel, the police station and an early log gaol. The Johnny Mullagh Cricket Centre, a celebration of the first Australian Aboriginal cricketer to travel overseas, is also located in town. Kelly's Garage and Transport Museum in Main St is popular with car enthusiasts, and the National Bush Billycart Championship is held here in Mar. 32 km SE.

Dergholm State Park: 26 km S; *see Casterton. Naracoorte Caves National Park:* World Heritage site of fabulous caves with extensive fossil history to explore; around 50 km W over SA border. *Fishing:* redfin, trout and yabbies in many lakes and swamps nearby. Availability depends on water levels; contact visitor centre for locations.

See also GRAMPIANS & CENTRAL WEST, pp. 46–7

TOWNS

Eildon

279 H1 | 282 D1 | 284 B5 | 289 F3

ℹ️ High St; (03) 5774 2909;
www.murrindinditourism.com.au

📻 97.3 FM ABC Local Radio, 106.9 UGFM
Upper Goulburn Community Radio

Eildon established itself as a town to service
dam workers, and later holiday-makers, when
the Goulburn River was dammed to create Lake
Eildon. This is the state's largest constructed
lake, irrigating a vast stretch of northern
Victoria and providing hydro-electric power.
In recent years low water levels have revealed
homesteads that were submerged when the dam
was constructed; they stand on the lake bed in
a more or less preserved state. The lake and the
surrounding national park are popular summer
holiday destinations, especially for watersports,
fishing and boating.

🎆 *Lions Club Monster Market:* Easter.
Opening of Fishing Season Festival: Sep.

🧭 **Lake Eildon National Park** Comprising
the lake and surrounding woodlands, hills and
wilderness areas, this national park provides
a venue for many water- and land-based
activities. When full, Lake Eildon has 6 times
the capacity of Sydney Harbour. Hire a kayak,
boat or houseboat from the outlets in Eildon
to explore the waters, or enjoy the thrills of
waterskiing with the picturesque foothills of
the Australian Alps providing a backdrop. In
the surrounding hills and woodlands there
are various nature walks, scenic drives and
panoramic lookout points. Many of the walks
start at the campgrounds; details from visitor
centre, or from Parks Victoria on 13 1963.

Lake Eildon Wall Lookout: 1 km N. *Eildon
Pondage and Goulburn River:* for excellent
fishing – there is no closed season for trout in
Lake Eildon. *Mt Pinniger:* for views of Mt Buller,
the alps and the lake; 3 km E. *Freshwater
Discovery Centre:* native-fish aquariums and

displays; Snobs Creek; 6 km SW. *Waterfalls:*
include Snobs Creek Falls and Rubicon Falls;
18 km SW via Thornton. *Eildon Trout Farm:*
towards Thornton on Back Eildon Rd.

See also HIGH COUNTRY, pp. 52–3

Emerald

279 F3 | 281 H1 | 282 B4 | 287 C4 | 289 F4

ℹ️ Dandenong Ranges Information
Centre, 1211 Burwood Hwy,
Upper Ferntree Gully; (03) 9758 7522;
www.dandenongrangestourism.com.au

📻 97.1 FM 3MDR Mountain District
Radio, 774 AM ABC Local Radio

Emerald is a delightful little town set in
the Dandenong Ranges, which lie behind
Melbourne's eastern suburbs. Over the weekend
many people flock from the city into 'the hills'
to take in the scenic forests and visit the many
cafes, galleries, and antique and craft stores.

🏠 **Emerald Lake** The lake is a lovely, tranquil
spot ideal for picnics and walks. Attractions
include the largest model railway display in the
Southern Hemisphere, paddleboats, cafe and
tearooms, fishing, free wading pool (summer
months) and a variety of walking trails. Picnic
shelters are available for hire throughout the
year. Puffing Billy stops at Emerald Lake and
many passengers spend a day here before
returning on the train in the late afternoon.
Emerald Lake Rd.

Galleries and craft shops: a wide variety,
specialising in locally made products; along
Main St.

🎆 *PAVE (Performing and Visual Arts in
Emerald) Festival:* Apr. *Great Train Race:*
runners attempt to race Puffing Billy from
Belgrave to Emerald Lake Park; 1st Sun in May.

🧭 **Puffing Billy** Victoria's favourite steam
train runs between Belgrave and Gembrook,

stopping at Emerald Lake. The view outside the red carriage windows is of tall trees and ferny gullies, and if you time your trip for the last Sat of the month you could catch the local craft and produce market at Gembrook station. Also at Gembrook is the Motorist Cafe and Museum. Puffing Billy operates every day of the year, except Christmas Day; 24 hr recorded timetable and fare information on 1900 937 069, all other inquiries (03) 9757 0700; Belgrave 9 km w, Gembrook 14 km e.

Menzies Creek This town is home to Cotswold House, where visitors enjoy gourmet food amid fantastic views. Nearby is Cardinia Reservoir Park, where picnic spots are shared with free-roaming kangaroos, and Lake Aura Vale, a popular spot for sailing. Belgrave–Gembrook Rd; 4 km NW.

Sherbrooke Equestrian Park: trail-rides; Wellington Rd; 3 km w. *Australian Rainbow Trout Farm:* Macclesfield; 8 km N. *Sherbrooke Art Gallery:* impressive collection of local artwork; Monbulk Rd, Belgrave; 11 km NW. *Bimbimbie Wildlife Park:* Mt Burnett; 12 km SE.

See also YARRA & DANDENONGS, pp. 32–3

Euroa

284 A3 | 287 D1 | 289 F2

ℹ️ **Strathbogie Ranges Tourism Information Service,** BP Service Centre, Tarcombe St; 1300 134 610; www.strathbogieregion.com.au

📻 97.7 FM ABC Local Radio, 98.5 FM

Euroa was the scene of one of Ned Kelly's most infamous acts. In 1878 the notorious bushranger staged a daring robbery, rounding up some 50 hostages and making off with money and gold worth nearly £2000. The Strathbogie Ranges, once one of the Kelly Gang's hideouts, now provide a pretty backdrop to the town, and the region really comes to life in spring, when stunning wildflowers bloom. During this time and in autumn a number of private gardens are open to the public.

🏠 **Farmers Arms Historical Museum** The museum features displays explaining the history of Ned Kelly and Eliza Forlonge; Eliza and her sister are said to have imported the first merino sheep into Victoria. Open Fri–Mon afternoons; Kirkland Ave.

Walking trail: self-guide trail to see the rich history and architecture of the town, including the National Bank building and the post office, both in Binney St; brochure available from visitor centre. *Seven Creeks Park:* good freshwater fishing, particularly for trout; Kirkland Ave.

🎆 *Miniature steam-train rides:* Turnbull St; last Sun each month. *Wool Week:* Oct.

🧭 *Faithfull Creek Waterfall:* 9 km NE. *Longwood:* includes the delightful White Hart Hotel and horse-drawn carriage rides; 14 km SW. *Gooram Falls:* a scenic drive takes in the falls and parts of the Strathbogie Ranges; 20 km SE. *Locksley:* popular for gliding and parachuting; 20 km SW. *Polly McQuinns Weir:* historic river crossing and reservoir; Strathbogie Rd; 20 km SE. *Mt Wombat Lookout:* spectacular views of surrounding country and the Australian Alps; 25 km SE. *Blue Wren Lavender Farm:* lavender products and Devonshire tea; Boho South; 28 km E. *Avenel Maze:* Ned Kelly–themed maze; open Thurs–Mon, school and public holidays; 37 km SW.

See also GOULBURN & MURRAY, pp. 50–1

Flinders

279 E5 | 281 E4 | 287 C5 | 289 E4

i Nepean Hwy, Dromana; (03) 5987 3078 or 1800 804 009.

📻 98.7 3RPP FM, 774 AM ABC Local Radio

Flinders is set on the south coast of the Mornington Peninsula, a region famous for its wineries. During the 1880s, Flinders became known as a health and recreation resort and a number of guesthouses and hotels began to emerge. Today Flinders remains a popular holiday spot, with its renowned cliff-top golf course and gastropub. Heritage buildings have wide verandahs, often shading antique and curio shops or excellent cafes, giving the town an enchanting and historic air. This, combined with taking in the view across the bay to The Nobbies and Seal Rocks, makes it easy to understand the town's perennial appeal.

🏠 *Foreshore Reserve:* popular for picnics and fishing from the jetty. *Studio @ Flinders:* small but unique art gallery with emphasis on ceramics, also exhibits handcrafted jewellery, glass, textiles, wood and paintings; Cook St. *Historic buildings:* 'Bimbi', built in the 1870s, is the earliest remaining dwelling in Flinders; King St. 'Wilga' is another fine Victorian-era home; King St. *Flinders Golf Links:* great views across Bass Strait; West Head, Wood St.

🎆 *Peninsula Piers and Pinots:* the region's winemakers showcase their pinots with local food and produce at Flinders Pier; Mar long weekend.

🧭 **Red Hill** This is fine wine country, where vineyards are interspersed with noted art galleries, farm gates, cafes and restaurants. The Red Hill Market is legendary and held on the first Sat of each month from Sept to May. It specialises in local crafts, clothing and fresh produce. The town also features a number of galleries and The Cherry Farm, where you can 'pick your own' cherries and berries in a pleasant setting (in season); Arkwells La. The Mornington Peninsula Winter Wine Fest is held annually on the Queen's Birthday weekend (June) and the Cool Climate Wine Show is in Mar.

Mornington Peninsula National Park The park covers 2686 ha and features a diverse range of vegetation, from the basalt cliff-faces of Cape Schanck to banksia woodlands, coastal dune scrubs and swampland. One of the park's many attractions is the Cape Schanck Lighthouse, built in 1859, which provides accommodation in one of the lighthouse keepers' houses. Historic Pt Nepean retains its original fortifications and has information displays and soundscapes. Also available here is a 'hop-on, hop-off' tractor train with commentary, and bicycle hire. There are ocean beaches for swimming and surfing, while the Bushranger Bay Nature Walk, starting at Cape Schanck, and the Farnsworth Track at Portsea are just 2 of the many walks on offer. Contact Parks Victoria on 13 1963; access to Cape Schanck from Rosebud–Flinders Rd; 15 km w.

French Island National Park French Island once served as a prison where inmates kept themselves entertained with their own 9-hole golf course. This unique reserve features a range of environments from mangrove saltmarsh to open woodlands. During spring more than 100 varieties of orchids come into bloom. The park is home to the most significant population of koalas in Victoria. Long-nosed potoroos and majestic sea-eagles can also be spotted. There is a variety of walking tracks on the island and bicycles can be hired from the general store. There are also guesthouses, and camping and picnic facilities. Contact Parks Victoria on 13 1963; access is via a 30 min ferry trip from Stony Pt, 30 km NE of Flinders.

Ashcombe Maze and Lavender Gardens: a large hedge maze surrounded by beautifully landscaped gardens; closed Aug; Red Hill Rd, Shoreham; 6 km N. *Ace Hi Horseriding and Wildlife Park:* beach and bush trail-rides and a native-animal sanctuary; Cape

Schanck; 11 km w. *Main Ridge:* Sunny Ridge Strawberry Farm – pick your own berries in season; Mornington–Flinders Rd. Also The Pig and Whistle, English-style pub, Purves Rd; 11 km NW. *Pt Leo:* great surf beach; 12 km NE via Shoreham. *Balnarring:* hosts a market specialising in handmade crafts; 3rd Sat each month Nov–May; 17 km NE. Nearby is Coolart Homestead, an impressive Victorian mansion with historical displays, gardens, wetlands and a bird-observation area.

See also MORNINGTON PENINSULA, pp. 34–5

Foster

289 F5

ⓘ Stockyard Gallery, Main St; 1800 630 704; www.visitpromcountry.com.au

📻 89.5 3MFM South Gippsland, 100.7 FM ABC Local Radio

Foster was originally a goldmining town settled in the 1870s. The town boasts close access to Wilsons Promontory – affectionately called 'the Prom' – and is a popular base for visitors. Set in the centre of a rich agricultural area, Foster is the main shopping precinct for the Prom and beaches of Corner Inlet and Waratah Bay.

🏠 *Historical Museum:* in old post office; Main St. *Stockyard Gallery:* Main St. *Hayes Walk:* view the site of Victory Mine, Foster's largest goldmine; starts in town behind the carpark. *Pearl Park:* picturesque picnic spot.

🎆 *Tastes of Prom Country:* Jan. *Great Southern Portrait Prize:* Jan. *Prom Coast Seachange Festival:* Apr. *Mt Best Art Show:* Apr. *Prom Country Challenge:* fun run; Aug. *Promontory Home Produce and Craft Market:* Nov–Apr.

🧭 **Wilsons Promontory National Park**
The Prom is well loved across the state for its wild and untouched scenery. Its 130 km coastline is framed by granite headlands, mountains, forests and fern gullies. Bordered on all sides by sea, it hangs from Victoria by a thin, sandy isthmus. Limited road access means opportunities for walking are plentiful. The park features dozens of walking tracks, ranging from easy strolls to more challenging overnight hikes that take visitors to one of 11 campsites only accessible by foot. Hikes range from beginner to intermediate, and permits are required. Detailed information is provided at the park's own visitor centre: the remnants of a commando training camp from WW II. Contact Parks Victoria on 13 1963; 32 km S.

Toora An internationally recognised wetland site located on Corner Inlet, it is renowned for the huge variety of migratory birds that nest in the area. Points of interest in Toora include Agnes Falls, Toora wind farm, Toora Lavender Farm and the Bird Hide where you can watch the migratory and indigenous birdlife. 12 km E.

Foster North Lookout: 6 km NW. *Wineries:* Windy Ridge Winery; 10 km S. *Fish Creek:* A rural village, which attracts many visitors en route to the Prom. From the novelty of the giant mullet on top of the Promontory Gate Hotel to the fish-shaped seats around town, there is more to this unusually themed town than meets the eye. Galleries and vineyards are located in the area. Access the Great Southern Trail and walk, ride or cycle your way to Foster. Nearby Mt Nicol offers a lookout with spectacular views; 13 km SW. *Turtons Creek Reserve:* features mountain ash, blackwood and tree ferns, and a small waterfall. Bush camping is available; 18 km N. *Coastal towns:* popular bases during summer months; Sandy Pt, 22 km S; Waratah Bay, 34 km SW; Walkerville, 36 km SW. *Cape Liptrap:* views over rugged coastline and Bass Strait; 46 km SW.

See also PHILLIP ISLAND & GIPPSLAND, pp. 36–7

TOWNS

🟧 RADIO STATION   🏠 IN TOWN   🎆 WHAT'S ON   🧭 NEARBY

Geelong

see inset box on page 98

Glenrowan

284 C2 | 289 G2

i Wangaratta Visitor Information Centre, 100 Murphy St, Wangaratta; 1800 801 065; www.visitwangaratta.com.au

📻 101.3 Oak FM, 106.5 FM ABC Local Radio

Glenrowan is a town well known to most Victorians as the site of Ned Kelly's final showdown with the police in 1880. Most of the attractions in Glenrowan revolve around the legends surrounding Kelly's life – a giant statue of Kelly himself towers over shops in Gladstone Street. Almost as legendary as Ned Kelly are the numerous wineries and fruit orchards in the area.

🏛 *Kate's Cottage Museum:* with an extensive collection of Kelly memorabilia as well as a replica of the Kelly homestead and blacksmith shop; Gladstone St. *Cobb & Co Museum:* an underground museum featuring notorious stories of Kelly and other bushrangers; Gladstone St. *Kellyland:* a computer-animated show of Kelly's capture; Gladstone St. *Kelly Gang Siege Site Walk:* discover the sites and history that led to the famous siege on this self-guide walk (brochure available). *Wine and produce outlets:* over 22 local wines are offered for tastings and sales at the Buffalo Mountain Wine Centre; Gladstone St. Gourmet jams and fruit products are also available at Smiths Orchard and The Big Cherry; Warby Range Rd. *White Cottage Herb Garden:* herb sales; Hill St.

🎆 *Trails, Tastings and Tales wine and food event:* June.

🛡 **Warby Range State Park** The 'Warbys', as they are known locally, extend for 25 km north of Glenrowan. The steep ranges provide excellent viewing points, especially from Ryans Lookout. Other lookouts include the Pangarang Lookout near the Pine Gully Picnic Area and the Mt Glenrowan Lookout, the highest point of the Warbys at 513 m. There are well-marked tracks for bushwalkers and a variety of pleasant picnic spots amid open forests and woodlands, with wildflowers blossoming during the warmer months. Access from Taminick Gap Rd.

See also HIGH COUNTRY, pp. 52–3

Halls Gap

see inset box on page 104

Hamilton

288 B3

i Lonsdale St; (03) 5572 3746 or 1800 807 056; www.sthgrampians.vic.gov.au

📻 94.1 FM ABC Local Radio, 99.3 Coastal FM

Hamilton is a prominent rural centre in the heart of a sheep-grazing district. This industry is such an important part of the town's economy that it has been dubbed the 'Wool Capital of the World'. It is both the geographical and business hub of the Western District. A thriving country city, Hamilton is filled with cultural experiences, whether gazing at botanical, artistic or architectural beauty, browsing through great shops or putting in a bid as part of a 50 000-head sheep sale.

🏛 **Hamilton Art Gallery** This gallery is said to be one of regional Australia's finest, featuring a diverse collection of fine arts and museum pieces dating back to the earliest European settlements in Australia. Many trinkets and treasures of the region's first stately homes are on display, as well as English and European glass, ceramic and silver work. There is also a good collection of colonial art from the Western District. Guided heritage tours of the gallery and district are available. Brown St.

Botanic Gardens First planted in 1870 and classified by the National Trust in 1990, these gardens have long been regarded as one of the most impressive in rural Victoria. Designed by the curator of the Melbourne Botanic Gardens, William Guilfoyle, the gardens feature his 'signature' design elements of sweeping lawns interrupted by lakes, islands, and contrasting plant and flower beds. Keep an eye out for the free-flight aviary, enormous English oaks and historic band rotunda. French St.

Lake Hamilton: attractive landscaped man-made lake used for swimming, sailing, yachting and rowing, and featuring an excellent walking/bike track; off Ballarat Rd. *Sir Reginald Ansett Transport Museum:* birthplace of Ansett Airlines, the museum tells the story of the Ansett empire with memorials and displays of aviation history in one of the airline's original hangars; Ballarat Rd. *Hamilton Pastoral Museum:* features farm equipment, tractors, engines, household items and small-town memorabilia; Ballarat Rd. *Big Wool Bales:* built in the shape of 5 giant wool bales and surrounded by native red gums, the Wool Bales tell the fascinating story of Australia's wool industry; Coleraine Rd. *Mt Baimbridge Lavender:* set on 12 acres. Wander through gardens and browse the gallery; Mt Baimbridge Rd; tours available by appt (03) 5572 4342. *Hamilton History Centre:* features the history of early Western District families and town settlement; Gray St.

Hamilton Farmer's Market: last Sat each month. *Harvest Rally:* Jan. *Beef Expo:* Feb. *Hamilton Cup:* Apr. *Promenade of Sacred Music:* Apr. *Plough and Seed Rally:* May. *Sheepvention:* promotes the sheep and wool industries; Aug.

Grampians National Park *See Halls Gap.* 35 km NE.

Mt Eccles National Park The key feature of this park is a large volcanic crater lake. A range of walks let visitors explore the scoria cones and caves formed thousands of years ago by volcanoes. The 3 main craters hold a 700 m long lake, Lake Surprise, fed by underground springs. Contact Parks Victoria on 13 1963; near Macarthur; 40 km S.

Tarrington: established by German settlers and originally named Hochkirch, this area is fast becoming a well-known 'pinot noir' grape-producing area; 12 km SE. *Waterfalls:* Nigretta Falls has a viewing platform; 15 km NW. Also Wannon Falls; 19 km W. *Mt Napier State Park:* features Byaduk Caves (lava caves) near the park's western entrance. Only 1 cave is accessible to the public; 18 km S. *Cavendish:* a small town en route to the Grampians, notable for the 3 beautiful private gardens open during the Southern Grampians Open Gardens Festival each Oct; 25 km N. *Penshurst:* a lovely historic town at the foot of Mt Rouse. Excellent views from the top of the mountain, where there is a crater lake. Country Muster each Feb; 31 km SE.

See also GRAMPIANS & CENTRAL WEST, pp. 46–7

Healesville

279 G2 | 282 B3 | 287 D3 | 289 F3

i **Yarra Valley Visitor Information Centre,** Old Courthouse, Harker St; (03) 5962 2600; www.visityarravalley.com.au

99.1 Yarra Valley FM, 774 AM ABC Local Radio

To the west of Yarra Ranges National Park and within easy reach of Melbourne, Healesville has a charming rural atmosphere. There are good restaurants and cafes in town, all focusing

TOWNS

GEELONG

NORTH
GEELONG

RIPPLESIDE

LIVERPOOL ST

Rippleside Pier

Rippleside Park

Rippleside
Beach

BELL PDE

GRANDVIEW
GV

DRUMCONDRA

GLENLEITH

Chifley on the
Esplanade

Griffins Gully
Jetty

Corio Bay

0   500 m

N

GEELONG
WEST

Sparrow
Park

West
Park

Cunningham
Pier

Steampacket
Gardens

Marina

Limeburners
Point

ABERDEEN

Johnstone
Park

Ford
Discovery
Centre

National
Wool
Museum

Geelong
Art Gallery

2 Faces

Four
Points by
Sheraton
Geelong

Fishermen's
Pier

Geelong
Waterfront

Eastern

Swimming
enclosure
Beach

The
Beach
House

Corio
Villa

Pevensey
Park

Merchiston
Hall

Eastern
Park

East
Geelong
Golf
Course

Moorak
Park

Mercure
Hotel
Geelong

Haymarket
Boutique
Hotel

Christ
Church

Wintergarden

MCKILLOP

Geelong
South

Rose
Garden

Geelong
Botanic
Gardens

EAST
GEELONG

Kardinia
Park

Hopetoun
Park

Richmond
Oval

Sladen
Park

Chilwell
Reserve

Frier
Reserve

WEST
FYANS

Barwon
Grange
Homestead

Barwon Valley
Park

BARRABOOL

SOUTH
GEELONG

John
Landy
Athletics
Field

Eastern
Cemetery

Thomson
Recreation
Reserve

Belmont
Common

CARR

Geelong
Showgrounds

THOMSON

Jerringot
Wildlife
Res &
Wetlands

Barwon
Valley
Golf
Course

Breakwater

BREAKWATER

Geelong
Racecourse

St
Albans
Res

278 C4 | 280 A2 | 287 A4 | 288 D4

ℹ️ **Cnr Princes Hwy and St Georges Rd, Corio; (03) 5275 5797 or 1800 620 888; www.visitgreatoceanroad.org.au**

📻 94.7 The Pulse FM, 774 AM ABC Local Radio

Situated on Corio Bay, Geelong is the largest provincial city in Victoria. Geelong was traditionally a wool-processing centre, and the National Wool Museum in Brougham Street details its early dependence upon the industry. The town was first settled by Europeans in the 1830s, but Geelong and its surrounds were originally home to the Wathaurong people, with whom the famous convict escapee William Buckley lived for many years. Buckley later described the unique culture of the Aboriginal tribes who welcomed him into their lives, and his writing is now one of the most priceless historical records of Indigenous culture in southern Australia. Geelong is a beautifully laid-out city, and a drive along the scenic Esplanade reveals magnificent old mansions built during its heyday.

🏠 **Waterfront Geelong** This superbly restored promenade stretches along Eastern Beach and offers a variety of attractions. Visitors can relax in the historic, 1930s-built sea-baths, enjoy fine dining in seaside restaurants and cafes or stroll along the famous Bollards Trail featuring colourful sculptures. The Waterfront district is on Eastern Beach Rd, with the beautiful old Cunningham Pier as a centrepiece.

National Wool Museum Housed in a historic bluestone woolstore, the centre features audiovisual displays plus re-created shearers' quarters and a mill-worker's cottage. There is a licensed restaurant and bar in the cellar, and a souvenir shop selling locally made wool products. Cnr Moorabool and Brougham sts; (03) 5227 0701.

Geelong Art Gallery: this regional gallery is considered one of the finest in the state. The focus is on late-19th- and early-20th-century paintings by British artists and members of the Royal Academy, such as Tom Roberts and Arthur Streeton; Little Malop St. **Historic buildings:** there are over 100 National Trust classifications in Geelong, including Merchiston Hall, Osborne House and Corio Villa. 'The Heights' is a 14-room prefabricated timber mansion set in landscaped gardens; contact visitor centre for details of open days; Aphrasia St, Newtown. Christ Church, still in continuous use, is the oldest Anglican Church in Victoria; Moorabool St. **Ford Discovery Centre:** Geelong has long been a major manufacturing centre for Ford and this centre details the history of Ford cars with interactive displays; closed Tues; Cnr Brougham and Gheringhap sts. **Wintergarden:** a historic building housing a gallery, a nursery, antiques and a giftshop; McKillop St. **Botanic Gardens:** overlooking Corio Bay and featuring a good collection of native and exotic plants; part of Eastern Park; Garden St. **Johnstone Park:** picnic and barbecue facilities; Cnr Mercer and Gheringhap sts. **Queens Park:** walks to Buckley Falls; Queens Park Rd, Newtown. **Balyang Bird Sanctuary:** Shannon Ave, Newtown. **Barwon River:** extensive walking tracks and bike paths in parkland by the river. **Norlane Water World:** water slides and fun park (summer only); Princes Hwy, Norlane. **Corio Bay beaches:** popular for swimming, fishing and sailing; boat ramps provided.

🎆 **Steampacket Gardens Market:** on foreshore at Eastern Beach; 1st Sun each month. **Geelong Farmers Market:** Little Malop St; 2nd Sat each month. **Skandia Geelong Week:** Jan. **Pako Festa:** Victoria's premier multicultural event; Pakington St; last Sat in Feb. **Highland Gathering:** Mar. **National Celtic Folk Festival:**

continued overleaf

TOWNS

📻 RADIO STATION   🏠 IN TOWN   🎆 WHAT'S ON   🧭 NEARBY

GEELONG continued

COLOURFUL BOLLARDS ALONG GEELONG'S WATERFRONT

June. *Geelong Show:* Oct. *Geelong Cup:* Oct. *Christmas Carols by the Bay:* Eastern Beach; Dec. *Geelong New Year Waterfront Festival:* New Year's Eve, New Year's Day.

You Yangs Regional Park These granite outcrops that rise 352 m above Werribee's lava plains have an ancient link to the Wathaurong people as they provided a much-needed water source – rock wells were created to catch water, and many of them can still be seen at Big Rock. The park is a popular recreational area: activities include the 12 km Great Circle Drive and the climb to Flinders Peak for fantastic views of Geelong, Corio Bay, Mt Macedon and Melbourne's skyline. Contact Parks Victoria on 13 1963; 24 km N.

Werribee Park and Open Range Zoo The key feature of Werribee Park is a beautifully preserved 1870s mansion with the interior painstakingly restored to its original opulence. The mansion is surrounded by 12 ha of gardens, including a grotto and a farmyard area, complete with a blacksmith. Within the grounds is the Victoria State Rose Garden with over 500 varieties of flowers. Next to the park is the Werribee Open Range Zoo, developed around the Werribee River. The zoo covers 200 ha and has a variety of animals native to the grasslands of Africa, Asia, North America and Australia, including giraffes, rhinos, meerkats, cheetahs and vervet monkeys. Guided safaris through the replicated African savannah are a must. Access from the Princes Hwy; Werribee Park 13 1963; Open Range Zoo (03) 9731 9600; 40 km NE.

Fyansford: one of the oldest settlements in the region, with historic buildings including the Swan Inn, Balmoral Hotel and Fyansford Hotel. The Monash Bridge across the Moorabool River is thought to be one of the earliest reinforced-concrete bridges in Victoria; outskirts of Geelong; 4 km W. *Adventure Park:* Victoria's first waterpark, with 22 attractions and rides; open Oct–Apr; Bellarine Hwy, Wallington; 15 km SE. *Avalon Airfield:* hosts the Australian International Air Show in odd-numbered years; off Princes Hwy; 20 km NE. *Serendip Sanctuary:* a wildlife research station that includes nature trails, bird hides and a visitor centre; just south of the You Yangs. *Fairy Park:* features miniature houses and scenes from fairytales; north of Anakie (29 km N). *Steiglitz:* once a gold town, Steiglitz is now almost deserted. The restored courthouse is open on Sun; 37 km NW. *Little River Earth Sanctuary:* 200 animals live here in the open grassy woodland, including species that had been extinct in Victoria for over 100 years and were reintroduced right here. Take the Wildlife Adventure Walk at sunset to see such creatures as potoroos and pademelons. Also on-site is the set used in the film *Ned Kelly*; guided tours only, bookings (03) 5283 1602; 45 km NE. *Geelong Wine Region:* stretching north past Anakie, around Geelong and south along the Bellarine Peninsula, this region produces a diverse range of red and white wines. Cellar doors offer tastings and sales; map from visitor centre.

See also WERRIBEE & BELLARINE, pp. 40–1

on quality local produce, especially the world-class Yarra Valley wines. On top of this is a host of art and craft boutiques and two major attractions – TarraWarra Museum of Art and the famous Healesville Sanctuary, one of the best places in Victoria to experience Australia's unique wildlife close-up.

🏠 *Silvermist Studio Gallery:* handmade gold and silver jewellery; Maroondah Hwy. *Open-air trolley rides:* from Healesville railway station; open Sun and public holidays. *Giant Steps/Innocent Bystander Winery:* thoroughly modern cellar door in the town centre with an excellent bakery, bistro serving mouth-watering pizzas, and cheese room; 336 Maroondah Hwy; (03) 5962 6111 or 1800 661 624.

🎆 *Market:* River St; 1st Sun each month. *Grape Grazing Festival:* variety of events held throughout wine district to celebrate the harvest; Feb. *Australian Car Rally Championship:* Sept.

🧭 **Healesville Sanctuary** Australia is famous for its unique animal species and they are all on show at this 32 ha reserve.

The sanctuary is also one of the few places in the world to have successfully bred platypus in captivity. Allow at least half a day to fully explore the sanctuary with the extra options of visiting the animal hospital or going on a keeper tour (bookings (03) 5957 2800). Badger Creek Rd; 4 km S.

TarraWarra Museum of Art TarraWarra Estate has been operating as a vineyard since 1983, producing a selection of fine chardonnay and pinot noir. Now there is a striking building housing an extensive private collection of modern art. The collection focuses on the 3 key themes of Australian Modernism – landscape, figuration and abstraction – and works by artists such as Howard Arkley, Arthur Boyd and Brett Whiteley can be found within. Healesville–Yarra Glen Rd; (03) 5957 3100.

Hedgend Maze: giant maze and fun park; Albert Rd; 2.5 km S. *Corranderrk Aboriginal Cemetery:* once the burial ground for an Aboriginal mission, and the final resting place of well-known Wurundjeri leader William Barak; 3 km S. *Maroondah Reservoir Park:* a magnificent park set in lush forests

TOWNS

with walking tracks and a lookout nearby; 3 km NE. *Donnelly's Weir Park:* starting point of the 5000 km Bicentennial National Trail to Cooktown (Queensland). The park also has short walking tracks and picnic facilities; 4 km N. *Badger Weir Park:* picnic area in a natural setting; 7 km SE. *Mallesons Lookout:* views of Yarra Valley to Melbourne; 8 km S. *Mt St Leonard:* good views from the summit; 14 km N. *Toolangi:* attractions include the Singing Gardens of C. J. Dennis, a beautiful, formal garden; the Toolangi Forest Discovery Centre, for a fascinating insight into the local forests and how they were formed; and Toolangi Pottery; 20 km NW. *Wineries:* around 85 in the area open for tastings and sales. Tours available; details from visitor centre. *See also Yarra Glen.*

See also YARRA & DANDENONGS, pp. 32–3

Heathcote

287 B2 | 289 E2

i Cnr High and Barrack sts; (03) 5433 3121; www.heathcote.org.au

91.1 FM ABC Local Radio, 100.7 Highlands FM

Heathcote is located near the outskirts of the scenic Heathcote–Graytown National Park, with the McIvor Creek flowing by the town. Heathcote was established during the gold rush, but is now known as a prominent wine region with good red wines produced from a number of new vineyards.

Courthouse Crafts: displays relating to the gold rush, plus arts and crafts; High St. *Pink Cliffs:* eroded soil from gold sluices gave the cliffs their remarkable pink colour; Pink Cliffs Rd, off Hospital Rd. *McIvor Range Reserve:* walking tracks; off Barrack St; details

of walks from visitor centre. *Heathcote Winery:* this winery, in the old Thomas Craven Stores building, has an art gallery and cellar-door sales; High St.

World's Longest Lunch: Mar. *Rodeo:* Mar long weekend. *Heathcote Wine and Food Festival:* 1st weekend in Oct.

Heathcote–Graytown National Park

Compared with many of Victoria's national parks, Heathcote–Graytown was declared quite late as part of a statewide plan to preserve box-ironbark forest. Now protecting the largest forest of this type in the state, the park is not only an important nature reserve but also has a long history of settlement. Take one of the many walks or scenic drives to explore evidence of Aboriginal, goldmining and pioneering history, or take in scenic views from the lookouts at Mt Black, Mt Ida and Viewing Rock (just near Heathcote). Contact Parks Victoria on 13 1963; access from Northern Hwy and Heathcote–Nagambie Rd.

Wineries Heathcote shiraz makes wine lovers go weak at the knees. Its depth is the result of the dark, red Cambrian soil and the continental climate. Jasper Hill is the most exclusive name in the area. Its elegant red wines can be hard to come by, so if you manage to find a bottle, it is worth purchasing it on the spot. Other good wineries include Heathcote Winery with its cellar door located on the town's main street, Shelmerdine Vineyards, Wild Duck Creek Estate and Red Edge. To find most of the region's wines under one roof, head to Cellar and Store, which also stocks a full range of local gourmet produce.

Lake Eppalock: one of the state's largest lakes, great for fishing, watersports and picnics; 10 km W.

See also GOULBURN & MURRAY, pp. 50–1

Hopetoun

288 B1 | 291 B4

ℹ️ **Gateway Beet, 75 Lascelles St; (03) 5083 3001; www.hopetounvictoria.com.au**

📻 92.9 3MBR-FM Mallee Border Radio, 594 AM ABC Local Radio

This small Mallee town, south-east of Wyperfeld National Park, was named after the first governor-general of Australia, the Earl of Hopetoun. The Earl was a friend of Edward Lascelles, who played a major role in developing the Mallee Country by eradicating vermin, developing water strategies to cope with the dry conditions, and enticing settlers to the region.

🏠 *Hopetoun House:* the residence of Lascelles, this majestic building is now National Trust–classified; Evelyn St. *Mallee Mural:* depicts history of the region; wall of Dr Pete's Memorial Park, cnr Lascelles and Austin sts. *Lake Lascelles:* good for boating, swimming and fishing when filled, presently dry. Camping facilities available; access from end of Austin St.

🏖️ *Hopetoun Bowl Club Annual Carnival:* Apr. *Hopetoun A & P Society Annual Show:* Oct.

🧭 **Wyperfeld National Park** Outlet Creek connects the network of lake beds that are the main highlight for visitors to this park. They fill only when Lake Albacutya overflows, which in turn fills only when Lake Hindmarsh overflows. Once a corroboree ground, the main lake bed, Wirrengren Plain, has flooded only once in the last 100 years. Eastern grey kangaroos can be seen grazing on Wirrengren and the other lake beds, and the Eastern Lookout Nature Drive is a great way to see the range of vegetation in the park – river red gums, black box, mallee and cypress pine, and wildflowers in spring. A variety of walking trails leave from the two campgrounds – Wonga Campground in the south and Casuarina Campground in the north, near the lakes. Contact Parks Victoria on 13 1963; 50 km NW.

Patchewollock: the northern gateway to the Wyperfeld National Park, and also home of the Patchewollock Outback Pub; 35 km NW.

See also MALLEE COUNTRY, pp. 48–9

Horsham

288 B2 | 291 B5

ℹ️ **20 O'Callaghan Pde; (03) 5382 1832 or 1800 633 218; www.grampianslittledesert.com.au**

📻 96.5 Triple H FM, 594 AM ABC Local Radio

Horsham is an important centre for the Wimmera district. Prior to European settlement, Horsham and its surrounds were occupied by the Jardwa and Wotjobaluk Aboriginal people, who referred to the region as 'Wopetbungundilar'. This term is thought to have meant 'place of flowers', a reference to the flowers that grow along the banks of the Wimmera River. Flowers continue to play an important role in Horsham, which is considered to be one of the prettiest regional towns in Victoria – the town prides itself on its clean streets and picturesque gardens. Although the Wimmera is a renowned wheat-growing region, Horsham is also a centre for fine wool production.

🏠 **Horsham Regional Art Gallery** This is one of Victoria's key regional galleries, with an extensive collection housed in a 1930s Art Deco building. Most of the artwork is centred on the Mack Jost collection of Australian art, with contemporary Australian photography another specialty. 80 Wilson St; (03) 5362 2888.

📻 RADIO STATION   🏠 IN TOWN   🎆 WHAT'S ON   🧭 NEARBY

HALLS GAP

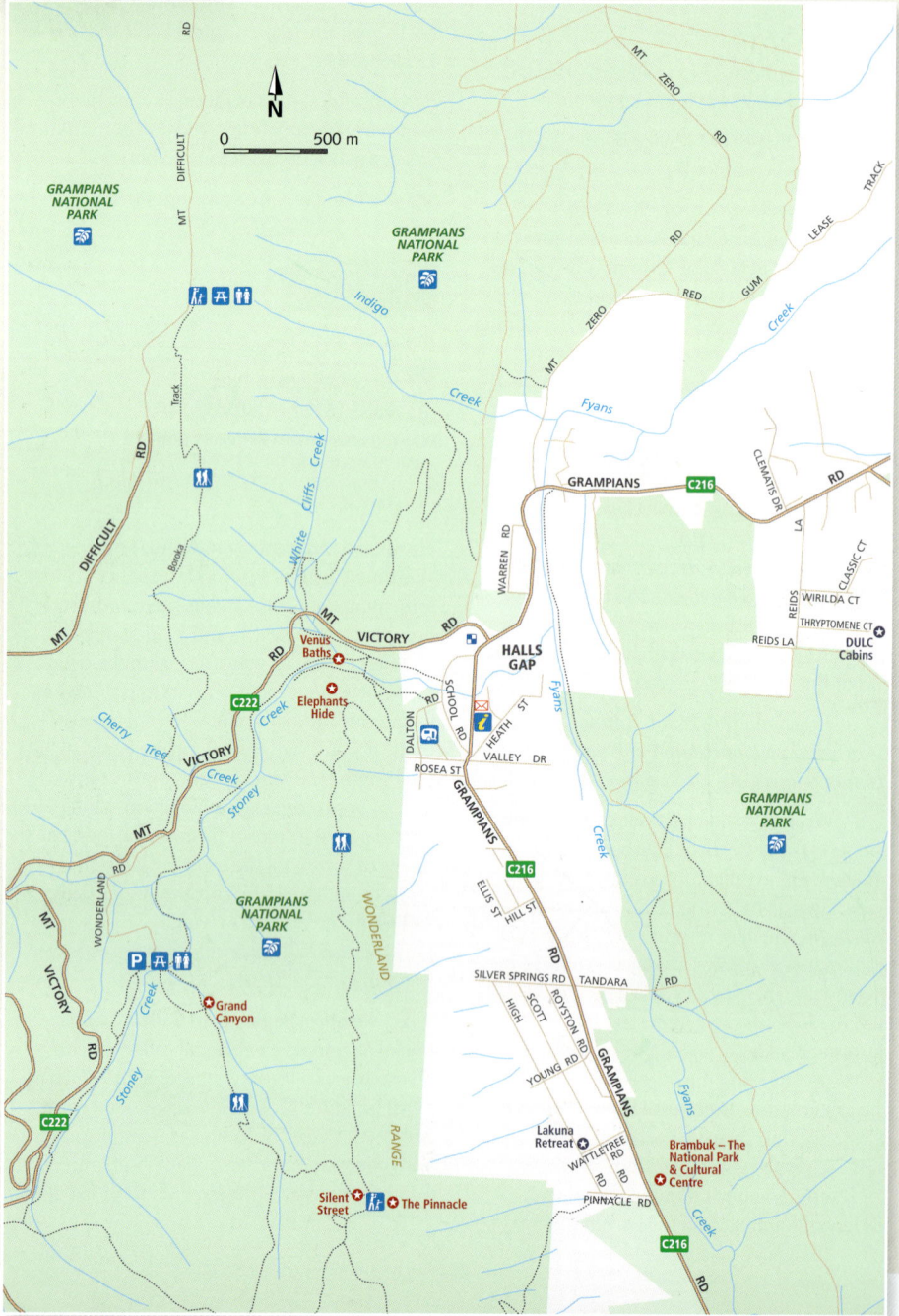

Map of Halls Gap area showing Grampians National Park, with roads including C216, C222, Mt Victory Rd, Mt Difficult Rd, Grampians Rd, and Wonderland Rd. Points of interest include Venus Baths, Elephants Hide, Grand Canyon, Silent Street, The Pinnacle, Lakuna Retreat, Brambuk – The National Park & Cultural Centre, and DULC Cabins.

BOROKA LOOKOUT, GRAMPIANS NATIONAL PARK

288 B3

ⓘ Grampians Rd; (03) 5356 4616 or 1800 065 599; www.grampianstravel.com.au

📻 94.1 FM ABC Local Radio, 99.9 VoiceFM

The little village of Halls Gap is set in the heart of the Grampians. It was named after Charles Browing Hall, who discovered the gap and valley in 1841. The valley was later developed by cattle-station owners, but the town really took off in the early 1900s when tourists, nature lovers and botanists caught on to the beauty and diversity of the mountain ranges that would later become Grampians National Park. The town itself has its own charm – shops, galleries and cafes lend a laid-back atmosphere that befits the location, while in the evening long-billed corellas arrive to roost opposite the shops in the main street.

🎆 **Grampians Jazz Festival:** Feb. **Grampians Grape Escape:** wine and food festival; May. **Wildflower Exhibition:** Oct.

🧭 **Grampians National Park** Aboriginal occupation of the area known as the

Grampians dates back over 5000 years (some evidence suggests up to 30 000 years). To local Koorie communities, this magnificent landscape of rock-encrusted mountain ranges perched high above the agricultural plains of the Western District is known as Gariwerd. Within the 168 000 ha park is a startling array of vegetation and wildlife, including 200 bird species and a quarter of Victoria's native flora species. The Grampians are renowned for striking displays of wildflowers each spring – the heathlands abound in colourful shows of Grampians boronia, blue pincushion lily and Grampians parrot-pea. Twenty of the park's 800 plant species are not found anywhere else in the world. Brambuk – The National Park and Cultural Centre, a short walk or drive south of Halls Gap, is an excellent first stop in the park. It features interactive displays and written information about the park's attractions, bringing to life the culture of the local Jardwadjali and Djab Wurrung people. Natural highlights of the Grampians include MacKenzie Falls, the largest of the park's

continued overleaf

📻 RADIO STATION   🏠 IN TOWN   🎆 WHAT'S ON   🧭 NEARBY

HALLS GAP *continued*

many picturesque waterfalls; Zumsteins picnic ground, a beautiful spot with tame and friendly kangaroos; and the Balconies, a rock ledge once known as the Jaws of Death, offering views over Victoria Valley. The most popular section of the park is the Wonderland Range, true to its name with features including Elephants Hide, Grand Canyon, Venus Baths and Silent Street. There are over 90 bushwalks available in the park, all varying in length and degree of difficulty. Visitors are advised to consult a ranger before embarking on one of the longer treks. For further information, contact Brambuk – The National Park and Cultural Centre on (03) 5361 4000.

The Gap Vineyard: cellar-door tastings and sales of award-winning white and red wine varieties, as well as port; closed Mon and Tues; Pomonal Rd; 2 km E. *Grampians Adventure Golf:* world-class minigolf, 18-hole course set on 2 acres; 481 Grampians Rd; 4 km s near Lake Bellfield. *Halls Gap Zoo:* explore the park's nature track and view the animals, many of which are free-range; (03) 5356 4668; 7 km SE. *Grampians Horse Riding Adventures:* morning and afternoon rides lasting 2 hrs, also has on-site accommodation; Brimpaen; (03) 5383 9225; 44 km w.

See also GRAMPIANS & CENTRAL WEST, pp. 46–7

Botanic Gardens: picturesquely set on the banks of the Wimmera River; Cnr Baker and Firebrace sts. *The Wool Factory:* produces extra-fine wool from Saxon-Merino sheep, with tours daily; Golf Course Rd. *Wimmera River:* key attraction for the town, with scenic picnic spots along the river's edges. Visit the river at dusk for spectacular sunsets.

Market: showgrounds on McPherson St; 2nd Sun each month. *Haven Recreation Market:* 1st Sat each month. *Wimmera Machinery Field Days:* Longerenong; Mar. *Art Is:* community festival; Apr. *Awakenings Festival:* largest Australian festival involving disabled patrons; Oct. *Spring Garden Festival:* Oct. *Horsham Show:* Oct. *Kannamaroo Rock 'n' Roll Festival:* Nov. *Karkana Strawberry Festival:* Nov.

Murtoa This town lies on the edge of Lake Marma, a small but scenic lake stocked with trout and redfin. The Water Tower Museum (open Sun) displays the history of the area as well as James Hill's 1885–1930 taxidermy collection of some 500 birds and animals. On the eastern side of town, among the grain silos, is an unusual relic called the Stick Shed. The roof of this now empty storage shed is held up with 640 unmilled tree trunks, and the interior is an evocative sight (open once a year in Oct); 31 km NE.

Jung: market on last Sat each month; 10 km NE. *Fishing:* redfin and trout in local lakes, depending on water levels. Reasonable levels at Taylors Lake; 18 km SE. *Mount Zero Olives:* the largest olive grove in the Southern Hemisphere, with tastings and sales of olive oil; Laharum; 30 km s.

See also GRAMPIANS & CENTRAL WEST, pp. 46–7

Inglewood

283 B1 | 287 A1 | 288 D2 | 291 D5

i Loddon Visitor Information Centre, Wedderburn Community Centre, 24 Wilson St, Wedderburn; (03) 5494 3489; www.loddonalive.com.au

89.5 The Fresh FM, 91.1 FM ABC Local Radio

North along the Calder Highway from Bendigo is the 'Golden Triangle' town of Inglewood. Sizeable gold nuggets were found in this area during the gold rush and are still being unearthed. Inglewood is also known as Blue Eucy town, due to the once vigorous and still active blue mallee eucalyptus oil industry. The town is also the birthplace of Australian aviator Sir Reginald Ansett.

Old eucalyptus oil distillery: not in operation but can be viewed; Calder Hwy, northern end of town. **Old courthouse:** local historical memorabilia; open by appt; Southey St. **Streetscape:** historic buildings are solid evidence of the town's goldmining history.

Kooyoora State Park The park sits at the northern end of the Bealiba Range and features extensive box-ironbark forests. The Eastern Walking Circuit offers a great opportunity for bushwalkers, passing through strange rock formations and giant granite slabs. The Summit Track leads to Melville Caves Lookout. The caves were once the haunt of the notorious bushranger Captain Melville. Camping is allowed around the caves. Contact Parks Victoria on 13 1963; 16 km w.

Bridgewater on Loddon: fishing and watersports, Old Loddon Vines Vineyard, Water Wheel Vineyards and horse-drawn caravans for hire; 8 km SE. **Loddon Valley wineries:** the warm climate and clay soils of this region are known for producing outstanding red varieties and award-winning chardonnays. Taste the wines at cellar doors like Pandalowie at Bridgewater on Loddon (8 km SE) and Kingower (11 km SW); winery map from visitor information centre.

See also GOLDFIELDS, pp. 44–5

Inverloch

279 G5 | 287 D5 | 289 F5

A'Beckett St; 1300 762 433; www.visitbasscoast.com

88.1 3MFM South Gippsland, 100.7 FM ABC Local Radio

Inverloch is a small seaside resort set on the protected waters of Anderson Inlet, east of Wonthaggi. It is characterised by long stretches of pristine beach that offer good surf and excellent fishing.

Bunurong Environment Centre: natural history displays with special focus on dinosaur diggings; also sales of natural products; The Esplanade. **Shell Museum:** The Esplanade.

Inverloch Food and Wine Festival: Feb. **Annual Dinosaur Dig:** Feb/Mar. **Inverloch Jazz Festival:** Mar. **Inverloch Billy Cart Derby:** Nov.

Bunurong Coastal Drive Stretching the 14 km of coastline between Inverloch and Cape Paterson is this spectacular coastal drive with magnificent views to Venus Bay and beyond. Carparks offer access to beaches and coastal walks along the drive. The waters offshore are protected within Bunurong Marine National Park, and offer opportunities to surf, snorkel, scuba dive or simply explore the numerous rockpools that are dotted along the coast.

Anderson Inlet: the most southerly habitat for mangroves in Australia. This calm inlet is popular for windsurfing and watersports, and nearby Townsend Bluff and Maher's Landing offer good birdwatching; adjacent to town. **Fishing:** in nearby waterways such as the Tarwin River; 20 km SE.

See also PHILLIP ISLAND & GIPPSLAND, pp. 36–7

TOWNS

Jeparit

288 B1 | 291 B4

ⓘ **Wimmera–Mallee Pioneer Museum,** Charles St; (03) 5397 2101.

📻 96.5 Triple H FM, 594 AM ABC Local Radio

This little town in the Wimmera is 5 kilometres south-east of Lake Hindmarsh, which was once the largest natural freshwater lake in Victoria. Sadly, it has been empty for the past several years. Former prime minister Sir Robert Menzies was born here in 1894.

🏠 **Wimmera–Mallee Pioneer Museum** This unique museum details what life was like for early settlers in the Wimmera through a collection of colonial buildings furnished in the style of the period. The buildings on display are spread over a 4 ha complex and include log cabins, a church and a blacksmith's shop. The museum also features displays of restored farm machinery. Southern entrance to town, Charles St; (03) 5397 2101.

Menzies Sq: site of the dwelling where Menzies was born; Cnr Charles and Roy sts. *Wimmera River Walk:* 6 km return; starts at museum.

🧭 **Lake Hindmarsh** Victoria's largest freshwater lake has seen dire water levels for the past several years. It was fed by the Wimmera River. Boating, waterskiing and fishing were all popular pastimes (Schulzes Beach has a boat ramp), with pelicans and other waterbirds existing at the lake in breeding colonies. Picnic and camping spots are available on the lake's shores. A historic fisherman's hut can also be seen. Contact the visitor centre for an update on water levels. 5 km NW.

Rainbow: a charming little Wimmera township, with Pasco's Cash Store, an original country general store, and Yurunga Homestead, a beautiful Edwardian home with a large collection of antiques and original fittings (northern edge of town, key available); 35 km N.

Pella: former German settlement with Lutheran church and old schoolhouse; 40 km NW via Rainbow. *Lake Albacutya:* fills only when Lake Hindmarsh overflows; 44 km N. *Wyperfeld National Park:* great for bushwalking; known for its birdlife, including the endangered mallee fowl, and wildflowers in spring; 60 km NW via Rainbow; *for details see Hopetoun.*

See also GRAMPIANS & CENTRAL WEST, pp. 46–7

Kerang

288 D1 | 291 D4

ⓘ **Sir John Gorton Library, cnr Murray Valley Hwy and Shadforth St; (03) 5452 1546; www.gannawarra.vic.gov.au**

📻 99.1 Smart FM, 102.1 FM ABC Local Radio

Kerang, situated on the Loddon River just south of the New South Wales border, lies at the southern end of the Kerang wetlands and lakes. They extend from Kerang 42 kilometres north-west to Lake Boga and offer a wonderland for watersports enthusiasts and birdwatchers; the lakes contain what are reputedly the world's largest ibis breeding grounds. The town itself is a service centre for its agricultural surrounds.

🏠 **Lester Lookout Tower:** town views; Cnr Murray Valley Hwy and Shadforth St. **Historical Museum:** focuses on cars and antique farm machinery; Riverwood Dr.

🎆 **Races:** Easter and Boxing Day. *Tour of the Murray River:* cycling race; late Aug/early Sept.

🧭 **Reedy Lakes:** a series of 3 lakes. Apex Park, a recreation reserve for swimming, picnicking and boating, is set by the first lake, and the second features a large ibis rookery. Picnic facilities are available at the third lake; 8 km NW. *Leaghur State Park:* on the Loddon River flood plain, this peaceful park is a perfect spot for a leisurely walk through the black box woodlands and wetlands; 25 km SW.

Murrabit: a historic timber town on the Murray surrounded by picturesque forests, with a country market 1st Sat each month; 27 km N. **Quambatook:** hosts the Australian Tractor Pull Championship each Easter; 40 km SW. **Lake Boga:** popular for watersports, with good sandy beaches; 42 km NW. **Fishing:** Meran, Kangaroo and Charm lakes all offer freshwater fishing; details from visitor centre.

See also GOULBURN & MURRAY, pp. 50–1

Kilmore

279 E1 | 287 C2 | 289 E3

i Library, 12 Sydney St; (03) 5781 1319.

📻 97.1 OKR FM, 774 AM ABC Local Radio

Kilmore is Victoria's oldest inland town, known for its historic buildings and many horseracing events. Like many towns in the central goldfields, Kilmore was the scene of a Kelly family saga. In this case, it was Ned Kelly's father who had a run-in with the law. In 1865 John 'Red' Kelly was arrested for killing a squatter's calf to feed his family, and was locked away in the Kilmore Gaol for six months. It was a crime that Ned had actually committed. Soon after Red's release, he died of dropsy and was buried in the small town of Avenel, where the Kelly family lived for some time.

🏠 **Old Kilmore Gaol** An impressive bluestone building, established in 1859, that is now a privately owned auction house; Sutherland St.

Hudson Park: picnic/barbecue facilities; Cnr Sydney and Foote sts. **Historic buildings:** Whitburgh Cottage, Piper St, and a number of 1850s shops and hotels along Sydney St; brochure from visitor centre.

🎆 **Kilmore Celtic Festival:** June. **Kilmore Cup:** harness racing; Oct.

🧭 **Tramways Heritage Centre at Bylands:** extensive display of cable cars and early electric trams, with tram rides available; open Sun only; just south of town. **Broadford:** a small town featuring a historic precinct on High St; 17 km NE. **Mt Piper Walking Track:** wildlife and wildflowers can be spotted along the way (1 hr return); near Broadford. **Strath Creek:** walks to Strath Creek Falls and a drive through the Valley of a Thousand Hills; starts at outskirts of Broadford.

See also SPA & GARDEN COUNTRY, pp. 38–9

Koo-wee-rup

279 F4 | 281 H3 | 287 D4 | 289 F4

i Newsagency, 277 Rossiter Rd; (03) 5997 1456.

📻 103.1 3BBR FM West Gippsland Community Radio, 774 AM ABC Local Radio

Koo-wee-rup and the surrounding agricultural area exist on reclaimed and drained swampland. It has given rise to Australia's largest asparagus-growing district. The town's name derives from the Aboriginal name meaning 'blackfish swimming', a reference to the fish that were once plentiful in the swamp.

🏠 **Historical Society Museum:** local history; open Sun; Rossiter Rd.

🧭 **Swamp Observation Tower:** offers views of remaining swampland and across to Western Port. A market with local produce operates regularly at the base; South Gippsland Hwy; 2 km SE. **Bayles Fauna Reserve:** native animals; 8 km NE. **Harewood House:** restored 1850s house with original furnishings; South Gippsland Hwy towards Tooradin. **Tooradin:** offers good boating and fishing on Sawtells Inlet; 10 km W. **Caldermeade Farm:** originally one of the region's premier beef cattle properties but now a fully operational

TOWNS

modern dairy farm focused on educating and entertaining visitors; 10 km se. *Pakenham:* now considered a suburb of Melbourne, Pakenham is home to the Military Vehicle Museum, Army Rd, and the Berwick Pakenham Historical Society Museum, John St; 13 km n. *Tynong:* attractions include Victoria's Farm Shed, featuring farm animals and shearing, and Gumbaya Park, a family fun park; 20 km ne. *Royal Botanic Gardens Cranbourne:* renowned, wonderfully maintained native gardens; 22 km nw. *Grantville:* hosts a market 4th Sun each month; 30 km s.

See also Phillip Island & Gippsland, pp. 36–7

Korumburra

279 G5 | 287 D5 | 289 F4

ⓘ **Prom Country Information Centre,** South Gippsland Hwy; (03) 5655 2233 or 1800 630 704; www.visitpromcountry.com.au

📻 88.1 3MFM South Gippsland, 100.7 FM ABC Local Radio

Established in 1887, Korumburra stands firmly as the heritage centre of South Gippsland. The township was a primary producer of black coal for Victoria's rail industry until the last mine closed in 1958. Korumburra is set in the rolling green hills of South Gippsland, with scenic drives found in any direction.

🏠 **Coal Creek Heritage Village** Coal Creek is an open-air museum that offers all the fascination of life in a 19th-century coalmining village, including history and memorabilia of the area. The village contains beautiful picnic areas, bush tramway and cafe, and community events are held throughout the year. South Gippsland Hwy; (03) 5655 1811.

Korumburra Federation Art Gallery: South Gippsland Hwy. *Whitelaw Antiques & Collectibles:* 9 Mine Rd.

🌺 *Korumburra Farmers Market:* Railway

Siding; 3rd Sat each month. *Korumburra Agricultural Show:* Feb. *Rotary Club of Korumburra Art Show:* Feb.

🧭 **South Gippsland Tourist Railway** This railway travels to Leongatha, Korumburra, Loch and Nyora, and provides a scenic way to view the ever-changing South Gippsland landscape. Trains operate Sun and public holidays with a Wed service during school holidays. The grand Edwardian Railway Station behind the main street is also worth a visit. (03) 5658 1111.

Loch: a thriving art and craft village with cosy eateries, antique stores and galleries; 14 km nw. *Poowong:* beautiful country town nestled among the rolling hills of South Gippsland with Poowong Pioneer Chapel, est. 1878; 18 km nw.

See also Phillip Island & Gippsland, pp. 36–7

Kyneton

278 D1 | 283 D3 | 287 B2 | 289 E3

ⓘ **Jean Haynes Reserve,** High St; (03) 5422 6110; www.visitmacedonranges.com

📻 91.1 FM ABC Local Radio, 100.7 Highlands FM

Part of Victoria's picturesque spa and garden country, Kyneton is a well-preserved town with many attractive bluestone buildings. Caroline Chisholm, who helped many migrants find their feet in this country, lived in Kyneton, where her family owned a store and her husband worked as a magistrate. While living in the town, she established a series of affordable, overnight shelters for travellers on the Mount Alexander Road (now the Calder Highway), a road frequented by gold prospectors. Remnants of the shelters can be seen at the historic township of Carlsruhe, south-east of Kyneton.

🏠 *Kyneton Museum:* in a former bank building, with a drop-log cottage in the grounds; open Fri–Sun; Piper St. *Wool on Piper:* features a spinning mill, with yarns and handmade garments for sale; Piper St. *Botanic Gardens:* 8 ha area scenically located above Pipers Creek. The gardens feature rare varieties of trees; Clowes St. *Historic buildings:* many in town, including mechanics institute on Mollison St and old police depot, Jenning St. *Campaspe River Walk:* scenic walk with picnic spots; access from Piper St.

Farmers market: farmgate produce; Piper St; 2nd Sat each month. *Kyneton Daffodil and Arts Festival:* Sept. *Kyneton Cup:* Nov.

Trentham and Wombat State Forest This picturesque spa-country town has a mixed history of gold, timber and farming. It has a charming streetscape and attractions include a historic foundry and Minifie's Berry Farm, where you can pick your own berries in season. Just north-east of town is Wombat State Forest – deep within is Victoria's largest single-drop waterfall, Trentham Falls. Cascading 32 m onto a quartz gravel base, the falls are an impressive backdrop for a picnic. 22 km sw.

Reservoirs: several offering scenic locations for walks and picnics. Upper Coliban, Lauriston and Malmsbury reservoirs all nearby. *Paramoor Farm and Winery:* a former Clydesdale horse farm, now winery and B&B; Carlsruhe; 5 km se. *Malmsbury:* a town noted for its old bluestone buildings. It features historic Botanic Gardens and The Mill, National Trust–classified, not open to the public. Also wineries in the area; 10 km nw. *Turpins and Cascade Falls:* with picnic area and walks; near Metcalfe; 22 km n.

See also Spa & Garden Country, pp. 38–9

Lakes Entrance

see inset box on next page

Leongatha

279 G5 | 287 D5 | 289 F5

i Michael Place Complex; (03) 5662 2111; www.visitpromcountry.com.au

88.1 3MFM South Gippsland, 100.7 FM ABC Local Radio

Leongatha is a thriving town, considered the commercial centre of South Gippsland. Idyllically positioned as a gateway to Gippsland destinations and attractions, any major road departing Leongatha provides access to popular attractions, all within an easy one hour's drive.

Historical Society Museum: McCartin St. *Leongatha Gallery:* Cnr McCartin St and Michael Pl. *Mushroom Crafts:* craft sales and gallery; 40 Blair St. *Great Southern Rail Trail:* commencement of 50 km rail trail that winds between Leongatha and Foster.

South Gippsland Golf Classic: Feb. *Music for the People Concert:* Mossvale Park; Feb. *Mossvale Music Festival:* Mar. *Raw Vibes Youth Festival:* Mar. *Daffodil Festival:* Sept. *Garden and Lifestyle Expo:* Nov.

Koonwarra Situated between Leongatha and Meeniyan on the South Gippsland Hwy, Koonwarra became the first eco-wise town in Australia. The town prides itself on its commitment to sustainable lifestyles. Drop in to the Koonwarra Fine Food & Wine Store to purchase local wines, cheese and pantry items. On the first Sat of each month, Koonwarra holds a farmers market. The town also boasts an organic cooking school, day spa, specialty shops, pottery and winery nearby. 8 km se.

Meeniyan: great place to visit for the art and craft enthusiast. Places of interest include Meeniyan Art Gallery, South Gippsland Craft Merchants, Beth's Antiques and Lacy Jewellery. Meeniyan hosts an annual art and craft exhibition over the Melbourne Cup

TOWNS

RADIO STATION   IN TOWN   WHAT'S ON   NEARBY

LAKES ENTRANCE

289 H4 | 290 B4

i **Lakes and Wilderness Tourism, cnr Esplanade and Marine Pde; (03) 5155 1966 or 1800 637 060; www.discovereastgippsland.com.au**

📻 90.7 FM 3REG Radio East Gippsland, 100.7 FM ABC Local Radio

Lakes Entrance is a lovely holiday town situated at the eastern end of the Gippsland Lakes, an inland network of waterways covering more than 400 square kilometres. The artificially created 'entrance' of the town's name allows the Tasman Sea and the lakes to meet, creating a safe harbour that is home to one of the largest fishing fleets in Australia. While many of the attractions in Lakes Entrance are based around the water, there is also the opportunity for

gourmets to indulge themselves with a variety of cafes and restaurants lining The Esplanade, plus sales of fresh fish and local wines.

🏠 **Seashell Museum:** The Esplanade.

🎆 **Markets:** Lakes Entrance Primary School, Myer St; 3rd Sat each month. **Arts Festival:** Forest Tech Living Resource Centre; Mar long weekend. **Lakes Motor Fest:** biannual; Apr. **New Year's Eve Entertainment and Fireworks:** Dec.

🧭 **Gippsland Lakes** Five rivers end their journey to the sea here, forming a vast expanse of water tucked in behind Ninety Mile Beach. The lakes are a true playground for anyone with an interest in water activities, especially fishing and boating. Explore the lakes on a sightseeing cruise, including one to Wyanga Park Winery, or on the ever-popular houseboats that can be hired over summer. Details from visitor centre.

Jemmys Point: great views of the region; 1 km w. **Lake Bunga:** nature trail along foreshore; 3 km E. **Lake Tyers:** sheltered waters ideal for fishing, swimming and boating. Cruises depart from Fishermans Landing in town. Lake is 6–23 km NE, depending on access point. Lake Tyers Forest Park is great for bushwalking, wildlife-spotting, picnicking and camping; 20 km NE. **Nyerimilang Heritage Park:** 1920s homestead, with original farm buildings and the wonderfully maintained East Gippsland Botanic Gardens. Rose Pruning

SCRUB, SAND AND SEA IN LAKES ENTRANCE

Day, with demonstrations, is held in July; 10 km NW. **Swan Reach:** Rosewood Pottery; Malcolm Cameron Studio Gallery, open weekends; 14 km NW. **Metung:** a scenic town on Lake King with boat hire, cruises and a marina regatta each Jan. Chainsaw Sculpture Gallery has chainsaw sculpture and a display of Annemieke Mein's embroidery art; 15 km W.

Nicholson River Winery: 22 km NW. **East Gippsland Carriage Co:** restored horse-drawn carriages and tours; 30 km E. **Bataluk Cultural Trail:** driving tour taking in Aboriginal cultural sites in the East Gippsland region; self-guide brochure from visitor centre.

See also EAST GIPPSLAND, pp. 54–5

weekend; 16 km SE. **Mossvale Park:** tranquil setting for a picnic or barbecue. Music concerts and festivals are held here in Feb and Mar; 16 km NE. **Mirboo North:** situated among the picturesque Strzelecki Ranges, the township is decorated with murals depicting the history of the area. Grand Ridge Brewery, Lyre Bird Forest Walk and the Grand Ridge Rail Trail are also located here; 26 km NE.

See also PHILLIP ISLAND & GIPPSLAND, pp. 36–7

Lorne

278 B5 | 286 C2 | 287 A5 | 288 D4

i 15 Mountjoy Pde; (03) 5289 1152; www.visitgreatoceanroad.org.au

🔸 94.7 The Pulse FM, 774 AM ABC Local Radio

Lorne is one of Victoria's most attractive and lively coastal resorts. The approach into town along the Great Ocean Road is truly

---

🔸 RADIO STATION   🏠 IN TOWN   🎆 WHAT'S ON   🧭 NEARBY spectacular, with the superb mountain scenery of the Otways on one side and the rugged Bass Strait coast on the other. The village of Lorne was established in 1871 and quickly became popular with pastoralists from inland areas, leading to its development around the picturesque Louttit Bay. When the Great Ocean Road opened in 1932 Lorne became much more accessible; however, the area has remained relatively unspoiled with good beaches, surfing, fishing and bushwalking in the hills – activities made all the more enjoyable by the area's pleasant, mild climate.

Teddys Lookout: excellent bay views; behind the town, at the end of George St. *Shipwreck Walk:* walk along the beach taking in sites of the numerous shipwrecks along this stretch of coast; details from visitor centre. *Foreshore Reserve:* great spot for a picnic, with paddleboats available for hire. *Qdos:* contemporary art gallery; Allenvale Rd. *Lorne Fisheries:* on the recently opened new pier with daily supplies.

Pier to Pub Swim: Jan. *Mountain to Surf Foot Race:* Jan. *Great Ocean Road Marathon:* May. *Anaconda Adventure Race:* Dec. *Falls Festival:* Dec–Jan.

Great Otway National Park The park covers 103 000 ha and includes a range of environments, from the timbered ridges of the eastern Otways to fern gullies, waterfalls and a coastline with tall cliffs, coves and sandy beaches. Around Lorne there are more than 100 walking tracks and the rock platforms along the coast provide ideal spots for ocean fishing. The Falls Festival, a major rock-music festival, is held over New Year's Eve at a property near the Erskine Falls, 9 km NW. These popular falls are a peaceful location and drop 30 m over moss-covered rocks. As well as driving, you can walk to the falls from Lorne along the river. The park surrounds Lorne and can be accessed from various points along the Great Ocean Rd. Contact Parks Victoria on 13 1963.

Cumberland River Valley: walking tracks and camping; 4 km SW. *Mt Defiance Lookout:* 10 km SW. *Wye River:* a small coastal village, good for rock and surf fishing, surfing and camping; 17 km SW. *Old Lorne Road Olives:* olive grove, cafe and gallery; closed Tues and Wed; Deans Marsh Rd; 22 km N. *Gentle Annie Berry Gardens:* pick your own; open Nov–Apr; 26 km NW via Deans Marsh. *Scenic drives:* west through the Otway Ranges, and south-west or north-east on the Great Ocean Rd.

See also SOUTH-WEST COAST, pp. 42–3

Maffra

289 G4

ℹ️ 96 Johnson St; (03) 5141 1811; www.tourismwellington.com.au

📻 100.7 FM ABC Local Radio, 104.7 Gippsland FM

Maffra, settled in the 1840s, retains the charm and old-style hospitality of another era. Named after Maffra in Portugal because many of the early Gippsland settlers had fought in that area of Europe during the Peninsula War, the town's early days were fraught with drought until a sugar beet industry established in the 1890s provided a major boost. The Glenmaggie Irrigation Scheme of 1919 also signalled a new heyday and ensured the viable and lengthy success of today's dairy industry. The sugar beet factory closed in 1948 owing to World War II's labour shortages and the competing dairy industry, but Maffra continues to support its rich agricultural surrounds. It also holds a great sense of history in its original shop verandahs and grand homesteads.

Maffra Sugar Beet Historic Museum: local history museum with special interest in the sugar beet industry; open Sun afternoon; River St. *Mineral and gemstone display:* large collection of rare gemstones and fossils at the information centre; Johnson St. *All Seasons*

Herb Garden: Foster St. *Gippsland Vehicle Collection:* outstanding rotating display of interesting vehicles; located in a historic vegetable dehydrating factory; Maffra–Sale Rd; (03) 5147 3223. *Gippsland Plains Rail Trail:* recreational trail for cycling and walking that passes through town; still under development but when complete will link Stratford in the east to Traralgon in the west by traversing dairy country.

Gippsland Harvest Festival: Mar. *Mardi Gras:* Mar.

Stratford: the scenic Avon River flows through town. Knobs Reserve is a site where the local Aboriginal people once sharpened axe heads on sandstone grinding stones – it is part of the Bataluk Cultural Trail, which takes in significant Indigenous sites throughout East Gippsland. Stratford hosts the Shakespeare Celebration in May; 9 km E. *Australian Wildlife Art Gallery and Sculpture:* Princes Hwy near Munro; 25 km E. *Robotic Dairy:* the first Australian dairy farm to install 4 'Astronaut Milking Robots' where the cows decide when to be milked; open on public visitor days or by appt; Toongabbie Rd, Winnindoo; (03) 5199 2212; 26 km w. *Lake Glenmaggie:* popular watersports venue; 42 km NW via Heyfield. *Alpine National Park:* sprawls from Licola, 75 km NW, to the NSW border. Near Licola is Lake Tali Karng, which lies 850 m above sea level and is a popular bushwalking destination during the warmer months. *Scenic drives:* the Traralgon to Stratford Tourist Route highlights attractions of the area. For stunning scenery, drive north along Forest Rd, through the Macalister River Valley to Licola and Mt Tamboritha in Alpine National Park; or to Jamieson (166 km NW via Heyfield), with access to snowfields or Lake Eildon.

See also EAST GIPPSLAND, pp. 54–5

Maldon

283 C2 | 287 A2 | 288 D2

i High St; (03) 5475 2569; www.maldon.org.au

91.1 FM ABC Local Radio, 106.3 Radio KLFM

Maldon is one of Victoria's best known gold towns and a popular spot for a weekend getaway for Melburnians. The town has been wonderfully preserved, with the wide, tree-lined main street featuring delightful old buildings and shopfronts. It seems the town has hardly changed since the gold rush, aside from the cafes and galleries that now prosper. Maldon was declared Australia's first 'notable town' by the National Trust in 1966.

Historic town walk: grab a brochure from the visitor centre and take to the wide, old footpaths to discover the historic delights of Maldon. See preserved 19th-century shopfronts and old stone cottages. Highlights include the restored Dabb's General Store in Main St, and the Maldon Hospital in Adair St. *Museum:* displays on mining as well as domestic memorabilia from Maldon's past, in heritage building; open 1.30–4pm daily; High St. *The Beehive Chimney:* southern end of Church St. *Anzac Hill:* the walk to the top is rewarded with magnificent views of the area; southern end of High St.

Fair: Easter. *Vintage Car Hill Climb:* Oct. *Folk Festival:* Oct–Nov.

Porcupine Township This award-winning tourist attraction is a reconstruction of an early 1850s goldmining town, with an array of slab, shingle and mudbrick buildings moved here from other goldfields. The village, complete with a blacksmith's, a doctor's surgery and even a bowling alley, is located in rugged bushland on the site of the original Porcupine diggings, where the first gold discovery between

TOWNS

RADIO STATION   IN TOWN   WHAT'S ON   NEARBY

Castlemaine and Bendigo was made. Visitors to the township can pan for gold, handfeed emus or take a ride on the Little Toot train, which does a circuit through the diggings. Cnr Maldon–Bendigo and Allans rds; (03) 5475 1000; 3 km NE.

Mt Tarrangower Lookout Tower: town views; 2 km w. *Carman's Tunnel Mine:* guided mine tours feature relics from goldmining days; 2 km sw. *Nuggetty Ranges and Mt Moorol:* 2 km N. *Cairn Curran Reservoir:* great for watersports and fishing, water levels permitting; features picnic facilities and a sailing club near the spillway; 10 km sw. *Victorian Goldfields Railway:* historic steam trains run from Maldon Railway Station (Hornsby St) through scenic forest to Castlemaine; operates Wed, Sun and public holidays; bookings (03) 5470 6658.

See also GOLDFIELDS, pp. 44–5

Mallacoota

290 D4

i Visitor Information Shed, Main Wharf; (03) 5158 0800; www.visitmallacoota.com

101.7 FM 3MGB Wilderness Radio, 104.9 FM ABC Local Radio

Mallacoota is a popular holiday centre in far East Gippsland, surrounded by the scenic Croajingolong National Park, which features Point Hicks, notable for being the first land on the east coast of Australia to be sighted by Europeans. There are spectacular surf beaches near the town, with Mallacoota Inlet offering great fishing.

WW II bunker and museum: restored and located at the airport. *Information shed:* a mural depicting Mallacoota's history is painted on the external walls; Main Wharf. *The Spotted Dog Gold Mine:* established in 1894, this was the most successful goldmine in the Mallacoota district.

Holiday markets: Easter and Christmas. *Bream Fishing Classic:* Mar (round 1) and June (round 2). *Tour of Gippsland Cycling Event:* July/Aug. *Flora and Fauna weekend:* 1st weekend in Nov.

Croajingolong National Park This park takes up a vast portion of what has been dubbed the Wilderness Coast. It protects remote beaches, tall forests, heathland, rainforest, estuaries and granite peaks, as well as creatures such as wallabies, possums, goannas and lyrebirds. Offshore, you might be lucky enough to spot dolphins, seals or southern right and humpback whales. Pt Hicks Lighthouse is a popular spot to visit, and Tamboon and Mallacoota inlets are good spots for canoeing. Access the park via a track west of town or various roads south of the Princes Hwy; contact Parks Victoria on 13 1963.

Surf beaches: Bastion Point, 2 km s; Bekta, 5 km s. *Gabo Island Lightstation Reserve:* take a scenic daytrip or stay in the Lightkeeper's Residence; 11 km E (offshore). *Gipsy Pt:* a quiet holiday retreat overlooking the Genoa River; 16 km NW.

See also EAST GIPPSLAND, pp. 54–5

Mansfield

284 B4 | 289 F3

i The Station Precinct, 173 Maroondah Hwy; 1800 039 049; www.mansfield-mtbuller.com.au

99.7 FM Radio Mansfield, 103.7 FM ABC Local Radio

Mansfield is located in Victoria's High Country at the junction of the Midland and Maroondah highways. It is within easy reach of Lake Eildon's network of rivers, Alpine National Park and Mansfield State Forest. Activities ranging from hiking to horseriding to skiing make it an ideal destination for anyone with a love of outdoor adventure, no matter what the season.

Troopers' Monument: monument to police officers shot by Ned Kelly at Stringybark Creek; Cnr High St and Midland Hwy. **Mansfield Mullum Wetlands Walk:** along reclaimed railway line; starts from behind the visitor centre. **Self-guide town walk:** take in many buildings of historical significance.

The High Country Autumn Festival and Merrijig Rodeo: Mar long weekend. **High Country Spring Arts Festival:** 24 Oct – 4 Nov.

Mt Buller Victoria's largest and best alpine skiing resort is Mt Buller, whose summit stands 1804 m above sea level. The 24 lifts, including the new 6-seater Holden chairlift (first of its kind in Australia), give access to 180 ha of ski trails, from gentle 'family runs' to heart-stopping double black diamond chutes. If you are a beginner, take on the friendly Bourke Street (Green Run) to find your 'ski legs', or join one of the ski schools there. There is also a half pipe at Boggy Creek and Terrain Park, or cross-country skiing at nearby Mt Stirling. Mt Buller Village offers resort accommodation, and the ski season runs between early June and late Sept. (03) 5777 6077; 47 km E.

Craig's Hut The High Country is synonymous with courageous and hardy cattlemen, transformed into Australian legends by Banjo Paterson's iconic ballad 'The Man from Snowy River'. The men would build huts on the high plains for shelter during summer cattle drives. Craig's Hut on Mt Stirling is a replica of one such shelter, used as a set on the 1983 film *The Man from Snowy River*. It burnt down in the 2006 bushfires, but was rebuilt and reopened in January 2008. The last 2 km of the track to the hut is 4WD or 1.5 km via a fairly steep walking track. 50 km E.

Delatite Winery: Stoneys Rd; 7 km SE. **Mt Samaria State Park:** scenic drives, camping and bushwalking; 14 km N. **Lake Eildon:** houseboat hire, fishing and sailing; 15 km S;

see Eildon for further details. **Lake Nillahcootie:** popular for boating, fishing and watersports; 20 km NW. **Jamieson:** an old goldmining town on the Jamieson River with historic buildings; 37 km S. **Alpine National Park:** begins around 40 km SE (*see Mount Beauty*). **Scenic drive:** take the road over the mountains to Whitfield (62 km NE), in the King River Valley, passing through spectacular scenery, including Powers Lookout (48 km NE) for views over the valley. **Lake William Hovell:** for boating and fishing; 85 km NE. **Mt Skene:** great for bushwalking, with wildflowers in summer; 85 km SE via Jamieson. **Fishing:** good spots include the Delatite, Howqua, Jamieson and Goulburn rivers. **Horse trail-riding:** a different way to explore the region, from 2 hr rides to 10-day treks; details from visitor centre. **Mountain-biking:** summer months reveal an expanding network of downhill and cross-country trails at Mt Buller and Mt Stirling.

See also HIGH COUNTRY, pp. 52–3

Maryborough

283 B2 | 288 D2

i Cnr Alma and Nolan sts; (03) 5460 4511 or 1800 356 511; www.visitmaryborough.com.au

99.1 Goldfields FM, 107.9 FM ABC Local Radio

Maryborough is a small city set on the northern slopes of the Great Dividing Range. Its historic 19th-century buildings, particularly around the civic square, are a testament to the riches brought by the Maryborough gold rush of the 1850s. Take a stroll through the streets to enjoy the cafes, craft shops and magnificent buildings, such as the National Trust–listed courthouse, post office and town hall.

Maryborough Railway Station So immense and impressive is this building that

RADIO STATION   IN TOWN   WHAT'S ON   NEARBY

Mark Twain, on his visit to the town, remarked that Maryborough was 'a station with a town attached'. Rumour has it that the building was actually intended for Maryborough in Queensland. The beautifully preserved station houses the visitor centre, the extensive Antique Emporium, the Woodworkers Gallery (open weekends only), and Twains Wood and Craft Gallery. Station St.

Pioneer Memorial Tower: Bristol Hill. *Worsley Cottage:* a historical museum featuring local relics; open Sun; Palmerston St. *Central Goldfields Art Gallery:* features an impressive collection of local artworks, housed in the old fire station; Neill St. *Phillips Gardens:* Alma St.

Maryborough Highland Gathering: New Year's Day. *Energy Breakthrough:* energy expo; Nov.

Paddys Ranges State Park This park offers the chance to enjoy red ironbark and grey box vegetation on one of the scenic walks or drives. The majority of walks start from the picnic area – see old goldmines and relics, enjoy the spring wildflowers, or keep an eye out for the rare painted honeyeater and other birdlife. There is also fossicking within the park, but in designated areas only. Access to the park is just south of Maryborough. The scenic Golden Way Tourist Drive travels through parts of the ranges. Contact Parks Victoria on 13 1963.

Aboriginal wells: impressive rock wells; 4 km s. *Carisbrook:* holds a popular tourist market 1st Sun each month; 7 km e.

See also GOLDFIELDS, pp. 44–5

Marysville

279 G2 | 282 C2 | 287 D3 | 289 F3

ℹ️ 11 Murchison St; (03) 5963 4567; www.marysvilletourism.com

📻 98.5 UGFM Upper Goulburn Community Radio, 774 AM ABC Local Radio

The historic town of Marysville was almost totally destroyed by bushfire on 7 February 2009. The community and state and federal governments have vowed to rebuild this once idyllic township.

Cathedral Range State Park The word 'imposing' does not do justice to the 7 km rocky ridge that forms the backbone of this park. Gentle walks reveal a landscape of mountain streams and historic sites, while the challenging hikes up the ridge to lookout points offer unparalleled views to the valley below. Walks can include overnight stays at the Farmyard, so named because lyrebirds imitate the noises of the domestic animals in the farmyards below. Contact Parks Victoria on 13 1963; 15 km n.

Lake Mountain Renowned for first-rate cross-country skiing, Lake Mountain has 37 km of scenic ski routes through the snow gum forests, plus a new visitor centre and bistro. It is also a great venue for tobogganing, snow tubing and sled rides. When the snow melts and the wildflowers bloom, hikers can take the Summit Walk (4 km return) over the mountain, stopping at lookouts with spectacular views. Ski and walk brochure available from visitor centre.

Lady Talbot Forest Drive: this 46 km route begins east of town and takes in ferny gullies, tall gum trees and gushing waterfalls. Stop en route to enjoy picnic spots, walking tracks and lookouts. *Buxton:* this town's attractions include the oldest trout farm in Victoria; 11 km n. *Scenic walks:* many tracks in the area, including a short walk to Steavenson Falls, from Falls Rd; 4 km loop walk in Cumberland Memorial Scenic Reserve, 16 km e; 4 km Beeches Walk through ancient beech and mountain ash forests (accessed via Lady Talbot Forest Dr). *Big River State Forest:* camping, fishing and gold fossicking; 30 km e.

See also YARRA & DANDENONGS, pp. 32–3

Milawa

284 C2 | 289 G2

i Wangaratta Visitor Information Centre, 100 Murphy St, Wangaratta; 1800 801 065; www.visitwangaratta.com.au

97.7 FM ABC Local Radio, 101.3 Oak FM

Milawa is the perfect destination for lovers of fine food and wine. It is positioned on the Snow Road that links Oxley, Markwood and Wangaratta to the north-west and the Great Alpine Road to the east. The Milawa gourmet region boasts over 13 wineries, including the renowned Brown Brothers vineyard. Other fresh local produce outlets sell olives, honey, cheese, chocolates and berries. This 'culinary crossroads' is home to wineries where you can meet the winemakers at their friendly cellar doors or the growers at their farm gates.

Milawa Mustards: a wide range of locally produced mustards; set in attractive cottage gardens; Snow Rd. **Milawa Cheese Company:** sales and tastings of specialist, gourmet cheeses; Factory Rd. **Milawa Muse Gallery:** ever-changing collection of various art mediums complementing the fine quality of the region; Milawa Cheese Factory complex. **Brown Brothers:** cellar-door tastings and sales; Bobinawarrah Rd. **EV Olives:** working olive grove open for tastings and sales; Everton Rd, Markwood.

A Weekend Fit for a King: be treated like a king at the King Valley wineries festival; Queen's Birthday weekend, June. **Beat the Winter Blues and Jazz Festival:** July. **King Valley Shed Show:** Oct. **La Dolce Vita:** wine and food festival at the Milawa/King Valley wineries; Nov.

King Valley Wine Region Stretching from Milawa and Oxley south to Whitfield and Cheshunt, this region produces wines with a distinctly Italian influence. The first vines were planted in the 1890s, and varieties including cabernet sauvignon, merlot, pinot noir, riesling and chardonnay are offered for tastings at various cellar doors, as well as the Italian varieties of sangiovese, pinot grigio and nebbiolo. Winery map from visitor centre.

Oxley: home to many wineries as well as the Blue Ox Blueberry Farm and King River Cafe; 4 km w.

See also HIGH COUNTRY, pp. 52–3

Mildura

see inset box on next page

Moe

279 H4 | 289 F4

i Latrobe Visitor Information Centre, The Old Church, Southside Central, Princes Hwy; 1800 621 409; www.visitlatrobevalley.com

100.7 FM ABC Local Radio, 104.7 Gippsland FM

Moe, located at the western end of the Latrobe Valley, is the gateway to the goldfields of Walhalla and the snowfields of Mount Baw Baw and Mount St Gwinear. Like many of the towns in this region it is supported by the power industry, but it has managed to avoid becoming a grim industrial centre. Instead Moe has a small-town feel and is home to a number of pretty gardens and public parks.

Gippsland Heritage Park Also known as Old Gippstown, this is a re-creation of a 19th-century community with over 30 restored buildings and a fine collection of fully restored horse-drawn carriages. Lloyd St; (03) 5127 8709.

TOWNS

RADIO STATION   IN TOWN   WHAT'S ON   NEARBY

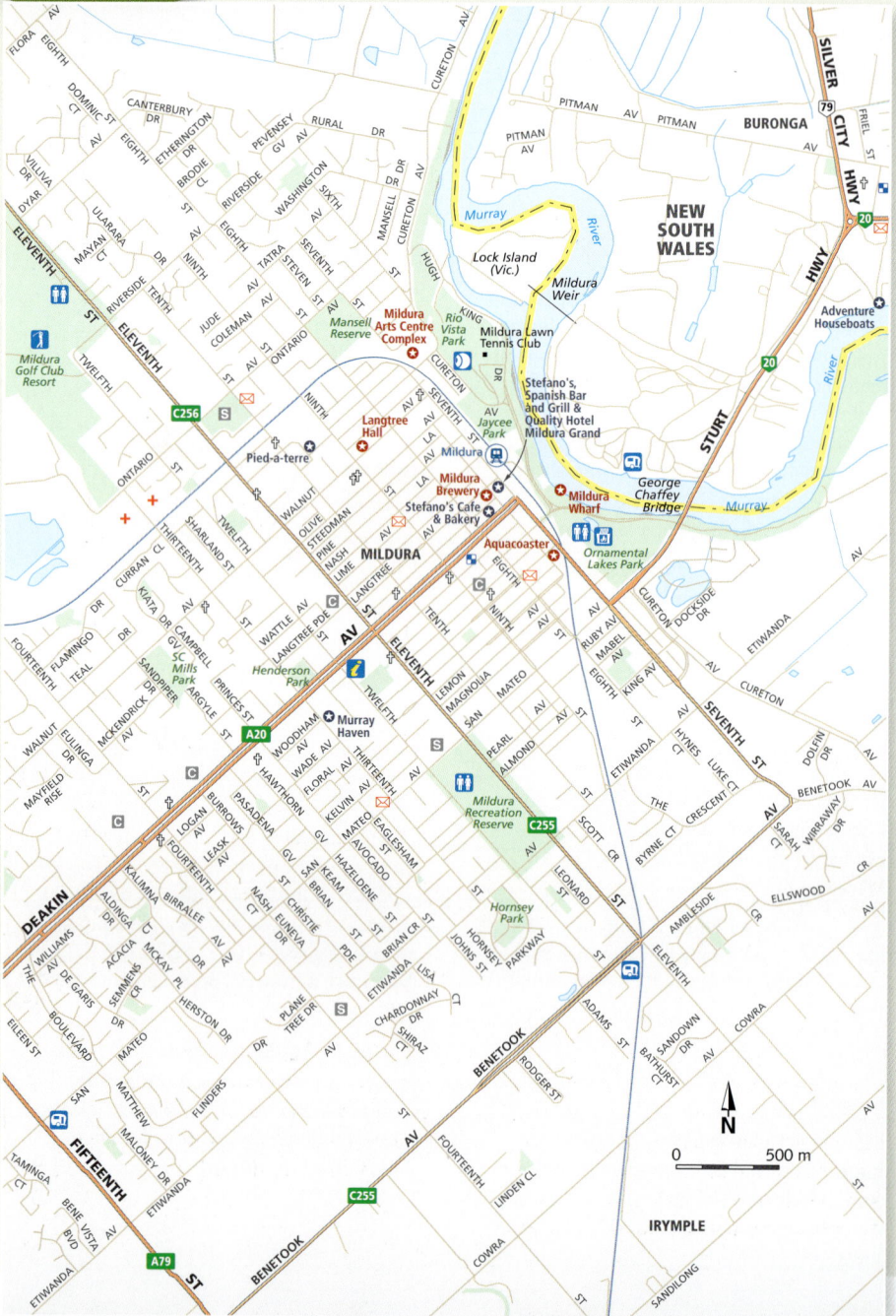

MILDURA

291 B2

i Alfred Deakin Centre, 180–190 Deakin Ave; (03) 5018 8380 or 1800 039 043; www.visitmildura.com.au

📻 104.3 FM ABC Local Radio, 106.7 HOTFM Sunraysia Community Radio

Mildura offers a Riviera lifestyle, with the Murray River flowing by the town and sunny, mild weather throughout the year. One of Victoria's major rural cities, Mildura's development has been aided by the expansion of irrigation, which has allowed the city to become a premier fruit-growing region.

🏠 **Mildura Arts Centre Complex** The complex is set on the banks of the Murray River and includes an art gallery, an amphitheatre and the Rio Vista museum. Rio Vista was the home of the town's founders, the Chaffey brothers, and is now preserved as a museum displaying colonial household items. The art gallery houses an impressive permanent collection and includes Australia's largest display of Brangwyn and Orpen paintings, as well as frequent temporary exhibitions. Outside, a delightful Sculpture Trail winds through the landscaped gardens surrounding the centre. Cureton Ave; (03) 5018 8330.

The Alfred Deakin Centre: interactive exhibitions and displays of the region; Deakin Ave. *Mildura Brewery:* produces natural and specialty beers inside the former Astor Theatre; view the brewing process or eat at the Brewery Pub; Langtree Ave; (03) 5021 5399. *Langtree Hall:* Mildura's first public hall now contains antiques and memorabilia; open Tues–Sun; Walnut Ave. *Mildura Wharf:* paddlesteamers departing here for river cruises include PS *Melbourne*, PS *Avoca* for lunch cruises on Sun, and PV *Rothbury* for daytrips to Trentham Winery each Thurs. Access from Madden Ave. *Snakes and Ladders:* fun park

AERIAL VIEW OF THE MURRAY RIVER

featuring 'dunny' collection; Seventeenth St. *Aquacoaster waterslide:* Cnr Seventh St and Orange Ave. *Stefano's:* Italian restaurant in the majestic Grand Hotel, featuring the culinary skills of television chef Stefano di Pieri; Seventh St.

🎆 *Arts Festival:* Mar. *Cup Carnival:* May. *Writers Festival:* July. *Golf Week:* July. *Country Music Festival:* Sept. *Vintage Tractor Pull:* Sept. *Jazz Food and Wine Festival:* Nov.

🧭 **Murray Darling Wine Region** The Mediterranean-style climate mixed with irrigated lands has contributed to making this wine region Victoria's largest. Noted mainly for its bulk table wine, the region is well regarded

continued overleaf

MILDURA continued

for its varieties of chardonnay, cabernet sauvignon and shiraz. Among the large-scale wineries such as Lindemans Karadoc, smaller boutique wineries offer specialty wines for tastings and sales. Brochure available from visitor centre.

Orange World: tours of citrus-growing region; 6 km N. *Australian Inland Botanic Gardens:* farmers market held 1st and 3rd Sat each month; garden tour with lunch last Sun each month; open daily; 8 km N. *Kings Billabong Wildlife Reserve:* situated on the Murray River floodplain, home to majestic river red gums and a large variety of birdlife. Attractions include Psyche Pump Station, Bruce's Bend Marina and Kings Billabong Lookout; 8 km SE. *Angus Park:* dried fruits and confectionery; 10 km SE. *Red Cliffs:* an important area for the citrus and dried fruit industries. The town features the 'Big Lizzie' steam traction engine; 15 km S. *Hattah–Kulkyne National Park:* 70 km S; *see Ouyen. Murray–Sunset National Park:* attractions near Mildura include Lindsay Island, for boating, swimming and fishing; access from Sturt Hwy, about 100 km W of Mildura. *See Murrayville for further details on park. Mungo National Park:* 104 km NE over NSW border.

See also MALLEE COUNTRY, pp. 48–9

Cinderella Dolls: Andrew St. *Race track:* picturesque country horse track with regular meetings; Waterloo Rd.

Old Gippstown Market: at Gippsland Heritage Park, with local crafts and produce; last Sat each month Sept–May. *Fairies in the Park:* Feb. *Jazz Festival:* Mar. *Blue Rock Classic:* cross-country horserace; Mar. *Moe Cup:* horserace; Oct.

Baw Baw National Park The landscape of Baw Baw ranges from densely forested river valleys to alpine plateaus and the activities on offer are equally varied – from canoeing river rapids and fishing for trout to skiing, horseriding and bushwalking. Wildflowers carpet the alpine areas in spring. Baw Baw Alpine Resort is located 90 km north of Moe, while the popular Aberfeldy picnic and camping area is accessed via a track north of Walhalla. Contact Parks Victoria on 13 1963.

Edward Hunter Heritage Bush Reserve: 3 km S via Coalville St. *Trafalgar Lookout and Narracan Falls:* near Trafalgar; 10 km W. *Old Brown Coal Mine Museum:* explore the history and memorabilia of the original township known as 'Brown Coal Mine' and the establishment of the power industry in the Latrobe Valley; Cnr Third St and Latrobe River Rd, Yallourn North; 10 km E. *Blue Rock Dam:* fishing, swimming and sailing; 20 km NW. *Thorpdale:* a town renowned for its potatoes. A bakery sells potato bread and a potato festival is held each Mar; 22 km SW. *Walhalla Mountain River Trail:* leads to the picturesque old mining township of Walhalla; Tourist Route 91; details from visitor centre. *See Walhalla.*

See also PHILLIP ISLAND & GIPPSLAND, pp. 36–7

Mornington

279 E4 | 281 E3 | 287 C4 | 289 E4

ℹ️ **Mornington Peninsula Visitor Information Centre, Point Nepean Rd, Dromana; (03) 5987 3078 or 1800 804 009; www.visitmorningtonpeninsula.org**

98.7 3RPP FM, 774 AM ABC Local Radio

Mornington was once the hub of the Mornington Peninsula, which is the reason this long arm of land was eventually given the same name. Today Melbourne's urban sprawl has just about reached the town, and it has virtually become a suburb. It still retains a seaside village ambience, particularly with a historic courthouse and post office museum that provide a glimpse of the past. The Rocks restaurant on the harbour provides a stunning view over the famous yachts. In the distance, colourful bathing boxes line Mills Beach.

Historic Mornington Pier: built in the 1850s, the pier remains popular today for walks and fishing. *Mornington Peninsula Regional Gallery:* print and drawing collection, including works by Dobell, Drysdale and Nolan; open Tues–Sat; Dunns Rd. *World of Motorcycles Museum:* Tyabb Rd. *Old post office:* now home to a local history display; Cnr Main St and The Esplanade. *Mornington Tourist Railway:* 10 km journey on steam train; departs from cnr Yuilles and Watt rds; 1st, 2nd and 3rd Sun each month, with additional trips running on Thurs in Jan.

Street Market: Main St; each Wed. *Mornington Racecourse Craft Market:* 2nd Sun each month. *RACV Vintage Car Rally:* Jan. *Mornington Food and Wine Festival:* Oct.

Arthurs Seat State Park At 309 m, Arthurs Seat is the highest point on the Mornington Peninsula. The summit can be reached by foot or vehicle and offers panoramic views of the bay and surrounding bushland. Picnic facilities and a restaurant are on the summit. There are many short walks, plus the historic Seawinds Park with gardens and sculptures. The Enchanted Maze Garden is set in superb gardens, with a variety of mazes and the Maize Maze Festival in Feb–Apr. Contact Parks Victoria on 13 1963; Arthurs Seat Rd, near Dromana; 16 km sw.

Mornington Peninsula Wine Region Although the first vines were planted in 1886, the wine industry on the peninsula did not truly take off until the 1970s. Comprising over 170 vineyards, the region consists predominantly of boutique wineries, with more than 50 cellar doors. While enjoying the sunshine, beaches and coastal resorts, it seems appropriate to try the crisp chardonnay that is famed in this region – or even a pinot noir or cabernet sauvignon as the chilly sea breeze kicks in of an evening. Wine festivals include Pinot Week each Mar, Queen's Birthday Wine Weekend each June and the Cool Whites Festival each Nov. Winery map from visitor centre.

Mount Martha: here is The Briars with a significant collection of Napoleonic artefacts and furniture. The town also features many gardens, plus wetlands great for birdwatching and bushland walks; 7 km s. *Ballam Park:* historic, French-farmhouse-style homestead built in 1845; open Sun; Cranbourne Rd, Frankston; 14 km ne. *Mulberry Hill:* former home of artist Sir Daryl Lindsay and author Joan Lindsay, who wrote *Picnic at Hanging Rock*; open Sun afternoons; Golf Links Rd, Baxter; 14 km ne. *Tyabb Packing House Antique Centre:* Australia's largest collection of antiques and collectibles; Mornington–Tyabb Rd, Tyabb; 16 km e. *Hastings:* coastal town on Western Port with 2 km walking trail through wetlands and mangrove habitat; 21 km se. *Moonlit Sanctuary Wildlife Conservation Park:* wildlife park featuring endangered native Australian animals; visit 11am–5pm or take an evening tour; night tour bookings (03) 5978 7935; 550 Tyabb–Tooradin Rd, Pearcedale; 24 km e. *Beaches:* the stretch of coast between Mornington and Mount Martha features sheltered, sandy bays popular with holiday-makers.

See also MORNINGTON PENINSULA, pp. 34–5

Morwell

289 G4

ℹ️ **Latrobe Visitor Information Centre, The Old Church, Southside Central, Princes Hwy, Traralgon; 1800 621 409; www.visitlatrobevalley.com**

📻 100.7 FM ABC Local Radio, 104.7 Gippsland FM

Morwell is primarily an industrial town and Victoria's major producer of electricity. Nestled in the heart of the Latrobe Valley, it contains one of the world's largest deposits of brown coal. Among all the heavy machinery is the impressive Centenary Rose Garden, featuring over 4000 rose bushes and regarded as one of the finest rose gardens in the Southern Hemisphere.

🏠 **PowerWorks:** dynamic displays on the electrical industries; tours of mines and power stations daily; Ridge Rd. **Centenary Rose Garden:** off Commercial Rd. **Latrobe Regional Gallery:** hosts outstanding works of contemporary Australian art by local and national artists; Commercial Rd. **Gippsland Immigration Wall of Recognition:** acknowledges all immigrants who contributed to the development of the Gippsland region.

🎆 **Market:** Latrobe Rd; each Sun.

🧭 **Morwell National Park** This park protects some of the last remnant vegetation of the Strzelecki Ranges, including pockets of rainforest and fern gullies. The area was once occupied by the Woollum Woollum people, who hunted in the ranges. In the 1840s European settlers cleared much of the surrounding land. On the Fosters Gully Nature Walk, keep your eyes peeled for orchids (over 40 species are found here) and native animals such as koalas, kangaroos and greater gliders. Contact Parks Victoria on 13 1963; 16 km s.

Hazelwood Pondage: warm water ideal for year-round watersports; 5 km s. **Arts Resource Collective:** housed in an old butter factory; Yinnar; 12 km sw. **Lake Narracan:** fishing and waterskiing; 15 km NW. **Narracan Falls:** 27 km w. **Scenic drives:** routes along the Strzelecki Ranges and Baw Baw mountains offer impressive views over the Latrobe Valley.

See also PHILLIP ISLAND & GIPPSLAND, pp. 36–7

Mount Beauty

285 E3 | 289 H2 | 290 A2

ℹ️ **Alpine Discovery Centre, 31 Bogong High Plains Rd; (03) 5754 1962 or 1800 111 885; www.visitalpinevictoria.com.au**

📻 92.5 Alpine Radio FM, 720 AM ABC Local Radio

At the foot of Mount Bogong, Victoria's highest mountain at 1986 metres, Mount Beauty was originally an accommodation town for workers on the Kiewa Hydro-electric Scheme. Today, the town is regarded as an adventure mecca and a focal point for a variety of adventure activities, with mountain-biking, hang-gliding and bushwalking just a few on offer. The pairing of adventure with more leisuirely outdoor activities like golf, swimming and fishing makes Mount Beauty an ideal holiday destination.

🏠 **Mt Beauty Pondage:** for watersports and fishing; just north of Main St. **Wineries:** cool-climate vineyards at Annapurna Estate, Bogong Estate and Recline. **Scenic walks:** several scenic walking tracks; details from visitor centre.

🎆 **Markets:** Hollonds St; 1st Sat each month. **Bogong Cup:** Jan. **MTBA National Series:** mountain-biking championships; Jan. **Music Muster:** Apr. **Mitta Mitta to Mount Beauty Mountain Bike Challenge:** Oct.

🧭 **Alpine National Park** Covering 646 000 ha in 4 sections, this is Victoria's largest park, containing the highest mountains in the state. Most of Australia's south-east rivers, including the mighty Murray, have their source here. The area is known for its outstanding snowfields during winter, and bushwalking and wildflowers in the summer months. Other activities include horseriding, canoeing, rafting and mountain-bike riding. 30 km SE.

Falls Creek Surrounded by Alpine National Park, Falls Creek is a winter playground for downhill and cross-country skiers. When the snow is falling, the ski resort caters for skiers and snowboarders with a variety of runs and terrain, including some to suit beginners. Novelty tours are also available, such as the Snowmobile Tours. Each Aug, Falls Creek hosts the Kangaroo Hoppet cross-country ski race. In spring and summer, take a walk on the Bogong High Plains or fly-fish in one of the lakes and rivers nearby; 30 km SE.

Tawonga Gap: features a lookout over valleys; 13 km NW. *Bogong:* scenic walks around Lake Guy and nearby Clover Arboretum for picnics; 15 km SE. *Scenic drives:* to Falls Creek and the Bogong High Plains (not accessible in winter beyond Falls Creek); details from visitor centre.

See also HIGH COUNTRY, pp. 52–3

Murrayville

291 A3

ⓘ **Ouyen Information Centre,** 17 Oke St, Ouyen; (03) 5092 2006; www.visitmildura.com.au/murrayville

📻 103.5 3MBR-FM Mallee Border Radio, 594 AM ABC Local Radio

Murrayville is a small town on the Mallee Highway near the South Australia border. It is near three major, remote national parks: Murray–Sunset National Park; Wyperfeld National Park; and Big Desert Wilderness Park, one of Victoria's largest wilderness zones.

🏠 *Historic buildings:* include the restored railway station and the old courthouse.

Walking tracks: several, including the Pine Hill Walking Trail in the town.

🧭 **Murray–Sunset National Park** Millions of years ago this area was submerged beneath the sea. When the sea retreated, large sand ridges and dunes were left. Now there is a variety of vegetation including grasslands, saltbush and mallee eucalypts. In spring, wildflowers abound; look out for Victoria's largest flower, the Murray lily. Access roads to the park are off Mallee Hwy. The Pink Lakes saltwater lakes, with a distinctive, pinkish hue, are a key attraction and are especially remarkable at sunset. There are many good walking tracks near the lakes, as well as excellent camping facilities. Lakes access via Pink Lakes Rd (turn-off at Linga, 50 km E); contact Parks Victoria on 13 1963. *For north section of park see Mildura.*

Cowangie: a small, historic town with several 19th-century buildings, including Kow Plains Homestead; 19 km E. *Big Desert Wilderness Park:* a remote park with no access other than by foot. True to its name, this park has remained relatively untouched by Europeans and includes many reptile species and plants adapted to arid conditions; the track south of town takes you close to the park boundary. *Wyperfeld National Park:* access via Underbool or by 4WD track south of Murrayville; *for further details see Hopetoun.*

See also MALLEE COUNTRY, pp. 48–9

Myrtleford

284 D3 | 289 G2

ⓘ **Post Office Complex, Great Alpine Rd;** (03) 5752 1044; www.visitalpinevictoria.com.au

📻 91.7 FM ABC Local Radio, 101.3 Oak FM

Myrtleford is a pretty town in Victoria's alpine High Country. Originally called Myrtle

TOWNS

📻 RADIO STATION   🏠 IN TOWN   🎆 WHAT'S ON   🧭 NEARBY

Creek Run in the early 1800s, it is a thriving agricultural district and gateway to Mount Hotham.

The Phoenix Tree: a sculpture created by Hans Knorr from the trunk of a red gum; Lions Park. *The Big Tree:* a huge old red gum; Smith St. *Old School:* the town's original school, now fully restored; open Thurs, Sun or by appt; Albert St. *Swing Bridge over Myrtle Creek:* Standish St. *Reform Hill Lookout:* a scenic walking track from Elgin St leads to the lookout, which has great views across town; end of Halls Rd. *Parks:* Rotary Park in Myrtle St and Apex Park in Standish St are both delightful picnic spots. *Michelini Wines:* Great Alpine Rd. *Murray to the Mountains Rail Trail:* the cycle touring loop from Bright to Wangaratta runs through the town.

Market: local produce; Great Alpine Rd; each Sat Jan–Apr. *Alpine Classic Bike Ride:* to Bright; Jan. *Myrtleford Festival:* Mar. *Golden Spurs Rodeo:* Dec.

Mt Buffalo National Park: 7 km s; *see Bright. Wineries:* several in the region, including Rosewhite Vineyards and Winery; open weekends, public holidays and throughout Jan; Happy Valley Rd; 8 km SE. *Gapsted:* home to the Victorian Alps Winery, offers tours and sales; 8 km NW. *Eurobin:* a number of farms near the town with sales of local produce, including Red Stag Deer Farm and Bright Berry Farm, offering homemade jams and berries Dec–Mar; 16 km SE. *Fishing:* in the Ovens and Buffalo rivers and Lake Buffalo (25 km s).

See also HIGH COUNTRY, pp. 52–3

Nagambie

287 C1 | 289 E2

i 319 High St; (03) 5794 2647 or 1800 444 647; www.nagambielakestourism.com.au

97.7 FM ABC Local Radio, 98.5 FM

Nagambie is found between Seymour and Shepparton on the Goulburn Valley Highway. The town is on the shores of Lake Nagambie, which was created by the construction of the Goulburn Weir in 1891. Activities such as waterskiing, speedboating and especially rowing are popular on this man-made lake.

The Jetty: fine dining, lakeside apartments and spa; High St. *The Grapevine by the Lake:* sales of nuts and local produce; High St. *Nagambie Lakes Entertainment Centre:* renovated 1890s building with bars, gaming lounge and non-motorised boat hire; High St.

Rowing Regatta: Jan–Mar. *Head of the River:* Mar. *Nagambie On Water Festival:* Mar long weekend. *After Vintage Festival:* May. *Shiraz Challenge:* a search for the best shiraz in the region; Nov. *Fireworks over the Lake:* New Year's Eve.

Goulburn Valley Wine Region In the 1850s a group of farmers got together and planted some vines; they were to form the Tahbilk Vineyard Proprietary that would become the Tahbilk Winery, one of the most successful in the region. The vineyard features National Trust–classified buildings, plus a museum detailing the history of the estate. The Goulburn Valley's warm climate and proximity to the Goulburn River has allowed for a prosperous industry, with the vineyards producing high-quality grenache and mourvedre varieties as well as the old-time favourites. Brochure and map detailing Tahbilk and other wineries available from visitor centre.

Goulburn Weir The construction of this weir resulted in the expansive waterway of Lake Nagambie. It is the diversion weir on the Goulburn River for the Goulburn Valley Irrigation area and feeds water by channel and pipeline to Bendigo, among other places. A walkway runs across the weir offering views of the structure and lake. Picnic and barbecue facilities are available; 12km N.

See also GOULBURN & MURRAY, pp. 50–1

Natimuk

288 B2 | 291 B5

🛈 National Hotel, Main St; (03) 5387 1300.

📻 96.5 Triple H FM, 594 AM ABC Local Radio

Natimuk is part of the state's Wimmera region, and is popular for its proximity to Mount Arapiles, a 369-metre sandstone monolith that has been described as 'Victoria's Ayers Rock'. The mountain was first climbed by Major Mitchell in 1836, and today is a popular rock-climbing destination with over 2000 marked climbing routes. Brigitte Muir, the first Australian woman to climb Mount Everest, trained here.

🏠 *Arapiles Historical Society Museum:* housed in the old courthouse; open by appt; Main St. *Arapiles Craft Shop:* features local arts and crafts; Main St. *The Goat Gallery:* showcases works of local and regional artists; Main St. *Self-guide heritage trail:* details from visitor centre.

🎆 *Nati Frinj:* biennial arts festival; Oct/Nov.

🧭 **Mt Arapiles–Tooan State Park** This park is divided into 2 blocks, the larger Tooan block and the smaller Mt Arapiles block; Mt Arapiles offers rock climbing and is by far the most popular. Mitre Rock presents a smaller climbing challenge if required. Should you choose not to scale one of the various rock faces, great views are still available from the walking tracks, or you can drive to the summit. Nature study is another possibility – a huge 14% of the state's flora is represented in the Mt Arapiles section alone. Contact Parks Victoria on 13 1963; access is from the Wimmera Hwy; 12 km sw.

Banksia Hill Flower Farm: 10 km E. *Duffholme Museum:* 21 km w.

See also GRAMPIANS & CENTRAL WEST, pp. 46–7

Nhill

288 A1 | 291 A5

🛈 Victoria St; (03) 5391 3086.

📻 96.5 Triple H FM, 594 AM ABC Local Radio

The name of this town may be derived from the Aboriginal word 'nyell', meaning 'white mist on water'. Nhill is exactly halfway between Melbourne and Adelaide, and claims to have the largest single-bin silo in the Southern Hemisphere. The town is a good starting point for tours of Little Desert National Park.

🏠 *Historical Society Museum:* open Thurs, Fri or by appt; McPherson St. *Cottage of John Shaw Neilson (lyric poet):* open by appt; Jaypex Park, Victoria St. *Boardwalk:* scenic walk from Jaypex Park to Nhill Lake. *Lowana Craft Shop:* local crafts; Victoria St. *Self-guide historical walk:* details from visitor centre.

🎆 *Boxing Day Races:* Dec.

🧭 *Little Desert National Park:* the Little Desert Lodge is in the central section of the park, south of Nhill, and is a departure point for day tours and a popular place to stay. There are walking trails in the central and western sections. 15 km s. *See also Dimboola.* *Mallee Dam:* lately dry, once offered fantastic birdwatching with bird hides provided; 20 km sw.

See also GRAMPIANS & CENTRAL WEST, pp. 46–7

Ocean Grove

278 D4 | 280 B3 | 286 D1 | 287 B4 | 289 E4

🛈 Geelong Visitor Information Centre, Stead Park, Princes Hwy, Corio; (03) 5275 5797 or 1800 620 888; www.visitgreatoceanroad.org.au

📻 94.7 The Pulse FM, 774 AM ABC Local Radio

TOWNS

Ocean Grove is a popular summer-holiday destination near the mouth of the Barwon River. The town's main street is at the top of a hill with excellent views of the pristine coastline along Bass Strait. The beaches around Ocean Grove offer great surfing and safe swimming, with surf patrols operating during the summer months.

Ocean Grove Nature Reserve This reserve contains the only significant example of woodland on the Bellarine Peninsula, preserved virtually as it was prior to European settlement. There are a number of good walks in the park, which is known as a haven for birdlife. A bird hide lets visitors look out for any number of the 130 different species that live here, including the eastern rosella and red-browed finch. Contact Parks Victoria on 13 1963; Grubb Rd.

Barwon Heads This is a pretty seaside town on the Barwon River, made famous as the location for the television series *SeaChange*. There are several good restaurants in the area, including one right on the Barwon River that provides a scenic environment for fine dining. The Barwon Heads Golf Club is one of the top 3 public courses in the state. The Jirrahlinga Koala and Wildlife Reserve on Taits Rd lets visitors encounter the delightful, yet often elusive, koala in a natural environment. Barwon Heads is a short drive from Ocean Grove. 3 km s.

Lake Connewarre State Game Reserve: with mangrove swamps and great walks, the game reserve is home to a variety of wildlife, including wallabies; 7 km N. *Wallington:* on the Bellarine Hwy between Geelong and Ocean Grove, the town is home to A Maze'N Games, a timber maze with minigolf, picnic/barbecue facilities and a cafe, Koombahla Park Equestrian Centre, Adventure Park and Bellarine Adventure Golf. A strawberry fair is held in Wallington in Nov; 8 km N.

See also WERRIBEE & BELLARINE, pp. 40–1

Olinda

279 F3 | 282 A4 | 287 C4 | 289 E4

i Dandenong Ranges Information Centre, 1211 Burwood Hwy, Upper Ferntree Gully; (03) 9758 7522; www.olindavillage.com.au

98.1 Radio Eastern FM, 774 AM ABC Local Radio

Olinda is in the centre of the Dandenong Ranges, a landscape of towering mountain ash forests, lush fern gullies, waterfalls, English gardens and picnic spots. The ranges have been a retreat for Melburnians since the 1800s. Olinda and nearby Sassafras are known for their many galleries and cafes, particularly the numerous tearooms serving traditional Devonshire teas.

Rhododendron and Daffodil Festivals: Aug–Nov.

Dandenong Ranges National Park This park offers great walking tracks and picnic facilities. Visitors may be lucky enough to spot an elusive lyrebird, a species renowned for its ability to mimic sounds – from other bird calls to human voices and even chainsaws. Most walking tracks leave from picnic grounds, such as the Thousand Steps Track from Ferntree Gully Picnic Ground (south-west via the Mt Dandenong Tourist Rd) and the walk to Sherbrooke Falls from the Sherbrooke Picnic Ground (via Sherbrooke Rd from the Mt Dandenong Tourist Rd). The park extends to the east and west of town. Contact Parks Victoria on 13 1963; 2 km NE, 6 km SW.

William Ricketts Sanctuary William Ricketts was a well-known artist and conservationist whose intricate sculptures focus on Aboriginal people and the complexities of Australia's native vegetation. Many sculptures are displayed in a lovely bushland setting on the scenic Mt Dandenong Tourist Rd. Contact Parks Victoria on 13 1963; 3 km N.

National Rhododendron Gardens: the gardens begin just east of town and are something of a mecca for garden enthusiasts, with superb displays of rhododendrons and azaleas in season. *R. J. Hamer Arboretum:* good walking tracks through 100 ha of rare and exotic trees; Olinda–Monbulk Rd, shortly after turn-off to Rhododendron Gardens. *Cloudehill Gardens:* twilight concerts are held here in summer; south of R. J. Hamer Arboretum. *Mt Dandenong Lookout:* spectacular views over Melbourne; picnic/barbecue facilities; 3 km N. *Alfred Nicholas Gardens:* a quaint ornamental lake with the original boathouse and the George Tindale Memorial Garden, with flowering plants beneath mountain ash trees. The original Nicholas family home (built 1920s) is here; Sherbrooke; 4 km SE. *Kawarra Australian Plant Garden:* an impressive collection of native plants; Kalorama; 4.5 km N. *Markets:* art, craft, plants and homemade goods; nearby markets include Kallista Market, 6 km S, 1st Sat each month, and Upper Ferntree Gully Market, 12 km SE, every Sat and Sun. *Burrinja Gallery:* a memorial to artist Lin Onus, with Aboriginal and Oceanic sculptures and paintings; Upwey; 10 km SW. *Silvan:* prominent flower-growing region with many tulip farms. The famous Tesselaar's Tulip Farm hosts a popular festival each Sept–Oct with sales of flowers and bulbs, and traditional Dutch music and food; Monbulk Rd; 15 km NE. *Silvan Dam:* an area to the north of this major Melbourne water supply has walking tracks and picnic/barbecue facilities; turn-off after Silvan. *Mont De Lancey:* wonderfully preserved house, built in 1882 and set in landscaped gardens; includes a museum and a chapel; open 2nd Sat each month; Wandin North; 22 km NE via Mt Evelyn.

See also YARRA & DANDENONGS, pp. 32–3

Omeo

285 G5 | 289 H3 | 290 A3

ℹ️ **Omeo Country Colours and Visitor Information Centre,** 152 Great Alpine Rd; (03) 5159 1679; www.omeoregion.com.au

📻 90.9 FM High Country Radio, 720 AM ABC Local Radio

Omeo is an Aboriginal word meaning mountains – appropriate for this picturesque town in the Victorian Alps. Today Omeo is a peaceful farming community, but it wasn't always so. During the 1800s gold rush, Omeo was an unruly frontier town, which early Australian novelist Rolf Boldrewood described as the roughest goldfield in Australia. Despite taking damage in the 1939 Black Friday bushfires, several historic buildings still remain.

🏠 **A. M. Pearson Historical Park** The park preserves a piece of Omeo's rich history in a peaceful, bushland setting. Buildings on display include the old courthouse, which now houses a museum, a log gaol, stables and a blacksmith's. Day Ave (Great Alpine Rd).

Historic buildings: many distinctive structures from the 19th century can be seen around town, including the post office, primary school and shire offices; Day Ave. *Shops:* several unique stores, including the German Cuckoo Clock Shop, Petersen's Gallery, High Country Paintings and Octagon Bookshop; Day Ave.

🎆 *High Country Calf Sales:* Mar. *Alpine Discovery Festival and Picnic Races:* Mar. *Rodeo, Easter Market and Easter Egg Hunt:* Easter. *Cobungra Polo Match:* Apr.

🧭 **Oriental Claims** The Claims was a major goldmining area, and remains the highest alluvial goldfield in Australia. French-Canadians, Americans and Europeans all worked alongside Australians and Chinese during the gold boom. The word 'Oriental' in the mine's name may conjure an image of

TOWNS

thousands of Chinese workers scurrying about with shovels, but 'Oriental Claims' was actually the name of a European company. The Omeo Sluicing Company, however, was Chinese. There are a variety of walks around the site and visitors should look out for the variety of flora, including wild orchids. High cliffs, left by the hydraulic sluicing process, offer impressive views across town, and signs throughout the Parks Victoria–managed site explain the history of the Claims. Contact Parks Victoria on 13 1963; 1.5 km w on Great Alpine Rd.

Mt Hotham This popular downhill ski resort is suited to both budding and experienced skiers. Skiing areas range from the beginners' Big D Playground through to the more advanced slopes around Mary's Slide and the black diamond chutes of Heavenly Valley. In summer, the mountain is a popular hiking and mountain-bike-riding destination. (03) 5759 3550; 56 km w.

Livingstone Park and Creek: walking tracks and swimming area adjacent to the Oriental Claims. *Mt Markey Winery:* on the site of the old Cassilis Hotel, on the touring loop from Omeo to Swifts Creek; Cassilis Rd, Cassilis; 15 km s. *Lake Omeo:* scenic natural landscape, dry for most parts of the year; Benambra; 21 km NE. *Benambra:* gateway to the Alpine National Park; 24 km N. *Anglers Rest:* historic Blue Duck Inn, a good base for horseriding, whitewater rafting and fly-fishing; 29 km NW. *Swifts Creek:* this town situated at the junction of Swifts Creek and Tambo River has the Great Alpine Art Gallery; 40 km s. *Taylors Crossing suspension bridge:* part of the scenic Australian Alps Walking Track and also a great base for camping and fishing the Mitta Mitta River; off Tablelands Rd; 44 km NE. *Dinner Plain:* relaxed village surrounded by the Alpine National Park that offers many activities such as skiing, walking, horseriding and Australia's first indoor-outdoor alpine spa; 46 km w. *Ensay:* small but picturesque town that is home to the well-known Ensay

Winery; 70 km s. *Great Alpine Rd:* covers over 300 km from the High Country to Gippsland Lakes and offers 6 individual self-guide touring routes with a diverse combination of scenery; details from visitor centre. Note that some drives cross state forests or alpine areas, so be alert for timber trucks and check conditions in winter. Omeo is located on this road. *Mitta Mitta and Cobungra rivers:* great trout fishing, waterskiing and whitewater rafting (only available in spring); details from visitor centre. *High Country tours:* explore the high plains around Omeo – on horseback, by 4WD or, for keen hikers, on challenging bushwalks; details from visitor centre.

See also HIGH COUNTRY, pp. 52–3

Orbost

290 B4

ℹ️ Slab Hut, 39 Nicholson St; (03) 5154 2424; www.lakesandwilderness.com.au

📻 90.7 FM 3REG Radio East Gippsland, 97.1 FM ABC Local Radio

Situated on the banks of the legendary Snowy River, Orbost is on the Princes Highway and surrounded by spectacular coastal and mountain territory. For those who love arts and crafts, there are many shops in the area supplying and displaying local products.

🏠 *Visitor Information Centre:* display explains complex rainforest ecology; Slab Hut, 39 Nicholson St. *Old Pump House:* behind relocated 1872 slab hut; Forest Rd. *Historical Museum:* details local history with displays of artefacts; Ruskin St. *Snowy River Country Craft:* Forest Rd. *Netherbyre Gemstone and Art Galley:* Cnr Browning and Carlyle sts. *Exhibition Centre:* equipped with 2 galleries, one dedicated to the National Collection of Australian Wood Design, the other presenting monthly exhibitions; Nicholson St. *Mirrawong Woolworks:* sells wool and felt handmade items;

295 Nicholson St. *The Paddle Boat Shed:* community project rebuilding the paddle steamer *Curlip. Heritage walk:* weaves its way through town with storyboards, fingerboards and plaques explaining the historic buildings; begins at Slab Hut.

Australian Wood Design Exhibition: Jan.

Errinundra National Park The park is one of the largest remaining stands of cool temperate rainforest in Victoria, and features giant eucalypt forests – take a stroll along the rainforest boardwalk for a closer look at these majestic, ancient trees. For keen hikers there are walking tracks, as well as camping and picnic facilities. Enjoy superb views from Ellery View, Ocean View Lookout and the peak of Mt Morris. In winter, snow and rain can make access difficult. Errinundra Rd, off Princes Hwy; contact Parks Victoria on 13 1963; 54 km NE.

Marlo: a popular fishing spot also known for its galleries and Bush Races in Jan; 14 km s. *Cape Conran Coastal Park:* rugged coastal scenery and excellent walks. Turn south after Cabbage Tree Creek (26 km E) or take the coastal route from Marlo. *Cabbage Tree Palms Flora Reserve:* 27 km E. *Bemm River Scenic Reserve:* a 1 km signposted rainforest walk and picnic facilities; off Princes Hwy; 40 km E. *Snowy River National Park:* in the south of the park is Raymond Creek Falls. A 40 min return walk leads to the falls, with a further 1 hr walk leading to the Snowy River; 42 km N; 2WD access, check road conditions. McKillops Bridge, 148 km N via Deddick, is one of the most accessible parts of this park; *for more details see Buchan. Sydenham Inlet:* a good spot for bream fishing; 58 km E. *Tranquil Valley Tavern:* on the banks of the Delegate River near the NSW border; about 115 km NE. *Baldwin Spencer Trail:* a 262 km scenic drive following the route of this explorer, taking in old mining sites and Errinundra National Park; details from visitor centre.

See also EAST GIPPSLAND, pp. 54–5

Ouyen

291 B3

ⓘ 17 Oke St; (03) 5092 2006; www.visitmildura.com.au/ouyen

92.9 3MBR-FM Mallee Border Radio, 594 AM ABC Local Radio

Ouyen was once little more than a station on the Melbourne–Mildura train route, but it has since grown to become an important service town. Ouyen is at the centre of the Mallee region, which was developed in the early 1900s – relatively late when compared with other regions of rural Victoria. This was mainly due to the difficulties in clearing the land as well as the harsh climate. The current success of agriculture in the region, in particular wheat-growing, is a testament to the hardiness of early farmers and settlers.

Roxy Theatre: newly restored and functioning tropical-style theatre, only one of its type in southern Australia; Oke St.

Great Australian Vanilla Slice Triumph: 1st Fri in Sept.

Hattah–Kulkyne National Park This park protects an area of 48 000 ha that includes typical mallee country with both low scrub and open native pine woodlands. The freshwater Hattah Lakes are seasonally filled by creeks connected to the Murray River, which brings the area to life with plants and waterbirds. Activities within the park include bushwalking, canoeing, fishing and scenic drives. There are picnic and camping facilities at Mournpall and Lake Hattah. Contact Parks Victoria on 13 1963; off the Calder Hwy; 35 km N.

Speed: Mallee Machinery Field Days held here in Aug; 39 km s.

See also MALLEE COUNTRY, pp. 48–9

TOWNS

RADIO STATION   IN TOWN   WHAT'S ON   NEARBY

Paynesville

289 H4 | 290 A4

ℹ️ **Community Craft Centre, Esplanade;** (03) 5156 7479; www.lakesandwilderness.com.au

📻 90.7 FM 3REG Radio East Gippsland, 100.7 FM ABC Local Radio

Paynesville is a popular tourist resort close to the rural city of Bairnsdale, on the McMillan Straits. The town is set on the Gippsland Lakes and the beaches of the Tasman Sea, making it a favourite destination for fishing and waterskiing.

🏠 *St Peter-by-the-Lake Church:* built in 1961, this unique structure incorporates seafaring images in its design; The Esplanade. *Community Craft Centre:* displays and sells local arts and crafts; The Esplanade.

🎆 *Market:* Gilsenan Reserve; 2nd Sun each month. *Jazz Festival:* Feb. *Marlay Pt Paynesville Overnight Yacht Race:* Mar long weekend.

🧭 **Gippsland Lakes** This area incorporates The Lakes National Park, Gippsland Lakes Coastal Park and the famous Ninety Mile Beach – an incredible stretch of scenic coastline offering great swimming beaches. Lake cruises, boat charters and organised scenic tours of the region are all available; details from visitor centre.

Eagle Pt: a small fishing community set by Lake King. The Mitchell River empties here, where it forms curious silt jetties that stretch out into the distance. The town hosts the annual Australian Powerboat Racing Championships at Easter; 2 km NW. *Raymond Island:* Koala Reserve and Riviera Meadows, an animal farm that specialises in miniature breeds; the island is just east of Paynesville and can be accessed by a ferry that departs from the foreshore.

See also EAST GIPPSLAND, pp. 54–5

Phillip Island

see Cowes

Port Albert

289 G5

ℹ️ **Old Courthouse, 9 Rodgers St, Yarram;** (03) 5182 6553.

📻 100.7 FM ABC Local Radio, 104.7 Gippsland FM

Port Albert is a tranquil port on the south-east coast. Looking at this peaceful village now, it is hard to believe that it was the first established port in Victoria, with ships from Europe and America once docking at its jetty. Ships from China arrived here during the gold rush, bringing thousands of prospectors to the Gippsland goldfields. Still a commercial fishing port, the sheltered waters of Port Albert are popular with anglers and boat owners, which sees its population swell considerably during summer.

🏠 **Port Albert Hotel** This attractive old building has wide verandahs, and offers genuine country hospitality and a glimpse into the area's past. The hotel was first licensed in 1842, which makes it one of the oldest hotels in Victoria still operating. Wharf St.

Historic buildings: include original government offices and stores, and the Bank of Victoria, which now houses a maritime museum with photographs and relics from the town's past. Georgian and Victorian architectural styles are evident in over 40 buildings; Tarraville Rd. *Warren Curry Art:* a gallery featuring country-town streetscapes; Tarraville Rd.

🎆 *Fishing Contest:* Mar.

🧭 **Nooramunga Marine and Coastal Park** Surrounding Port Albert and comprising the waters and sand islands offshore, this marine park is a fishing enthusiast's delight. Snapper, flathead and Australian salmon can be caught from the surf beaches or from a boat. The Aboriginal middens that dot the shorelines prove that fishing has been carried on here for many thousands of years. This park is an important reserve for migratory wading birds. Camping is allowed but permits must be obtained. Contact Parks Victoria on 13 1963.

Christ Church: built in 1856, this was the first church to be established in Gippsland; Tarraville; 5 km NE. *Beaches:* Manns, for swimming, 10 km NE; and Woodside, on Ninety Mile Beach, for good surfing, 34 km NE. Note that both beaches are patrolled during summer. *St Margaret Island:* a protected area featuring a wildlife sanctuary; 12 km E.

See also PHILLIP ISLAND & GIPPSLAND, pp. 36–7

Port Campbell

286 C5 | 288 C4

ℹ️ **12 Apostles Visitor Information Centre, 26 Morris St; 1300 137 255; www.visit12apostles.com.au**

📻 103.7 3WAY-FM, 774 AM ABC Local Radio

This peaceful seaside resort – the base of a small crayfishing industry – is in the centre of Port Campbell National Park on the Great Ocean Road. The Twelve Apostles, one of Victoria's most famous attractions, can be found nearby.

🏠 *Historical Museum:* open Wed, Thurs and Sat; Lord St. *Fishing:* good from rocks and pier; boat charters available.

🎆 *Market:* Lord St; each Sun in summer and Easter.

🧭 **Port Campbell National Park** The park is a major attraction on the Great Ocean Rd,

with magnificent rock formations jutting out into the ocean. Particularly impressive when viewed at dusk (when penguins can be seen) and dawn, the key coastal features are The Arch, 5 km W; London Bridge, 6 km W; Loch Ard Gorge, 7 km SE; and the world-famous Twelve Apostles, which begin 12 km SE of Port Campbell and stretch along the coast. Other notable features are The Grotto, Bay of Islands and Bay of Martyrs. There are walking tracks throughout the park, and the Historic Shipwreck Trail marks 25 sites along the coast between Moonlight Head and Port Fairy (sites are also popular with divers – a charter company is based in Port Campbell; details from visitor centre). For the ultimate view of this coastline, take an ever-popular scenic flight (details from visitor centre).

Mutton Bird Island: attracts short-tailed shearwaters, best viewed at dawn and dusk Sept–Apr; just off coast. *Great Ocean Walk:* between Apollo Bay and the Twelve Apostles. The 91 km walk offers stunning views; walkers must register to use campgrounds en route; further information available at greatoceanwalk.com.au *Timboon:* a pretty town in the centre of a dairy district. Timboon Farmhouse Cheese offers tastings and sales of gourmet cheeses, while Timboon Railway Shed Distillery offers a variety of spirits. A scenic drive goes from Port Campbell to the town. It is also on one end of the Camperdown–Timboon (Crater to Coast) Rail Trail. Pick your own berries in season at nearby Berry World; 16 km N. *Otway Deer and Wildlife Park:* 19 km SE. *Gourmet Food and Wine Loop:* map from visitor centre.

See also SOUTH-WEST COAST, pp. 42–3

TOWNS

📻 RADIO STATION   🏠 IN TOWN   🎆 WHAT'S ON   🧭 NEARBY

Port Fairy

286 A4 | 288 B4

ℹ️ **Railway Place, Bank St; (03) 5568 2682; www.visitportfairy.com**

📻 103.7 3WAY-FM, 1602 AM ABC Local Radio

Port Fairy was once a centre for the whaling industry and one of the largest ports in Australia. Today many visitors are attracted to it for its charming old-world feel, its legacy of historic bluestone buildings, the small fleet of fishing boats that line the old wharf, and its great beach and lively atmosphere in summer. The town truly comes alive in March, when the Port Fairy Folk Festival is held. International folk and blues acts play, and tickets are best booked well in advance.

🏛️ *History Centre:* displays relating to local history housed in the old courthouse; Gipps St. *Battery Hill:* old fort and signal station at the river mouth; end of Griffith St. *Port Fairy Wharf:* sales of fish and crayfish when in season. *Historic buildings:* many are National Trust–classified, including the splendid timber home of Captain Mills, Gipps St; Mott's Cottage, Sackville St; Caledonian Inn, Bank St; Seacombe House, Cox St; St John's Church of England, Regent St; and the Gazette Office, Sackville St.

🎡 *Port Fairy Folk Festival:* Mar. *Spring Music Festival:* Oct. *Moyneyana Festival:* family entertainment; Dec.

🧭 **Griffiths Island** Connected to town by a causeway, this island is home to a large colony of short-tailed shearwaters. Each year they travel across the Pacific Ocean from North America to nest in the same burrows (Sept–Apr). Also on the island is a much-photographed lighthouse.

The Crags: rugged coastal rock formations; 12 km w. *Yambuk:* a small township centred on an old inn with Yambuk Lake, a popular recreation area, nearby; 17 km w. *Lady Julia Percy Island:* home to a fur seal colony; charters can be arranged from Port Fairy Wharf; 22 km off coast. *Codrington Wind Farm:* Victoria's first wind-power station; 27 km w. *Mahogany Walk to Warrnambool:* a 6–7 hr walk (one way, can return by bus) taking in a magnificent stretch of coastline; details from visitor centre. *Historic Shipwreck Trail:* between Port Fairy and Moonlight Head with 25 wreck sites signposted along the way.

See also SOUTH-WEST COAST, pp. 42–3

Portland

288 A4

ℹ️ **Lee Breakwater Rd; (03) 5523 2671 or 1800 035 567; www.visitgreatoceanroad.org.au**

📻 96.9 AM ABC Local Radio, 99.3 Coastal FM

Portland is the most westerly of Victoria's major coastal towns and the only deep-water port between Melbourne and Adelaide. It was also the first permanent settlement in Victoria, founded in 1834 by the Hentys. The township, which features many National Trust–classified buildings, overlooks Portland Bay. The Kerrup–Tjmara people, who once numbered in the thousands, were the original inhabitants of the district and referred to it as 'Pulumbete' meaning 'Little Lake' – a reference to the scenic lake now known as Fawthorp Lagoon.

🏛️ **Portland Maritime Discovery Centre** The centre features a 13 m sperm whale skeleton, and the lifeboat used to rescue 19 survivors from the *Admella* shipwreck in 1859. Another wreck, the *Regia*, is displayed in 2 m of water. The centre shares the building with the information centre. Lee Breakwater Rd.

Botanical Gardens: established in 1857, with both native and exotic plant life. A restored

1850s bluestone worker's cottage is within the grounds and open to the public; Cliff St. *Historical buildings:* more than 200 around town, many National Trust–classified. The best way to explore buildings such as the courthouse, Steam Packet Inn and Mac's Hotel is to take either a guided or self-guide walk; details from visitor centre. *History House:* a historical museum and family research centre in the old town hall; Charles St. *Burswood:* a bluestone, regency-style mansion that was once the home of pioneer settler Edward Henty. The house is set amid 5 ha of gardens; Cape Nelson Rd. *Fawthorp Lagoon:* prolific birdlife; Glenelg St. *Powerhouse Car Museum:* Percy St. *Watertower Lookout:* displays of WW II memorabilia on the way up the 133 steps to magnificent 360-degree views across Portland and the ocean, where whales and dolphins can sometimes be spotted; Percy St. Another good spot for whale-watching is Battery Hill.

Anzac Day Floral Display: Apr. *Portland Bay Festival:* Nov. *3 Bays Marathon:* Nov.

Cape Bridgewater This cape is home to a 650-strong colony of Australian fur seals. A 2 hr return walk leads to a viewing platform, or you can take a 45 min boat ride that leads into the mouth of a cave to see them up close (bookings essential, (03) 5526 7247). Across the cape towards Discovery Bay are the Petrified Forest and the Blowholes – spectacular during high seas. 21 km sw.

Lower Glenelg National Park The Glenelg River is a central feature of the park. It has cut an impressive 50 m deep gorge through a vast slab of limestone. Keep an eye out for platypus, water rats, moorhens and herons around the water's edge. Bushwalking, camping, fishing and canoeing are all popular, and Jones Lookout and the Bulley Ranges offer great views. Also in the park are the Princess

Margaret Rose Caves on the north side of the river – you can drive there via Nelson or Dartmoor. Alternatively, boat tours operate from Nelson. Contact Parks Victoria on 13 1963; 44 km nw.

Cape Nelson: here a lighthouse perches on top of tall cliffs and lightstation tours are available; 11 km sw. *Narrawong State Forest:* a short walk leads to Whalers Pt, where Aboriginal people once watched for whales; 18 km ne. *Discovery Bay Coastal Park:* Cape Bridgewater is included in this park, though the majority of it is remote and relatively untouched. The Great South West Walk (*see below*) offers the best chance to take in the park's scenery. Behind Cape Bridgewater are the Bridgewater Lakes (19 km w) – popular for waterskiing and fishing. A walking track leads from here to the beach. *Mt Richmond National Park:* a 'mountain' formed by an extinct volcano. The area has abundant spring wildflowers and native fauna, including the elusive potoroo; 25 km nw. *Heywood:* home to the Bower Birds Nest Museum, and the Wood, Wine and Roses Festival in Feb. Budj Bim National Heritage Landscape, the traditional lands of the Gunditjmara people, is located here also. Visitors can experience the aquaculture system including stone eel traps, permanent stone houses and smoking trees; Budj Bim Tours (03) 5527 1699; 28 km n. *Nelson:* a charming hamlet near the mouth of the Glenelg River. There is good waterskiing in the area; 70 km nw. *Great South West Walk:* this epic 250 km walking trail takes in the full range of local scenery – the Glenelg River, Discovery and Bridgewater bays and Cape Nelson are some of the highlights. It is possible to do just small sections of the walk; maps and details from visitor centre.

See also SOUTH-WEST COAST, pp. 42–3

TOWNS

RADIO STATION   IN TOWN   WHAT'S ON   NEARBY

Pyramid Hill

288 D1 | 291 D4

ℹ️ **Loddon Visitor Information Centre,**
Wedderburn Community Centre,
24 Wilson St, Wedderburn; (03) 5494 3489;
www.pyramidhill.net.au

📻 91.1 FM ABC Local Radio,
104.7 Radio EMFM

Pyramid Hill's namesake is an unusually shaped, 187-metre-high hill. The town, which is located in a wheat-growing district about 30 kilometres from the New South Wales border, was a source of inspiration to notable Australian author Katherine Susannah Pritchard, who based a character in her book *Child of the Hurricane* on a woman she met while staying in Pyramid Hill during World War I.

🏠 **Pyramid Hill** A climb to the top of this eerily symmetrical hill reveals views of the surrounding irrigation and wheat district. There are abundant wildflowers in spring.

Historical Museum: features local story displays; open Sun afternoons or by appt; McKay St.

🧭 **Terrick Terrick National Park** The park is a large Murray pine forest reserve, with numerous granite outcrops, including Mitiamo Rock. There is a variety of good walking tracks, and the park is a key nesting area for the distinctive brolga. Contact Parks Victoria on 13 1963; access is via the Pyramid Hill–Kow Swamp Rd; 20 km SE.

Mt Hope: named by explorer Major Mitchell, who 'hoped' he would be able to spot the sea from the mountain's peak. Now known for its wildflowers; 16 km NE. ***Boort:*** nearby lakes provide a habitat for swans, ibis, pelicans and other waterbirds, and a place for watersports, fishing and picnics; 40 km W.

See also GOULBURN & MURRAY, pp. 50–1

Queenscliff

278 D4 | 280 C3 | 287 B4 | 289 E4

ℹ️ **55 Hesse St; (03) 5258 4843;**
www.queenscliffe.vic.gov.au

📻 94.7 The Pulse FM, 774 AM ABC Local Radio

Queenscliff is a charming seaside town on the Bellarine Peninsula. It began life as a resort for wealthy Victorians in the 1800s, as testified by lavish buildings such as the Queenscliff Hotel, with its ornate lattice work and plush interiors. The town's wide main street is lined with cafes and restaurants, plus an array of art galleries, and the nearby beaches become a playground for holiday-makers during summer. A ferry runs between Queenscliff and Sorrento, a resort town across Port Phillip Bay.

🏠 **Queenscliff Maritime Museum** The museum explores the town's long association with ships and the sea through a collection of maritime memorabilia. It features a re-created fisherman's cottage, a diving-technology display and an array of navigational equipment. Weeroona Pde; (03) 5258 3440.

Marine Discovery Centre This is a great family destination where visitors can learn all about the local marine life. It has a number of aquariums and touch-tanks. The centre also runs various tours, including boat cruises off Port Phillip and 'rockpool rambles'. Adjacent to the Maritime Museum, Weeroona Pde; (03) 5258 3344.

The Blues Train An incredibly popular attraction that provides a unique dining and entertainment experience on board a steam train. Round trips provide 4 carriages, each with a different blues musician. Guests can change carriages at stops on the journey and purchase drinks from the mobile bar at each station platform. Operates Sat nights Oct–May.

Departs from and returns to Queenscliff Railway Station; bookings at Ticketek on 132 849, or contact visitor centre for more information.

Fort Queenscliff: built during the Crimean War, it includes the unique 'Black Lighthouse'. Tours of the fort run most days; details from visitor centre. **Queenscliff Historical Museum:** open daily 2–4pm; Hesse St. **Bellarine Peninsula Railway:** beautifully restored steam trains run between Queenscliff and Drysdale. There are many engines on display around the station. Trains run Sun, public holidays and other times during school holidays; Symonds St. **Bellarine Rail Trail:** 32.5 km track that extends from South Geelong to Queenscliff; on reaching Drysdale it runs along the Bellarine Peninsula Railway and ends in the town.

Market: with crafts and second-hand goods; Princes Park, Gellibrand St; last Sun each month except winter. **Queenscliff Music Festival:** major event attracting local and international music acts; Nov.

Pt Lonsdale This peaceful holiday town offers gorgeous beaches suitable for either surfing or swimming. A lookout from the cliff-top provides a great view of the treacherous entrance to Port Phillip known as 'The Rip'. A market is held here on the 2nd Sunday of each month. 6 km sw.

Lake Victoria: an important waterbird habitat; 7 km sw via Pt Lonsdale. **Harold Holt Marine Reserve:** incorporates Mud Island and coastal reserves. Guided boat tours can be arranged from the Marine Discovery Centre.

See also WERRIBEE & BELLARINE, pp. 40–1

Robinvale

291 C2

i **Kyndalyn Park Information Centre,** Bromley Rd; (03) 5026 1388; www.murrayriver.com.au/html/towns/ robinvaleeuston.html

90.7 HOTFM Sunraysia Community Radio

Robinvale is set on the New South Wales border by a pretty stretch of the Murray River. The Robinswood Homestead, built in 1926, was home to the town's founder, Herbert Cuttle (you can find the homestead in River Road). Herbert's son, Robin, was killed during World War I, so he named both the homestead and the town in Robin's honour. As another form of remembrance, the town has a sister city in France, near where young Robin died.

Rural Life Museum: housed in the information centre, with locally grown almonds for sale; open by appt; Bromley Rd. **Murray River:** the beaches around Robinvale are popular for picnics and fishing, while in the river waterskiing and swimming are favourite summer pastimes.

Ski Race: Mar. **Tennis Tournament:** Easter. **Almond Blossom Festival:** Aug.

Euston Weir and Lock on Murray: created as an irrigation water store, it features a 'fish ladder' that enables fish to jump over the weir. Picnic and barbecue facilities are provided; Pethard Rd, south-west edge of town. **Robinvale Organic and Bio-dynamic Wines:** tastings and sales of these distinctive, preservative-free wines. Also a children's playground; Sea Lake Rd; 5 km s. **Olive oil:** this region is renowned for producing award-winning olive oil. Robinvale Estate offers farmgate sales and tastings; Tol Tol Rd; 8 km SE. There is also Boundary Bend Estate; Boundary Bend; Murray Valley Hwy; 1 km s

TOWNS

of the Murray River. *Robinvale Indigenous Arts and Crafts:* learn about the local bush tucker; River Rd. *Hattah–Kulkyne National Park:* 66 km sw; *see Ouyen.*

See also MALLEE COUNTRY, pp. 48–9

Rochester

289 E2

ⓘ Council offices, 43 Mackay St; (03) 5484 4500; www.rochester.org.au

🔳 91.1 FM ABC Local Radio, 104.7 Radio EMFM

On the Campaspe River, near Echuca, Rochester is the centre of a rich dairying and tomato-growing area. There are several lakes and waterways near town, making Rochester a popular destination for freshwater fishing.

🏠 **The 'Oppy' Museum** The museum details the history of Sir Hubert Opperman, affectionately known as Oppy, a champion cyclist who competed in the Tour de France. There is a collection of memorabilia related to Oppy's career as a cyclist, as well as artefacts from the town's past. A statue of Oppy is opposite the museum. Moore St.

Heritage walk: take in the town's attractive old buildings. *Campaspe River Walk:* a pleasant, signposted walk by the river.

🧭 **Kyabram Fauna Park** This park, owned by the Kyabram community, is home to over 140 animal species – everything from wombats to waterfowl. It has been built from the ground up on a piece of degraded farmland, and is now heavily involved in breeding programs for endangered species such as the eastern barred bandicoot. Check out the walk-through aviary and Australia's first energy-efficient reptile house. (03) 5852 2883; 35 km NE.

Campaspe Siphon: an impressive engineering feat, where the Waranga–Western Main irrigation channel was redirected under the

Campaspe River; 5 km N. *Fishing:* nearby channels, rivers and lakes are popular with anglers for redfin and carp. Lakes include Greens Lake and Lake Cooper (14 km SE), also popular for picnicking and watersports. *Elmore:* here is the Campaspe Run Rural Discovery Centre, which explains Koorie and colonial history and heritage. Elmore Field Days are held each Oct; 17 km S.

See also GOULBURN & MURRAY, pp. 50–1

Rushworth

287 C1 | 289 E2

ⓘ 33 High St; (03) 5856 1117; www.campaspe.vic.gov.au/community/ rushworth/main.htm

🔳 97.7 FM ABC Local Radio, 98.5 FM 98.5

Situated in central Victoria off the Goulburn Valley Highway, this delightful little town was once a goldmining settlement. The original site of the township was known as Nuggetty owing to the numerous gold nuggets found during the 19th century. Rushworth has retained much of its original character, with well-preserved early buildings lining the main street.

🏠 *Historic buildings:* many along High St are National Trust–classified, including the Church of England, the Band Rotunda, the former Imperial Hotel, the Glasgow Buildings and the Whistle Stop. Take the High St Heritage Walk to see these and others; map from visitor centre. *History Museum:* housed in the old mechanics institute with displays relating to the town's goldmining heritage; Cnr High and Parker sts. *Growlers Hill Lookout Tower:* views of the town, Rushworth State Forest and the surrounding Goulburn Valley; Reed St.

🧭 **Rushworth State Forest** The largest natural ironbark forest in the world, Rushworth State Forest is also renowned for the orchids and wildflowers that blossom here in spring.

Picnics and bushwalks are popular activities in this attractive reserve where over 100 species of birds, along with echidnas and kangaroos, can be seen. Access via Whroo Rd; 3 km s.

Jones's Eucalyptus Distillery: eucalyptus oil is extracted from blue mallee gum; Parramatta Gully Rd, just south of town. *Waranga Basin:* an artificial diversion of the Goulburn weir constructed in 1916, now a haven for boating, fishing, swimming and watersports; 6 km NE. *Whroo Historic Reserve:* Balaclava Hill, an open-cut goldmine, along with camping and picnic facilities, the Whroo cemetery and an Aboriginal waterhole; 7 km s. *Murchison:* a small town picturesquely set on the Goulburn River. Town attractions include the Italian war memorial and chapel; Meteorite Park, the site of a meteorite fall in 1969; Longleat Winery; and Campbell's Bend Picnic Reserve; 19 km E. *Days Mill:* a flour mill with buildings dating from 1865; 39 km NE via Murchison. *Town ruins:* goldmining played a huge role in the development of this region, but not all towns survived the end of the gold rush. Ruins of Angustown, Bailieston and Graytown are all to the south of Rushworth.

See also GOULBURN & MURRAY, pp. 50–1

Rutherglen

284 D1 | 289 G1

i 57 Main St; (02) 6033 6300 or 1800 622 871; www.rutherglenvic.com

101.3 Oak FM, 106.5 FM ABC Local Radio

Rutherglen is the centre of one of the most important winegrowing districts in Victoria, with a cluster of vineyards surrounding the town. Many of the local wineries are best known for their fortified wines. Rutherglen's main street features preserved late-19th-century architecture.

Rutherglen Wine Experience: interpretive displays of Rutherglen's wine history; visitor centre, Main St. *Common School Museum:* local history displays and a re-creation of a Victorian-era schoolroom; behind Main St. *Historic tours:* the best way to explore the town's numerous old buildings is to take a self-guide walk, bike ride or drive, following maps provided at the visitor centre. *Lake King:* originally constructed in 1874 as Rutherglen's water storage, it is now a wildlife sanctuary and offers a scenic walk.

Tastes of Rutherglen: celebration of the region's gourmet food and wine; Mar. *Rutherglen and District Art Society Show:* Mar. *Easter in Rutherglen:* Easter. *Winery Walkabout:* June. *Country Fair:* June. *Wine Show:* Sept. *Tour de Rutherglen:* cycling and wine event; Oct. *Young Bloods and Bloody Legends:* food and wine event; Oct.

Rutherglen Wine Region In Rutherglen, the most difficult task you'll face will be finding the time to visit all the fantastic wineries in the region. At many of them the appeal extends beyond cellar-door tastings and sales, such as at the All Saints Estate, 10 km NW, which features a National Trust–classified, castle-like building and a fine restaurant. A Day on the Green concert is held here in Feb. In the grounds of the Bullers Calliope Vineyard, 6 km W, is a bird park, with over 100 native and exotic species. Gehrig Estate, 21 km E, is Victoria's oldest continuously operating vineyard. It displays historic farming implements and has a charming restaurant.

Great Northern Mine: marked by mullock heaps associated with the first alluvial goldmine in the district. Historical details are provided on-site; Great Northern Rd, 5 km E. *Lake Moodemere:* found near the winery of the same name, the lake is popular for watersports and features ancient Aboriginal canoe trees by the shores; 8 km W. *Old customs house:* a relic from the time when a tax was payable on goods from NSW; 10 km nw.

See also HIGH COUNTRY, pp. 52–3

St Arnaud

288 C2 | 291 C5

ℹ️ 4 Napier St; (03) 5495 1268 or 1800 014 455.

📻 91.1 FM ABC Local Radio, 99.1 Goldfields FM

A former goldmining town surrounded by forests and scenic hill country, St Arnaud is a service centre for the district's farming community, yet retains a peaceful rural atmosphere. The main street is lined with well-preserved historic buildings, many of which feature impressive ornate lacework. Together, these buildings form a nationally recognised historic streetscape.

🏠 *Self-guide historic tour:* brochure available from visitor centre. **Queen Mary Gardens:** great spot for a picnic; Napier St. **Old Post Office:** now a B&B and restaurant; Napier St. **Police lock-up:** built in 1862; Jennings St.

🎆 **Heritage Festival:** Nov.

🧭 **St Arnaud Range National Park** The park protects an oasis of dense box-ironbark forest and woodland surrounded by agricultural land. Over 270 different species of native flora have been recorded here and provide a glimpse of what the area would have looked like before the land-clearing that occurred during and after the gold rush. Within the park are the Teddington Reservoirs, popular for brown trout and redfin fishing. The rugged terrain throughout provides a great opportunity for keen bushwalkers or 4WD enthusiasts. Wedge-tailed eagles can be seen soaring above the steep, forested ranges. Contact Parks Victoria on 13 1963; Sunraysia Hwy; 15 km s.

Great Grape Rd: wine-themed circuit through Stawell and Ballarat; details from visitor centre.

See also GOLDFIELDS, pp. 44–5

Sale

289 G4

ℹ️ **Wellington Visitors Information Centre,** Princes Hwy; (03) 5144 1108 or 1800 677 520; www.tourismwellington.com.au

📻 104.7 Gippsland FM, 828 AM ABC Local Radio

Situated by the Thomson River near the Latrobe River junction, Sale grew on the back of the gold rush and became Gippsland's first city in 1950. Although largely considered an industrial town, with the nearby Bass Strait oilfields providing a large part of the town's economy, Sale has a lot more to offer. The Port of Sale is being redeveloped into a modern recreational precinct. There are many good cafes and restaurants, and a number of fine-art galleries and craft outlets. The lakes near Sale are home to the unique Australian black swan – the bird that has become a symbol for the town.

🏠 **Gippsland Arts Gallery** The gallery was developed to promote the work of artists and craftspeople in central Gippsland. Works range from traditional landscapes to visual statements on environmental and cultural issues, and may be in any medium from painting and photography to film and video. Foster St; (03) 5142 3372.

Lake Guthridge Parklands This major recreational area within Sale comprises the Lake Guthridge and Lake Guyatt precincts, the Sale Botanic Gardens and the Regional Aquatic Complex. The precinct showcases over 35 ha of historically significant botanic gardens, walking trails, Indigenous artworks and a contemporary fauna park. It also provides sensory gardens, abundant seating, an adventure playground for children and tennis courts. Foster St.

Historical Museum: local history memorabilia; Foster St. *Ramahyuck Aboriginal Corporation:* offers local arts and crafts and is part of the Bataluk Cultural Trail, which takes in sites of Aboriginal significance in the region; Foster St. *Historical buildings:* include Our Lady of Sion Convent in York St; Magistrates Court and Supreme Court, Foster St; St Paul's Anglican Cathedral featuring fine stained-glass windows, Cunninghame St; St Mary's Cathedral, Foster St. Bicentennial clock tower in the mall utilises the original bluestone base, ironwork and clock mechanisms; Raymond St. *RAAF base:* home of the famous Roulettes aerobatic team; Raglan St. *Sale Common and State Game Refuge:* protected wetland area with a boardwalk; south-east edge of town. *Textile art:* Sale is the home of internationally recognised textile artist Annemieke Mein. Her work is on permanent display in the foyer of the Port of Sale Civic Centre, ESSO BHP Billiton Wellington Entertainment Centre and St Mary's Cathedral; Foster St.

🎆 **Sale Cup:** Greenwattle Racecourse; Oct.

🧭 **Holey Plains State Park** The open eucalypt forests in this park are home to abundant wildlife, while swamps provide a habitat for many frog species. There is a good swimming lake, and a series of fascinating fossils can be seen nearby in a limestone quarry wall. Bushwalking, picnicking and camping are all popular activities, particularly around Harriers Swamp. Access from Princes Hwy; 14 km sw.

Fishing: good fishing for trout in the Avon River near Marlay Pt and also in the Macalister, Thomson and Latrobe rivers, especially at Swing Bridge; 5 km s. *Marlay Pt:* on the shores of Lake Wellington with boat-launching facilities provided. The yacht club here sponsors an overnight yacht race to Paynesville each Mar; 25 km E. *Seaspray:* a popular holiday spot on Ninety Mile Beach; offers excellent surfing and fishing; 32 km s. *Golden*

and Paradise beaches: two more townships on Ninety Mile Beach with great surfing and fishing; 35 km SE. *Loch Sport:* set on Gippsland Lakes and popular for camping and fishing; 65 km SE. *For details on Gippsland Lakes see Lakes Entrance and Paynesville.* *Howitt Bike Trail:* 13-day round trip beginning and ending in Sale; details from visitor centre. *Bataluk Cultural Trail:* takes in sites of Indigenous significance from Sale to Cann River; brochure from visitor centre.

See also EAST GIPPSLAND, pp. 54–5.

Seymour

287 C2 | 289 E3

ℹ️ Old Courthouse, Emily St; (03) 5799 0233.

📻 87.6 Seymour FM, 97.7 FM ABC Local Radio

Seymour is a commercial, industrial and agricultural town on the Goulburn River. The area was recommended for a military base by Lord Kitchener during his visit in 1909. Nearby Puckapunyal became an important training place for troops during World War II, and remains a major army base today.

🏠 **Royal Hotel:** featured in Russell Drysdale's famous 1941 painting *Moody's Pub*; Emily St. *Old Courthouse:* built in 1864, it now houses local art; Emily St. *Fine Art Gallery:* in the old post office; Emily St. *Goulburn River:* a walking track goes by the river and the Old Goulburn Bridge has been preserved as a historic relic. *Goulburn Park:* for picnics and swimming; Cnr Progress and Guild sts. *Seymour Railway Heritage Centre:* restored steam engines and carriages; open by appt; Railway Pl. *Australian Light Horse Memorial Park:* Goulburn Valley Hwy.

🎆 **Market:** Kings Park; 3rd Sat each month. *Alternative Farming Expo:* Feb. *Tastes of* *the Goulburn:* food and wine festival; Oct. *Seymour Cup:* Oct.

Tallarook State Forest Tallarook is a popular destination for bushwalking, camping, rock climbing and horseriding. The key features are Mt Hickey, the highest point in the park and the location of a fire-lookout tower, and Falls Creek Reservoir, a scenic picnic spot. Warragul Rocks offers great views over the Goulburn River. 10 km s.

Travellers note: *Lookout from Warragul Rocks can only be accessed via private property. The landowner requests that any visitor contact him first to arrange access: Ron Milanovic, 0413 402 744.*

Wineries: several in the area, including Somerset Crossing Vineyards, 2 km s; Plunketts Winery, 21 km NE; Tahbilk, 26 km N; Mitchelton, 28 km N. *RAAC Memorial and Army Tank Museum:* Puckapunyal army base; 10 km w.

See also GOULBURN & MURRAY, pp. 50–1

Shepparton

287 D1 | 289 F2

534 Wyndham St; (03) 5831 4400 or 1800 808 839; www.greatershepparton.com.au

97.7 FM ABC Local Radio, 98.5 FM

Shepparton has recently become a popular destination for conferences and sporting events, and so has plenty of modern accommodation and good restaurants in town. Indeed, Shepparton is a thriving city and is considered the 'capital' of the Goulburn Valley. It is home to many orchards irrigated by the Goulburn Irrigation Scheme.

Art Gallery: features Australian paintings and ceramics; Welsford St. *Bangerang Cultural Centre:* displays and dioramas on local Aboriginal culture; Parkside Dr. *Historical Museum:* in the Historical Precinct; open

even-dated Sun afternoons; High St. *Emerald Bank Heritage Farm:* displays of 1930s farming methods; Goulburn Valley Hwy. *Victoria Park Lake:* scenic picnic spot; Tom Collins Dr. *Reedy Swamp Walk:* prolific birdlife; at the end of Wanganui Rd. *Moooving Art:* mobile interactive public art in the form of life-size 3-D cow sculptures; various parks throughout Shepparton including Monash Park, Queens Gardens and Murchison riverbank. *Factory sales:* Pental Soaps and Campbells Soups.

Trash and treasure market: Melbourne Rd; each Sun. *Craft market:* Queens Gardens, Wyndham St; 3rd Sun each month. *International Dairy Week:* Jan. *Bush Market Day:* Feb. *Shepparton Fest:* major local arts festival with family entertainment; Mar. *Spring Car Nationals:* car competitions; Nov.

SPC Ardmona KidsTown: a fun tourist attraction with a maze, flying fox, enormous playground and miniature railway, and camel rides on the weekends; Midland Hwy; (03) 5831 4213; 3 km w. *Mooroopna:* a small town in the fruit-growing district. It hosts the popular Fruit Salad Day in Feb. SPC Ardmona also has a factory sales supermarket here; 5 km w. *Kialla:* Ross Patterson Gallery, with displays and sales of local artwork. Also here is Belstack Strawberry Farm, where you can pick your own berries; Goulburn Valley Hwy; 9 km s. *Tatura:* a museum with displays on local WW II internment camps. Taste of Tatura is held each Mar; 17 km sw. *Wunghnu:* the town (pronounced 'one ewe') is centred on the well-known Institute Tavern in the restored mechanics institute building. A tractor-pull festival is held each Easter; 32 km N.

See also GOULBURN & MURRAY, pp. 50–1

Sorrento

see inset box on page 144

Stawell

288 C2

ℹ️ **Stawell and Grampians Visitor Information Centre, 50–52 Western Hwy; (03) 5358 2314 or 1800 330 080.**

📻 96.5 Triple H FM, 594 AM ABC Local Radio

Pastoral runs were established in the Stawell region in the 1840s, but it was the discovery of gold in 1853 by a shepherd at nearby Pleasant Creek that was the catalyst for creating a town. Stawell remains a goldmining centre with Victoria's largest mine. However, it is actually better known as the home of the Stawell Gift, Australia's richest footrace, and the gateway to the Grampians.

🏠 **Stawell Gift Hall of Fame Museum** In 1878 the Stawell Athletic Club was formed by local farmers and businessmen who were keen to have a sports day each Easter. The club put up the prize pool of £110, and the race was on. The annual Stawell Gift has run almost continuously since and is now one of the most prestigious races in the world. The race has been run at Central Park since 1898. Visit the museum to discover the glory and heartbreak of the race since its inception. Open 9–11am Mon–Fri; Main St; (03) 5358 1326.

Big Hill Lookout and Stawell Gold Mine viewing area: the Pioneers Lookout at the summit of this local landmark presents magnificent 360-degree views of the surrounding area. Continue down Reefs Rd to Stawell Gold Mine viewing area to hear about the daily operations of Victoria's largest gold-producing mine. *Casper's Mini World:* miniature tourist park with working models of famous world attractions such as the Eiffel Tower and including dioramas and commentaries; London Rd. *Fraser Park:* displays of mining equipment; Main St. *Pleasant Creek Court House Museum:* local

history memorabilia; Western Hwy. *Stawell Ironbark Forest:* spring wildflowers, including rare orchids; northern outskirts of town, off Newington Rd.

🎆 *SES Market:* Drill Hall, Sloane St; 1st Sun each month. *Farmer's Market:* Harness Racing Club, Patrick St; last Sun each month. *Stawell Gift:* Easter.

🧭 **Bunjil's Shelter** This is Victoria's most important Aboriginal rock-art site. It depicts the creator figure, Bunjil, sitting inside a small alcove with his 2 dingoes. Bunjil created the geographical features of the land, and then created people, before disappearing into the sky to look down on the earth as a star. The site is thought to have been used for ceremonies by the local Djab Wurrung and Jardwadjali people. Off Pomonal Rd; 11 km s.

The Sisters Rocks: huge granite tors; beside Western Hwy; 3 km SE. *Great Western:* picturesque wine village with Seppelt Great Western Winery, est. 1865, featuring National Trust–classified underground tunnels of cellars and Champagne Picnic Races in Jan; 16 km SE. *Tottington Woolshed:* rare example of a 19th-century woolshed; road to St Arnaud; 55 km NE. *Great Grape Rd:* circuit through Ballarat and St Arnaud, stopping at wineries; details from visitor centre.

See also GRAMPIANS & CENTRAL WEST, pp. 46–7

Swan Hill

291 D3

ℹ️ **Swan Hill Region Information Centre, cnr McCrae and Curlewis sts; (03) 5032 3033 or 1800 625 373; www.swanhillonline.com**

📻 99.1 Smart FM, 102.1 FM ABC Local Radio

In 1836, explorer Thomas Mitchell named this spot Swan Hill because of the black swans that

TOWNS

SORRENTO

POINT KING

278 D4 | 280 C3 | 287 B5 | 289 E4

i Mornington Peninsula Visitor Information Centre, 359B Pt Nepean Rd, Dromana; (03) 5987 3078 or 1800 804 009.

98.7 3RPP FM, 774 AM ABC Local Radio

Just inside Port Phillip Heads on the Mornington Peninsula, in 1803 Sorrento was the site of Victoria's first European settlement. The town is close to historic Point Nepean and major surf and bayside beaches. Its population swells significantly over summer as visitors flock to soak up the holiday-resort atmosphere. A ferry links Sorrento to Queenscliff on the Bellarine Peninsula.

Collins Settlement Historic Site: marks the state's first European settlement and includes early graves; on Sullivan Bay. **Historic buildings:** include Sorrento Hotel on Hotham Rd and Continental Hotel on Ocean Beach Rd. Both are fine examples of early Victorian architecture, with the latter reputed to be the largest limestone building in the Southern Hemisphere; the visitor centre can give details of self-guide historical walks. **Nepean Historical Society Museum and Heritage Gallery:** a collection of local artefacts and memorabilia in the National Trust–classified mechanics institute. Adjacent is Watt's Cottage and the Pioneer Memorial Garden; Melbourne Rd. **Dolphin and seal cruises:** depart from the pier; not in winter months.

Craft market: primary school, cnr Kerferd and Coppin rds; last Sat each month. **Street Festival:** Oct.

Mornington Peninsula National Park The park incorporates Sorrento, Rye and Portsea back beaches and stretches south-east to Cape Schanck and beyond (see Flinders). Walks, picnics and swimming are the main attractions, but there is also the unique rock formation of London Bridge, at Portsea. The rugged coastline offers good surfing. Pt Nepean and historic Fort Nepean can be accessed by a daily transport service departing from Portsea. A former Quarantine Station on Pt Nepean offers tours, which include a visit to the Army Health Services Museum, on Sun and public holidays. Contact Parks Victoria on 13 1963.

Portsea: an opulent holiday town with good, safe swimming beaches. It hosts the Portsea Swim Classic each Jan; 4 km NW. **Popes Eye Marine Reserve:** an artificially created horseshoe-shaped island and reef, now a popular spot for diving. Gannets nest here. Cruises available; details from visitor centre; 5 km offshore at Portsea. **Rye:** a beachside holiday spot with horseriding trips on offer and the annual Beach Sand Sculpting Championship each Feb; 8 km E. **Peninsula Hot Springs:** relaxing, outdoor, naturally heated pools. Private mineral pools, baths and massage therapies available; Springs La, Rye. **Moonah Links Golf Course:** 2 fantastic 18-hole golf courses, one designed specifically for the Australian Open; Peter Thompson Dr, Fingal. **Rosebud:** a bayside resort town with gorgeous, safe swimming beaches. Summer fishing trips depart from Rosebud pier. A film festival is held here each Nov; 15 km E. **McCrae Homestead:** National Trust–classified drop-slab property built in 1844; open afternoons; McCrae; 17 km E.

See also MORNINGTON PENINSULA, pp. 34–5

kept him awake all night. The town's swans remain, but there are many other attractions in this pleasant city on the Murray Valley Highway.

Swan Hill Pioneer Settlement This museum re-creates the Murray and Mallee regions from the 1830s to the 1930s. Wander through the street lined with barber shops and chemists, and take a ride on the PS *Pyap* or a horse-drawn cart. There is also the Sound and Light Tour; bookings required. End of Gray St on Little Murray River.

Swan Hill Regional Art Gallery: an impressive permanent collection plus touring exhibitions; opposite the Pioneer Settlement Museum.

Market: Curlewis St; 3rd Sun each month. **Racing Cup Carnival:** June. **Australian Inland Wine Show:** Oct.

Swan Hill Wine Region The region, which starts around Tresco to the south-east and ends around Piangil to the north-west, takes advantage of the Murray River and the Mediterranean-style climate. The first vines were planted here in 1930, but the proliferation of vineyards really began when Sicilian immigrants arrived on the Murray after WW II. Today cellar doors offer tastings and sales of predominantly shiraz, colombard and chardonnay varieties. Winery map from visitor centre.

Lake Boga The town has an interesting history as an RAAF flying-boat repair depot during WW II. The depot serviced over 400 flying boats, one of which can be seen at the Flying Boat Museum. The underground museum is in the original communications bunker in Willakool Dr. At Lake Boga, the water mass is popular for watersports, fishing and camping, and is home to a variety of bird species that can be seen on the various walks. A yachting regatta is held here each Easter. 17 km SE.

Lakeside Nursery and Gardens: over 300 varieties of roses; 10 km NW. *Tyntyndyer Homestead:* built in 1846; open Tues and Thurs 10am–4pm or by appt; Murray Valley Hwy; 20 km NW. *Nyah:* good market with local produce; 2nd Sat each month; 27 km NW. *Tooleybuc:* situated in NSW, it has a tranquil riverside atmosphere and good fishing, picnicking and riverside walks. The Bridgekeepers Cottage has sales and displays of dolls and crafts; 46 km N.

See also MALLEE COUNTRY, pp. 48–9

When the old town of Tallangatta was going to be submerged in 1956 after the level of the Hume Weir was raised, the residents simply moved the entire township 8 kilometres west. Tallangatta now has an attractive lakeside location and sits directly north of Victoria's beautiful alpine region.

The Hub: local art and craft, and Lord's Hut, the only remaining slab hut in the district; Towong St.

Farm and Water Festival: Apr. *Fifties Festival:* Oct. *Garage Sale Festival:* Oct.

Lake Hume Tallangatta is on the shores of this enormous and attractive lake, formed when the then largest weir in the Southern Hemisphere was constructed. It is now a picturesque spot for swimming, waterskiing, windsurfing and fishing. The foreshore reserves are perfect for barbecues.

Eskdale: craft shops, and trout fishing in the Mitta Mitta River; 33 km S. *Lake Dartmouth:* great for trout fishing and boating; hosts the Dartmouth Cup Fishing Competition over the June long weekend. Also here is The Witches Garden featuring unique medicinal plants; 58 km SE. *Mitta Mitta:* remnants of a large open-cut goldmine. Also a gallery, Butcher's Hook Antiques and Bharatralia Jungle Camp. Hosts the Mitta Muster on Sun on the long weekend in Mar; 60 km S. *Australian Alps Walking Track:* passes over Mt Wills; 108 km S via Mitta Mitta. *Scenic drives:* to Cravensville, to Mitta Mitta along Omeo Hwy and to Tawonga and Mount Beauty.

See also HIGH COUNTRY, pp. 52–3

Tallangatta

285 F2 | 289 H2 | 290 A2

i 50 Hanson St, Corryong; (02) 6076 2277; www.pureuppermurrayvalleys.com

101.3 Oak FM, 106.5 FM ABC Local Radio

Terang

286 C4 | 288 C4

i Old Courthouse, 22 High St; (03) 5592 1984.

103.7 3WAY-FM, 774 AM ABC Local Radio

Terang is in a fertile dairy-farming district. It is a well-laid-out town with grand avenues of deciduous trees, and is known throughout the state for its horseracing carnivals.

Cottage Crafts Shop: in the old courthouse on High St. *District Historical Museum:* old railway station and memorabilia; open 3rd Sun each month; Princes Hwy. *Lions Walking Track:* 4.8 km, beside dry lake beds and majestic old trees; begins behind Civic Centre on High St. *Historic buildings:* many examples of early-20th-century commercial architecture. A Gothic-style Presbyterian church is in High St.

Terang Cup: Nov.

Demo Dairy: demonstrates dairy-farming practices; Princes Hwy, 4 km w. *Lake Keilambete:* 2.5 times saltier than the sea and reputed to have therapeutic properties; must obtain permission to visit as it is surrounded by private land; 4 km NW. *Model Barn Australia:* collection of model cars, boats and planes; open by appt; Robertson Rd; 5 km E. *Noorat:* birthplace of Alan Marshall, author of *I Can Jump Puddles*. The Alan Marshall Walking Track here involves a gentle climb to the summit of Mt Noorat, an extinct volcano, with excellent views of the crater, the surrounding district and the Grampians; 6 km N.

See also SOUTH-WEST COAST, pp. 42–3

Torquay

278 C4 | 280 A3 | 286 D1 | 287 A5 | 288 D4

ℹ️ Surfworld Australia, Surf City Plaza, cnr Surfcoast Hwy and Beach Rd; (03) 5261 4219 or 1300 614 219; www.visitsurfcoast.com

📻 94.7 The Pulse FM, 774 AM ABC Local Radio

Torquay was one of the first resort towns on Victoria's coast, and remains one of the most popular today. It was named in honour of the famous English resort, but its heritage is very different. Not only does Torquay and its coast have some of the best surf beaches in the world, it was also the birthplace of world leaders in surfboards, wetsuits and other apparel, including Rip Curl and Quiksilver, founded here in the 1960s and '70s.

Surf City Plaza This modern plaza houses some of the biggest names in surfing retail alongside smaller outlets. The complex also boasts the world's biggest surfing museum, Surfworld. See how board technology has developed over the last century, find out exactly what makes a good wave, and learn about the history of surfing at Bells Beach. A theatre here screens classic 1960s and '70s surf flicks and the latest surf videos. Beach Rd.

Fishermans Beach: good spot for fishing, with a sheltered swimming beach and a large sundial on the foreshore. *Tiger Moth World:* theme park based around the1930s Tiger Moth biplane. Joy-flights available; Blackgate Rd. *Surf schools:* programs available to suit all abilities, with many courses run during summer school holidays; details from visitor centre.

Cowrie Community Market: foreshore; 3rd Sun each month Sept–Apr. *Danger 1000 Ocean Swim:* Jan. *Surf for Life Surfing Contest:* Jan. *Kustom Jetty Surf Pro:* Jan. *Rip Curl Pro:* Easter. *Hightide Festival:* fireworks display; Dec.

The Surf Coast It is no wonder the coast that runs from Torquay through to Eastern View (past Anglesea) has dubbed itself the Surf Coast. Submerged reefs cause huge waves that are a surfer's paradise. Most famous is Bells Beach, around 5 km SW of Torquay. The clay cliffs provide a natural amphitheatre for one of the best surf beaches in the world. It is also home to the longest running surf competition,

TOWNS

RADIO STATION   IN TOWN   WHAT'S ON   NEARBY

the Rip Curl Pro, which started in 1973 and still attracts the top competitors each Easter. Other good surf beaches include Jan Juc, Anglesea and Fairhaven. To see the coast on foot, take the 30 km Surf Coast Walk, starting at Torquay and travelling south to Moggs Creek.

Hinterland: delightful towns like Bellbrae, Deans Marsh and Birregurra are dotted along the vista of the Surf Coast hinterland; starts 8 km w. *Bicycle lane:* runs along Surfcoast Hwy from Grovedale to Anglesea.

See also SOUTH-WEST COAST, pp. 42–3

Traralgon

289 G4

ℹ️ Latrobe Visitor Information Centre, The Old Church, Southside Central, Princes Hwy; 1800 621 409; www.visitlatrobevalley.com

📻 100.7 FM ABC Local Radio, 104.7 Gippsland FM

Traralgon is one of the Latrobe Valley's largest towns; a commerical hub located on the main Gippsland rail and road routes. Primarily a service centre for neighbouring agricultural communities, timber and electricity production, it also retains a certain village atmosphere with historic buildings in its wide streets and attractive public gardens.

🏠 *Historic buildings:* include the old post office and courthouse; Cnr Franklin and Kay sts. *Victory Park:* a great spot for picnics. Also here is a band rotunda and miniature railway; Princes Hwy.

🎆 *Farmers market:* 4th Sat each month. *International Junior Tennis Championships:* Jan. *Traralgon Cup:* Nov.

🧭 *Walhalla Mountain Rivers Trail:* this scenic drive (Tourist Route 91) winds through pretty hills to the north of town. *Loy Yang power station:* tours available; 5 km s. *Toongabbie:* a small town that hosts the Festival

of Roses each Nov; 19 km NE. *Hazelwood Cooling Pond:* year-round warm water makes this a popular swimming spot; outskirts of Churchill; 20 km SW. *Tara–Bulga National Park:* temperate rainforest; 30 km s.

See also PHILLIP ISLAND & GIPPSLAND, pp. 36–7

Walhalla

289 G4

ℹ️ Latrobe Visitor Information Centre, The Old Church, Southside Central, Princes Hwy, Traralgon; 1800 621 409.

📻 100.7 FM ABC Local Radio, 104.7 Gippsland FM

This tiny goldmining town is tucked away in dense mountain country in Gippsland – in a steep, narrow valley with sides so sheer that some cemetery graves were dug lengthways into the hillside. The town has a tiny population and is a relic from a long-gone era – it was only connected to electricity in 1998.

🏠 **Long Tunnel Gold Mine** This was one of the most prosperous goldmines in the state during the 19th century with over 13 tonnes of gold extracted here. Guided tours take visitors through sites such as Cohen's reef and the original machinery chamber 150 m below the ground. Tours operate daily at 1.30pm; Main St.

Historic buildings and goldmining remains: include the old post office, bakery and Windsor House, now a B&B. *Walks:* excellent walks in the town area, including one to a cricket ground on top of a 200 m hill. Another walk leads to a historic cemetery with graves of early miners; details from visitor centre. *Old Fire Station:* with hand-operated fire engines and firefighting memorabilia; open weekends and public holidays. *Museum and Corner Store:* local history displays plus goldmining artefacts; Main St. *Walhalla Goldfields Railway:* wonderfully restored old steam engine; departs from Thomson Station on Wed, Sat, Sun and public holidays. *Gold panning:* try your luck along pretty Stringers Creek, which runs through town. *Ghost tours:* spook yourself with a night-time guided ghost tour of Walhalla using old-fashioned lanterns; details from visitor centre.

Deloraine Gardens: terraced gardens; just north of town. *Thomson River:* excellent fishing and canoeing; 4 km s. *Rawson:* a town built to accommodate those who helped construct the nearby Thomson Dam. Mountain trail-rides are available; 8 km sw. *Erica:* visit this small timber town to see a timber-industry display at the Erica Hotel. The King of the Mountain Woodchop is held in town each Jan; 12 km sw. *Baw Baw National Park:* park areas accessible from Walhalla include the Aberfeldy River picnic and camping area; 12 km N. *See Moe. Moondarra State Park:* great for walks and picnics. Moondarra Reservoir is nearby; 30 km s. *4WD tours:* to gold-era 'suburbs' such as Coopers Creek and Erica. Tours can be organised through Mountain Top Experience, (03) 5134 6876. *Australian Alps Walking Track:* starts at Walhalla and goes for an incredible 655 km. It can be done in sections; details from visitor centre.

See also PHILLIP ISLAND & GIPPSLAND, pp. 36–7

Wangaratta

284 C2 | 289 G2

ℹ️ 100 Murphy St; 1800 801 065; www.visitwangaratta.com.au

📻 101.3 Oak FM, 106.5 FM ABC Local Radio

Wangaratta lies in a rich agricultural district in north-eastern Victoria that produces a diverse range of crops including kiwifruit, wine grapes, walnuts and wheat. An entry for both the Murray to the Mountains Rail Trail and the Great Alpine Road, it offers all the services of a bustling rural city while retaining the warm welcome of a country town. A short drive in any direction will lead to world-class wineries, gourmet food and some spectacular views.

Self-guide historical walk: historic sites and buildings, such as the majestic Holy Trinity cathedral, Vine Hotel Cellar Museum and the Wangaratta Historical Museum; details from visitor centre. *Wangaratta Cemetery:* headless body of infamous bushranger Daniel 'Mad Dog' Morgan is buried here; Tone Rd. *Wangaratta Exhibitions Gallery:* changing exhibitions by national and regional artists; Ovens St. *Brucks Textile Factory:* a factory outlet for Sheridan sheets; Sicily Ave. *Australian Country Spinners:* an outlet for local wool products; Textile Ave.

Wangaratta Trash and Treasure Market: Olympic Swimming Pool carpark, Swan St; each Sun. *Wangaratta Stitched Up Festival:* textile displays; June/July. *Wangaratta Show:* agricultural show; Oct. *Festival of Jazz:* well-known jazz festival; Oct/Nov.

Warby Range State Park The steep ranges of the 'Warbys', as they are known locally, provide excellent viewing points, especially from Ryan's Lookout. Other lookouts include the Pangarang Lookout, near Pine Gully Picnic Area, and Mt Glenrowan Lookout, the highest point of the Warbys at 513 m. There are well-marked tracks for bushwalkers and a variety of pleasant picnic spots amid open forests and woodlands, with wildflowers blossoming during the warmer months. 12 km w.

Eldorado Eldorado is a fascinating old goldmining township named after the mythical city of gold. The main relic of the gold era is a huge dredge, the largest in the Southern Hemisphere, which was built in 1936. There is a walking track with information boards around the lake where the dredge now sits.

TOWNS

The Eldorado Museum provides details of the town's mining past, alongside WW II relics and a gemstone collection. 20 km NE.

Wombi Toys: old-fashioned, handmade toys for sale; Whorouly; 25 km SE. **Reids Creek:** popular with anglers, gem fossickers and gold panners; near Beechworth; 28 km E. **Newton's Prickle Berry Farm:** pick your own blackberries and buy organic berry jams; Whitfield; 45 km S. **Scenic drives:** one goes for 307 km along the Great Alpine Rd through the alps to Bairnsdale. The road south leads through the beautiful King Valley and to Paradise Falls. A network of minor roads allows you to fully explore the area, including a number of tiny, unspoiled townships such as Whitfield, Cheshunt and Carboor. **Murray to the Mountains Rail Trail:** following historical railway lines with 94 km of bitumen sealed track, the trail ventures into pine forests, natural bushland and open valleys. It links several townships. Suitable for both cycling and walking; a gentle gradient makes the track appropriate for all ages and levels of fitness.

See also HIGH COUNTRY, pp. 52–3

Warburton

279 G3 | 282 C4 | 287 D4 | 289 F4

ℹ️ **Water Wheel Visitor and Information Centre,** 3400 Warburton Hwy; (03) 5966 9600; www.warburtononline.com

📻 99.1 Yarra Valley FM, 774 AM ABC Local Radio

Warburton was established when gold was discovered in the 1880s, but its picturesque location and proximity to Melbourne meant it quickly became a popular tourist town, with many guesthouses built over the years. It lies in the foothills of the Great Dividing Range, and the Yarra River flows through town. Its tree-lined banks provide great spots for picnics

and walks. Look closely at the river and you may spot an elusive platypus. There are many fine cafes and antique and craft shops in town.

🏠 **Information Centre:** local history display and an old-style, operating water wheel, 6 m in diameter. A wood-fired bakery is adjacent to the centre; Warburton Hwy. **River Walk:** 9 km return walk, following a pretty stretch of the Yarra River; starts at Signs Bridge on Warburton Hwy. **Upper Yarra Arts Centre:** cinema with regular screenings and a variety of live performances held during the year; Warburton Hwy. **Warburton Golf Course:** with great views across the river valley; Dammans Rd. **O'Shannassy Aqueduct Trail:** good walking and cycling track that follows the historic open channelled aqueduct; details from visitor centre.

🎆 **Film Festival:** Upper Yarra Arts Centre; June. **Winterfest:** wood festival; July.

🧭 **Yarra Ranges National Park** Here, tall mountain ash trees give way to pockets of cool temperate rainforest. Mt Donna Buang, a popular daytrip destination – especially during winter, when it is often snow-covered – is 17 km NW of Warburton. The recently built Rainforest Gallery on the southern slopes of the mountain features a treetop viewing platform and walkway. Night walk tours here reveal some of Victoria's unique nocturnal creatures. Acheron Way is a scenic 37 km drive north through the park to Marysville. Along the way are views of Mt Victoria and Ben Cairn. Drive starts 1 km E of town.

Yarra Centre: indoor sports and swimming; Yarra Junction, Warburton Hwy; 9 km SW. **Yarra Junction Historical Museum:** local history displays; open 1–5pm Sun or by appt; Warburton Hwy; 10 km SW. **Upper Yarra Reservoir:** picnic and camping facilities; 23 km NE. **Walk into History:** takes in the goldmining and timber region from Warburton East to Powelltown (25 km S); details from visitor centre. **Ada Tree:** a giant mountain ash over 300 years old; access from Powelltown. **Yellingbo State Fauna Reserve:** good for nature spotting. Home to the helmeted honeyeater, a state emblem; 25 km sw. **Vineyards:** several in the region, many with tastings and sales. They include the Yarra Burn Winery, the Five Oaks Vineyard and the Brahams Creek Winery. **Rail trails:** former railway tracks now used for walking, bikeriding or horseriding, the main one being the Lilydale to Warburton trail; details from visitor centre.

See also Yarra & Dandenongs, pp. 32–3

Warracknabeal

288 B1 | 291 B4

🛈 119 Scott St; (03) 5398 1632; www.wag.wimmera.com.au

📻 96.5 Triple H FM, 594 AM ABC Local Radio

The town's Aboriginal name means 'the place of the big red gums shading the watercourse', a name that is both beautifully descriptive and accurate, especially for the part of town around Yarriambiack Creek. Warracknabeal is a major service town at the centre of a wheat-growing district.

🏠 **Historical Centre:** includes a pharmaceutical collection, clocks, and antique furnishings of child's nursery; open afternoons; Scott St. **Black Arrow Tour:** a self-guide driving tour of historic buildings. **Walks:** including the Yarriambiack Creek Walk; details from visitor centre. **National Trust–classified buildings:** include the post office, the Warracknabeal Hotel and the original log-built town lock-up. **Lions Park:** by the pleasant Yarriambiack Creek with picnic spots and a flora and fauna park; Craig Ave.

🎆 **Y-Fest:** golf, horseracing, machinery and country music; Easter.

🧭 **North Western Agricultural Machinery Museum:** displays of farm machinery from the last 100 years; Henty Hwy; 3 km s.

See also Grampians & Central West, pp. 46–7

Warragul

279 H4 | 287 D4 | 289 F4

🛈 Gippsland Food and Wine, 123 Princes Hwy, Yarragon; 1300 133 309; www.bawbawcountry.com.au

📻 99.1 Yarra Valley FM, 104.7 Gippsland FM

Warragul is a thriving rural town with a growing commuter population, being the dairying centre that supplies much of Melbourne's milk. An excellent base to explore the delightful countryside including the Baw Baw snowfields and 'Gippsland Gourmet Country', it is surrounded by a patchwork of fields, emerald green hills, and dales complete with tiny bucolic hamlets. Travelling the web of back roads in the region, including the Old Sale Road, is a scenic indulgence. The town itself showcases 19th-century architecture, especially in the ornate facades and arched windows of Queen Street.

🏠 **West Gippsland Arts Centre** Part of the town's fantastic, architect-designed civic centre complex, the centre is a mecca for art lovers from across the state. It houses a good permanent collection of contemporary visual arts and is known for the variety of theatre productions and events held here throughout the year. Ask inside for a full program of events. Civic Pl; (03) 5624 2456.

🎆 **Harvest of Gippsland:** Mar. **Gippsland Field Days:** Mar/Apr.

🧭 **Mt Worth State Park** This park protects a rich variety of native flora including the silver wattle and the Victorian Christmas bush. The Giant's Circuit is a walk that takes in a massive

TOWNS

old mountain ash that is 7 m in circumference. Other walks include the Moonlight Creek and MacDonalds tracks, both of which are easily accessible. No camping is permitted. Contact Parks Victoria on 13 1963; access via Grand Ridge Rd; 22 km SE.

Yarragon Nestled in the foothills of the Strzelecki Ranges and with views of green rolling hills, Yarragon is a wonderful destination with an abundance of delightful shops and accommodation options. It boasts one of Gippsland's leading antique stores and a unique gallery renowned for its quality original artwork, exquisite jewellery, beautiful handblown glass and much more. Sample local wines and gourmet produce, including award-winning cheeses from Tarago River and Jindi Cheese. 13 km SE.

Gippsland Gourmet Country: the renowned 'Gippsland Gourmet Country' takes in lush green pastures and state forests to reveal a diverse range of superb gourmet delights. Previously known as 'Gourmet Deli Country', Gippsland Gourmet encompasses some of the best food and wine producers in the region. Sure to tempt your tastebuds and tantalise the senses; details from visitor centre. *Darnum Musical Village:* a complex of buildings housing a collection of musical instruments dating back to the 1400s; Princes Hwy; 8 km E. *Oakbank Angoras and Alpacas:* sales of yarn and knitted goods; near Drouin, 8 km W. *Waterfalls:* Glen Cromie, Drouin West (10 km NW); Glen Nayook, south of Nayook; and Toorongo Falls, just north of Noojee. *Neerim South:* visit Tarago Cheese Company for tastings and sales of top-quality cheeses, or enjoy a picnic or barbecue at the pleasant reserve near the Tarago Reservoir. Scenic drives through mountain country start from town; 17 km N. *Grand Ridge Road:* 132 km drive that starts at Seaview, 17 km S, and traverses the Strzelecki Ranges to Tarra–Bulga National Park *(see Yarram for park details).* *Nayook:* good fresh produce, a fruit-and-berry farm, and the Country Farm Perennials Nursery

and Gardens; 29 km N. *Childers:* Sunny Creek Fruit and Berry Farm, and Windrush Cottage; 31 km SE. *Noojee:* a mountain town featuring a historic trestle bridge and the Alpine Trout Farm; 39 km N.

See also PHILLIP ISLAND & GIPPSLAND, pp. 36–7

Warrnambool

see inset box on page 154

Wedderburn

288 D2 | 291 D5

ℹ️ Loddon Visitor Information Centre, Wedderburn Community Centre, 24 Wilson St; (03) 5494 3489; www.loddonalive.com.au

📻 91.1 FM ABC Local Radio, 99.1 Goldfields FM

Wedderburn, part of the 'Golden Triangle', was once one of Victoria's richest goldmining towns. Many large nuggets have been unearthed here in the past and – for some lucky people – continue to be discovered today. The town's annual Detector Jamboree, with music, historical re-enactments and family entertainment, is growing every year and recognises the importance of gold in the development of so many towns in Victoria.

🏠 **Hard Hill Tourist Reserve** Hard Hill is a fascinating former mining district with original gold diggings and Government Battery. There is a good walking track through the site, where old mining machinery can be seen. Hard Hill is in a pleasant bushland setting, and picnic facilities are provided. Nearby is a fully operational eucalyptus distillery offering tours and selling eucalyptus products. Northern outskirts of town.

Coach House Cafe and Museum: a 1910 building restored to its original appearance, with authentic, old-fashioned stock and coach-builders quarters; High St. *Bakehouse Pottery:* old bakery now used as a pottery, also home to gold pistachio nuts; High St. *Nardoo Creek Walk:* takes in the key historic buildings around town; map from visitor centre.

Wedderburn Detector Jamboree: gold festival; Mar long weekend. *Historic Engine Exhibition:* Sept.

Mt Korong: bushwalking; 16 km SE. *Wychitella Forest Reserve:* wildlife sanctuary set in mallee forest, home to mallee fowl; 16 km N. *Kooyoora State Park: see Inglewood for details. Fossickers Drive:* takes in goldmining sites, places of Aboriginal significance, local wineries and the Melville Caves; details from visitor centre.

See also GOLDFIELDS, pp. 44–5

Welshpool

289 G5

ℹ️ **Old Courthouse, 9 Rodgers St, Yarram;** (03) 5182 6553.

📻 89.5 3MFM South Gippsland, 828 AM ABC Local Radio

Welshpool is a small dairying community in South Gippsland. On the coast nearby, Port Welshpool is a deep-sea port servicing the local fishing and oil industries. Barry Beach Marine Terminal, a short distance west of Port Welshpool, services the offshore oil rigs in Bass Strait.

Port Welshpool This popular coastal town has all the natural attractions that a seaside village could want. It is frequented by families who enjoy the safe beaches and fabulous coastal walks, and has fantastic views across to Wilsons Promontory. Fishing enthusiasts should drop a line from the historic jetty, or try from a boat. The port's long link with the sea is detailed in the Port Welshpool

and District Maritime Museum, which exhibits shipping relics and local history displays as well. 2 km s.

Franklin River Reserve: great bushwalking with well-marked tracks; near Toora; 11 km w. *Agnes Falls:* the highest single-span falls in the state, spectacular after heavy rain; 19 km NW. *Scenic drive:* head west to see magnificent views from Mt Fatigue; off South Gippsland Hwy. *Fishing and boating:* excellent along the coast.

See also PHILLIP ISLAND & GIPPSLAND, pp. 36–7

Winchelsea

278 B4 | 286 C1 | 287 A4 | 288 D4

ℹ️ **Old Library, Willis St (Princes Hwy);** open 11am–4pm Fri–Sun; 1300 614 219; www.historicwinchelsea.com.au

📻 94.7 The Pulse FM, 774 AM ABC Local Radio

This charming little town on the Barwon River west of Geelong was first developed with cattle runs in the 1830s. Many of the historic buildings that grew from this development can still be seen around town, the most impressive being the nearby Barwon Park Homestead – a mansion built by famous settlers of the district, Thomas and Elizabeth Austin. Winchelsea soon became a key stopover for travellers taking the road from Colac to Geelong, and it still serves that purpose for travellers on the Princes Highway.

Barwon Bridge: an impressive arched bridge, built from stone in 1867; Princes Hwy. *Antiques and collectibles:* many shops in town that outline its history; Main St and Princes Hwy. *Winchelsea Historical Trail:* map available from visitor information centre, or check township information boards. *Barwon Hotel:* known locally as the 'bottom

WARRNAMBOOL

286 B4 | 288 B4

ℹ️ Adjacent Flagstaff Hill Maritime Museum, Merri St; (03) 5564 7837; www.warrnamboolinfo.com.au

📻 103.7 3WAY-FM, 594 AM ABC Local Radio

Warrnambool lies at the end of the Great Ocean Road on a notorious section of coastline that has seen over 80 shipwrecks. The best known was the *Loch Ard* in 1878, which claimed the lives of all but two of those on board. While the wreck site itself is closer to Port Campbell, impressive relics from the ship are held at the Flagstaff Hill Maritime Museum in town. Warrnambool, as Victoria's fifth largest city,

offers first-rate accommodation and dining as well as a fantastic swimming beach. The southern right whales that migrate here in winter are another major drawcard.

Flagstaff Hill Maritime Village This reconstructed 19th-century maritime village is complete with a bank, hotel, schoolhouse and surgery. There are also 2 operational lighthouses and an authentic keeper's cottage, now housing the Shipwreck Museum, where relics retrieved from the *Loch Ard* – including the famous earthenware Loch Ard Peacock – are kept. On display is the Flagstaff Hill tapestry, an intricate work depicting themes of Aboriginal history, sealing, whaling, exploration, immigration and settlement. At night, visitors can watch the

and market in front of former Fletcher Jones factory; Raglan Pde, eastern approach to town. *History House:* local history museum; open 1st Sun each month or by appt; Gilles St. *Portuguese Padrao:* monument to early Portuguese explorers; Cannon Hill, southern end of Liebig St. *Heritage walk:* 3 km self-guide walk taking in the many historic buildings around town; details from visitor centre. *Hopkins River:* great for fishing and boating, with Blue Hole, at the river's mouth, a popular spot for family swimming and rockpool exploration. Cruises are available; east of town. *Proudfoots Boathouse:* National Trust–classified boathouse on the Hopkins. *Wollaston Bridge:* an unusual bridge, built over 100 years ago; northern outskirts of town. *Tours and charters:* fishing, whale-watching and diving tours (including shipwreck sites); details from visitor centre.

Trash and treasure market: showgrounds on Koroit St; each Sun. *Hillside market:* Flagstaff Hill; operates throughout summer. *Wunta Fiesta:* family entertainment, food stalls and music; Feb. *Tarerer Festival:* Indigenous culture and music; Mar. *Racing Carnival:* May. *Fun 4 Kids:* children's festival; June. *Melbourne–Warrnambool Cycling Classic:* Oct. *Flower Shows:* held in spring.

Tower Hill State Game Reserve This is a beautiful piece of preserved bushland featuring an extinct volcano and a crater lake, with tiny islands. Nature walk starts at the Worn Gundidj Visitor Centre in the reserve. For further information contact (03) 5561 5315; 12 km NW, just after the turn-off to Koroit.

Logans Beach Each year in June, southern right whales return to the waters along the south coast of Australia to give birth, raise their young and start the breeding cycle again. Each female seems to have a favourite spot to give birth, which means that many familiar faces keep reappearing at Warrnambool's Logans

sound-and-light show 'Shipwrecked', which details the story of the *Loch Ard*. Merri St; (03) 5559 4600.

Main beach: a safe swimming beach, with a walkway along the foreshore from the Breakwater to near the mouth of the Hopkins River. *Lake Pertobe Adventure Playground:* a great spot for family picnics; opposite main beach, Pertobe Rd. *Art Gallery:* local artwork, plus European and avant-garde collections; Timor St. *Customs House Gallery:* Gilles St. *Botanic Gardens:* pretty regional gardens designed by Guilfoyle (a curator of Melbourne's Royal Botanic Gardens) in 1879; Botanic Rd. *Fletcher Jones Gardens/Mill Markets:* award-winning landscaped gardens

WARRNAMBOOL continued

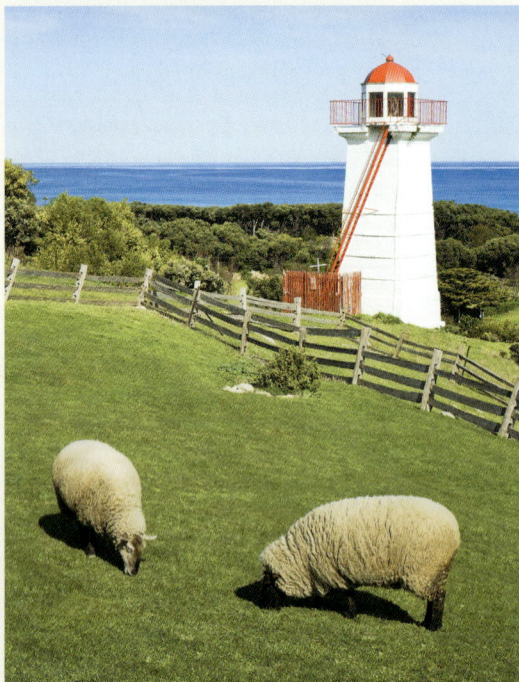

SHEEP OUTSIDE THE FLAGSTAFF HILL MARITIME VILLAGE

Beach. The beach features a purpose-built viewing platform above the sand dunes (binoculars or telescopes are recommended), and the local visitor centre releases information on whale sightings daily.

Allansford Cheeseworld: for cheese tastings and sales; 10 km E. *Hopkins Falls:* scenic picnic spot, particularly spectacular in winter after heavy rain. In spring hundreds of baby eels migrate up the falls, creating a most unusual sight; 16 km NE. *Cudgee Creek Wildlife Park:* deer, crocodiles and other native fauna, plus an aviary. Picnic and barbecue facilities are provided; Cudgee; 18 km E. *Koroit:* National Trust–classified buildings, good local arts and crafts shops, botanic gardens and an Irish festival in Apr; 19 km NW.

See also SOUTH-WEST COAST, pp. 42–3

pub' of the town, offers country style; Main St. *Winchelsea Tavern:* recently renovated Art Deco 'top pub'; Princes Hwy. *Old Shire Hall:* beautifully restored bluestone building, now housing popular tearooms; Princes Hwy. *Old Library:* houses the visitor information centre; Princes Hwy. *Marjorie Lawrence Trail:* details the life of one of the world's most adored dramatic sopranos from the 1900s; details from visitor centre.

Winchelsea Festival: wool shearing, dog trials, wool classing, children's activities, local produce and market stall, plus more; Nov.

Barwon Park Homestead Only the greatest estate would satisfy Elizabeth Austin, and her husband, Thomas, acquiesced. Barwon Park, built in 1869, was the biggest mansion in the Western District. Featuring 42 rooms furnished largely with original pieces, the bluestone building is an impressive example of 19th-century design. The name Austin might be familiar: Thomas Austin reputedly imported the first of Australia's devastating rabbit population and Elizabeth Austin contributed to major charities, and established the Austin Hospital in Melbourne. Open 11am–4pm Wed and Sun; Inverleigh Rd; (03) 5267 2209; 3 km N.

Country Dahlias Gardens: beautiful gardens, best viewed during spring, with sales of dahlia plants; open Feb–Apr; Mathison Rd; 5 km s. *Killwarrie Cottage:* rose garden display, home-grown vegetables; open Nov–Mar; 7 km sw.

See also SOUTH-WEST COAST, pp. 42–3

Wodonga

285 E1 | 289 G2 | 290 A2

i Gateway Visitor Information Centre, Lincoln Causeway; 1300 796 222; www.destinationalburywodonga.com.au

106.5 FM ABC Local Radio, 107.3 Ten-73 Border FM

Wodonga and its twin town, Albury (in New South Wales), sit astride the Murray River. There are many attractions around the Murray and nearby Lake Hume, making the region a popular holiday destination.

Gateway Village: includes woodwork shops and cafes. Also houses the visitor centre; Lincoln Causeway. *Huon Hill Lookout:* maps from visitor centre. *Sumsion Gardens:* a pretty lakeside park with walking track, picnic and barbecue facilities; Church St. *Tennis Centre:* the largest grass court centre of its kind in Australia; Melrose Dr.

Wodonga Craft Market: Woodland Gr; 1st Sat each month. *Farmers market:* Gateway Village; 2nd Sat each month. *Wodonga Show:* Mar. *In My Backyard Festival:* raises environmental awareness; Mar. *Wine and Food Festival:* Oct.

Mt Granya State Park The park displays a great contrast between steep, rocky slopes and open eucalypt forests. Bushwalking is a popular pastime and the display of wildflowers in spring is magnificent. There is a pleasant picnic spot at Cottontree Creek, and a short walk leads to the Mt Granya summit, which offers spectacular views of the alps. Murray River Rd; 56 km E.

Military Museum: Bandiana; 4 km SE. *Hume Weir:* good spot for walks and picnics; 15 km E. *Tours:* winery and fishing tours, as well as scenic drives through the Upper Murray region, the mountain valleys of north-east Victoria and the Riverina; details from visitor centre.

See also HIGH COUNTRY, pp. 52–3

Wonthaggi

279 F5 | 287 D5 | 289 F5

i Watt St; 1300 854 334; www.visitbasscoast.com

88.1 3MFM South Gippsland, 100.7 FM ABC Local Radio

Once the main supplier of coal to the Victorian Railways, Wonthaggi, near the beachside town of Cape Paterson, is South Gippsland's largest town. There are good tourist facilities in town and a number of pretty beaches nearby.

Bass Coast Rail Trail: 16 km trail that runs between Wonthaggi and Anderson. Suitable for walking and cycling, it is the only coastal rail trail in Victoria with landscape that varies from flat farmland and bushland to rugged coastline.

Energy and Innovation Festival: Mar.

State Coal Mine The demand for black coal created a thriving industry in Wonthaggi from 1909 until 1968, and the mine site has been retained to show visitors the lifestyle and working conditions of the miners. Daily underground tours offer close-up views of the coalface, a short walk into the East Area Mine and a cable-hauled skip ride to the surface. Above ground, visit the museum for an introduction to the history of the mine and

TOWNS

RADIO STATION   IN TOWN   WHAT'S ON   NEARBY

of Wonthaggi itself, or take a walk around the historic buildings. Inquiries (03) 5672 3053 or Parks Victoria on 13 1963; Cape Paterson Rd; 1.5 km s.

Cape Paterson: waters offshore are protected by Bunurong Marine and Coastal Park and are good for surfing, swimming, snorkelling and scuba diving; 8 km s. **George Bass Coastal Walk:** starts at Kilcunda; 11 km NW. Ask at visitor centre for details of other walks. **Gippsland Gourmet Country:** takes in central Gippsland's gourmet food and wine producers; details from visitor centre.

See also PHILLIP ISLAND & GIPPSLAND, pp. 36–7

Woodend

278 D1 | 283 D4 | 287 B3 | 289 E3

ⓘ High St, beside Five Mile Creek; (03) 5427 2033 or 1800 244 711; www.visitmacedonranges.com

📻   100.7 Highlands FM, 774 AM ABC Local Radio

During the gold rushes of the 1850s, travellers sought refuge from mud, bogs and bushrangers at the 'wood's end' around Five Mile Creek, where a town eventually grew. In the late 19th century Woodend became a resort town, and its lovely gardens and proximity to spectacular natural sights, such as Hanging Rock and Mount Macedon, still make it a popular daytrip and weekend getaway for visitors from Melbourne.

🏛 **Bluestone Bridge:** built in 1862, the bridge crosses Five Mile Creek on the northern outskirts of town. **Clock Tower:** built as a WW I memorial; Calder Hwy. **Courthouse:** historic structure built in 1870; Forest St.

🎪 **Craft market:** 3rd Sun each month Sept–May. **Woodend Winter Arts Festival:** June. **Macedon Ranges Budburst Festival:** held throughout the wine district; Nov.

🧭 **Hanging Rock** A massive rock formation made famous by *Picnic at Hanging Rock*, the novel by Joan Lindsay that was later made into a film. The story, about schoolgirls who mysteriously vanished while on a picnic in the reserve, became something of a legend. There is certainly something eerie about Hanging Rock with its strange rock formations and narrow tracks through dense bushland. Hanging Rock is renowned for the annual races held at its base, especially the New Year's Day and Australia Day races. Other events include a Vintage Car Rally and Harvest Picnic, both held in Feb. The reserve also has a discovery centre and cafe. Access from South Rock Rd, off Calder Hwy; 8 km NE.

Macedon: a town at the foot of Mt Macedon. Home to the Church of the Resurrection, with stained-glass windows designed by Leonard French, and excellent plant nurseries; 8 km SE. **Mt Macedon:** a township located higher up the mountain, 2 km from Macedon, renowned for its beautiful gardens, many open to the public in autumn and spring. **Macedon Regional Park:** bushwalking and scenic drives. The Camels Hump marks the start of a signposted walk to the summit of the mountain where there stands a huge WW I memorial cross. Access via turn-off after Mt Macedon township. **Wineries:** several in region include Hanging Rock Winery at Newham; 10 km NE; details from visitor centre. **Gisborne:** a variety of craft outlets. Gisborne Steam Park holds a steam-train rally each May; 16 km SE. **Glen Erin at Romsey/Cope-Williams Winery:** tastings and sales, surrounded by charming English-style gardens, tennis courts and a cricket green; Romsey; 19 km E. **Lancefield:** historic buildings and wineries. Mad Gallery and Bankart Gallery offer contemporary and fine art, respectively. The town is also home to a woodchopping competition in Mar and a farmers market, for local produce, 4th Sat each month; 25 km NE. **Monegeetta:** in town is the Mintaro Homestead, a smaller replica of

Melbourne's Government House, but not open to the public; 27 km E via Romsey.

See also Spa & Garden Country, pp. 38–9

Wycheproof

288 C1 | 291 C4

i **Wycheproof Community Resource Centre, 280 Broadway; (03) 5493 7455; www.wycheproof.vic.au**

📻 99.1 Goldfields FM, 102.1 FM ABC Local Radio

Wycheproof is renowned for the long wheat trains that travel right down the middle of the main street, towing up to 60 carriages behind them. There are many historic buildings in town, as well as rare, old peppercorn trees. Mount Wycheproof, at a mere 43 metres, has been named the smallest mountain in the world.

🏠 **Mt Wycheproof** A walking track leads up and around the mountain. Emus and kangaroos can be seen up close in a fauna park at the mountain's base.

Willandra Museum: farm machinery, old buildings and historical memorabilia; open by appt; Calder Hwy. *Centenary Park:* aviaries, 2 log cabins and barbecue facilities; Calder Hwy.

🎆 *Music on the Mount:* Oct. *Racing Carnival:* Oct/Nov.

🧭 *Tchum Lakes:* artificially created lakes, great for fishing and watersports dependent on water levels; 23 km W. *Birchip:* visitors to town are greeted by the town's beloved 'Big Red' mallee bull in the main street. Also in town is the Soldiers Memorial Park with large, shady Moreton Bay fig trees, a great spot for a picnic; 31 km W.

See also Grampians & Central West, pp. 46–7

Yackandandah

285 E2 | 289 G2

i The Athenaeum, High St; (02) 6027 1988; www.uniqueyackandandah.com.au

📻 101.3 Oak FM, 106.5 FM ABC Local Radio

Yackandandah, with its avenues of English trees and traditional buildings, is so rich with history that the entire town is National Trust–classified. It is situated south of Wodonga in the heart of the north-east goldfields region. In fact, many of the town's creeks still yield alluvial gold.

🏠 *Historic buildings:* the post office, several banks and general stores, with the Bank of Victoria now preserved as a museum, open Sun and school holidays. Explore these and other buildings on a self-guide walk; details from visitor centre; High St. *Ray Riddington's Premier Store and Gallery:* displays and sales of local art; High St. *The Old Stone Bridge:* a beautiful old structure, built in 1857; High St. *Arts and crafts:* many outlets in town, including Yackandandah Workshop, cnr Kars and Hammond sts, and Wildon Thyme, High St. *Antiques:* Finders Bric-a-Brac and Old Wares, High St; Frankly Speaking, High St; and Vintage Sounds Restoration, specialising in antique gramophones, radios and telephones, Windham St. *Rosedale Garden and Tea Rooms:* Devonshire teas; Kars St.

🎆 *Folk Festival:* 3rd weekend Mar. *Spring Migration Festival:* Sept. *Flower Show:* Oct.

🧭 *Kars Reef Goldmine:* take a tour of this fascinating old goldmine, or try your hand at gold panning (licence required); details of tours from visitor centre; Kars St. *Lavender Patch Plant Farm:* sales of plants and lavender products; Beechworth Rd; 4 km W. *Kirbys Flat Pottery and Gallery:* Kirbys Flat Rd; open weekends or by appt; 4 km S. *Indigo Valley:*

TOWNS

a picturesque area with a scenic drive leading along the valley floor to Barnawatha; 6 km NW. *Allans Flat:* a great destination for food lovers, with The Vienna Patisserie for coffee, ice-cream and delicious Austrian cakes (closed Tues). Also here are Parks Wines and Schmidt's Strawberry Winery, both with tastings and sales; 10 km NE. *Wombat Valley Tramways:* a small-gauge railway; open Easter or by appt for groups; Leneva; 16 km NE.

See also HIGH COUNTRY, pp. 52–3

Yarra Glen

279 F2 | 282 B3 | 287 C3 | 289 F3

ⓘ **Yarra Valley Visitor Information Centre, Old Courthouse, Harker St, Healesville; (03) 5962 2600; www.yarraglen.com.au**

📻 99.1 Yarra Valley FM, 774 AM ABC Local Radio

Yarra Glen is in the heart of the Yarra Valley wine region, nestled between the Yarra River and the Great Dividing Range. A gorgeous area featuring lush, vine-covered hills and fertile valleys; all within easy reach of Melbourne. Indulgence – in fine wines and top-quality local produce – is definitely the focus here. Fascinating antique, specialty gift and clothing shops, and not forgetting restaurants, are also in town to entice. For the more adventurous, Yarra Glen is home to hot-air ballooning, scenic helicopter flights over the valley and even skydiving at nearby Coldstream airfield. The bushfire of February 2009 came very close to the township of Yarra Glen, and some businesses and townsfolk were directly affected.

🏛 *Yarra Glen Grand Hotel:* imposing heritage-listed and National Trust–classified hotel, built in 1888 with a recently refurbished restaurant, stands like a sentinel in the main street; Bell St. *Hargreaves Hill Brewing Co:* the old Colonial Bank building houses a fine-dining restaurant specialising in local produce

and an extensive choice of Yarra Valley and European boutique beers; Bell St. *Tea Leaves:* a treasure chest containing Melbourne's largest range of premium-quality teas, novelty teapots and tea accessories: Bell St. *Den of Antiquities and Yarra Valley Antique Centre:* amazing establishments with large collections of genuine antique furniture, china and glass, vintage radios and other collectibles; Bell St. *Yarra Glen Railway Station:* old station on the 1888 Healesville–Lilydale railway line, rebuilt in 1915 and now being restored as part of the Yarra Valley Tourist Railway; King St.

🎆 *Yarra Valley Farmers Market:* Historic Barn at Yering Station; 3rd Sun each month. *Gulf Station Farmers Market:* Gulf Station Historic Farm; 4th Sun each month. *Craft market:* racecourse; 1st Sun each month Sept–June. *Grape Grazing Festival:* wine, food and music throughout the valley; Feb. *Shortest Lunch:* midwinter fine food and wine at the smaller boutique wineries; June. *Melba Festival and Melba Wine Trail:* arts, culture, food and wine event; Oct.

🧭 **Yarra Valley Wine Region** Victoria's first vines were planted in the Yarra Valley by the Ryrie brothers in 1838 – these plantings would develop into Yering Station, today home to one of the region's finest wineries and restaurants. It produces excellent shiraz viognier as well as award-winning pinot noir. With over 55 cellar door outlets and around 100 wineries, the Yarra Valley is also home to other exceptional names. The De Bortoli Winery in Dixons Creek is Australia's oldest family-owned winery; Domaine Chandon, owned by the legendary Moët & Chandon, makes sophisticated sparkling wines that can be enjoyed in the glass-walled tasting room overlooking the vines. To combine wine with art, head to TarraWarra Estate, well known for its chardonnay and pinot noir, and its modern gallery that holds exhibitions of work by Australian greats from Arthur Boyd to Peter Booth; *see Healesville*. Excellent restaurants abound throughout the valley, many at wineries. Tour companies offer bus tours and personalised winery tours by car through the Yarra Valley region. The ever-popular Grape Grazing Festival is celebrated each Feb, and the smaller wineries' Shedfest wine festival is held in Oct. Winery map available from visitor centre.

Kinglake National Park Kinglake's beautiful messmate forests, fern gullies, panoramic lookouts and bushwalking tracks were devastated by the bushfire of February 2009, and the park is closed until further notice. Phone Parks Victoria on 13 1963 for an update on progress on the park's reopening.

Gulf Station: this National Trust–owned pastoral property, preserved as it was during pioneering days, features old-fashioned farming implements and early animal breeds; open Wed–Sun and public holidays; 2 km NE. *Yarra Valley Dairy:* a working dairy with sales of specialty cheeses, clotted cream and local produce; 4 km S. *Ponyland Equestrian Centre:* trail-rides and riding lessons; 7 km W. *Sugarloaf Reservoir Park:* sailing, fishing and walking, with barbecue and picnic facilities available; 10 km W. *Yarra Valley Regional Food Trail:* a self-guide tour, taking in the many gourmet food outlets in the region; details from visitor centre.

See also YARRA & DANDENONGS, pp. 32–3

Yarram

289 G5

ⓘ Old Courthouse, 9 Rodgers St; (03) 5182 6553; www.tourismwellington.com.au

📻 89.5 3MFM South Gippsland, 100.7 FM ABC Local Radio

Yarram is deep in the dairy country of South Gippsland, and at the heart of some of its most beautiful locales, from the splendour of Ninety Mile Beach to the refreshingly cool atmosphere of Tarra–Bulga National Park. Yarram was originally settled on a swamp, and its name is derived from an Aboriginal word meaning 'plenty of water'. In town are some notable examples of early architecture, including the recently restored Regent Theatre and the historic courthouse.

🏠 *Regent Theatre:* built in 1930, this theatre has been wonderfully restored. Cinemas operate on weekends and school holidays; Commercial Rd.

🎆 *Tarra Festival:* Easter.

🧭 **Tarra–Bulga National Park** Tarra–Bulga is a lovely, tranquil park where visitors will be amazed by the spectacular river and mountain views. Fern Gully Walk, starting from the Bulga picnic ground, takes in the dense temperate rainforests of mountain ash, myrtle and sassafras. The walk leads across a suspension bridge high among the treetops. A walk to Cyathea or Tarra falls, surrounded by lush fern gullies, completes the rainforest experience. Keep an eye out for rosellas, lyrebirds and the occasional koala. The Tarra–Bulga Visitor Centre is on Grand Ridge Rd near Balook; from Yarram, access the park from Tarra Valley Rd; 20 km NW.

Won Wron Forest: great for walks, with wildflowers in spring; Hyland Hwy; 16 km N. *Beaches:* there are many attractive beaches in the region, including Manns, for fishing, 16 km SE; McLoughlins, 23 km E; and Woodside Beach, which is patrolled in summer; 29 km E. *Tarra Valley:* there are many attractive gardens in the region, including Eilean Donan Gardens and Riverbank Nursery; located just north-west of Yarram. *Scenic drive:* a 46 km circuit goes from Yarram through Hiawatha and takes

TOWNS

---

in Minnie Ha Ha Falls on Albert River, where picnic and camping facilities are provided.

See also **PHILLIP ISLAND & GIPPSLAND, pp. 36–7**

Yarrawonga

284 B1 | 289 F1

ℹ️ Irvine Pde; (03) 5744 1989 or 1800 062 260; www.yarrawongamulwala.com.au

📻 101.3 Oak FM, 106.5 FM ABC Local Radio

Yarrawonga and its sister town Mulwala, across the New South Wales border, are separated by a pleasant stretch of the Murray River and the attractive Lake Mulwala. The 6000-hectare lake was created in 1939 during the building of the Yarrawonga Weir, which is central to irrigation in the Murray Valley. Yarrawonga's proximity to such great water features has made it a popular holiday resort. The sandy beaches and calm waters are ideal for watersports, and are also home to abundant wildlife.

🏠 *Yarrawonga and Mulwala foreshores:* great locations for walks and picnics, with shady willows, water slides, barbecue facilities and boat ramps. *Canning A.R.T.S Gallery:* work by local artists; Belmore St. *Tudor House Clock Museum:* Lynch St. *Cruises:* daily cruises along the Murray on paddleboats *Paradise Queen* or *Lady Murray*; depart from Bank St.

🎆 *Rotary Market:* local crafts and second-hand goods; showgrounds; 3rd Sun each month. *Powerboat Racing:* May. *Murray Marathon:* Dec.

🧭 *Fyffe Field Wines:* tastings and sales; Murray Valley Hwy; 19 km w. *Fishing:* Murray River for Murray cod and yellow-belly. *Guided tours:* local wineries; book at visitor centre.

See also **GOULBURN & MURRAY, pp. 50–1**

Yea

279 F1 | 282 B1 | 287 D2 | 289 F3

ℹ️ Old Railway Station, Station St; (03) 5797 2663; www.murrinditourism.com.au

📻 88.9 UGFM Upper Goulburn Community Radio, 97.7 FM ABC Local Radio

This town sits by the Yea River, a tributary of the Goulburn River. Hume and Hovell, the first explorers through the region, discovered this wonderfully fertile area – a discovery that led in part to the settlement of the rest of Victoria. Near the Yea–Tallarook Road there are beautiful gorges and fern gullies, a reminder of what Yea looked like thousands of years ago.

🏠 *Historic buildings:* Beaufort Manor, High St; General Store, now a restaurant, High St. *Wetlands Walk:* sightings of abundant birdlife and glider possums; eastern outskirts of town.

🎆 *Market:* local craft and produce; Main St; 1st Sat each month Sept–May. *Autumn Fest:* Mar.

🧭 *Murrindindi Reserve:* see the impressive Murrindindi Cascades and a variety of wildlife including wombats, platypus and lyrebirds; 11 km SE. *Ibis Rookery:* Kerrisdale; 17 km w. *Flowerdale Winery:* Whittlesea–Yea Rd; 23 km sw. *Grotto:* a beautiful old church set in the hillside; Caveat; 27 km N. *Berry King Farm:* pick your own fruit; Two Hills Rd, Glenburn; 28 km s. *Wilhelmina Falls:* spectacular falls and a great spot for walks and picnics; access via Melba Hwy; 32 km s. *Kinglake National Park:* 32 km s; *see Yarra Glen*. *Mineral springs:* Dropmore, off back road to Euroa; 47 km N. *Scenic drives:* many in the region. Best time is Aug–Sept when wattles are in bloom; maps from visitor centre.

See also **GOULBURN & MURRAY, pp. 50–1**

STRAWBERRY COULANT FILLED WITH WHITE
CHOCOLATE SOUP AND STRAWBERRY KEBABS,
VUE DE MONDE, MELBOURNE

victoria

Town entries are ordered alphabetically,
with places nearby listed at the end.

LEGEND

$	=	under $15
$$	=	$15–$25
$$$	=	$25–$35
$$$$	=	$35–$45
$$$$$	=	over $45

For the average price of a main meal

BYO AVAILABLE

CREDIT CARDS ACCEPTED

DISABLED ACCESS

DRESS CODE APPLIES

FAMILY FRIENDLY

LICENSED

OUTDOOR DINING

VEGETARIAN OPTIONS

Melbourne

ABLA'S

$$$
LEBANESE
Map ref. p. 6 D2

Owner/chef Abla Amad has been pleasing diners with her simple yet superb, authentic Lebanese cuisine in this unpretentious terrace house for 30 years. Regulars know to start with traditional dips such as creamy hummus and eggplant baba ganoush, super-fresh tabouli salad and homemade labna (yoghurt cheese), before moving on to perhaps kibbeh meatballs or tangy mint-flavoured cabbage rolls, lemon-marinated chicken kebabs or delicious chicken with almonds and rice. At weekends gather up your friends and literally make a feast of it – only banquets are served on Thursday, Friday and Saturday nights, with some 13 courses. Given notice, Abla will also prepare specific dishes and vegetarian banquets.

109 Elgin St, Carlton; (03) 9347 0006; open Thurs–Fri for lunch and Mon–Sat for dinner; www.ablas.com.au

BABKA BAKERY/CAFE

$
BAKERY CAFE
Map ref. p. 6 D2

If the queues that regularly spill from Babka's front door aren't hint enough of something special at this Brunswick Street bakery and cafe, then the aroma of freshly baked loaves, pies and cakes should have you joining the line. Small, closely packed and wonderfully homey, Babka takes Eastern Europe as its major influence – spot the graffiti-style Babushkas painted on the shop's exterior. The short, regularly changing menu is chock full of stroganoff, borscht, potato dumplings and sweet, cheesy blintzes. There are excellent sandwiches too – BLT with dill mayo or corned beef and house-made pickles – served on Babka's beautifully textured bread. Buy a loaf on the way out and relive the memory.

358 Brunswick St, Fitzroy; (03) 9416 0091; open Tues–Sun for breakfast and lunch

BECCO $$$$

ITALIAN
Map ref. p. 13

For more than a decade this big-hearted and soulful Italian eatery has captivated its loyal clientele of diners and wine lovers. The bar serves a clever concoction of options, including fantastic cocktails, but the dining room with its open kitchen is the hub of this spacious establishment. The menu of pasta dishes and meaty mains delights newcomers and entertains regulars with a feast of adventurous specials. Try the popular chilli-flour-dusted calamari, a perfect beef carpaccio or roast duck with muscatel sauce, and don't miss the caramel-laced panna cotta for dessert.

11–25 Crossley St; (03) 9663 3000; open Mon–Sat for lunch and dinner; www.becco.com.au

BRUNETTI $

ITALIAN BAKERY
Map ref. pp. 8, 6 D2

A bustling piece of loud, swirling Roman chaos in the midst of Melbourne's Little Italy, Brunetti is one of the city's quintessential cafe experiences. Multiple shopfronts, a large outdoor seating area and a sensational range of Italian-style cakes, pastries, breads and gelati are certainly part of the charm, but top-notch people-watching is also one of Brunetti's best attributes. Some of the hot food options can be hit-and-miss but the coffee is usually good and the sweet stuff – particularly Italian classics like cream-filled cannoli pastries – hit the spot in an authentically satisfying manner. As some locals

like to say, Brunetti is not so much a cafe as a state of mind.

194–204 Faraday St, Carlton; (03) 9347 2801; open daily for breakfast, lunch and dinner. Also Brunetti City Square, 214 Flinders La, (03) 9663 8085; and Brunetti Camberwell, 1/3 Prospect Hill Rd, (03) 9882 3100; www.brunetti.com.au

CAFE DI STASIO $$$$

ITALIAN
Map ref. p. 6 D5

At this iconic Latin restaurant on St Kilda's colourful Fitzroy Street, waiters with attitude serve fine authentic dishes. Tables are close, adding to the intimacy, and the feeling is one of pure theatre – from the outstretched hands that greet you as door handles on entering, to the facemask lamps adorning the wall. Do consider the daily specials – often more than a dozen – before perusing the printed menu. Regulars come for the freshly shucked oysters, fresh pasta of the day, calamari with radicchio or the house specialties – crayfish omelette, roast duckling and braised guinea fowl. The two-course lunch menu with a good selection of dishes and a glass of wine is great value.

31 Fitzroy St, St Kilda; (03) 9525 3999; open daily for lunch and dinner; www.distasio.com.au

CLAYPOTS $$$

SEAFOOD
Map ref. pp. 6 D2, 6 D5

This ultra-casual seafood specialist does a roaring trade, despite not taking bookings – so come early. In summer, head for a shared table in the taverna-style pebbled courtyard at the rear. The fish is bought fresh daily, with the blackboard menu based on what is available – perhaps trevally baked with couscous, fiery harissa and chermoula marinade, or swordfish filled with olive tapenade butter. Most dishes are whole fish meant to be shared, served grilled, poached, steamed or baked. If you like a bit more protein on your plate, opt for the seafood chilli stir-fry with prawns, mussels, pipis and clams. The eponymous claypots are ideal for individual serves with tasty seafood stews served on either rice or couscous.

213 Barkly St, St Kilda; (03) 9534 1282; open daily for dinner. Also at 153 Gertrude St, Fitzroy; (03) 9416 4116

CUMULUS INC $$

MODERN AUSTRALIAN
Map ref. p. 13

Housed in a beautifully designed former gallery space on the CBD's hippest small thoroughfare, Cumulus Inc could rest on its good-looking laurels and still attract a crowd. But whether you are sitting at one of the two bars – one black metal, the other white marble – ensconced on a banquette or at the round communal table, appearance becomes less important once the clever, skilfully cooked food begins to arrive. Oyster lovers are treated to a menu of often rare and always freshly shucked bivalves, while the list of shareable dishes might combine obscure and familiar ingredients like guinea fowl terrine, a fabulous salad of cracked wheat served with barberries or a simple golden chicken broth. A place of style and substance.

45 Flinders La; (03) 9650 1445; open Mon–Sat for breakfast, lunch and dinner; www.cumulusinc.com.au

EZARD $$$$$

MODERN AUSTRALIAN
Map ref. p. 8

Summer or winter, this basement venue has a good feel – cool and sleek when the mercury rises, cosy and welcoming in the cooler months. Chef and co-owner Teage Ezard's individual style of contemporary 'freestyle' cuisine is worth lingering over. While the menu is constantly evolving, some things never change – like Japanese-inspired oyster shooters, fried pork hock with chilli caramel, and the signature Sichuan duck. Desserts are knockouts: crème brûlée with Jerusalem artichoke and truffle oil, pineapple tart with coconut sorbet, and honeycrunch ice-cream with toasted gingerbread. Staff are knowledgeable and professional, and a full vegetarian/vegan degustation menu is available.

187 Flinders La; (03) 9639 6811; open weekdays for lunch and Mon–Sat for dinner; www.ezard.com.au

FLOWER DRUM $$$$$

CHINESE
Map ref. p. 13

Flower Drum is Melbourne's iconic Cantonese restaurant, the kind of place where visiting dignitaries reserve a table when they are in town and locals book for a special occasion. Impeccable produce, cooking perfection and discreet service for over 30 years have contributed to its formidable reputation. Dishes such as crayfish with ginger are magnificently fresh, and no diner should leave without trying the famous Peking duck. Bookings are essential, and often lunch at weekends can be a less busy option.

17 Market La; (03) 9662 3655; open daily for lunch and dinner; www.flower-drum.com

FRANCE SOIR $$$

FRENCH
Map ref. p. 6 D4

It's best to book at a place like this – they turned Mick Jagger away because they didn't have a table free. France Soir has been serving reliably great French food with flair and panache for more than 20 years. The menu never changes, the frenetic pace rarely shifts gear and the French accents of the staff just get a tad thicker. The day's specials are always worth considering and are written on

WHERE TO EAT

a mirrored wall. There might be scallops in a beurre blanc with basil but many come here simply for the steaks – rib eye, Scotch and eye fillet, porterhouse or the steak frite with French fries and green salad (their signature). Traditional desserts are a treat.

11 Toorak Rd, South Yarra; (03) 9866 8569; open daily for lunch and dinner; www.france-soir.com.au

GIUSEPPE ARNALDO & SONS $$$
ITALIAN
Map ref. p. 16

Walk into the riverside Giuseppe Arnaldo & Sons and you are immediately transported to a little slice of modern-day Rome. This eatery can be everything to everybody – a bar or trattoria, perfect for an intimate tête-à-tête or for a lively group. Tiled walls, grand yellow marble tables and handwritten feature walls add colour to an otherwise chic black expansive space. Authentic traditional dishes are best shared: perhaps a plate of mixed salumi meats to start, followed by grilled scallops with watercress and radish salad, and perfectly al dente spaghetti with crab, tomato and chilli baked in a paper bag. With a no-bookings policy, be prepared to wait or come early.

Riverside, Crown Complex, Southbank; (03) 9694 7400; open daily for lunch and dinner; www.idrb.com/giuseppe_main_flash.html

IL FORNAIO $$
ITALIAN BAKERY
Map ref. p. 6 D5

A constant stream of food lovers is attracted throughout the day to this smart Italian bakery-cum-bistro. The polished concrete floor and backstage ambience lure colourful locals and the odd celebrity for early breakfast pastries and rustic breads, morning or afternoon coffees and light lunch or brunch dishes. Breakfast specials might be grilled sardines on eggplant relish with toasted sourdough, hearty cheese kransky

on toasted baguette with Dijon mustard and caramelised onions, or corn fritters with fried free-range egg, leg ham, rocket and relish. For the sweet-toothed there's toasted French brioche with mixed berry compote and vanilla ice-cream. A daily risotto and pasta as well as popular steak sandwiches are also available.

2 Acland St, St Kilda; (03) 9534 2922; open daily for breakfast and lunch; www.ilfornaio.net.au

JACQUES REYMOND $$$$$
MODERN FRENCH
Map ref. p. 7 E5

Distinguished French chef Jacques Reymond transports guests from fine to grand dining. This award-winning restaurant, graciously housed in an elegant, beautifully restored 19th-century mansion overlooking a courtyard garden, exudes excellence from every one of its dining rooms. Jacques Reymond's passion for experimenting with French cuisine with imaginative Asian tones is responsible for the sublime menu of dishes like highland venison or kingfish with miso, green pea and mint purée. Various degustation and vegetarian menus are available, including a seven-course degustation tasting menu and three-, four- or five-course à la carte menus.

78 Williams Rd, Prahran; (03) 9525 2178; open Thurs–Fri for lunch and Tues–Sat for dinner; www.jacquesreymond.com.au

JOURNAL CANTEEN $$
ITALIAN
Map ref. p. 8

Not to be confused with the much-loved Journal Cafe downstairs, Journal Canteen is a bright and cheery lunch-only joint with a daily changing menu of simple, rustic and unfailingly delicious Sicilian-inspired food. With banks of windows overlooking Flinders Lane, a series of plywood and metal communal tables and an open kitchen that is very much part of the

room, there is a lovely hominess to the place, as if you are eating in someone's house. The food reflects this comfort zone, like the rustic antipasto that includes house-marinated olives and squares of pan-fried ricotta, the simple pasta dishes or Italian classics like veal saltimbocca. A tiny, all-Italian wine list keeps things simple and authentic.

Level 1, 253 Flinders La; (03) 9650 4399; open weekdays for lunch

KANTEEN $
CAFE
Map ref. p. 7 E4

Kanteen is the perfect place for hardcore city slickers to get a small, civilised dose of the great outdoors. Nestled in a leafy bend of the Yarra River, this was once an amenities block but a simple, very effective renovation that makes the most of the lovely views and riverside ambience makes it easy to forget the past. Much favoured by joggers, bikeriders and well-groomed pram-pushing mothers, Kanteen keeps things simple food-wise – poached eggs with smoked salmon and spinach for breakfast, rustic chunky soups and stuffed pide for lunch – but the real star here is the excellent, lovingly made coffee. Service can be slow in busy times but with the sun shining and the river flowing, who wants to hurry?

150 Alexandra Ave, South Yarra; (03) 9827 0488; open daily for breakfast and lunch; www.kanteen.net

MOVIDA BAR DE TAPAS Y VINO $$
SPANISH
Map ref. p. 8

Madrid meets Melbourne in this always-packed Spanish restaurant tucked down a graffitied cobblestone laneway. The terracotta-toned dining area is a flatteringly lit place for roaming through a rich, big-flavoured selection of tapas dishes, but the best and most authentic experience at MoVida comes from

sitting up at the bar, snacking on croutons topped with anchovies and tomato sorbet or superb acorn-fed jamon ham while working your way through a Spanish-heavy list of wines and sherries. The sweet end of the meal is also well worth considering as the churros (Spanish doughnuts) here are among the best in town. MoVida is deservedly popular so bookings are essential. The more casual MoVida Next Door is literally next door and has a no-bookings policy.

1 Hosier La; (03) 9663 3038; open daily for lunch and dinner; www.movida.com.au

STOKEHOUSE $$$$
MODERN AUSTRALIAN
Map ref. p. 6 D5

With its wonderful views of the bay, superb upstairs deck and an ongoing reputation for consistently pumping out some of the best food in Melbourne, Stokehouse should be on the must-do list for visitors and locals alike. Downstairs is a more casual bar and cafe that does a great line in wood-fired pizza and people-watching, but the true Stokehouse experience happens upstairs in the wooden-floored, stylishly casual dining room that makes the most of the seaside vista through banks of windows. The modern Mediterranean flavours are big and sometimes complicated but never lack for balance and finesse, and a superb, far-reaching wine list ensures there is something for everybody. A Melbourne classic.

Level 1, 30 Jacka Boulevard, St Kilda; (03) 9525 5555; open daily for lunch and dinner; www.stokehouse.com.au

TAXI DINING ROOM $$$$
MODERN JAPANESE
Map ref. p. 8

The views from Taxi Dining Room over the Yarra River, arts precinct and CBD are worth a visit in themselves, as is the dining area that channels 1960s airport glamour and

WHERE TO EAT

FAMILY FRIENDLY   LICENSED   OUTDOOR DINING   VEGETARIAN OPTIONS

a cinematically futuristic metal mesh and glass aesthetic. But Taxi's charm comes from more than its striking looks. The menu of contemporary food that shows influences from Japan, South-East Asia and Europe (but never on the same plate) might include both superb quality sashimi and duck and rabbit with foie gras. The excellent, lengthy wine list includes a comprehensive list of sake and is supported by top-quality, knowledgeable service.

Level 1, Transport Hotel, Federation Sq; (03) 9654 8808; open daily for lunch and dinner; www.transporthotel.com.au

THE PRESS CLUB $$$

🖪 ♿ 🛏 ♙ 🥕   MODERN GREEK
                              Map ref. p. 13

Melbourne has one of the biggest Greek populations outside of Greece, but before The Press Club came along, the city had to be content with the jolly but basic tavernas dotted throughout the suburbs. Big and bustling with smart modern lines, The Press Club adopts the taverna's hospitable attitude but combines it with smart service and a generous, exciting, modern take on Greek food that includes both the basic (spit-roasted lamb) and the more exotic (cumin-roasted beetroot salad). Greek wine is a highlight of the lengthy list and there is a superb and eye-opening list of ouzo for those really wanting to get into the Greek spirit.

72 Flinders St; (03) 9677 9677; open Sun–Fri for lunch and daily for dinner; www.thepressclub.com.au

VUE DE MONDE $$$$$

🖪 ♿ ♙ 🥕   MODERN FRENCH
                              Map ref. p. 11

This Melbourne restaurant has received some of the industry's highest accolades. Chef Shannon Bennett's modern French menu is strictly degustation in the evening, when diners pay upwards of $150 (sometimes a long way upwards). Expect magnificent creations cooked

with precision and a characteristic twist: perhaps braised abalone set in a sweetcorn taco shell or roast duck marinated in liquorice served with mandarin foam. To sample Bennett's master hand without such a hefty price tag, the restaurant does fixed-price à la carte menu lunches, offers informal dining at Bistro Vue and creates gourmet lunch boxes at Cafe Vue (both additional dining venues are on-site). Cafe Vue sibling establishments also exist at 401 St Kilda Road and at the Heidi Museum of Modern Art in Bulleen.

430 Little Collins St; (03) 9691 3888; open Tues–Fri for lunch and Tues–Sat for dinner; www.vuedemonde.com.au

Alexandra

MIA MIA TEA ROOMS $

🖊 🖪 🛏 ⛱ 🥕   CAFE

Welcome newcomer to Alexandra, the Mia Mia Tearooms are housed in a lovely heritage-listed building that indeed started life as the Mia Mia Tearooms back in the 1880s. With its gracious facade, sunlight streaming through the windows, you could almost think you were still back in that era as you mix with locals who have quickly come to regard the tearooms as a relaxed meeting place. The menu of homemade offerings includes good pies, cakes, soups and terrific platters of local produce such as smoked trout, local cheese and olive oil. There are always several good vegetarian and gluten-free options for main courses and cakes for dessert.

79 Grant St; (03) 5772 2122; open Wed–Sun for breakfast and lunch; www.marmalades.com.au

STONELEA COUNTRY ESTATE $$$

🖪 ♿ 🛏 ♙ ⛱ 🥕   VINEYARD RESTAURANT

The restaurant at this family-owned and operated country house offers an excellent

🖊 BYO AVAILABLE   🖪 CREDIT CARDS ACCEPTED   ♿ DISABLED ACCESS   👔 DRESS CODE APPLIES

regional menu that makes good use of outstanding local produce such as Yarra Valley salmon and caviar, whole Buxton trout, Dobsons gourmet potatoes from Acheron and rabbit, yabbies, quail and venison from Yarra Valley Game. The estate also boasts its own winery and offers estate-grown wines on the restaurant wine list. Try the breast of quail on chard with crispy prosciutto, roasted hazelnuts and vanilla citrus dressing with the 2004 Stonelea Pinot Noir.

Connellys Creek Rd, Acheron; (03) 5772 2222; open daily for breakfast, lunch and dinner; www.stonelea.com.au

TEA ROOMS OF YARCK $$$
ITALIAN

Don't be fooled by the Devonshire tea–evoking name. This quaint wooden cottage restaurant is all about big-flavoured rustic Italian food made with brilliant ingredients –many of them sourced locally – and an Italian-leaning wine list that is a perfect match for the Sardinian-inspired dishes. You can order à la carte but for those in no rush the chef's menu – five or six courses that include house-made pasta, antipasto and perhaps roasted veal or suckling pig – is the best way to appreciate the restaurant's substantial charms.

6585 Maroondah Hwy, Yarck; (03) 5773 4233; open weekends for lunch and Fri–Sun for dinner

Anglesea

LOCANDA DEL MARE $$
ITALIAN

Snap your fingers and transport this beachside eatery complete with courtyard, terracotta tiles and terrific Italian food to Italy, and it would be absolutely right at home – somewhere around the Ligurian coastline from where owner Massimiliano hails. He imports traditional ingredients such as prosciutto, artisanal pasta, taleggio and other regional cheeses to ensure his antipasto, pizzas and pasta dishes are authentic. Try his laganelle all limone (fine lemon-flavoured noodles served with local seafood), trofie al pesto (small, twisted pasta typically from Liguria, served with pesto) or half-moon-shaped mezzalune (filled with spinach and ricotta and served with creamy walnut sauce). As you'd expect, Italian wines dot the interesting wine list.

5 Diggers Pde; (03) 5263 2904; open Thurs–Tues for lunch and dinner; daily in summer

PETE'S PLACE $$$
SEAFOOD

This homely space overlooks the Anglesea River, but if you want a view of the sea, book Table 1.1 on the sundeck. Owner Pete produces everything in-house, including the terrific house bread crusted with garlic, oregano, sesame, parmesan and rock-salt topping. He specialises in local seafood from Port Arlington or buys direct from local fishermen in Lorne. Start with steamed mussels or bay scallops before moving on to his signature calamari – flash-fried and dusted with oregano, served with a yoghurt, garlic and cucumber dipping sauce. The wine list includes several regional labels.

113 Great Ocean Rd; (03) 5263 2500; open weekends for breakfast, Fri–Sun for lunch and Wed–Sun for dinner; and extended summer hours, closed mid-July–Aug

A LA GRECQUE $$$
GREEK

This informal Greek restaurant run by legendary restaurateur Kosta Talihmanidis is

WHERE TO EAT

just 11 kilometres south of Anglesea at Aireys Inlet. A crisp, modern Australian incarnation of Greek dining, the restaurant sparkles with energy. White walls are splashed with bright colour, and the wooden furnishings and pitched roof lined with straw add warmth and style. Local seafood features strongly – perhaps calamari or flathead, cooked simply but to perfection, and always with good-quality ingredients. The dining inside is great but you can also ask for a table on the deck or in the courtyard to eat under the gum trees in the ocean breeze. Kosta has effortlessly captured the essence of his homeland, charming visitors and locals with his zesty fare.

60 Great Ocean Rd, Aireys Inlet; (03) 5289 6922; open daily for breakfast, lunch and dinner from Christmas to Easter; other times Wed–Sun; closed June–Aug; www.alagrecque.com.au

Apollo Bay

BAY LEAF CAFE $$

CAFE

This welcoming shopfront cafe has been serving happy customers for 17 years. Hearty breakfasts include BLT and avocado bagel with dill mayonnaise, pancakes with banana and maple syrup, and vegetarian zucchini and feta fritters served with grilled tomato, mushrooms and hummus. Lunch might be salt-and-pepper squid or grilled local fish with coriander and lime on Asian coleslaw, while for dinner there's pasta marinara or lamb rump stuffed with feta and red capsicum. In between, regulars munch on homemade muffins and croissants, or sip hearty soups. A good wine list includes interesting local wines.

131 Great Ocean Rd; (03) 5237 6470; open daily for breakfast, lunch and dinner Nov–May, daily for breakfast and lunch May–Nov

CHRIS'S BEACON POINT RESTAURANT $$$

MEDITERRANEAN

From a lofty perch on the hillside above the Great Ocean Road and Bass Strait, Chris has created a haven from the bustle of daily life. Risen from the ashes of a disastrous fire, his new restaurant is bigger, better and more contemporary than its predecessor, but that spectacular view of the ocean through overhanging gums is the same. For more than 30 years, Chris' cuisine has attracted gourmet travellers from all over the globe and a long line of loyal clientele who come to enjoy fresh seafood and Greek-influenced dishes, along with Chris' legendary hospitality. Standouts are his seafood soup, fresh crayfish in season (November–April), and walnut baklava with rose petal ice-cream and Turkish delight. Excellent wine list.

280 Skenes Creek Rd; (03) 5237 6411; open daily for lunch and dinner; www.chriss.com.au

GREAT OCEAN ROAD HOTEL $$$

MODERN AUSTRALIAN

This friendly hotel is on the way out of town from Melbourne. Regulars come here for the porterhouse steaks and generous seafood platters for two piled high with prawns, oysters, crab, calamari, scallops, smoked salmon and fish. There are usually pastas and a risotto, plus a popular bar menu. Some of the 80-odd seats in the relaxed beer garden have views of the sea.

29 Great Ocean Rd; (03) 5237 6240; open daily for lunch and dinner

LA BIMBA RESTAURANT & CAFE $$$

MEDITERRANEAN

Overlooking the beach on Apollo Bay's main strip, this contemporary space fosters the work of local artists with paintings on the walls for

BYO AVAILABLE   CREDIT CARDS ACCEPTED   DISABLED ACCESS   DRESS CODE APPLIES

sale. Comfy wicker chairs on the balcony invite lunchtime customers to stay all day. The breakfast menu features interesting dishes such as Israeli eggs poached in Napoli sauce, served with crunchy sourdough and house-made baked beans. Tapas style dishes are the go for lunch, while whole local fish prepared with a variety of spices and flavours or the seafood paella are popular for dinner. The wine list features local labels as well as good examples of specific wine varieties such as shiraz from the Barossa and cabernet sauvignon from Coonawarra.

125 Great Ocean Rd; (03) 5237 7411; open daily for breakfast, lunch and dinner; closed Wed in winter

AIRE VALLEY RESTAURANT $$$
MODERN AUSTRALIAN

Having cooked at Balmoral Castle (the Scottish residence owned by the British royal family and Queen Elizabeth II's preferred summer retreat) and in a ski chalet in Courchevel in the French Alps, chef Annabel Tunley and her husband Martin operate this 1890s Federation farmhouse with great aplomb. The à la carte menu is based on local Apollo Bay seafood, Otway lamb, Western District beef, and whatever is available from the back garden. Their ever-expanding garden supplies all vegetables, fruit and herbs for the 20-seat restaurant. Salads can be so fresh that greens and herbs are picked to order – even during service!

2590 Great Ocean Rd, Hordern Vale; (03) 5237 9223; open daily for dinner, lunch for groups by arrangement; www.airevalleyguesthouse.com.au

Ararat

NECTAR AMBROSIA $$
CAFE PROVEDORE

This former pub was the tallest building outside of Melbourne when it was built in 1859. Today it has been transformed into a smart eatery and produce store championing local produce from olives to sheep's milk yoghurt, as well as the region's famous wines. Share a few tapas-style plates such as salt-and-pepper squid, pan-seared scallops, chargrilled kangaroo, lemon chicken skewers or perhaps chickpea and corn fritters served with couscous and tabouli salad. They specialise in aged Angus beef and are justly proud of their tender chargrilled steaks. All breads and pastas are made in-house, plus they make a good cup of coffee.

157–159 Barkly St; (03) 5352 7344; open daily for lunch and Thurs–Sun for dinner; www.nectarambrosia.com.au

Avoca

WARRENMANG VINEYARD & RESORT $$$
VINEYARD RESTAURANT

In the heart of the Pyrenees wine region near Avoca, Warrenmang Vineyard & Resort offers the full gourmet deal, effortlessly blending style and comfort with a warm welcome. After 20 years spent pioneering wine, food and accommodation in this remote region, the affable Bazzani family has perfected the art of hospitality. The award-winning restaurant, specialising in regional produce, offers casual alfresco lunches overlooking the estate vineyards and fine dining in the evenings, with all dishes designed to complement the estate's excellent wines. For lunch, start with

WHERE TO EAT

house-made charcuterie, local cheese and game, followed by Bazzani shiraz-braised lamb shanks and sticky orange pudding with burnt orange caramel and clotted cream. Dinner might offer carpaccio of smoked sugar-cured venison and slow-roasted duck.

188 Mountain Creek Rd, Moonambel; (03) 5467 2233; open daily for breakfast, lunch and dinner; www.bazzani.com.au

Bairnsdale

PAPER CHASE $
CAFE

This classy 100-seat cafe within the bustling Collins bookshop is named after the second part of local author Hal Porter's autobiography. Parisian-style green and white chairs and tables give way to the main cafe inside, which leads through to a lovely courtyard planted with citrus trees shading herbs and salad vegetables destined for the cafe's kitchen. A talented team of sibling chefs prepare all the food on the menu, from crunchy granola, salmon scrambles and Austrian-style pancakes for breakfast through to white chocolate and raspberry muffins, decadent rum baba and black forest cake. Open sandwiches are named after classic authors like Steinbeck and Hemingway. Try the homemade lemonade.

168 Main St; (03) 5152 5181; open daily for breakfast and lunch

Ballarat

EUROPA CAFE $$
CAFE
Map ref. p. 64

Over 14 years, this buzzy, family-friendly cafe in the town's main street has built up an enviable

reputation for its all-day breakfast. In fact, the full menu for breakfast, lunch and dinner is available all day – so if you feel like sitting down to their signature egg and bacon pide or French toast with bacon and maple syrup for dinner, or perversely Thai chicken broth or spaghetti bolognaise for breakfast, then that's just fine. Check the blackboard for up to 20 daily specials. It's a good-value, good-feel space where they make their own breads, muesli and more.

411 Sturt St; (03) 5338 7672; open daily for breakfast and lunch, and Thurs–Sun for dinner; www.europacafe.com.au

L'ESPRESSO $$
ITALIAN
Map ref. p. 64

This bustling, chic and groovy Italian cafe started life as a record shop more than 20 years ago. Today, this heritage is the wall of mostly jazz and blues CDs for sale to the throng of customers. There are wide windows looking out onto the main street and a warm wooden interior where everyone sits around small tables and feasts on the excellent meals from the surprisingly extensive menu. Try eggs Benedict or parmesan omelette for breakfast, smoked local Tuki trout or crab and avocado salad for lunch, or risotto made using authentic Ferron rice or a hearty Tuscan-style steak for dinner. L'espresso's exceptional regional cafe food, buzzing atmosphere and Italian open-hearted style has ensured success.

417 Sturt St; (03) 5333 1789; open daily for breakfast and lunch, and Fri–Sat for dinner; www.ballarat.com/lespresso.htm

MASONS CAFE & FOODSTORE $$
CAFE PROVEDORE
Map ref. p. 64

This beautiful old Victorian corner pub is a friendly haven any time of day. Call in for a morning or afternoon coffee and cake, a light lunch or more hearty dinner, or pick up

good food-to-go – all made on the premises. Blackboard lunchtime specials offer terrific value: homemade gnocchi, spaghettini with a simple sauce, or free-range chicken parmigiana and salad. For dinner, order a few entrée plates to share: Kashmiri-style lamb curry, homemade ravioli with lemon and spinach sauce, marmalade-glazed pork belly or maybe baked ricotta with caramelised fig and quince jam. Main courses are also appealing: gnocchi with prawns, Asian duck and shiitake mushroom pie or perhaps oven-roasted breast of chicken fillet with spiced pear and cranberry sauce.

32 Drummond St North; (03) 5333 3895; open Mon–Fri for lunch and Thurs–Fri for dinner

PHOENIX BREWERY $$$

MODERN AUSTRALIAN
Map ref. p. 64

Centrally located in Ballarat's historic arts precinct, this atmospheric eatery is housed in a converted newspaper building, not a brewery at all. However, it boasts one of the best wine lists in town with a good selection available by the glass. The contemporary menu offers Asian-influenced dishes such as Sichuan pepper-dusted squid and twice-cooked pork belly on a warm Asian salad for starters, followed perhaps by rack of spring lamb with pistachio, brie and mushroom filling or seafood and chicken tom yum. Imaginative vegetarian options might be homemade sweet potato and sage ravioli with wild mushrooms and spinach ragout.

10 Camp St; (03) 5333 2686; open weekdays for lunch and Mon–Sat for dinner; www.ballarat.com/phoenix

Beechworth

PROVENANCE RESTAURANT $$$

MODERN AUSTRALIAN

Talented chef Michael Ryan champions top-notch regional produce at this gracious two-storey former bank dating back to 1856. There could be Nug Nug goat form Myrtleford, Hume Weir trout, local Murray Grey beef and locally picked cherries. Complementing the extensive wine cellar housed in the bank's former vault, he offers an à la carte menu as well as a six-course degustation menu and similar vegetarian tasting feast; both degustations are available with or without matching wines. Dishes are multifaceted, like the chef's signature entrée of butter-sautéed cauliflower, Mount Buffalo hazelnut crumble, mustard sabayon and brown butter jelly. Save room for his amazing custard-like confection tocino del cielo or 'bacon from heaven'.

86 Ford St; (03) 5728 1786; open Fri and Sun for lunch and Wed–Sun for dinner; www.theprovenance.com.au

THE GREEN SHED BISTRO $$$

EUROPEAN

Housed in a historic 1860s printing office, where the local newspaper used to tell of infamous neighbour Ned Kelly's activities and eventual trial in Beechworth, this casual country bistro has colourful artworks and an open fire in winter. The European-inspired menu offers entrées such as cuttlefish risotto or oxtail-stuffed tomato with pesto. Main courses might be a rabbit pie floater made with homemade puff pastry on pea purée or baked blue-eye with bean, olive and potato salad. Good use is made of local produce as in a confit of local duck with Stanley apple, pear and walnut sauce with Pennyweight sherry.

WHERE TO EAT

FAMILY FRIENDLY   LICENSED   OUTDOOR DINING   VEGETARIAN OPTIONS

They cure their own salmon and make their own house wines and Marc Wine labels from their vineyard in Stanley.

37 Camp St; (03) 5728 2360; open weekends for lunch and Fri–Sun for dinner

THE OX AND HOUND $$

MODERN AUSTRALIAN

This casual bistro is a welcome addition to Beechworth's clutch of good eateries. The owners of Oxenbury Vineyard have played on the name to arrive at The Ox and Hound, while also serving some of their estate-grown Cow Hill wines – mainly pinot noir. Food is essentially French country cuisine with a strong emphasis on seafood and 'from farm to plate' themes. There might be local Harrietville smoked trout for lunch, terrific snapper pie for dinner and even their own farmed milk-fed lamb on the menu. In autumn, they join with a local chestnut grower to make their own farm pork and chestnut sausages. Also worth knowing about is their farmhouse terrine, Peking-style duck and decadent dark chocolate tart.

52 Ford St; (03) 5728 2123; open Fri–Sun for lunch and Thurs–Mon for dinner

WARDENS FOOD & WINE $$$

ITALIAN

After exploring historic Beechworth, treat yourself and dine at Wardens. This beloved eatery is housed in an old pub and comprises a beautiful dining room with polished floorboards, clean lines and plenty of natural light. The modern Italian fare focuses on seasonal local ingredients. Risotto might be Portobello mushrooms, baby leeks, toasted pine nuts and taleggio cheese, or try hearty dishes such as roasted quail with Sicilian flavours, pickled-fig sausage and fregola sarda. The tiramisu semifreddo should be obligatory.

All dishes are wine matched from their comprehensive list of mostly Italian and local wines; Wednesday is BYO night.

32 Ford St; (03) 5728 1377; open Wed–Sun for lunch and Wed–Sat for dinner; www.wardens.com.au

Benalla

BENALLA GALLERY CAFE $$

CAFE

Housed in the most visited regional art gallery outside of Melbourne, this contemporary cafe boasts a lovely sunny deck over Lake Benalla in the botanic gardens. With an emphasis on alfresco dining, it opens for dinner only during the months of daylight saving. Showcasing quality regional produce, the blackboard menu changes daily depending on what's seasonal and fresh. In winter, expect soul-warming soups and succulent eye fillet steaks; in summer, tables are laden with antipasto platters of local produce, seafood and dishes such as Cajun-style chicken salad, prawn and scallop salad or grilled asparagus topped with smoked salmon and dill.

Bridge St East; (03) 5762 3777; open daily for breakfast and lunch, and Fri–Sat for dinner during daylight saving; www.benallagallerycafe.com

GEORGINA'S $$$

MODERN AUSTRALIAN

A busy restaurant in a century-old building in Benalla's main street, Georgina's offers a menu of Australian home-style cuisine as well as a spicy, Asian-influenced range of dishes. Entrées might be goat's cheese salad, chilli prawns or perhaps warm kangaroo salad. Main courses include confit duck risotto, veal scaloppini with mushrooms, or sweet pork and cashew nut

curry. Daily specials are worth considering, with tempting dishes such as tempura-battered King George whiting, chips and salad.

100 Bridge St East; (03) 5762 1334; open Tues–Sun for dinner; www.georginas.net.au

NORTH EASTERN HOTEL $$
MODERN AUSTRALIAN

This 1905 Federation brick hotel has had a major overhaul to create an open-plan dining room with leather couches and open fires for winter warmth, and relaxing courtyard dining in summer. The menu of regional contemporary dishes gives a nod to Mediterranean and Asian flavours, and the lunchtime menu is a variation on the dinner menu with smaller serves. In season, look for fresh asparagus, antipasto plates and soft-shell crab and calamari salad. Porterhouse steak is always a good option, as is slow-cooked pork spare ribs served with Chinese vegetables and coconut rice.

1–3 Nunn St; (03) 5762 7333; open Wed–Sun for lunch and Tues–Sat for dinner

RAFFETY'S RESTAURANT $$$
MODERN AUSTRALIAN

There's a warm welcome at Raffety's, with a cosy fire in winter inside this 100-year-old heritage building and a side verandah with concertina doors that open for summer dining. There are also pavement tables and alcove seating on comfy leather couches for drinks before being seated for dinner. Everything is made on the premises, and local produce is sourced for the modern Australian fare. Start with tempura prawns on pickled vegetables with wasabi mayonnaise on a warm squid salad. As in most country places, steaks are popular, and their 250-gram fillet steak is no exception. There is always a pasta, risotto and

fish of the day, and locals won't let the owners take the lemon tart off the dessert menu.

55 Nunn St; (03) 5762 4066; open Tues–Sat for dinner; www.raffetys.com

Bendigo

GPO BENDIGO $$
MEDITERRANEAN
Map ref. p. 70

Opposite Bendigo's ornate GPO building, GPO Bendigo brings a touch of the city slicks to this historic part of town. The long narrow space, with its bare wooden tables, red banquettes and whitewashed walls, functions as bar, cafe and restaurant, depending on the time of day and your current mood. There are good pizzas topped with artisan toppings, house-made pasta, tapas-style snacks and a good selection of flame-grilled meat dishes. A favourite of Bendigo's younger set, GPO can get rowdy with cocktail swillers on weekends but it's a happy noise that suits the casual approach.

60–64 Pall Mall; (03) 5443 4343; open Sun for breakfast, and daily for lunch and dinner; www.gpobendigo.com.au

THE BRIDGE $$$
MODERN AUSTRALIAN
Map ref. p. 70

This smartly renovated pub offers two levels of dining: a casual, well-executed list of pub favourites like fish and chips or chicken pot pie in the front bar, and a more serious menu in the casually chic dining room at the rear of the building (think slow-roasted duck and excellent crispy pig trotters). It offers a similar level of high-quality, locally sourced ingredients and switched-on service no matter which end of the spectrum you choose. A wine list that includes local, national and

WHERE TO EAT

international wines provides plenty of joy for the buffs; Sunday is BYO night.

49 Bridge St; (03) 5443 7811; open Tues–Sun for lunch and dinner; www.thebridgebendigo.com.au

THE DISPENSARY $$$

EUROPEAN
Map ref. p. 70

Tucked away down a narrow laneway, this is a hidden gem worth unearthing. Owner Tim Baxter has had 20 years in the industry while chef Travis Rodwell has racked up several years at acclaimed Melbourne restaurants including L'Oustal and Circa, the Prince. Together they bring a fresh, sophisticated approach to Bendigo's dining scene – the pork-loving chef even raising his own pigs for charcuterie, and making his own chorizo sausages, ham and air-dried bresoala. The menu has French, Spanish and Italian flavours with local versions of niçoise salad or veal carpaccio with tuna mayonnaise for entrée. A Lyonnaise salad of confit duck leg or oregano, rosemary and garlic-stuffed lamb saddle, served on semolina gnocchi is among main course options.

9 Chancery La; (03) 5444 5885; open daily for breakfast and lunch, and Tues–Sat for dinner; www.thedispensaryenoteca.com

WHIRRAKEE RESTAURANT $$$

FRENCH
Map ref. p. 70

The Art Nouveau details and high ceilings of the former Royal Bank building provide the background to one of Bendigo's best fine diners. The menu is contemporary European, with a lean towards the French, particularly in its impressive sourcing and use of local ingredients. Dishes are quite intricate but are finessed rather than tricky. A potato and gorgonzola soufflé makes light work of potentially heavy ingredients, duck is served confit and roasted, and desserts lean towards

the fruity and refreshing. Smart service rounds out an impressive package.

17 View St; (03) 5441 5557; open Tues–Sun for lunch and dinner; www.whirrakeerestaurant.com.au

WILD MINT $$

MEDITERRANEAN
Map ref. p. 70

As part of the new Bendigo Bank complex, this restaurant/wine bar is so named because of its location and connection with money production. The large modern space has an outside deck overlooking the city's ornate fountain, Charing Cross and Rosalind Park. Although the space and menu are contemporary, the kitchen is traditional, making all its soups, sauces, stocks and bases from scratch, baking fresh bread daily and churning its own homemade ice-creams. Wild Mint caters to a wide sector of the community with quick coffee and homemade cakes, tapas plates in the wine bar and everything through to a full sit-down meal. The wine list reflects the best from the Bendigo region wineries.

Shop 11, Bendigo Bank Centre; (03) 5444 2060; open Mon–Sat for breakfast, lunch and dinner

WINE BANK ON VIEW $$

MEDITERRANEAN
Map ref. p. 70

This wine bar/bottle shop is located in a wonderfully atmospheric old bank building that combines high ceilings and wooden shelves crammed with bottles, cosy open fireplaces, comfy leather couches and great outdoor seating under impressive Corinthian columns. One of the best places in town for a coffee, it also has an excellent range of wine, both New and Old World, and a good casual menu that starts with tapas and moves through to generously proportioned steak sandwiches. Take advantage of the knowledgeable service and discover delicious local wines.

BYO AVAILABLE   CREDIT CARDS ACCEPTED   DISABLED ACCESS   DRESS CODE APPLIES

45 View St; (03) 5444 4655; open daily for lunch and dinner; www.winebankonview.com

Bright

POPLARS

$$$
FRENCH
Map ref. p. 76

There is a real mix of diners in this 40-seater restaurant: workers straight from the farm, suits from a business meeting or perhaps a starry-eyed couple out for a romantic evening. But the French-style brasserie takes it all in its stride, offering a selection of smaller entrée dishes that might move around the table before main courses are served. Classics include French onion soup, terrines, eye fillet with Café de Paris butter and pommes frites, coq au vin, beef bourguignon and confit of duck – all beautifully executed. Do factor in their signature soufflé flavoured with whatever's fresh and in season – peaches, blackberry, passionfruit or perhaps chocolate.

Shop 8, Star Rd; (03) 5755 1655; open Tues– Sat for dinner; www.poplars.com.au

SIMONE'S OF BRIGHT

$$$
ITALIAN
Map ref. p. 76

For more than 20 years, George and Patrizia Simone have been serving exceptional Italian cuisine at their award-winning restaurant in a welcoming converted Victorian home. Loyal gourmet food buffs come from around the state to sample Simone's rustic fare featuring quality regional produce. Popular dishes include braised Buckland Valley goat, roast farmed Yackandandah rabbit with fennel and garlic, and homemade gnocchi with truffle. With chef son Anthony joining Patrizia in the kitchen, expect even more interesting dishes such as local Roberts Creek duck breast filled with smoked eel and served with watercress salad and local raspberries. Meanwhile George reigns over a comprehensive cellar of classic regional, Australian and Italian wines.

98 Gavan St; (03) 5755 2266; open Tues–Sat for dinner; www.simonesrestaurant.com.au

VILLA GUSTO

$$$
ITALIAN

A Tuscan-style escape at the foot of Mount Buffalo, this small Italian restaurant serves good local food with regional wines. The menu is a set-price five-course degustation dinner, complemented by High Country and Italian wines. No two menus are the same and they often include local ingredients such as Kiewa Valley pork, Ovens Valley lamb, veal and beef, Roberts Creek duck, Milawa free-range quail and Mountain Fresh trout and salmon. Vegetables are bought direct from the farm and pastas are all house-made.

630 Buckland Valley Rd, Buckland; (03) 5756 2000; open daily for dinner; www.villagusto.com.au

Castlemaine

BOLD CAFE GALLERY

$
CAFE

On the approach into Castlemaine from Melbourne, look for this quirky cafe adjacent to the Bold Garden and opposite the venue for the Wesley Hill Saturday-morning market. A bakery during the gold-rush era, the building has maintained its historic integrity while integrating courtyard water features, private nooks and plants from its nursery neighbour. With Asian and Western chefs in the kitchen, it truly is an east-meets-west menu. Everything is made on the premises, with special dishes

WHERE TO EAT

offered on a specific day. For example, Fridays mean gluten-free chocolate roulade; laksa is offered on Sundays; and a traditional vegetarian monk dish is prepared on Fridays and at the weekends. There is always a daily curry and terrific cakes, many gluten-free.

146 Duke St; (03) 5470 6038; open Wed–Sun for lunch

SAFFS CAFE $$
                                  CAFE

The buzzy cafe is housed in an 1890s shopfront, with pavement seating at the front and two rooms inside that spill onto a rear deck and into a back garden with summer seating. Regulars come for eggs Benedict and eggs Florentine to kick-start the day, moving on to an extensive lunchtime menu and daily specials board. All tastes are catered for, from lentil and lamb burgers to risotto, pasta, a daily soup and choice of salads. Some dishes carry over to the dinner menu, which might also offer homemade gnocchi with sweet potato, Asian-style pork salad and caramelised beetroot tart, as well as steaks, curries and fish of the day.

64 Mostyn St; (03) 5470 6722; open daily for breakfast and lunch

THE EMPYRE $$$
                                  MODERN AUSTRALIAN

This 1860s two-storey hotel has been lovingly restored to become the most elegant accommodation in town once again, with a range of dining options. The former front bar morphs into a classy cafe for breakfast and lunch, and transforms by night into a chic restaurant with crisp linen tablecloths, serving excellent fare. The original side carriageway has been filled in to become a casual lounge, while the former 'Ladies' Lounge' has found new life as part of the restaurant and as an elegant private dining room. Local produce is sourced

for the menu – perhaps Holy Goat cheese baked in pastry with Waldorf-style salad, or eye fillet of Angus beef from nearby Kyneton with anchovy butter.

68 Mostyn St; (03) 5472 5166; open Wed–Sun for breakfast and lunch, and Wed–Sat for dinner; www.empyre.com.au

TOGS PLACE $
                                  CAFE

When this welcoming cafe opened 18 years ago in an old miner's cottage, it was the first cafe in town. Today it is so popular it has seats on a pavement verandah and even on the roof – the views over the rooftops of Castlemaine are one of the best kept secrets in town. Their fresh made-to-order eggs are renowned – try the bacon and egg jaffles. They sell muffins by the tonne –brandy-spiced apricot or raspberry, and savoury ones such as prosciutto, cheddar and ricotta. In winter, lunchtime soups might be pea and ham, lamb shank and barley or Moroccan vegetable and chickpea; in summer, perhaps fresh tomato and basil. They are also known for the curries – Indian, Asian, Thai, Malay and more.

58 Lyttleton St; (03) 5470 5090; open daily for breakfast and lunch

Cohuna

GUNBOWER FAMILY HOTEL $$
                                  TRADITIONAL AUSTRALIAN

This unassuming hotel just a few kilometres from the Murray River has created quite a buzz with the quality of its meat. It is not so hard to understand why when you realise that publican Richard McGillivray is also a butcher who grazes his own livestock (grass-fed Herefords and Wiltshire horn sheep) and operates an abattoir, so the paddock-to-plate trail is under constant scrutiny. Some Asian-influenced dishes are also on the menu, such as duck spring rolls, but it is the beef and lamb that has kept the chatter coming.

Murray Valley Hwy, Gunbower; (03) 5487 1214; open daily for lunch and dinner

Colac

OLD LORNE ROAD OLIVES $$
MEDITERRANEAN

Absorb the bucolic bliss of the olive grove as you sit on the deck of this Mediterranean-style cafe, whose menu combines much local produce with home-grown goods. Savour terrific smoked eel from nearby Parratte, blue or camembert-style cheeses from Apostle Whey, local pork, or ratatouille tart with bocconcini and estate-grown olives. There are also more substantial dishes such as stuffed chicken breast, pastas and Sardinian seafood ragout over chargrilled sourdough. Desserts and coffee are reliably good. Check the gallery of local artists' work and take home some of their olive oil, olives or olive-related products.

45 Old Lorne Rd, Deans Marsh; (03) 5236 3479; open Thurs–Mon for lunch; www.oldlorneroadolives.com.au

OTWAY ESTATE WINERY AND BREWERY $$
VINEYARD RESTAURANT

This winery and brewery has a cafe restaurant, art gallery and cellar door overlooking the Otway rainforest ranges and estate vineyard. Take a seat on the deck in summer for a cordial-tasting (they make about 30 different flavours), beer-tasting (12 are hand-crafted on the premises) or wine-tasting – the cool climate is ideal for rosé, pinot noir, chardonnay, riesling and sauvignon blanc.

Share a platter to start, then move on to perhaps a steak, poultry, seafood or game dish. Everything is made on the premises, with the menu changing each month.

10–30 Hoveys Rd, Barongarook; (03) 5233 8400; open daily for lunch and Sat for dinner; www.otwayestate.com.au

Cowes

HARRY'S ON THE ESPLANADE $$$
MODERN AUSTRALIAN
Map ref. p. 82

With an enviable location on the waterfront in front of the pier, this casual beachside restaurant enjoys panoramic views across Westernport Bay, with a retractable roof for year-round alfresco dining. The daily menu has a regional focus, revolving around fresh seafood sourced from local trawlers – perhaps succulent crayfish in season and King George whiting – as well as Phillip Island beef and lamb, and vegetables and herbs from market gardens from nearby Koo-wee-rup and Nar Nar Goon. An in-house bakery produces terrific farmers-style bread, baguettes and breads daily, and all ice-creams are homemade. Harry boasts an extensive wine list, many aged in his own private cellar.

Shop 5, 17 The Esplanade; (03) 5952 6226; open weekends for breakfast, and Tues–Sun for lunch and dinner; extended summer hours; www.harrysrestaurant.com.au

HOTEL $$
MODERN AUSTRALIAN
Map ref. p. 82

Across the road from the jetty in one of the oldest buildings in Cowes, this happy beach-house-style restaurant converts into a nightclub on Friday and Saturday evenings after dinner. Enjoy views over Westernport Bay to Stoney Point and Red Hill, and further

WHERE TO EAT

🛏 FAMILY FRIENDLY   🍷 LICENSED   ☂ OUTDOOR DINING   🥕 VEGETARIAN OPTIONS

to French Island as you contemplate the predominately seafood menu that caters for all tastes, including tender local Tooradin porterhouse steak and a good children's menu. Start with a trio of dips on toasted pita bread or perhaps toasted bruschetta with basil and tomato topping. Tuck into a Thai prawn salad or popular 'surf 'n turf' (freshly poached prawns atop porterhouse steak with hollandaise) before heading off to the penguin parade, just 15 minutes away.

11–13 The Esplanade; (03) 5952 2100; open daily for lunch and dinner

INFUSED RESTAURANT CAFE AND WINE BAR $$$

MODERN AUSTRALIAN
Map ref. p. 82

Away from the foreshore holiday crowds, this contemporary space houses local artwork and boasts a covered bar with couches where locals love to relax. A roll-down plastic awning swings into action if the weather sours. The modern Australian menu changes daily and is known for its freshly shucked oysters in season, presented eight different ways – four hot and four cold – so order a mixed dozen. Locals won't let the owners take the house-made duck spring rolls off the menu. The pork two ways – spiced confit of pork belly with a pork prosciutto and pistachio terrine – is recommended, as is the Phillip Island scotch fillet served with a warm tart of walnut, prosciutto and Swiss brown mushrooms.

115 Thompson Ave; (03) 5952 2655; open Wed–Mon for lunch and dinner; extended summer hours; www.infused.com.au

FORESHORE BAR AND RESTAURANT $$$

MODERN AUSTRALIAN
Map ref. p. 82

Rustic and chic, this restaurant is blessed with stunning 180-degree water views from its vantage point on Phillip Island in the quiet village of Rhyll. Take a seat on the deck to enjoy open-air seaside dining, making the most of the island location. The friendly atmosphere encourages guests to linger over drinks in the bar, relax in the lounge area and savour the extensive dining menu. Choose from light dishes such as freshly shucked oysters and open sandwiches, or heartier fare like port and rhubarb duck breast, Phillip Island rib-eye pork or locally made beef sausages for bangers and mash. There is always a pasta, risotto and fish of the day.

11 Beach Rd, Rhyll; (03) 5956 9520; open Wed–Mon for lunch and dinner; www.theforeshore.com.au

Creswick

HARVEST 383 $$$$

MODERN AUSTRALIAN

This contemporary dining room is the in-house restaurant for the new Novotel Forest Resort. The name was developed in line with the environmental philosophies of both the resort and executive chef Glenn Krumb, the number 383 representing the radius in kilometres around the resort within which produce for the menu is sourced. This encompasses Daylesford, Ballarat, Smeaton and Meredith, and includes pancetta and prosciutto from Istra Smallgoods in Musk, Tuki Springs lamb, Western Plains pork, venison from Spa Venison in Daylesford and Meredith cheese. Expect dishes such as roasted Tuki Springs lamb rack with braised fennel and ruby grapefruit or slow-cooked Western Plains pork belly.

Novotel Forest Resort Creswick, 1500 Midland Hwy; (03) 5345 9600; open daily for breakfast and dinner; www.novotel.forestresort.com.au

BYO AVAILABLE   CREDIT CARDS ACCEPTED   DISABLED ACCESS   DRESS CODE APPLIES

Daylesford

FRANGOS & FRANGOS $$$$

EUROPEAN
Map ref. p. 88

Among a number of exceptional dining experiences in Daylesford, Frangos & Frangos offers a taste of sophisticated Melbourne in the heart of Victoria's spa country. This celebrated emporium is divided into two spaces: its namesake, a chic and cosy formal dining room; and, as a cheaper, funkier alternative, Koukla, a bustling bohemian cafe with wood-fired pizza oven. The food brims with the top-quality regional produce visitors have come to expect while exploring this beautiful part of regional Australia.

82 Vincent St; (03) 5348 2363; dining room open weekends for breakfast and lunch, and Fri–Sat for dinner; Koukla open daily for breakfast, lunch and dinner; www.frangosandfrangos.com

LAKE HOUSE $$$$

MODERN AUSTRALIAN
Map ref. p. 88

Alla Wolf-Tasker is the woman behind Daylesford's beloved Lake House, regarded as one of regional Victoria's best restaurants, if not the best. The light-filled restaurant ranges over several levels overlooking Lake Daylesford. Menus reflect what's seasonal and regional, some dishes tipping their hat to Alla's Russian heritage. In autumn, look for locally bred free-range pork slow-cooked with chestnuts, and perhaps roasted quince with local honey panna cotta; in spring, local wild morel mushrooms might be paired with baby lamb, asparagus and broad beans. Patrons can choose either à la carte or an eight-course degustation; a vegetarian degustation is also available. The internationally acclaimed wine

cellar boasts three sommeliers, with selections from small-scale local winemakers as well as internationally renowned wines.

King St; (03) 5348 3329; open daily for breakfast, lunch and dinner; www.lakehouse.com.au

MERCATO @ DAYLESFORD $$$$

ITALIAN
Map ref. p. 88

This 1864 timber building radiates warmth and comfort, the glowing dining room accentuated by polished floorboards, high ceilings and a soothing cream colour scheme. The Italian menu is gaining a loyal following, with dishes such as the 'open ravioli' entrée of Tuki trout, baby leeks, wilted rocket, roasted truss tomatoes and Meredith goat's cheese. Dishes are a zesty duet of regional produce and urban style, and a comprehensive wine list showcases the region's favourites.

32 Raglan St; (03) 5348 4488; open Thurs–Tues for dinner and weekends for lunch; www.mercatorestaurant.com.au

THE FARMERS ARMS HOTEL $$$$

MODERN AUSTRALIAN
Map ref. p. 88

This award-winning restaurant nestled in an old-fashioned pub has a great atmosphere. The robust menu boasts sublime comfort food using superior Daylesford and Macedon produce. In summer, you might find rosemary and garlic pan-roasted baby chicken with sweet corn purée, asparagus and Istra prosciutto; in winter, hearty rabbit is braised in spiced red wine with cotechino sausage, soft carrots and lentils. In addition to a traditional front bar, this stylish tucked-away restaurant has an impressive wine list and wide range of ales from which to choose. There are comfortable couches with a selection of children's books as well as a pretty courtyard for families to

WHERE TO EAT

FAMILY FRIENDLY   LICENSED   OUTDOOR DINING   VEGETARIAN OPTIONS

unwind and relax at this favourite hotel that is so much more than a pub.

1 East St; (03) 5348 2091; open weekends for lunch and daily for dinner; www.farmersarms.com.au

COSY CORNER $$

MODERN AUSTRALIAN
Map ref. p. 88

As the name suggests, Cosy Corner is a quaint restaurant tucked away in one of Hepburn Springs' few side streets. The atmosphere is especially charming in winter when the fireplace is roaring. Menu items feature local produce and wines, as well as bread baked on the premises. But the most exciting aspect of this eatery is the very reasonable prices for good-quality food. A tender wine-roasted lamb rump and the Black Angus scotch fillet are both well under $30. Coupled with friendly staff, you're unlikely to find a more exceptional value-for-money experience in Victoria's spa country.

3 Tenth St, Hepburn Springs; (03) 5348 2576; open Sat–Sun for breakfast, and Thurs–Tues for lunch and dinner; www.cosy-corner.com.au

Drysdale

LOAM RESTAURANT $$

MODERN AUSTRALIAN

After a stint cooking overseas, former Portland boy Aaron Turner returned to open his own restaurant on the Bellarine Peninsula near Drysdale, with wife Astrid as front of house. Loam occupies the spacious upstairs dining space above Lighthouse Olive Oil, overlooking the olive grove. There are two menus: a small, rustic and produce-driven à la carte menu served 'On the Deck'; and constantly changing tasting menus in the dining room with options for two, four, seven or nine courses. Using fresh

and artisinal produce, with home-grown fruit, herbs and vegetables, Turner is happiest when showcasing passionate local producers such as Drysdale goats cheese, Portarlington mussels, and free-range eggs from Stonehaven. Local wines and beers are also on offer.

Lighthouse Olive Grove, 650 Andersons Rd; (03) 5251 1101; open Thurs–Sun for lunch and Fri–Sat for dinner; loamrestaurant.blogspot.com

PORT PIER CAFE $$$

SPANISH

Located in an old fish co-op, this popular Spanish restaurant is about as close to the water as you can get. For breakfast, locals come for egg-based dishes like Spanish omelette or eggs Flamenco – baked with artichoke and chorizo. If you're feeling ravenous, go for the Port Pier hunger breaker – breakfast with the lot and a bit more. The same menu is available for lunch and dinner, with at least two dozen tapas dishes, several paellas – seafood, mixed and vegetarian – lots of salads, steaks with a choice of sauces and the very popular seafood feast for two. There is also a good selection of Spanish, local and not-so-local wines.

Portarlington Foreshore, Pier St, Portarlington; (03) 5259 1080; open daily for breakfast, lunch and dinner; reduced winter hours

THE OL' DUKE HOTEL $$$

MODERN AUSTRALIAN

The first hotel in town when it was built in 1855, The Ol' Duke had been derelict and de-licensed for around 60 years when new owners bought it in 2000, renovated it and reopened it as a trendy bar and restaurant serving contemporary cuisine. Breakfast regulars come for the light and tasty corn and asparagus fritters served with smoked salmon, poached egg and lemon mayonnaise. For lunch

and dinner, they know to go for the terrific crispy skin duck served with bok choy, Chinese sausage and hoi sin sauce. There are always plenty of options, including good local seafood such as the famous Port Arlington mussels and fresh calamari from Port Phillip Bay.

40 Newcombe St, Portarlington; (03) 5259 1250; open daily for breakfast, lunch and dinner; www.theolduke.com.au

Dunkeld

GOURMET PANTRY $
CAFE PROVEDORE

This cafe and larder champions the best local produce. Take a seat in the front courtyard under the shade sail and enjoy the view over to Mount Sturgeon in the Grampians. Everything is made on the premises, including beef and red wine or chicken and leek pies, huge sausage rolls, vegetarian pasties and quiches. There are Turkish rolls ready to fill with chicken and ham to go, and terrific homemade cakes, many of which are gluten-free. Stock up on a great range of local cheese – made from goat, sheep and buffalo milk, yoghurt, olives, olive oil and Dunkeld wines. There are lots of old-fashioned lollies in jars, too.

109 Parker St; (03) 5577 2288; open daily for breakfast and lunch, and Fri–Sat for dinner

ROYAL MAIL HOTEL $$$$
MODERN AUSTRALIAN

Housed in an 1855 Art Deco–style renovated hotel, this restaurant has won many awards for its exceptional cuisine. Its outstanding wine list has also been acclaimed by prestigious UK magazine *Wine Spectator*. The restaurant serves only degustation menus to showcase the incredible culinary skills chef

Dan Hunter has gleaned after several years in top Melbourne kitchens, and more recently during his four years at the two-Michelin-star Mugaritz in Spain. Every dish is a delicate and flavoursome work of art, using edible flowers and leaves straight from the back garden. A meal (together with matching wines) may be pricey, but it will certainly be one of the most memorable meals of your life. The more reasonably priced bistro serves hearty country-style food such as slow-cooked Western District lamb and Hopkins River sirloin. There is also a most affordable bar menu.

Glenelg Hwy; (03) 5577 2241; open daily for breakfast, lunch and dinner; www.royalmail.com.au

Echuca

CERES $$$
MODERN AUSTRALIAN

Named after the Roman goddess of tillage (cereal crops and grains), this 1881-built former flour mill is the perfect setting for this lovely contemporary space. With polished cement floors, chandeliers and rugs, a casual dining area invites patrons to relax in leather lounges at coffee tables as they share tapas and sip coffee or wine. Elsewhere, the main restaurant serves an appealing modern menu that might have such entrées as beef tartare, fresh oysters with champagne sorbet and salmon roe or lightly deep-fried salt-and-pepper calamari. Popular main courses include double-roasted duck, whole baby snapper, pan-roasted chicken breast or dry-hung aged locally grown beef. And to finish: share an assiette of desserts – a little taste of all the menu's sweet offerings.

2 Nish St; (03) 5482 5599; open Mon–Sat for lunch and dinner; www.ceresechuca.com.au

WHERE TO EAT

FAMILY FRIENDLY   LICENSED   OUTDOOR DINING   VEGETARIAN OPTIONS

LEFT BANK $$$

MODERN AUSTRALIAN

This restaurant and wine bar, located in a beautiful 1862 former bank building, is more like a Melbourne restaurant that has been happily transported to the country. Recent refurbishment sees polished floorboards in the bar where tapas is served, with leather banquette seating, wrought-iron chairs and white table linen in the restaurant. Sourcing much regional produce, the menu might have an entrée of chargrilled quail with spiced carrot purée and red wine jus, and main courses such as dry-aged Angus Murray Grey scotch fillet or confit duck leg and crispy skin duck breast. Finish with vanilla-baked locally grown strawberries with mascarpone cream.

551 High St; (03) 5480 3772; open Tues–Sat for dinner

OSCAR W'S WHARFSIDE $$$

MODERN AUSTRALIAN

Perched right on the Murray River, this popular restaurant and bar is away from the main tourist precinct. Take a seat at the bar, in the lounge or in the Red Gum Grill restaurant – all have river views and one menu serves the whole space. Share some tapas or perhaps consider the chargrilled spicy boned quail or flash-fried calamari with chorizo to start. Steaks are enormously popular here, likewise the locally farmed barramundi from nearby Moama and locally grown lamb. There is an extensive list of wines available by the glass, carafe or bottle.

101 Murray Espl, Port of Echuca; (03) 5482 5133; open daily for lunch and dinner; www.oscarws.com.au

PS EMMYLOU $$

INTERNATIONAL

This 1981-built paddlesteamer is a faithful reproduction of earlier vessels that plied the mighty Murray River. On day cruises, morning and afternoon teas are available as well as an à la carte menu. At night, a set-price three-course dinner is offered with a good selection for each course. Start with Japanese pancakes, scallops brochette or pâté, before moving on to Angus porterhouse steak, muscovy duck, marinated Asian-style chicken fillet or Tasmanian ocean trout with French onion tart. Dessert might be brown-sugar panna cotta, chocolate fondant or lemon and lime tart with King Island double cream. The *Emmylou* often cruises the upper reaches of the Murray for several days at a time, so check availability before booking for a dinner or lunchtime cruise.

57 Murray Espl; (03) 5482 5244; open daily for lunch and dinner; www.emmylou.com.au

Emerald

ELEVATION AT EMERALD $$

MODERN AUSTRALIAN

This purpose-built modern restaurant was built to maximise the views over the velvet green hills of Emerald. Polished concrete floors and coloured suede couches welcome guests to the light-filled contemporary space. There is a good selection of tapas dishes for starters before more serious main course dishes such as duck ballotine, beef Wellington, flathead tails in beer batter, pastas, risottos and a variety of good steaks. The menu is constantly changing, with a daily lunchtime three-course special deal that is also available on Monday and Tuesday evenings for dinner.

374 Main Rd; (03) 5968 2911; open daily for lunch and dinner

Euroa

RUFFY PRODUCE STORE $$
CAFE PROVEDORE

Apart from a fire shed with a few trucks, there's not much in Ruffy (population: a handful) in the heart of the Strathbogie Ranges. So what a delightful surprise to happen upon this culinary oasis that offers simple, flavoursome fare championing quality local produce. Enjoy good coffee on the lawn, or hop into a terrific breakfast of bircher muesli with Di's rhubarb and yoghurt, panettone French toast with lemon curd and crème fraîche or indeed bacon and eggs with perhaps side orders of mushrooms with lemon and tarragon or hearty bushman's sausages. For lunch, try the produce platter of an amazing array of homemade goodies, local Donnybrook and Yea cheeses and fresh Euroa ciabatta.

26 Nolans Rd, Ruffy; (03) 5790 4387; open weekends and public holidays for breakfast, and Fri–Sun and public holidays for lunch; www.ruffy.com.au

Flinders

FOXEYS HANGOUT $
VINEYARD RESTAURANT

Foxeys Hangout's cellar door, housed in a smart wood and glass building overlooking the vineyard, also incorporates an excellent little eatery that offers a series of small dishes. These work equally well as a quick snack with a glass of wine or, ordered en masse, as a more substantial meal. Local ingredients feature prominently, like mushrooms wrapped in vine leaves, and there is usually excellent barbecued quail and spiced meatballs. A brief, well-selected range of cheeses, chosen to complement the winery's output, seems as good a reason as any to linger longer.

795 White Hill Rd, Red Hill; (03) 5989 2022; open weekends and public holidays for lunch; www.foxeys-hangout.com.au

MERRICKS GENERAL STORE $$
FRENCH

Dating back to the 1920s, and with a fairly recent refurbishment under its belt, the Merricks General Store is certainly one of the more atmospheric pit stops on the Mornington Peninsula. Operating as a cellar door for three local wineries, the store is also a bistro dishing up rustic, French-influenced food. The charcuterie is always good and they also do a tasty line in tarts and flans, both sweet and savoury. Good wine and coffee complete a cheery and satisfying picture.

3458 Frankston–Flinders Rd, Merricks; (03) 5989 8088; open daily for breakfast and lunch; www.merricksgeneralstore.com.au

MONTALTO $$$$
VINEYARD RESTAURANT

Using the surrounding natural beauty as inspiration, this rammed-earth vineyard restaurant appears to have thought of everything. More than 1500 olive trees and 11 hectares of vineyards provide spectacular views through floor-to-ceiling windows while diners feast on dishes that feature organic herbs and vegetables from the winery gardens. The innovative French-influenced menu, backed by local flavours, offers wonderful dishes such as the Red Hill goat's cheese soufflé with truffle-scented cauliflower purée and herb salad. After lunch, view the sculpture park and take a wander through the wetlands on specially constructed boardwalks. In addition

WHERE TO EAT

FAMILY FRIENDLY   LICENSED   OUTDOOR DINING   VEGETARIAN OPTIONS

to its award-winning wine, Montalto produces its own olive oil and verjuice.

33 Shoreham Rd, Red Hill South; (03) 5989 8412; open daily for lunch and Fri–Sat for dinner; extended summer hours; www.montalto.com.au

TEN MINUTES BY TRACTOR $$$
VINEYARD RESTAURANT

There is a lot to like at this smart winery restaurant, starting with the wonderful view over rolling hills and lush vines from the expansive windows of the main dining room. The award-winning wine list – a well-annotated collection of wines from all over the world, chosen to compare and contrast with Ten Minutes' own, ever-improving output – is another reason to visit. The clever food takes advantage of much of the region's great produce, with seafood a strong point. They also know how to treat a steak with respect, an ideal reason to scour the wine list for a perfect match.

1333 Mornington–Flinders Rd, Main Ridge; (03) 5989 6080; open Thurs–Sun for lunch and Thurs–Sat for dinner; extended summer hours; www.tenminutesbytractor.com.au

Geelong

2 FACES $$$
MODERN AUSTRALIAN
Map ref. p. 98

This restaurant is housed in a former 1857-built bluestone bank that is heritage-listed and considered of state significance. Its rooms boast soaring ceilings with cornices, and the windows still sport the bars from its days as a bank. Cosy in winter and welcoming in summer, 2 Faces has earned a reputation for its twice-baked cheese and zucchini soufflé with mascarpone blue cheese sauce as an entrée, and

the seafood-filled bouillabaisse is exemplary. Other recommended dishes are twice-cooked Western Plains pork belly or local Chesterdale lamb rack with globe artichoke and haloumi fritters. Finish with the chef's dessert plate with a taste of everything sweet.

8 Malop St; (03) 5229 4546; open Tues–Sat for dinner; www.2faces.com.au

FISHERMEN'S PIER $$$
SEAFOOD
Map ref. p. 98

Sitting out over the water of Corio Bay, this enormously popular seafood restaurant has been pleasing locals since 1971. Embracing a simple, modern bistro style, the ever-changing menu has an emphasis on local seafood. Start with the local Queenscliff calamari with chorizo, rocket and garlic or the terrific seafood chowder made with fresh Port Arlington mussels and scallops. For main course, consider the sesame-crusted yellowfin tuna with red papaya salsa, or the enormously popular seafood selection for two with a variety of fresh and cooked seafood – and not a deep-fried prawn in sight. There is also a good variety of meat and vegetarian dishes, and since all food is prepared to order, all dietary requirements can be catered for.

Yarra St, Eastern Beach; (03) 5222 4100; open daily for lunch and dinner; www.fishermenspier.com.au

THE BEACH HOUSE $$$
MODERN AUSTRALIAN
Map ref. p. 98

On the beach at Waterfront Bay, this two-storey property on the promenade overlooks the children's swimming pool by day and the lights of Melbourne across the bay by night. The upstairs restaurant is light-filled with lots of glass and white furnishings to maximise the seaside views. Expect entrées such as steamed Port Arlington mussels, an antipasto plate

and a vegetarian tasting plate to start. Main courses might be oven-roasted rack of lamb, Thai yellow curry, linguini marinara, char-sui marinated pork belly or market-fresh local fish. A cafe downstairs offers a more casual menu of wraps and burgers, and is open daily for breakfast and lunch.

Eastern Beach Reserve, Waterfront Bay; (03) 5221 8322; open Fri–Sun for lunch and Wed–Sat for dinner; www.easternbeachhouse.com.au

PETTAVEL WINERY & RESTAURANT

$$$

VINEYARD RESTAURANT

Named after the visionary Swiss immigrant David Pettavel, this estate perches on a hilltop surrounded by hectares of shiraz vineyards. The restaurant was originally intended to complement the lush winery, but this thriving, award-winning family business is now a favourite port of call for foodies in its own right. Dishes are conceived according to the seasons and the region's own produce. A five-course degustation menu is offered with matched wines; an eight-course degustation is available on request. At the cellar door, the attention to detail is continued and the starter plate for two is the perfect accompaniment to wine-tasting.

65 Pettavel Rd, Waurn Ponds; (03) 5266 1120; open daily for lunch and Fri for dinner; www.pettavel.com

Glenrowan

BAILEYS OLD BLOCK CAFE

$$

VINEYARD RESTAURANT

This historic family property was settled in 1853, with vines planted in 1866 producing the first wine in 1870. Today the old handmade brick winery overlooks the Warby Ranges and Lake Mokoan and houses the welcoming gallery room that serves as a showcase for local art during the week and as a cafe at weekends. The ever-changing menu features what's fresh and seasonally available – perhaps a fresh prawn or Greek salad in summer, or soul-warming mulligatawny or pumkin soup in winter. There is also a popular grazing plate of local produce for two. All dishes complement the estate-grown wines, such as the double-chocolate brownies with tokay-soaked figs matched, of course, with tokay.

Baileys of Glenrowan, Taminick Gap Rd; (03) 5766 2392; open weekends for lunch; www.baileysofglenrowan.com.au

Hamilton

DARRIWILL FARM

$$$

CAFE PROVEDORE

Although the original farm is a few hours away at Bannockburn, this produce/wine store and cafe champions regional produce – selling through its retail outlet (it has even spawned outlets interstate) and featuring local fare on its menu. A typical entrée might be crumbed calamari with Greek-style salad using Mount Zero olives, Meredith goat's feta and Doodles Creek lemon and caper mayonnaise. More substantial dishes might be warm Western District beef salad with roasted marinated vegetables, oven-baked rack of grain-fed lamb with caramelised onion, or crisp-skinned duck breast with braised wild rabbit pie. They stock a huge variety of local wines as well as other Australian and imported ones.

169 Grey St; (03) 5571 2088; open Mon–Sat for breakfast and lunch, and Thurs–Sat for dinner; www.darriwillfarm.com.au/store-hamilton.html

WHERE TO EAT

FAMILY FRIENDLY   LICENSED   OUTDOOR DINING   VEGETARIAN OPTIONS

HAMILTON STRAND RESTAURANT $$$

ITALIAN

A former bank manager's residence has been turned into fine-dining restaurant, complete with high ceilings, chandeliers, open fires and an outdoor dining patio that overlooks a lovely English-style rose garden. The Italian menu represents good value for money, producing exemplary modern dishes such as the ever-popular homemade gnocchi served with double-braised beef cheek, red onion, tomato and herbs tossed with feta. Main course could be slow-roasted saltbush lamb rump, with a white chocolate panna cotta and local berry salad for dessert. The extensive wine list features many regional wines.

100 Thompson St; (03) 5571 9144; open Wed–Sat for lunch and Mon–Sat for dinner

ROXBURGH HOUSE $

MODERN AUSTRALIAN

Off the main street in a former doctor's two-storey Victorian home, this welcoming wine-bar-cum-cosy-cafe has evolved into a fully fledged restaurant serving terrific tapas and great pizzas. Its intimate, homely rooms are furnished with antique leather couches, armchairs and the occasional dining table, with different music playing in each room. There's also a more formal dining room upstairs for sit-down monthly dinners with a set menu. Order an antipasto platter, a cheese board or a few tapas plates to share: garlic prawns, spicy meatballs, ranchos huevos (baked eggs), salt cod cakes, tuna turnovers and more. Pizza toppings are interesting and the wine list is good, with local wines the heroes.

64 Thompson St; (03) 5572 4857; open Tues–Sat for lunch and Thurs–Sat for dinner

CAFE CATALPA $$$

MODERN AUSTRALIAN

The only business in Tarrington – there's a church and a school – this former general store has been transformed into a lively cafe just 8 kilometres out of Hamilton. It is named after a 40-year-old catalpa Indian bean tree that stands nearby. Hunting pictures and memorabilia adorn the walls, reflecting the preponderance of game on the menu. Entrées might feature quail, smoked eel from Wangoom or local yabbies. Locals love the duck and shiitake mushroom pies, rabbit with Dijon mustard and slow-cooked hare with star anise. Even the beer-battered fish and chips, and old-fashioned hamburgers have regulars raving. On Sundays, diners often arrive in vintage and veteran cars and classic motorbikes. There's a good list of regional wines.

7921 Hamilton Hwy, Tarrington; (03) 5572 1888; open Wed–Sun for breakfast and lunch, and Wed–Sat for dinner

Healesville

3777 $$$

MODERN AUSTRALIAN

Boasting the best views in the Yarra Valley, 3777 would be able to draw a crowd on the strength of its vistas alone. But there is no laurel-resting in the smartly kitted-out restaurant of this small boutique retreat. Perched on the top of a hill, it is furnished in soothing natural shades of brown and green, with lots of natural light, open fireplaces and comfortable upholstery. The menu has influences from both Europe and Asia, and utilises the best ingredients the region offers, including local venison, salmon roe, stone fruit and chocolate. Local wine also gets a good showing.

BYO AVAILABLE   CREDIT CARDS ACCEPTED   DISABLED ACCESS   DRESS CODE APPLIES

Mt Rael Retreat, 140 Healesville–Yarra Glen Rd; (03) 5962 1977; open Thurs–Sun for lunch and dinner, and weekends for breakfast; www.mtrael.com.au/mtrael/dining.php

GIANT STEPS/INNOCENT BYSTANDER $$$

MODERN AUSTRALIAN

A bakery, cafe, cellar door and cheese room in one, Giant Steps/Innocent Bystander has a trendy, industrial feel that provides the setting for a multitude of gourmet experiences. Just off Healesville's main road, this modern complex is a large, light-filled space with steel and large windows. The artisan bakery displays breads, cakes and pastries (including delicious Portuguese tarts) that you can take away or enjoy in the central seating area overlooking the wine barrels. If you are interested in a more substantial meal, the kitchen produces terrific wood-fired pizzas, salads and 'pots' with the likes of cinnamon-baked chicken with tomato, air-dried chorizo and couscous. Wine and cheese tastings offer further indulgences.

336 Maroondah Hwy; (03) 5962 6111; open daily for lunch and dinner, and weekends for breakfast; www.innocentbystander.com.au

HEALESVILLE HOTEL $$$

MODERN AUSTRALIAN

You'll enjoy one of the best dining experiences in the Yarra Valley at this gastropub, where the timber floors, sandy-coloured walls and cane chairs add a touch of old-fashioned character. The owners and chef source produce from farms and backyards all over the valley and have won many awards for their endeavours. The same menu is offered for lunch and dinner, with changing specials such as local figs in Spanish jamon or Murramong lamb in baba ganoush. Entrées could be terrine of confit duck and poached pear or twice-cooked pork

belly with roast scallops. Main courses might include chorizo and muscatel-stuffed local quail, pan-fried snapper, roast wagyu beef or veal saltimbocca. The outstanding wine list has also won awards.

256 Maroondah Hwy; (03) 5962 4002; open daily for lunch and dinner; www.healesvillehotel.com.au

BELLA VEDERE $$$

VINEYARD RESTAURANT

Surrounded by the vines of Badger's Brook Estate, the atmosphere at Bella Vedere is rustic country style, casual but smart. The open-plan kitchen offers diners a view of the intricate food preparation undertaken by owner/chef Gary Cooper and his team. The menu offers exceptional food, comprising fresh regional produce meticulously prepared. Produce and bread baked on the premises can be purchased from the bakery, and there is a vegetable garden out the back door. Warming soups and comforting dishes of duck, corned beef, pork and baked salmon might feature in winter, while desserts might be locally made ice-creams or lightly poached creations and flavoursome tarts based on seasonal fruits such as raspberries, pears and quinces. Friday night is à la carte and on Saturday night there's a degustation menu.

874 Maroondah Hwy, Coldstream; (03) 5962 6161; open Wed–Sun for breakfast and lunch, and Fri–Sat for dinner; www.badgersbrook.com.au

Heathcote

EMEU INN $$$

INTERNATIONAL

The atmospheric Emeu Inn restaurant is housed in one of the town's oldest buildings

FAMILY FRIENDLY   LICENSED   OUTDOOR DINING   VEGETARIAN OPTIONS

(1857) in a region renowned for its first-class red wines. The seasonal menu is an eclectic mix of regional produce, with a selection of 'bush tucker' and dishes reflecting the owner's German origins. The truffle and porcini mushroom risotto has been on the menu since day one, and there is always a rabbit dish in winter and fruits from the orchard in summer. You might also find confit duck leg with sour cherries and puréed chestnuts, and an emu-meat shepherd's pie with red wine. The atmosphere is comfy and homey, with roaring log fires in winter and alfresco dining in the garden in summer. The wine list is impressive, with a dazzling array of labels representing Heathcote producers.

187 High St; (03) 5433 2668; open Thurs–Mon for lunch and dinner; www.emeuinn.com.au

Horsham

CAFE CHICKPEA $

CAFE

Just off the main road in Horsham, this homely little cafe has been serving hearty breakfasts and light lunches to locals and travellers alike for over 14 years. Most of the food is baked fresh daily on the premises, such as quiches, frittatas, zucchini bakes, and spinach and feta pies. Regulars come to breakfast on fresh fruit salad, cereal and local free-range eggs any way you like them. Any dietary requirement can be catered for including gluten-free, diabetic and lactose-intolerance. The local artwork that adorns the walls is for sale, and is rotated regularly.

30A Pynsent St; (03) 5382 3998; open daily for breakfast and lunch

Inverloch

TOMO $$

JAPANESE

This friendly Japanese restaurant in the main street of Inverloch is a contemporary space with walls displaying modern Japanese artworks and a Japanese-style bamboo garden at the back. Owner/chef Tomo Ezaki cooked at one of Melbourne's favourite Japanese restaurants for several years and already has a loyal following of locals here. If you are fond of chilli, let Tomo know and he'll spice things up for you. His dishes are designed to be shared – even the steak with wasabi mash is cut for that purpose. Recommended are the gyoza (Japanese-style dumplings) and spicy calamari legs with chilli and garlic. The stand-out main course is touban duck – a fillet of duck breast cooked in a rich broth with mushrooms, leeks, soy, mirin, miso and chilli.

Shop 1, 23 A'Beckett St; (03) 5674 3444; open Wed–Sun for lunch (daily in school holidays) and Tues–Sun for dinner

VELLA 9 $$$

MODERN AUSTRALIAN

Tony Richardson, ex-sous-chef of the Healesville Hotel, and his partner, Felicity O'Dea, have taken over the former Cafe Gabriel's. The modern Australian menu with Mediterranean influences is produce-driven and draws on Richardson's 16 years of experience behind the stoves including time spent in Spain and Italy, and an early childhood in the Barossa Valley with a thriving home garden. The restaurant serves his own homemade bread, ice-creams, sorbets, pastries and pasta, as well as tapas-style dishes such as white bean puree with olives, and goats cheese with chargrilled Turkish bread. Other menu delights could include Gippsland beef, organic lamb, crispy-skin duck with apricots and Pedro Ximénez or two-toned squid-ink tagliatelle with squid and prawns.

9 A'Beckett St; (03) 5674 1188; open Wed–Sun for lunch and dinner; limited hours in winter

Kyneton

ANNIE SMITHERS' BISTROT $$$

FRENCH

Talented chef Annie Smithers has worked at many top Melbourne restaurants and now focuses on her own country eatery. When she opened in 2005, this was possibly the only decent restaurant in town; today, Piper Street is a fabulous 'eat street' and foodies' precinct. On her farm at Malmsbury, Annie grows fruit and vegetables, runs free-range chooks and sources other fine local produce. Her unpretentious French provincial fare charms everyone visiting her high-ceilinged restaurant. Entrées might be deep-fried brains with Seville orange marmalade and bacon, or classic steak tartare. There is often confit duck leg and a special steak dish featuring local beef. Desserts are likely to be a delicious French-inspired crème brûlée or crème caramel. She also has a takeaway wine licence so visitors can try local labels.

72 Piper St; (03) 5422 2039; open Wed–Sun for lunch and Thurs–Sat for dinner; www.anniesmithers.com.au

LITTLE SWALLOW CAFE $

FRENCH

A newcomer to the Piper Street scene is this little European-style cafe owned and run by Steve and Sarah Rogers, who both spent several years honing their culinary skills in Jacques Reymond's celebrated Melbourne restaurant. Having lived in France, their aim is to bring southern Mediterranean flavours to the Victorian country through their warm and welcoming cafe. Start the day with a classic eggs Benedict, baked eggs or roasted field mushrooms with baby spinach and goat's curd. For lunch, try the white bean salad with marinated anchovies, leek and gruyère tart or more substantial dishes such as braised lamb with Mount Zero olives on soft polenta. Sarah used to run Reymond's pastry section, so be sure to check her range of cakes, tarts and homemade nougat.

58A Piper St; (03) 5422 6241; open Wed–Sun for breakfast and lunch; www.littleswallowcafe.com

PIZZA VERDE $$

ITALIAN

This warm and welcoming restaurant was designed for the locals – several have regular weekly bookings. Chef Damian Sandercock uses the wood-fired oven not only for his crisp, thin-based, Roman-style pizzas, but also for oven-baked dishes like spinach and ricotta balls and even to toast the bread that might go into his Tuscan tomato and bread panzanella salad. In winter there is a Sunday roast; in summer, a Sunday salad. There are always daily specials – perhaps scallops wrapped in pancetta – and the antipasto selection includes plenty of regional produce. Popular pizza toppings include pork and fennel sausage with cherry tomatoes, parmesan and oregano, and the bianco pizza has a base of caramelised onion topped with potatoes, pancetta, sage and assiago cheese. There's a rear courtyard with pavement dining in summer.

62 Piper St; (03) 5422 7400; open Sun for lunch and Thurs–Mon for dinner; www.pizzaverde.com

WHERE TO EAT

FAMILY FRIENDLY   LICENSED   OUTDOOR DINING   VEGETARIAN OPTIONS

ROYAL GEORGE HOTEL $$$

MEDITERRANEAN

While the Royal George falls into the category of spruced-up country gastropub, it still retains the relaxed and hospitable vibe of the old-time hotel. The dining room may be all quality linen cloths, good stemware and designer salt – a good fit with a menu full of deftly cooked, quality ingredients – but the service and ambience are neither stuffy nor snooty. You feel as if they want you to have a good time, which is easy to do with dishes like local lamb teamed with Moroccan spices, salt cod croquettes and a good selection of local cheeses. The wine list gives you a chance to sample the region's best.

24 Piper St; (03) 5422 1390; open Thurs–Sun for lunch and Wed–Sat for dinner; www.royalgeorge.com.au

STAR ANISE BISTRO $$$

INTERNATIONAL

In a lovely old Victorian house with polished floorboards, dark wooden furniture, open fireplaces and an eclectic collection of chairs, this intimate 25-seater has a warm, European bistro feel. Using as much local, free-range, organic and seasonal produce as possible, the menu reflects Asian, Italian and Middle Eastern influences and ingredients. Popular entrées are seared scallops on fennel, apple and mint salad, or vegetarian spinach crepe pinwheels filled with roast pumpkin and drizzled with sage butter sauce. Main courses might include star-anise-spiced duck salad with roasted beets and orange and cherry dressing, or slow-cooked pork belly in soy, ginger and star anise served with scallops and chilli jam.

29A Piper St; (03) 5422 2777; open Wed–Sun for lunch and Thurs–Sat for dinner; www.staranisebistro.com

Lakes Entrance

BOATHOUSE RESTAURANT $$$

SEAFOOD
Map ref. p. 112

Part of the Bellevue on the Lakes hotel complex, this stand-alone restaurant specialises in local seafood and has been voted one of the top ten seafood restaurants in Victoria. The contemporary restaurant has linen-clad tables and exudes a good atmosphere. Lovers of seafood can't see past the three-course seafood banquet, where the stars of the menu arrive in three distinct courses. First, cold seafood arrives: a selection of oysters, chilled prawns and aioli. Then, hot seafood: prawn spring rolls, salt-and-pepper calamari, garlic prawns, Thai-style fish cakes and scallops with chorizo sausage. The last course comprises salmon fillet, crumbed flathead tails, battered gummy shark and chips. Carnivores should go for the terrific eye fillet. Happy hour is from 5pm to 6pm.

201 The Esplanade; (03) 5155 3055; open daily for breakfast and dinner

FERRYMAN'S SEAFOOD CAFE $$$

SEAFOOD
Map ref. p. 112

Walk over the gangplank to this floating restaurant for some of the freshest seafood around. Built on the pontoon base of a former Raymond Island car ferry, this seafood eatery has three sunny decks, including one that is heated and can be enclosed with blinds when the weather turns chilly. The restaurant works with three deep-sea trawlers to source fresh fish – hapuka, rockling, blue-eye, snapper and flathead tails. It is known for its fish and chips, seafood platters and bouillabaisse.

Middle Boat Harbour, The Esplanade; (03) 5155 3000; open daily for brunch, lunch and dinner; www.ferrymans.com.au

MIRIAM'S

$$
SEAFOOD
$$
Map ref. p. 112

Take a seat on the balcony of this first-floor restaurant overlooking the vast waters of the lakes and the trawlers that dock there after a day's fishing. Locals come for the warm bruschetta of smoky red peppers, feta, grilled prawns and oregano, or freshly shucked oysters done three ways: chilled with lemon wedges, in tempura batter or roasted with semi-dried tomatoes, bacon and parsley. They also plump for the roasted fillet of chicken filled with prawn, tomato and feta, or the very versatile Miriam's Greek fisherman's plate that can be ordered all hot, all cold or half and half. In season it comprises crabmeat, crayfish, mussels, fish, oysters, prawns, calamari, Balmain bugs and more.

Level 1, cnr The Esplanade & Bulmer St; (03) 5155 3999; open daily for dinner

THE METUNG GALLEY

$$$
MODERN AUSTRALIAN

A culinary highlight in often sleepy Metung, this lively cafe serves good coffee, a flexible menu and a good wine list that locals really appreciate. Kick-start the day with the Galley breakfast choice of Turkish bread topped with spinach, fried eggs and melted tasty cheese with spicy tomato relish. Light lunch dishes include chicken and salmon baguettes or focaccia, or go for more substantial dishes like salt-and-pepper calamari or Gippsland lamb cutlets stuffed with olive and parmesan. Local Lakes Entrance scallops and mussels are super fresh – pan-fried and steamed, respectively. Other popular dishes include linguini with Lakes Entrance seafood, rack of oven-roasted pork with salted apple salad, and Gippsland eye fillet on a white wine and basil risotto cake.

3/59 Metung Rd, Metung; (03) 5156 2330; open daily for lunch, and Tues–Sat for breakfast and dinner; extended summer hours; www.themetunggalley.com.au

Lorne

BA BA LU BAR AND RESTAURANT

$$$

SPANISH

This graceful heritage-listed building near the entrance to Lorne enjoys a quasi village atmosphere, overlooking green parks and the Erskine River. Since the French-Swiss owner used to run a Spanish restaurant in Spain, the menu here is strictly Spanish and tapas is king. Dishes are designed to share – Spanish meatballs, sherry-marinated mushrooms or perhaps authentic Spanish ham. The menu changes daily, the food is as fresh as can be, and it is all made in-house. Sunday is paella night, when this iconic seafood and rice dish is prepared with great ceremony in a huge communal paella pan, accompanied by live

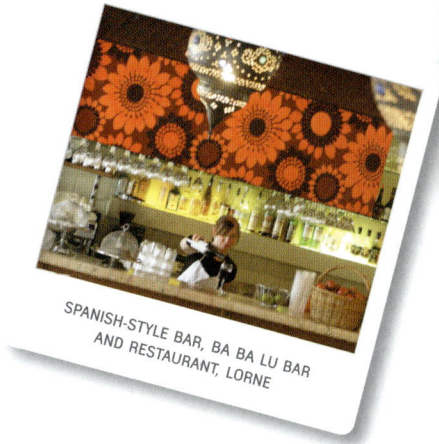

SPANISH-STYLE BAR, BA BA LU BAR AND RESTAURANT, LORNE

FAMILY FRIENDLY   LICENSED   OUTDOOR DINING   VEGETARIAN OPTIONS

music. Many Spanish wines, beers and sherries are available by the bottle or glass.

6A Mountjoy Pde; (03) 5289 1808; open daily for breakfast, lunch and dinner; www.babalubar.com.au

BISTRO C BAR & RESTAURANT $$$
SEAFOOD

With a big covered deck that enjoys uninterrupted views over the water to Aireys Inlet and beyond, this relaxed seafood eatery has one of the best locations in town. Recently freshened up, and given a new name (it was formerly Aqua), there is a new deck at Bistro C that puts diners even closer to the ocean. A blackboard announces daily specials – perhaps angel-hair pasta with scallops, mussels and cauliflower cream, or the catch of the day, maybe pan-fried snapper. The highly recommended seafood platter could comprise prawns, grilled scampi, smoked salmon, marinated crab, oysters, Tasmanian scallops and more. Seafood is sourced from Lorne and Geelong, and there is a special menu for children with games, pens and lots of fun.

Cumberland Lorne Resort, 150 Mountjoy Pde; (03) 5289 2455; open daily for breakfast, lunch and dinner Sept–Apr; reduced winter hours; www.cumberland.com.au

LORNE OVENHOUSE $$$
ITALIAN

Although the wood-fired oven has been moved inside the kitchen, you can still view this hallowed beast through windows and in winter sit in front of an open fire. Early birds catch the limited number of boned shoulder of lamb that has been slow-roasted in the oven for up to five hours with garlic and rosemary; others plump for the crispy, oven-baked whole baby snapper.

Pizzas include the crispy thin-based margherita topped with tomato, fior di latte cheese and fresh basil, and the Australiana of chicken breast with smoked bacon, caramelised onion and parmesan. Succulent seafood pizza is covered with king prawns, scallops, coriander, basil and a touch of chilli. For something different, the vegetable Goan-style curry is also a winner.

46A Mountjoy Pde; (03) 5289 2544; open weekends for breakfast and lunch, and daily for dinner; closed Tues–Wed end Apr–Nov; www.ovenhouse.com.au

QDOS $$$
EUROPEAN

Qdos is situated among the trees and wildlife of Great Otway National Park at the back of Lorne. You can either drive the kilometre up the hill or, if you're feeling energetic, walk. Enjoy a restorative drink at the bar while appreciating the international artworks in the gallery or cosy up in the lounge by the fire while considering the interesting menu. With experience in Michelin-star restaurants in Europe, the chefs here offer an exciting range of dishes, beginning with breakfasts of sautéed wild mushrooms with thyme and ricotta cheese, or blanched muesli, poached eggs and rhubarb with homemade yoghurt. In the evening, try the duck tart with parmesan pastry followed by marsala-baked figs. They bake their own breads, churn homemade ice-cream and harvest fresh produce from a kitchen garden.

35 Allenvale Rd; (03) 5289 1989; open daily for breakfast and lunch, and Thurs–Sat for dinner in summer; closed Tues–Wed in winter; www.qdosarts.com

Maldon

PENNY SCHOOL GALLERY/CAFE $$$
INTERNATIONAL

Housed in one of only six Victorian heritage-listed buildings in Maldon – itself classified by the National Trust as Australian's first notable town – this gallery cafe was a former denominational (Penny) school prior to the days of public education. Today it is a commercial fine art gallery, its walls lined with high-quality artworks. Lunch ranges from pasta, frittatas and antipasto platters to classic French terrines such as duck and pistachio. For dinner, perhaps start with a chickpea and prosciutto soup or prawn and water chestnut dumplings before trying a main course of Moroccan-style tagine of lamb with preserved lemon or a red Thai duck curry.

11 Church St; (03) 5475 1911; open daily for lunch and Fri–Sun for dinner; www.pennyschoolgallery.com.au

ZEN EDEN PRODUCE $
VEGETARIAN

A lovely little two-storey 1870-built shopfront is the perfect setting for this most agreeable vegetarian cafe and produce store. Admire the pressed-metal ceiling as you check out the fresh organic and biodynamic produce in the front of the shop, or make your way through to take a seat inside, on the rear deck, under the pergola or in the garden. The menu changes daily, depending on what is in season. There might be an eggplant stack, asparagus and bocconcini tart, vegetarian lasagne, bean and potato pie, rice and broccoli tart or a spinach and risotto crepe stack. Dine in or pick up prepared dishes to take away. Fair Trade coffee is served for morning and afternoon tea, and non-alcoholic wine is available.

6 Main St; 0408 319 188; open Tues–Sun for lunch

Mallacoota

LUCY'S NOODLES $
CHINESE

This family-owned and run noodle house believes in doing things properly. Lucy, who used to run her own restaurant in Nanning, the capital of Guangxi province in China, even grinds her own rice for the authentic noodles made fresh every morning, serving them with hydroponic produce fresh from her home garden. Other choices include local abalone and sea urchin roe, chicken, pork, tofu and popular cha'sui – classic barbecue pork and beef. She also makes homemade dumplings filled with vegetables, pork, prawns and more. When the population of this sleepy fishing village swells from 800 to 5000 in summer, the noodle shop buzzes from 7am till very late at night, as everything is prepared fresh.

64 Maurice Ave; (03) 5158 0666; open daily for breakfast, lunch and dinner

Mansfield

MANSFIELD HOTEL $$
MODERN AUSTRALIAN

This central 1862-built country hotel has been recently renovated, with big glass doors opening onto a rear courtyard that is shaded in summer for dining by a century-old pin-oak. There's a playground for children to keep them amused while adults can enjoy a few quiet drinks and dine in peace. Regulars drive from Melbourne and nearby towns just to enjoy the meals cooked on special heated granite

FAMILY FRIENDLY   LICENSED   OUTDOOR DINING   VEGETARIAN OPTIONS

WHERE TO EAT

stones. In DIY barbecue style, patrons cook their own choice of chicken, pork or steak over these intensely hot stones that are brought out to individual tables – accompanied by salads. The hotel also does a roaring trade with thin, crisp-crust gourmet pizzas from their wood-fired oven.

86 High St; (03) 5775 2101; open daily for lunch and dinner; www.mansfieldhotel.com.au

MANSFIELD REGIONAL PRODUCE STORE $$

CAFE PROVEDORE

Three yellow umbrellas identify this popular produce store and cafe housed in an 1895 building with high cathedral ceilings and exposed beams. Known locally as 'the proddy', it oozes colour and character with fresh produce, local artworks, a rear wine room with more than 80 regional wines, and the savvy cafe serving terrific food and great coffee. Like a 'bit of Melbourne in Mansfield', they bake their own breads and fill baguettes with rare roast beef, tandoori chicken and the like. Signature dishes include King Valley dips, sweet potato and macadamia nut fritters, and produce platters. The third Friday of the month is Bracket and Jam night, when top local musicians head up a quickly booked-out jam session.

68 High St; (03) 5779 1404; open Tues–Sun for lunch and Fri for dinner; www.theproducestore.com.au

THE MAGNOLIA RESTAURANT $$$

MODERN AUSTRALIAN

Surrounded by an established garden with the eponymous 110-year-old magnolia in front, this gracious, century-old, two-storey, twin-gabled cottage is the perfect setting for dining out in the country. Although they serve modern Australian dishes, you can expect the occasional European accent to appear since the chef and

co-owner is indeed Austrian. While the menu might feature High Country beef and farmed barramundi, locals know that Wednesday is schnitzel night, with a choice of beef, pork or chicken schnitzels with various toppings. On Thursdays a degustation menu is offered, available with matching wines.

190 Mt Buller Rd; (03) 5779 1444; open Thurs–Sat for dinner; www.magnoliamansfield.com.au

JAMIESON BREWERY $$

BREWERY RESTAURANT

There was a Jamieson Brewery in this historic town during the gold-rush days of the 1850s – in fact there were three. Brewer Jeff White and his wife, Jeanette, built the new brewery in 2001 and today brew six different ales. The menu complements their hand-crafted ales, with a beer suggestion for each dish. If you can't make up your mind, start with a tasting tray of the four beers they have on tap. Popular dishes are beef and beer pie with Pale Ale and lamb shanks cooked in Mountain Ale. There are several daily specials such as kranskys on creamy mashed potato and a children's menu that includes dessert.

Eildon Rd, Jamieson; (03) 5777 0515; open daily for lunch and dinner; www.jamiesonbrewery.com.au

Milawa

RESTAURANT MERLOT $$$

MODERN AUSTRALIAN

Overlooking estate vines to Mount Buffalo, this contemporary space is the stylish dining room of Lindenwarrah Country House Hotel. The seasonally changing menu features quality local produce from the celebrated Milawa gourmet region. A typical entrée might be King

Valley free-range pork sausage with Milawa Capricornia goat's cheese, red apple salad, Milawa honey mustard and pomegranate orange dressing. Main course might be Milawa free-range chicken on spiced polenta with wilted baby spinach and pomegranate yoghurt, or Meadow Creek beef fillet on potato röesti with sautéed green beans, crème fraîche and beetroot and horseradish dressing.

Lindenwarrah Country House Hotel, Milawa–Bobinawarrah Rd; (03) 5720 5777; open Fri–Sun for lunch and Thurs–Sun for dinner; www.lindenwarrah.com.au/merlot.html

THE AGEING FROG BISTROT $$
MODERN AUSTRALIAN

Housed in a former 1915 butter factory, this bistro is part of the Milawa Cheese Company's multi-pronged tourist complex. And although French chef Michel Renoux has moved on, current chef Bob Langmead continues Renoux's French influence through the modern Australian menu that also has a few touches of Italy. Smaller dishes are popular, such as pan-fried quail, prawns and saffron risotto or oven-baked scallops. The delicious country terrine of pork, chicken and game is recommended. More hearty dishes include braised, stuffed and rolled pork belly, and double-roasted duck leg with the famous local salad of Stanley apples and walnuts with a port and apple glaze. Finish with a local cheese platter, accompanied by sourdough bread from the on-site bakery.

Milawa Cheese Company, Factory Rd; (03) 5727 3589; open daily for lunch; www.milawacheese.com.au

THE EPICUREAN CENTRE $$
VINEYARD-RESTAURANT

The menu at this winery restaurant is designed to complement the terrific range of estate wines. Dishes are rustic in style, and each one is paired with two or three wine suggestions. Local vine-wrapped river trout slow cooked with baby fennel, lemon and white beans matches a non-vintage sparkling, the 2006 rosé or a 2007 chardonnay. Spatchcock roasted with truffle butter and fresh beans is matched with a 2005 tempranillo, 2008 viognier and 2007 chardonnay, while homemade gnocchi with local cherry tomatoes, chilli and fresh mint is matched with a 2008 sauvignon blanc, 2006 barbera and non-vintage pinot meunier. Parents can relax while children play in the terrific fenced-off playground.

Brown Brothers Vineyard, 239 Milawa–Bobinawarrah Rd; (03) 5720 5540; open daily for lunch; www.brownbrothers.com.au/ourplace/epicureancentre.aspx

Mildura

SPANISH BAR AND GRILL $$$$
STEAKHOUSE
Map ref. p. 120

The owners of this popular up-market steakhouse go to a lot of trouble obtaining premium cuts of meat, aged on the bone and cooked over a real charcoal fire of slow-burning red gum and mallee roots. Butchers from Loxton, Ouyen and Mildura source prime beef from local farmers; the chefs do the rest – usually to perfection. There are plenty of non-meat options, such as seafood and poultry, but not a lot of choices for vegetarians. The adjacent Seasons restaurant at the central wine bar offers a seasonally changing menu of modern Australian fare; it is open Monday to Saturday for dinner.

Quality Hotel Mildura Grand, Langtree Ave; (03) 5021 2377; open Tues–Sun for dinner; www.seasonsmildura.com.au

WHERE TO EAT

FAMILY FRIENDLY   LICENSED   OUTDOOR DINING   VEGETARIAN OPTIONS

STEFANO'S $$$$$

ITALIAN
Map ref. p. 120

The star of Mildura is Stefano's, the kind of place you dine at one night and love so much you go back again the next. This may have something to do with the restaurant's beautiful setting in a historic hotel cellar – and Stefano de Pieri's food. His passion for the Sunraysia region's produce and his dedication to seasonal cooking have given his northern Italian cuisine a unique flavour. The menu is degustation, with five different courses each night. Among them, you can expect handmade pastas and dishes featuring local beef, pork and lamb. This special culinary experience is so popular you might have to book well ahead.

Quality Hotel Mildura Grand, Langtree Ave; (03) 5023 0511; open Mon–Sat for dinner; www.stefano.com.au

STEFANO'S CAFE & BAKERY $

CAFE BAKERY
Map ref. p. 120

Not content to have just one restaurant serving some of the best food in the country, energetic chef Stefano de Pieri has opened this second outlet – a cafe, bakery, art gallery and wine bar – nearby. The bakery produces terrific breads – sourdough, grain, ciabatta and focaccia – as well as pastries, cakes, muffins and more. Start the day with Danish pastries or homemade bircher muesli with a great cup of coffee. Traditional breakfast dishes are made using free-range eggs and organic bacon; at weekends, breakfast is served all day. Stefano also makes Italian-style eggs poached in peperonata and Moroccan-style with Middle Eastern flavours. For lunch, there might be a whole range of pastas topped with Italian sausage, meatballs or trout, depending on the season.

27 Deakin Ave; (03) 5021 3627; open daily for breakfast and lunch; www.stefano.com.au

THE GOL GOL HOTEL $$

INTERNATIONAL

This historic country pub was first licensed in 1877 and served as a watering hole and stopover in the days of Cobb & Co. Just five minutes from Mildura over the bridge into New South Wales, it enjoys one of the best views of the Murray River. Houseboats can tie up at the hotel's mooring and guests can walk up the grassy slopes to dine on the pub's great-value country fare, choosing from the standard bar menu or à la carte bistro cuisine. Usual suspects include salt-and-pepper squid, garlic prawns and, in winter, lamb korma puffs. Main courses might be grain-fed porterhouse, chicken parmigiana or crumbed breast of Kulkyne chicken stuffed with mushrooms, onion, bacon and cheese, topped with hollandaise sauce.

Sturt Hwy, Gol Gol; (03) 5024 8492; open daily for lunch and dinner; www.golgolpub.com.au

TRENTHAM ESTATE RESTAURANT $$$

VINEYARD RESTAURANT

Enjoying one of the best positions on the banks of the Murray, just 13 kilometres out of Mildura, this winery restaurant has plenty of balcony and verandah tables with views for outside dining. The chef bakes bread daily, blends a version of Egyptian dukkah using local pistachio nuts, and also makes his own balsamic-style vinegar caramelised with raw sugar and bush tomato. Start perhaps with baked goat's cheese tart or Asian-style yabbie gowgee, before considering twice-cooked Asian duck on kipfler potatoes or citrus chicken using the local oranges for which the region is famous. Diners can also opt to DIY barbecue on the lawns. The cellar door is open daily.

Sturt Hwy, Trentham Cliffs; (03) 5024 8888; open Tues–Sun for lunch; www.trenthamestate.com.au

Mornington

AFGHAN MARCO POLO $$
AFGHAN

For more than 15 years the Shakoor family has been treating appreciative locals to their terrific family-style Afghan cuisine. Dishes are designed to be shared so you can taste the wide variety of flavours on offer. Start with a selection of mixed entrées, including borani bonjon (golden-fried eggplant with garlic yoghurt and tomato sauce), munto (spiced mincemeat with onions wrapped in pastry and steamed) and sambosa (deep-fried curried vegetable pastry parcels). Then choose kabuli palow – a rice dish with caramelised carrots and sultanas – or aashok, a zesty pasta dish; both can also be served vegetarian. Kebabs, curries and rice dishes are house specialties.

9–11 Main St; (03) 5975 5154; open daily for dinner

BRASS RAZU WINE BAR $$
WINE BAR

Brass Razu's patrons have a lot of fun amid the baroque, old-world decor of leather banquettes, velvet couches and chandeliers. Ask for a Long Island iced tea and the five-white-spirits cocktail arrives in a lovely silver teapot on a tray. Tennis anyone? Pimm's fruit cup comes in a gold-etched jug – again on a tray. Essentially a traditional European-style wine bar, food was originally a secondary consideration here but it has proved so popular it now takes near equal billing. You might like to accompany one of up to 24 wines available by the glass with French-style pâtés and terrines, gourmet pies such as rabbit and prune or duck, French-style sausages, gourmet pizzas – even a platter called Love Thy Neighbour from the Afghan restaurant next door.

13 Main St; (03) 5975 0108; open Tues–Sun for lunch and dinner

THE ROCKS $$$
SEAFOOD

Attached to the Mornington Yacht Club and adjacent to the Mornington pier, this is the place to be in summer – either on the casual cafe deck or inside in the more formal but relaxed restaurant, with views overlooking local fishing boats and yachts in the marina. The dining room specialises in live seafood, plucking crayfish, mud crabs and Moreton Bay bugs from tanks in the open kitchen. Start with a tasting plate of oysters from four different regions or seafood antipasto. The modern seafood selection also boasts a large sashimi menu and offers four to five different fish of the day. Popular dishes include the Spanish paella and the mixed seafood grill.

Mornington Yacht Club, 1 Schnapper Point Dr; (03) 5973 5599; open daily for breakfast, lunch and dinner; www.therocksmornington.com.au

Myrtleford

PLUMP HARVEST $
CAFE PROVEDORE

This regional produce store and bakery-cum-cafe is housed in a huge converted warehouse with seating for around 90 diners. Start the day with a big hearty cooked breakfast on sourdough bread, or savour one of their famous homemade tarts – raspberry and almond, lemon or perhaps chocolate and hazelnut – to accompany some of the best coffee in the region. Stock up on a selection of Plump Harvest preserves and specialty farm-gate produce from some 20 small

FAMILY FRIENDLY   LICENSED   OUTDOOR DINING   VEGETARIAN OPTIONS

suppliers in the area, and sample local beers and wines.

72 Great Alpine Rd; (03) 5752 2257; open Wed–Sun for breakfast and lunch; extended summer hours; www.plumpharvestproduce.com.au

THE BUTTER FACTORY $$

CAFE PROVEDORE

Housed in a converted 1906 butter factory, this charming produce store/cafe sources good local produce in season to make their own jams, sauces, preserved lemons and more. They hand-churn their own ice-cream, make their own gnocchi, bake fresh bread daily and offer a range of home-baked cakes. Locals know to order the baked chorizo for breakfast – baked in the oven with rich tomato sauce and olives, and topped with an egg. Or perhaps you'd prefer to opt for the Butter Factory breakfast of eggs Florentine-style with smoked local trout. Many dishes are Mediterranean-influenced, such as baked ricotta gnocchi or sun-dried tomato and ricotta gnocchi with blue cheese and white wine cream sauce.

15 Myrtle St; (03) 5752 2300; open Thurs–Tues for breakfast and lunch, Fri–Sat for dinner, Sun for dinner in winter; www.thebutterfactory.com.au

Nagambie

MITCHELTON WINES $$$

VINEYARD RESTAURANT

With its imposing observation tower and sprawling, whitewashed Spanish-style buildings, Mitchelton is easy to find and hard to forget. The restaurant is located in an airy high-ceilinged room with a large open fireplace and banks of windows that take in the slow glide of the Goulburn River. Local ingredients are a feature on a menu that mainly lingers in Europe and the Middle East – lamb koftas, chicken breast wrapped in prosciutto – with the occasional venture further afield, as with an African-style eggplant curry. Mitchelton wines are a feature, including some styles and vintages unavailable elsewhere.

Mitchells Town Rd; (03) 5736 2221; open daily for lunch; www.mitchelton.com.au

TAHBILK WETLANDS CAFE $$

VINEYARD RESTAURANT

Located in a dramatic ironbark, stone and corrugated-iron building with a large deck overlooking beautifully restored wetlands, the Tahbilk Wetlands Cafe is the perfect place to fortify yourself before setting off for a stroll through the wildlife reserve or to the tasting room in the landmark Tahbilk winery buildings. The food is simple and wholesome, with grazing plates and cheese plates making the most of locally produced meats, cheeses, fruit and nuts. Breakfast is also served and the cafe features the winery's Dalfarras range of wines.

Tahbilk Winery, 254 O'Neils Rd; (03) 5794 2555; open weekends for breakfast and daily for lunch; www.tahbilk.com.au/wetlands

THE JETTY $$$

MODERN AUSTRALIAN

Part of a lakeside complex comprising apartment-style accommodation and a health retreat with views over Lake Nagambie, this modern cafe-style restaurant offers casual dining under market umbrellas in a courtyard – ideal for leisurely lunches. There are also candlelit tables inside for more intimate dinners. The modern Australian menu has Mediterranean and sometimes Asian influences with dishes such as bruschetta topped with

mild chilli pancetta, or ricotta, basil and baby spinach served with pan-fried cherry tomatoes and pine-nut butter. The local flame-grilled steaks are recommended, as is any duck dish – perhaps roasted breast with aromatic honey jus. Dessert might be kaffir lime panna cotta with berry soup and pistachio biscotti.

317 High St; (03) 5794 1964; open Fri–Sun for lunch, Thurs–Sat for dinner and Sun for breakfast; www.thejetty.com.au

Olinda

WILD OAK RESTAURANT AND WINE BAR
$$$

MODERN AUSTRALIAN

Overlooking the floral splash of a neighbouring nursery, this contemporary eatery has always been popular with locals and visitors alike. Serving modern Australian food with a French influence, it offers a good-value set-price two- or three-course lunch. On Sunday, start the day with the 'big breakfast' of 'the lot' or savour fluffy buttermilk pancakes with local berries and cream. For lunch or dinner you don't have to be a vegetarian to appreciate the flavoursome rotolo of roasted butternut pumpkin, thyme and semi-dried tomatoes. Duck three ways has become a signature dish at Wild Oak – comprising confit duck leg and local cherry tart with pan-roasted duck breast and duck sausage. And for dessert, perhaps try the bombe Alaska.

Cnr Ridge and Mt Dandenong rds; (03) 9751 2033; open Sun for breakfast, and Wed–Sun for lunch and dinner; www.wildoak.com.au

LADYHAWKE CAFE
$$

MIDDLE EASTERN

Named after a 1980s Michelle Pfeiffer movie, Ladyhawke is a place that relishes eccentricity.

The converted 1920s homestead has a labyrinth of quirkily decorated rooms and a wonderfully homey atmosphere, complete with couches and open fireplaces. There are views to the quarter acre of well-kept gardens – the perfect place to walk off breakfast or lunch. Middle Eastern and European flavours are at the fore here, perhaps in a chicken and date tagine or a salad of marinated eggplant, peppers and haloumi. There are plenty of vegetarian options and a convivial attitude.

1365–1367 Mt Dandenong Tourist Rd, Mount Dandenong; (03) 9751 1104; open Thurs–Mon for breakfast and lunch

MISS MARPLE'S TEA ROOM
$

CAFE

In nearby Sassafras, this ever-bustling tearoom in an English Tudor-style cottage is evidence that the Devonshire tea tradition is alive and well in the Dandenongs. Visit the Tea Leaves shop next door for an incredible range of teas and teapots while you inevitably wait for a table. Fresh scones with homemade raspberry jam are hard to beat, and are one reason for the large crowds. For more substantial fare, choose from traditional dishes such as hearty

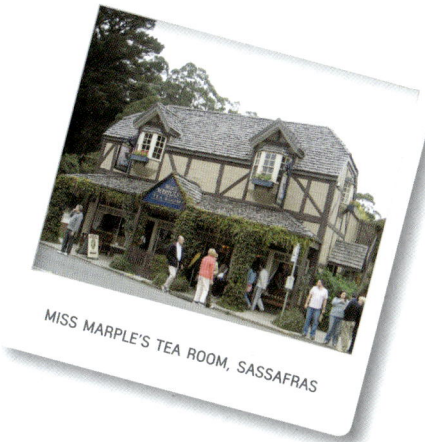

MISS MARPLE'S TEA ROOM, SASSAFRAS

FAMILY FRIENDLY   LICENSED   OUTDOOR DINING   VEGETARIAN OPTIONS

WHERE TO EAT

chicken or beef cottage pie, ploughman's lunch, quiche Lorraine, English-style fish and chips or a Pimlico pastie. Serves are large, so come with an appetite. Be warned: ice-cream sundaes are massive; the bread and butter pudding is sheer comfort food. There are also gluten-free options.

382 Mt Dandenong Tourist Rd, Sassafras; (03) 9755 1610; open daily for lunch; www.missmarples.com.au

RIPE – AUSTRALIAN PRODUCE $$
CAFE

Again in Sassafras, this gem of a place is a haven for foodies who travel from near and far to sample the delights of the food store and cafe. Housed in what appears as a rustic dwelling, it is set back from the street without a sign, but any local can tell you where to find it. Inside is a wood-panelled space with floor-to-ceiling shelves of preserves and wines, and a conglomeration of seating: a large communal table by the fireplace, smaller tables squeezed into nooks and crannies, and a large deck out the back where magenta rhododendrons bloom

THE QUAINT INTERIOR OF RIPE – AUSTRALIAN PRODUCE, SASSAFRAS

in spring. The menu is handwritten each day and features soups, pastas, more substantial dishes, cakes and hot chocolate made with Lindt chocolate.

376–378 Mt Dandenong Tourist Rd, Sassafras; (03) 9755 2100; open daily for breakfast and lunch

Omeo

THE GOLDEN AGE HOTEL MOTEL $$
MODERN AUSTRALIAN

This contemporary restaurant is within the 1940s Art Deco walls of a comfortable two-storey country hotel, overlooking the main street of Omeo and the surrounding hills. Just 50 minutes from Mount Hotham, it is a good spot to warm up before a taste of the snow. Popular entrées include salt-and-pepper calamari and beef satay stir-fry. Main courses might be Atlantic salmon, seafood pasta, and reef and beef – prawns, scallops, mussels and calamari atop a 300-gram steak. For dessert, you can't go past the apple and rhubarb crumble or a slice of their homemade cheesecake.

189 Day Ave; (03) 5159 1344; open daily for lunch and dinner; www.goldenageomeo.com.au

Orbost

A LOVELY LITTLE LUNCH $
CAFE

This welcoming apple-green building is in the middle of the main street in Orbost. It boasts local artworks on its walls and a lovely garden setting in the front for alfresco dining. Owner Juliet Webb bakes everything on the premises

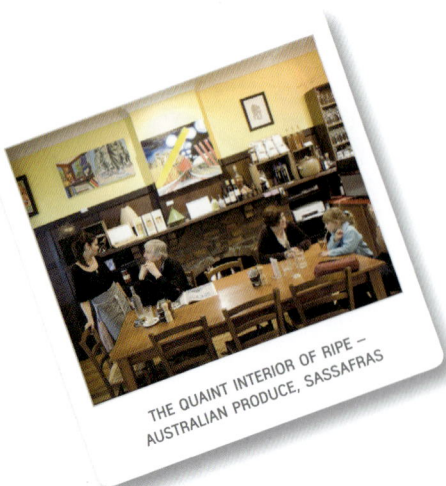

and also caters for specialty diets. Start the day with one of her big fluffy three-egg omelettes, perhaps filled with sun-dried tomato and feta, or munch into an egg and bacon roll. For lunch, her warm salad of marinated chicken and braised mushroom is renowned, likewise her baked cheesecake. She uses as much local and organic produce as possible.

125A Nicholson St; (03) 5154 1303; open Mon–Sat for breakfast and lunch

PS CURLIP II $

INTERNATIONAL

The PS *Curlip II* is a replica of the original paddlesteamer that used to carry corn and market-garden vegetables up the Murray River before it was swept out to sea in a wild storm some 100 years ago and broke up on the mouth of the Snowy River at Marlo. The local community of Orbost came together to build another, which was launched at the end of 2008 and now takes daytime cruises up the Brodribb River to Marlo, with dinner cruises planned for the future. Enjoy morning tea, lunch and afternoon tea on the hour-and-a-half cruise with local commentary.

PS Curlip Centre, 1 Browning St; (03) 5154 1699; open Wed–Sun for lunch; www.paddlesteamercurlip.com.au

Paynesville

CAFE ESPAS $$$

SEAFOOD

Vehicular ferry is a grand way to arrive on Raymond Island. Dolphins might be swimming by, certainly swans. And a walk around the island will confirm it has one of the largest populations of koalas in the area. This former fishing cottage turned artist's studio still boasts Brendon Sims' artworks – except he is now front of house, while his wife, Maria, prepares modern coastal-style cuisine using the wonderfully fresh seafood from nearby Lakes Entrance. Some dishes she daren't take off the menu: Thai-style seafood salad, squid-ink fettuccine with coriander pesto, and Moroccan-style lamb with orange and olive salad, preserved lemon and yoghurt. Fish of the day is also a good option. And to finish, try the trio of desserts.

Raymond Island; (03) 5156 7275; open Fri–Sun for lunch and Fri–Sat for dinner; daily during school and public holidays

Port Albert

WILDFISH $$$

SEAFOOD

Former professional fisherman Michael Hobson has set up this terrific new waterfront restaurant right on the wharf, with an adjacent fish and chippery and fresh fish sales. Guests can relax inside on comfy cushions while contemplating the menu that is heavy with local seafood, or dine outside overlooking the water while local children try their luck with fishing rods. Start with a tapas platter to share – calamari, salmon or maybe chicken liver pâté – before ordering crisp-battered King George whiting with chips or snapper fillet with lemon. A small wine list has some good local labels.

40 Wharf St; (03) 5183 2007; open Thurs–Mon for lunch and dinner; www.wildfishrestaurant.com.au

WHERE TO EAT

Port Campbell

ROOM SIX CAFE RESTAURANT $$
INTERNATIONAL

This new addition to the Port Campbell eating scene is owned by a couple, and both are chefs. One has a specialty in Mediterranean fare, the other in Asian cuisine – hence the menu features a fusion of both their styles. In a novel twist, patrons can select a live crayfish from the operation next door, bring it to the restaurant and have it cooked up and served with fresh crusty bread and salad. Freshly made sushi is available, to dine in or takeaway. If you do have a taste for sushi, it is best to order it the day before.

28 Lord St; (03) 5598 6242; open daily for lunch and dinner; www.roomsix-cafe-restaurant.com

THE CRAYPOT BISTRO $$
INTERNATIONAL

This family-friendly pub offers great value for money. There are good, big meals under $20 and also a children's menu. Even the scotch fillet steak with your choice of sauce won't break the bank. The crayfish come by way of the town's fishermen. Fairly priced bottles of wine are available from the bar. There is a beer garden for summer dining, and open fires in winter.

Port Campbell Hotel, 40 Lord St; (03) 5598 6320; open daily for dinner

TIMBOON RAILWAY SHED DISTILLERY $$
CAFE PROVEDORE

This distillery is run by the owners of Timboon Ice Cream. Housed in a beautifully renovated railway station, the venture is in part an ode to the local characters that ran bootleg whisky operations hereabouts. The smell of the distilling whisky can seep, ever so subtly, through this popular cafe. There is plenty of local produce on the menu and it can also be bought from the provedore, where local chocolate, cheese and smoked eel feature. This new addition to the Twelve Apostles scene is open on Friday night for handmade pizzas, and on Saturday night for à la carte.

630 Glenfyne–Brucknell Rd, Timboon; (03) 5598 3555; open daily for breakfast and lunch, and Fri–Sat for dinner; www.timboondistillery.com

Port Fairy

MERRIJIG INN $$$
MEDITERRANEAN

New life has been breathed into the Merrijig Inn, with an acclaimed menu of imaginative and well-crafted food that changes every few weeks and attracts food lovers from far and wide. For starters, you might find pan-seared local abalone, calamari with ham, or succulent local crayfish. Main courses are just as well thought out – perhaps local Western District lamb cutlet with dukkah-crusted shoulder, zucchini flower and Persian feta. Desserts are also unexpected – maybe a garlic take on the Greek semolina custard in pastry with blood orange sorbet and citrus, mint and date salad. There are also six- and nine-course tasting menus. The comprehensive wine list includes a good range of imports and local wines.

1 Campbell St; (03) 5568 2324; open Mon–Sat for dinner; www.merrijiginn.com

PORTOFINO ON BANK
$$$
MEDITERRANEAN

Transformed from an old 1868 bank building, Portofino on Bank is an elegant and popular restaurant serving fragrant and zesty dishes that display strong Mediterranean and Middle Eastern influences. Ingredients are sourced from the best local produce and the food rarely disappoints. Regulars love the kataifi – pastry-wrapped goat's cheese balls served with local honey and zaatar spice, the spaghettini with local crayfish, and the cardamom and honey-roasted duck breast with radish, mint and currant salad. The restaurant's owners, the Clancey brothers, have paid particular attention to their award-winning wine list, so take time to choose a wine to match the flavoursome fare or seek the advice of Andrew or Shane; they are consummate hosts and will be pleased to oblige.

26 Bank St; (03) 5568 2251; open Mon–Sat for dinner

SALTRA BRASSERIE
$$
MODERN AUSTRALIAN

Housed in former council offices, this space has undergone major renovations, including polished floorboards, a gorgeous oak bar, romantic lighting and comfy lounges. There is no pool table, TV, TAB or jukebox – it is all class from go to whoa, with good use of candles, mood music and masses of flowers. Sip on a signature lychee slipper cocktail (lychees, vodka and apple juice) as you consider perhaps a dozen oysters, each prepared in a different way, or local crayfish (in season) available in a variety of styles: thermidore, mornay, garlic butter, whisky butter or vanilla-bean butter. Popular desserts are the house-made ice-creams and sorbets.

20 Bank St; (03) 5568 3058; open Tues–Sun for lunch and dinner

TIME & TIDE
$
CAFE

This wonderful gallery-cum-cafe is a well-kept secret, located away from the tourist bustle of Port Fairy's main streets. The town has so much to offer that you could easily miss this oceanside gem tucked away off the main road a few minutes out of town (you turn left off the main highway, shortly after departing town heading west). You will find it hard to resist the gourmet bread rolls overflowing with tasty fillings or the delicious cakes and sweets for morning or afternoon tea. The menu focuses on organic ingredients such as bircher muesli and Zeally Bay organic breads from Torquay, gluten-free produce and locally smoked Demmington trout. The contemporary artworks are always of interest and, along with great food and coffee, the views are sensational.

21 Thistle Pl; (03) 5568 2134; open Thurs–Sun and public holiday Mon for breakfast and brunch; extended summer hours

Portland

CLOCK BY THE BAY
$$$
MODERN AUSTRALIAN

Housed in the old post office in the town centre, this 1882 building overlooks Portland Bay. An up-market restaurant, it serves contemporary dishes. For starters, try seared scallops with crispy pork belly, apple and rocket salad with a green ginger glaze, or calamari with paprika and garlic served with yoghurt and a herb dipping sauce. Main course might be a seafood stack with crispy won tons,

WHERE TO EAT

tomato and cucumber salsa with salad greens, or winter warmers like confit duck legs with stir-fried vegetable and soba noodles.

Cnr Cliff and Bentinck sts; (03) 5523 4777; open Mon–Sat for dinner; www.clockbythebay.com.au

LIDO LARDER $
CAFE PROVEDORE

Housed in a lovely Federation-style heritage building, this contemporary cafe bakes everything fresh on the premises – frittatas, quiches, chicken and coriander sausage rolls, delicious slices and cakes. It fills crusty baguettes with gourmet fillings and makes tasty and healthy lunch boxes, as well as freshly prepared seasonal fruit salad. Take a seat for casual pavement dining with views of the sea or fill up your own holiday larder for self-catering with quality comestibles – homemade pesto, Meredith goat's cheese, Simon Johnson and Maggie Beer goodies, and more.

5 Julia St; (03) 5521 1741; open Mon–Sat for breakfast and lunch

BRIDGEWATER BAY BEACH CAFE $$
CAFE

The original kiosk overlooking the ocean, the beach and the bluff to the seal colony has morphed in recent years into this casual licensed cafe with outside deck. It is worth the 15-minute detour by car west of Portland for the views alone, but most come for the fisherman's basket (fish, prawns, calamari, scallops, chips and a bowl of salad), great hamburgers, and signature fish and chips. They also do vegetarian lasagne and rolls, sandwiches and wraps, and serve good coffee.

1611 Bridgewater Rd, Cape Bridgewater; (03) 5526 7155; open daily for breakfast and lunch, and Fri–Sun for dinner; www.bridgewaterbay.com.au

Queenscliff

APOSTLE QUEENSCLIFF $$$
MODERN AUSTRALIAN

With its impressive New Zealand kauri vaulted ceiling, stained-glass windows and central rosette window, the Gothic architecture of this 1888 former Methodist church is an atmospheric backdrop for this well-regarded restaurant. Start the day with an Apostle big breakfast with the lot, or truffled eggs with homemade baked beans and crusty bread. The fluffy homemade potato gnocchi with smoked salmon, dill and caper cream has become a signature dish, likewise the pan-fried scallop salad with garlic, lemon and fresh herbs. Pan-seared blue-eye trevally with asparagus spears and sautéed potatoes is a typical main course, while desserts are sheer comfort dishes such as crème brûlée and golden syrup dumplings.

79 Hesse St; (03) 5258 3097; open daily for breakfast and lunch, and Fri–Sat for dinner; daily in summer; www.apostlequeenscliff.com.au

ATHELSTANE HOUSE $$$
MODERN AUSTRALIAN

This lovely old 1860 former guesthouse has been restored and given a modern fit-out to suit the contemporary fare served in its restaurant. Both the menu and wine list focus on quality local produce – the wine list being nominated as one of the best in the region. Even breakfast dishes are made using free-range eggs from a nearby poultry farm, and tomatoes come from a local hydroponic farm. Simple dishes feature on the menu, such as local calamari and snapper, traditional corned beef, panna cotta and homemade ice-creams. They offer a two- or three-course deal which also includes a glass of wine.

4 Hobson St; (03) 5258 1024; open daily for breakfast and dinner, and weekends for lunch; www.athelstane.com.au

VUE GRAND HOTEL $$$$

MODERN AUSTRALIAN

Located in the heart of Queenscliff, the Vue Grand is an award-winning and beautifully restored boutique hotel. Dining is taken to a grand scale in the impressive dining room, where soaring ceilings adorned with chandeliers perfectly complement the classic, modern menu. Entrées might be seared scallops, ravioli of chicken, ricotta and pumpkin, or terrine of pancetta and rabbit. Main courses could be herb-crusted lamb loin, fillet of beef or braised pork belly. And for dessert, if you can't wait 15 minutes for the butterscotch soufflé, try the Tahitian lime baked Alaska instead, or the dark chocolate and marmalade tart. On-site Cafe Lure is open daily for lunch.

46 Hesse St; (03) 5258 1544; open Wed–Sun for dinner; www.vuegrand.com.au

Rutherglen

BEAUMONT'S CAFE $$$

MODERN AUSTRALIAN

This unassuming, quietly stylish cafe dishes up some of the best food in the neighbourhood, with a menu that leaps continents in a single bound but manages to land successfully, whether in Italy, Morocco, India or Thailand. There is a terrific, leafy courtyard out the back, friendly and personable service, and some skilled and interesting cooking that makes the most of what is produced locally.

The house-made gnocchi is well worth a try, and desserts like a chilled cardamom and orange rice pudding keep things interesting until stumps. A brief wine list sticks to the local labels.

84 Main St; (02) 6032 7428; open Fri–Sat for lunch and Tues–Sat for dinner; www.beaumontscafe.com.au

VINTARA WINERY, $
BREWERY & CAFE

VINEYARD RESTAURANT

This recently opened brewery and winery complex is all about matching the right food with the wines and beers. The locally brewed Bintara beers in particular have garnered some acclaim, and the Crystal Wheat, Black Beer, Pale Ale and Pilsner are all well suited to both the larger plates in the cafe (perhaps produce platters or more complex dishes like a twice-baked Milawa cheese soufflé) and to the excellent range of tapas-style offerings available in the bar (fried whitebait and Peking duck rolls among them). The winery and brewery are open daily for tastings and sales.

105 Fraser Rd; 0447 327 517; open Thurs– Mon for lunch and weekends for breakfast; www.vintara.com.au

PICKLED SISTERS CAFE $$

VINEYARD RESTAURANT

Located in a pitch-roofed tin shed next to the Cofield Winery's cellar door, Pickled Sisters is an airy, casual place with a friendly attitude and a straightforward approach towards the food it serves. The main theme is local, so you might get Murray cod served with zucchini and mash, or the vineyard platter with terrine, salami, local cheeses and bread – perfect with Cofield's sparkling shiraz. The colourful room is pretty

FAMILY FRIENDLY   LICENSED   OUTDOOR DINING   VEGETARIAN OPTIONS

basic but enthusiastic service and tasty food help make a virtue out of simplicity. Picnic hampers are available with 24 hours notice.

Cofield Wines, Distillery Rd, Wahgunyah; (02) 6033 2377; open Wed–Mon for lunch and Sat for dinner during daylight saving; www.pickledsisters.com.au

TERRACE RESTAURANT $$$

VINEYARD RESTAURANT

It is hard not to be impressed by the setting of the Terrace Restaurant, located in a mock Scottish castle built in 1880 at All Saints winery. But the brick-floored restaurant does not rest on its location laurels and has a well-deserved reputation as being one of the region's best and most consistent performers. The menu visits both Asia and Europe – the hoi sin–lacquered duck is a particular highlight – and there is a seven-course degustation option that is matched with All Saints and neighbouring St Leonard's vineyards' wines. There are also separate menus for vegetarians and children.

All Saints Estate, All Saints Rd, Wahgunyah; (02) 6035 2209; open Wed–Sun for lunch and Sat for dinner; www.prbwines.com.au

Sale

BIS CUCINA $$$

MODERN AUSTRALIAN

Part of the town's main entertainment centre, with adjacent live theatre and functions room, this bright and lively cafe has a menu that would be right at home somewhere chic in Melbourne. Locals come to breakfast on ricotta hotcakes or the Bis breakfast with the lot. By day, smart young mothers and families come in to snack on chicken wraps or rosemary lamb burgers, or perhaps rosemary-marinated mushrooms with

feta and lime on Hope Farm sourdough toast. Salt-and-pepper calamari is a popular entrée for lunch and dinner, with Gippsland eye fillet and fresh local fish absolute standouts.

100 Foster St; (03) 5144 3388; open daily for breakfast and lunch, and Tues–Sat for dinner; www.biscucina.com.au

IL NIDO $$$

ITALIAN

Housed in a refurbished Art Deco home, 'the nest' serves nurturing Italian fare, sourcing as much local produce as possible, including fresh local seafood and top-quality Gippsland lamb and beef. There are usually a few chef's specials worth considering – perhaps a seafood, risotto or pasta of the day. Grilled marinated octopus is recommended, likewise the hearty tomato-based seafood bisque filled with crab, prawns and more. Good local wines feature on the wine list.

29 Desailly St; (03) 5144 4099; open Mon–Sat for breakfast and lunch, and daily for dinner

RELISH @ THE GALLERY $$

CAFE

Part of the Gippsland Art Gallery in Sale, on the main highway, this busy cafe serves two menus – modern Australian and Thai – plus daily specials. Lunch suggestions might be an antipasto platter to share, followed by a warm chicken salad with mango, cashews and honey mustard dressing, a steak sandwich or a seafood marinara. There is always a daily risotto and pasta. If Asian is more to your palate, perhaps try the tandoori chicken fillet or Thai green chicken curry. Yum cha is also available, but requires 24 hours' notice when booking.

68–70 Foster St; (03) 5144 5044; open daily for breakfast, lunch and dinner

Seymour

PLUNKETT FOWLES CELLAR DOOR AND CAFE
$$

VINEYARD RESTAURANT

This winery cafe is an integral part of the cellar door that overlooks the vineyard to Mount Bernard and the start of the Strathbogie Ranges. The seasonally changing menu features local produce such as Avenel mushrooms from the farm down the road, gourmet sausages and smoked ham from the highly acclaimed Avenel butcher, and vegetables from the cafe's own organic garden. The menu is divided into antipasto (Yarra Valley smoked eel, calamari fritti, local mushrooms, slow-roasted tomatoes and goat's cheese), charcuterie (local smallgoods, house-made pork rillettes and terrine) and main courses (king prawn salad, eye fillet) – all with matching wine suggestions. If you just want a little something, try the wine flight of three wines to match three small tastes of food.

Cnr Hume Hwy and Lambing Gully Rd, Avenel; (03) 5796 2150; open daily for breakfast and lunch; www.plunkettfowles.com.au

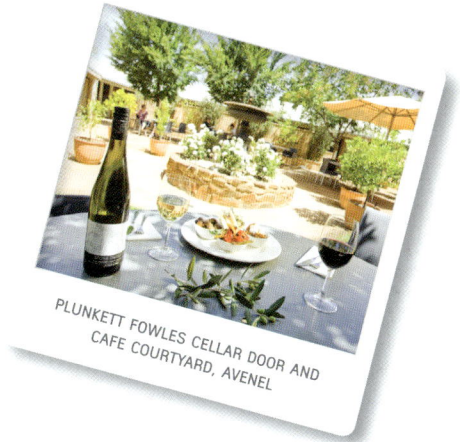

PLUNKETT FOWLES CELLAR DOOR AND CAFE COURTYARD, AVENEL

likewise the rack of lamb and chicken with lemongrass and lime on wild rice. Check out the large array of home-baked cakes and slices in the cabinet to eat in or take away. Local wines feature on the wine list.

2 Queen St, Avenel; (03) 5796 2122; open Wed–Sun for lunch and Thurs–Sat for dinner

THE TROUGH
$$$

MODERN AUSTRALIAN

Adjoining the old Avenel Post Office (now a beauty salon), this cafe-restaurant, gourmet deli and wine centre is in the centre of the lush north-eastern thoroughbred region – hence the name. A relative newcomer, its extensive menu includes popular dishes such as prawns baked in kataifi pastry with garlic butter, or rare beef salad with slow-baked sweet potato and beetroot drizzled with honey mustard sauce. Certified Angus beef is recommended,

TRAWOOL SHED CAFE
$$$

CAFE

Don't let the name of this country diner fool you into thinking you will be dining in a rustic farm shed, for this 'shed' is a slick contemporary building enjoying some of the most scenic views in the region. Located south of Seymour in historic Trawool Valley, it serves seasonal contemporary food with everything made fresh on the premises. Expect garden-fresh salads in summer (if only you could buy that dressing) and warming soups and hearty fare in winter. A lunchtime blackboard menu changes daily, with à la carte for dinner. They have earned a good reputation for their country steaks and flathead

WHERE TO EAT

FAMILY FRIENDLY   LICENSED   OUTDOOR DINING   VEGETARIAN OPTIONS

tails, and the tangy lemon tarts and chocolate fudge are fixtures.

RMB 5470 Goulburn Valley Hwy, Trawool; (03) 5799 1595; open Fri–Mon for morning tea and lunch, and Fri–Sat for dinner; www.trawoolshed.com.au/theshedcafe.html

Shepparton

BOHJASS $$
WINE BAR

One floor up above the main street, this friendly wine bar welcomes with its warm rustic decor, polished floorboards and bar made from 200-year-old oak wine barrels. Tapas is the go here. Share a few plates, such as their famous Asian-cut calamari, with a wine from one of the many Australian or New Zealand boutique wineries on the wine list, or cosy up on a couch with a good coffee. For something more substantial, popular dishes include chargrilled eye fillet on polenta, slow-cooked ox cheek and ox tail on risotto, or Moroccan-style chicken tagine.

276B Wyndham St; (03) 5822 0237; open Mon–Sat for dinner; www.bohjass.com.au

CELLAR 47 RESTAURANT $$$
& WINE BAR
MEDITERRANEAN

This popular restaurant has been serving the people of Shepparton for more than 30 years. Businessmen come for relaxed lunches, while families and couples come for intimate dinners at night. A wood-fired oven is used for some of the Mediterranean-style dishes such as quail and whole baked barramundi, as well as pizzas. Popular entrées include fresh oysters and sweet chilli prawns, with main courses of lamb

shanks, eye fillet and wagyu beef. And as you'd expect of a cellar, the wine list is excellent.

166–170 High St; (03) 5831 1882; open Mon–Sat for lunch and dinner; www.cellar47.com.au

LETIZIA'S $$
JAPANESE

This central restaurant has two levels of dining: a family-friendly ground floor and a romantic basement cellar. Owners chef Mario and pastry chef Joanne Letizia offer a contemporary cross-cultural menu that reflects Mario's Asian and Italian heritage, and valuable time spent running the Japanese section of celebrated Anton Mosimann's London restaurant. Dishes are designed to be shared, with three different bento boxes and four different table platters: yum cha, kebabs, antipasto and fresh king prawns. Known for their seafood, they do a roaring trade in whole crayfish and their version of reef and beef with king prawns, scallops and a half crayfish atop a thick-cut rib-eye fillet. Locals know to keep room for Joey's indulgent chocolate desserts. Complimentary yum cha is served from 5pm to 7pm on Fridays.

67 Fryers St; (03) 5831 8822; open Tues–Sun for lunch and dinner

TELLER $$$
MODERN AUSTRALIAN

At Mooroopna, former city chef Matthew Milsome returned to the countryside and created this slick award-winning restaurant infused with Melbourne sophistication. Housed in a heritage-listed building that was once a bank, Milsome presents casual lunchtime fare such as fish pie, before dimming the lights in the formal dining room for evening service. The cuisine is modern Australian with Asian

BYO AVAILABLE   CREDIT CARDS ACCEPTED   DISABLED ACCESS   DRESS CODE APPLIES

and European influences – perhaps confit rabbit and mushroom spring rolls or Sichuan smoked duck with local peaches. On Sunday evenings there's a six-course degustation menu with BYO wine (no corkage). There is also an extensive wine list.

108 McLennan St, Mooroopna; (03) 5825 3344; open Wed–Sun for lunch and dinner, and weekends for breakfast

Sorrento

ACQUOLINA $$$
ITALIAN
Map ref. p. 144

The owners of this friendly Italian trattoria make an annual pilgrimage back to Italy to cook in restaurant kitchens, gleaning new ideas for their menu. They make their own pasta and fill ravioli cushions with tasty things like pumpkin or rabbit, or Bergamo-style with beef, pork, veal, prosciutto, pancetta and more. Much of the antipasto plate is house-made: yoghurt cheese, marinated olives, mushrooms and tuna mousse – ideal to share. Other recommended dishes include sizzling Spanish-style king prawns, homemade fettucini marinara, mare monte, classic veal saltimbocca, and pasta served with prawns and porcini mushrooms. Australian and Italian wine list.

26 Ocean Beach Rd; (03) 5984 0811; open Thurs–Mon for dinner; extended summer hours

LOQUAT RESTAURANT & BAR $$$
MEDITERRANEAN
Map ref. p. 144

Originally a general store, this comfortable space has evolved over the years to become the intimate restaurant that it is today. Alcoves add atmosphere and should be requested when booking. The modern Mediterranean menu might offer entrées of chargrilled quail with pomegranate salad, oysters with a pear, coriander and champagne vinaigrette, or trout rillettes. Main courses range from barramundi and South Australian prawns to twice-cooked free-range Otway pork belly served on a hot lentil salad, or a duo of duck with seared breast and confit leg, braised red cabbage and fennel gratin. For dessert, opt for the chocolate fondant or saffron brûlée. Two- and three-course dinners are offered on Saturdays. The excellent wine list features many Mornington Peninsula wines by the glass.

3183 Point Nepean Rd; (03) 5984 4444; open Sun for lunch and Thurs–Sun for dinner; extended summer hours; loquat.homestead.com

SMOKEHOUSE SORRENTO $$
MEDITERRANEAN
Map ref. p. 144

This popular pizzeria has been pleasing locals and holiday-makers since 1992. They come for the wood-fired pizzas and fresh, simply flavoured Mediterranean-style food. Many dishes are roasted in the oven – barramundi, saddle of rabbit – even steaks are sometimes finished off in there. Salads range from classic Caesar or Greek with creamy Yarra Valley feta to niçoise using their own preserved tuna. Vegetarians are well catered for, with options such as the seven-vegetable tagine with couscous. Popular pizza toppings include Moroccan-style slow-cooked lamb with fresh rocket and a yoghurt dressing, smoked salmon with horseradish cream and French Boursin cheese on a pesto base with mozzarella, hot salami, sun-dried tomatoes and roasted capsicum. The wine list includes local wines and beer.

182 Ocean Beach Rd; (03) 5984 1246; open Wed–Sun for dinner; extended summer and public holiday hours

WHERE TO EAT

FAMILY FRIENDLY   LICENSED   OUTDOOR DINING   VEGETARIAN OPTIONS

THE BATHS $$

INTERNATIONAL
Map ref. p. 144

On the sands near the Queenscliff ferry, this heritage-listed building has been a commercial premises since around 1870: a bathing pavilion, tearooms, a boat hire business – even a local fish market where the boats would bring their catch. A relaxed restaurant for the past eight years, if it was any closer to the beach you'd have sand between your toes as you eat. The broad menu has something for everyone, from homemade muffins and French toast for breakfast to steaks, lamb and seafood specials for lunch and dinner. Regulars come for The Baths fish and chips – either fried in crispy beer batter or grilled – and for the tender marinated and grilled calamari.

3278 Point Nepean Rd; (03) 5984 1500; open daily for lunch and dinner, and weekends and school holidays for breakfast; www.thebaths.com.au

Swan Hill

CARRIAGES RESTAURANT $$$

INTERNATIONAL

Housed in two old train carriages (with an extra upstairs dining room), this novel restaurant sees hospitality students from Swan Hill International College cooking and waiting on table for up to 150 patrons as part of their curriculum program. They cook and serve dishes such as Moroccan lamb, calamari salad or old-fashioned prawn cocktails as entrées before creating classic main courses such as camembert chicken, roast duck, carpetbag steak, lamb cutlets and fisherman's platters. Desserts might be homemade strawberry or mango cheesecake, tiramisu or sticky date pudding.

423 Campbell St; (03) 5033 2796; open Tues–Sun for lunch and dinner; www.carriagesrestaurant.com.au

JAVA SPICE $$$

THAI & INDONESIAN

Indonesian language teacher Peter Morrison and his wife, Trish, didn't set out to open a restaurant, but such was their love for Asian culture and architecture, it just sort of happened. All the buildings, including the five grass huts as gazebos, were prefabricated in Java and Bali, taken down, shipped and reassembled in situ in Swan Hill, and are now appropriately surrounded by lush tropical gardens and palms. The restaurant specialises in Thai and Indonesian food that is prepared by chefs from those countries. The à la carte menu is divided into sections for soups, salads, curries, vegetarian, seafood and so on, with half a dozen banquet suggestions for a minimum of four diners.

17 Beveridge St; (03) 5033 0511; open Thurs–Fri and Sun for lunch, and Tues–Sun for dinner; www.javaspice.com.au

QUO VADIS $$$
ITALIAN

Three generations of the Tripodi family have been involved in the running of this popular Italian restaurant and pizza parlour for more than 20 years. It is spread over three shops in the town's main street: the pizza parlour occupies one, the restaurant serving good Italian fare the other two. The menu changes every month but some dishes are always featured, such as their signature garlic prawns and terrific spaghetti marinara. The antipasto is also good, likewise their aged rib-eye beef. Italians love their sweets, so finish with a tiramisu or an excellent soufflé of the day. The extensive wine list includes everything from Penfolds Grange to the best of the local wines.

255–259 Campbell St; (03) 5032 4408; open daily for dinner; www.quo-vadis.com.au

YUTAKA SAWA $$
JAPANESE

Meaning 'good harvest', this simple Japanese restaurant in the town's main street produces consistently high-quality dishes that are slightly larger than the normal Tokyo-style offerings, which pleases appreciative local diners no end. They come back again and again for the royal tataki eye fillet of beef prepared with vinegar, wine and garlic, and appreciate the lightness of the tempura seafood and vegetables. All dishes are designed to be shared, from the exemplary sushi and sashimi through to the deliciously spiced stir-fried pork mince and tofu. Finish with saki or umeshu (sweet plum wine).

107 Campbell St; (03) 5032 3515; open Wed–Sat and Mon for lunch, and Wed–Mon for dinner; www.yutakasawa.com.au

Torquay

GROWLERS $$
INTERNATIONAL

This welcoming place has a unique spot right on the water, with deck, courtyard and restaurant views over the sparkling ocean. It is a typical seaside venue, where patrons come in for traditional breakfasts, with all homemade sauces and trimmings, stepping up to an up-market cafe-style menu for lunch. But come dinner time, linen napkins appear, table lanterns are lit and the beautiful space becomes almost formal. Try local Port Arlington oysters – natural, Kilpatrick,

Rockefeller or with Thai nahm phrik sauce – before considering the terrific seafood bisque, beer-battered King George whiting or grilled porterhouse steak with Cafe de Paris butter. An absolute bonus for dinner guests is the 12-seater courtesy bus that will pick you up and deposit you back home safely after a few wines.

23 The Esplanade; (03) 5264 8455; open daily for breakfast, lunch and dinner; www.growlers.com.au

SCORCHED $$$
MODERN AUSTRALIAN

This stylish shopfront restaurant offers pavement dining with lovely beach views and a casual but refined style of dining. For those who can't make up their mind what to have from the contemporary Australian menu, there is a six-course degustation menu. Recommended entrées are pan-seared Atlantic scallops or rabbit ravioli. Main courses might be wild barramundi fillet, crumbed Otway free-range pork rib-eye with Waldorf salad, or terrific local eye fillet with baby root vegetables. Sweet-tooths are well catered for with yoghurt panna cotta with mixed berries and mint, triple chocolate tart with rocky road ice-cream, and an excellent apple tarte tartin. The wine list is outstanding.

17 The Esplanade; (03) 5261 6142; open Wed–Sun for lunch and daily for dinner Dec–Apr, Wed–Sun for dinner May–Nov, and weekends for breakfast; scorched.yokall.com

THE SURF RIDER $$$
MODERN AUSTRALIAN

This family-owned and operated restaurant offers relaxed casual dining some 200 metres from the beach, but the surf interest is actually inside. The surf-loving family has turned The Surf Rider into a quasi surfing museum with lots of local history, photos and surfing

WHERE TO EAT

FAMILY FRIENDLY   LICENSED   OUTDOOR DINING   VEGETARIAN OPTIONS

memorabilia. Dishes on the modern fusion menu are well executed. A typical entrée might be seared local scallops on grilled chorizo, dauphin potatoes, chilli jam and a sweet basil and rocket salad. A popular main course is twice-cooked honey and soy farm duck with pears, pink-eye potatoes, gingered bok choy and teriyaki sauce. And for dessert, hot Belgian chocolate soufflé with raspberry caramel and French vanilla ice-cream.

26 Bell St; (03) 5261 6477; open daily for dinner in summer, Wed–Sun May–Aug; www.thesurfrider.com.au

SUNNYBRAE RESTAURANT AND COOKING SCHOOL $$$

MODERN AUSTRALIAN

Part cooking school and part restaurant, Sunnybrae is one of regional Victoria's hidden gems. It is overseen by renowned chef George Biron, a staunch advocate of the philosophy of slow food. The regionally sourced lunches he creates in this farmhouse surrounded by gardens are set-priced and multi-coursed, and reveal the wonder of eating things that have been pulled from the ground or plucked from the bush a short time before. Excellent local snapper might rest on a bed of samphire greens or homemade cheese on wilted cucumber. Sunnybrae is convivial, homely and very special.

Cnr Cape Otway and Lorne rds, Birregurra; (03) 5236 2276; open weekends for lunch; sunnybraerestaurantandcookingschool. blogspot.com

Traralgon

CAFE AURA $$

MODERN AUSTRALIAN

This busy cafe-deli-cum-restaurant serves terrific cafe food, from egg dishes for breakfast

to decent steaks for dinner. Kick-start the day with eggs Benedict. For lunch perhaps consider a homemade crepe filled with chicken, leek and mushrooms, a tender steak sandwich or crunchy baguette filled with chicken, avocado, crispy bacon and homemade aioli, or rare roast beef with homemade chilli jam. As well as steaks, the dinner menu offers several grazing dishes to share for starters, a daily risotto and several pastas – perhaps linguini marinara or spaghetti with tiger prawns.

Shop 3, 19–25 Seymour St; (03) 5174 1517; open daily for breakfast and lunch, and Tues–Sat for dinner

IIMIS CAFE $$

GREEK

Meaning 'we are' or 'all of us' in Greek, Iimis is a bright and colourful cafe that serves Mediterranean-style food with a strong leaning towards traditional Greek dishes. Expect to find an array of dips, filo pastry parcels such as spanakopita and tiropita, grilled saganaki cheese, calamari, souvlakis and lots of bite-sized mezze dishes to share. The mega mezze plate is especially popular – a selection of Greek dips, seafood and grilled meats, ideal for one or more. Consider desserts; they can be extra good.

28 Seymour St; (03) 5174 4577; open daily for breakfast and lunch, and Mon–Sat for dinner

NEILSONS $$$

MODERN AUSTRALIAN

Housed in an old Californian-style bungalow, this welcoming restaurant seats diners in three intimate dining rooms. Talented chef and co-owner Lewis Prince offers a contemporary à la carte menu as well as an eight-course tasting menu or vegetarian degustation menu, available with matching wines. Using local produce, he delights with flavoursome dishes such as tempura zucchini flowers filled with Tarago

River goat's cheese, or wagyu ox-cheek ragout cooked slow and low, with sticky tamarind glaze, dukkah cucumber salad and smoked yoghurt. Desserts don't disappoint either: try the kaffir-lime panna cotta with blood-orange sorbet and candied pistachios.

13 Seymour St; (03) 5175 0100; open Tues–Sat for lunch and dinner; www.neilsons.com.au

TERRACE CAFE $$$
INTERNATIONAL

Part of the Century Inn accommodation and conference centre, this modern cafe is located in the front of the complex on the Princes Highway. It is the place for a light lunch such as a filled baguette, or a two-course lunch special including a glass of wine. At night, expect to find glazed Asian duck, rack of local Gippsland lamb or perhaps pork cutlets. It is environmentally friendly, with a green AAA rating, and serves terrific Rainforest Alliance–certified coffee.

5 Airfield Rd; (03) 5173 9400; open weekdays for lunch and Mon–Sat for dinner; www.centuryinn.com.au/terrace-cafe

Walhalla

PARKER'S RESTAURANT $$$
MODERN AUSTRALIAN

The dining room of Walhalla's stylish Star Hotel was named after one of the hotel's original owners, who in 1878 carried out renovations that gave the building the form that is replicated today. While the exterior might say gold-rush era, the interior is indeed contemporary. The dinner menu is à la carte and changes daily. Generally there is a choice of four dishes for each course, with mains including a selection of fish, poultry and red meat dishes. Popular entrées include sweet

Thai chilli prawns and house-made terrine, while favourite main courses are Gippsland lamb and rosemary pie or roast pork belly with apple relish. Desserts include evergreens: rich chocolate mud cake and lemon tart. The wine list features several regional labels. Reservations are required.

Walhalla's Star Hotel, Main Rd; (03) 5165 6262; open daily for dinner; www.starhotel. com.au/restaurant.html

Wangaratta

QUALITY HOTEL WANGARATTA $$$
GATEWAY
INTERNATIONAL

This hotel dining room offers a contemporary à la carte menu that pleases locals and visitors alike. The menu covers the full gamut of flavours, with imaginative offerings such as duck rillettes with chilli dipping pot, chicken and veal terrine with pear and thyme chutney, salt-and-pepper squid, or pumpkin gnocchi with bocconcini, caramelised onion and roasted eggplant. Main courses might be fish of the day, Moroccan lamb fillets, grain-fed scotch and veal fillets, or green chicken curry.

29–37 Ryley St; (03) 5721 8399; open daily for breakfast and dinner; www.wangarattagateway.com.au

RINALDO'S $$
ITALIAN

It was only a matter of time before passionate chef Adam Pizzini moved from the King Valley, bringing his Italian fare to appreciative diners in nearby Wangaratta. Yet, Pizzini's mixed menu of modern Australian and traditional Italian dishes still reflects the valley's four distinct seasons, working with

FAMILY FRIENDLY   LICENSED   OUTDOOR DINING   VEGETARIAN OPTIONS

quality local produce such as King Valley free-range goat, Milawa free-range chicken and duck, Black Range river trout, Welsh Black beef from neighbouring Myrrhee Valley, Milawa cheese and local honey. Adam grows much of his own fruit and vegetables including Italian herbs, radicchio and heritage tomatoes to ensure a constant fresh supply. His Dutch cream potato gnocchi – perhaps in beef or goat ragù – is a standout. Check the day's specials for seasonal dishes.

8–10 Tone Rd; (03) 5721 8800; open Sat for breakfast, Tues–Sat for lunch and Wed–Sat for dinner; www.rinaldos.com.au

TREAD $$

INTERNATIONAL

With its expansive deck overlooking the Ovens River, this relative newcomer to Wangaratta's dining scene is so named because it is housed in a former tyre shop. It offers a mainly tapas-style menu that covers a wide variety of cuisine styles but is ideal to share. Perhaps start with salt-and-pepper squid, patatas bravas (Spanish-style spicy fried potatoes) and Japanese fried chicken. Main courses might include medallions of premium eye fillet with roasted beetroot or tender lamb backstrap. All desserts are homemade, such as the orange and chocolate tart, mixed berry compote or coconut panna cotta with fresh pineapple. There are some good local wines listed.

56–58 Faithful St; (03) 5721 4635; open Wed–Sun for breakfast and lunch, and Wed–Sat for dinner; www.treadrestaurant.com.au

Warburton

WILD THYME $$

CAFE

Muso Alan Seppings runs this bohemian cafe in the middle of the main street in Warburton. He encourages local bands with an 'open mike' jam night on the first Saturday of the month, and invites bands from Melbourne and touring bands from interstate to play for his appreciative diners. Using as much organic and Fair Trade produce as possible, he also sources local produce and has a thriving organic kitchen garden on the banks of the Yarra immediately behind. Locals come for the vegetarian Greek-style breakfast of tomato, olives, feta, dill and scrambled eggs on sourdough toast. Other popular dishes include smoked trout risotto, curried potato and spicy lentil roti wrap, stuffed mushrooms and huge T-bone steaks.

3391 Warburton Hwy; (03) 5966 5050; open daily for breakfast and lunch, and Wed–Sun for dinner

BULONG ESTATE WINERY & $$
RESTAURANT

VINEYARD RESTAURANT

Nestled among the vines in a natural amphitheatre looking east to Mount Donna Buang and the Brittannia Ranges, this modern winery restaurant has spacious decks and established oak trees for alfresco dining accompanied by happy birdsong. Third-generation French chef Antoine Cheron, from Normandy, produces a modern French menu with classics such as snails with Parisian garlic butter, traditional French-style mussels, confit duck or wild barramundi. He sources much Yarra Valley produce, free-range eggs and terrific local seasonal berries that might end up in desserts such as his exceptional almond three-berry torte. Ask the knowledgeable wait staff to suggest appropriate estate-grown wines.

70 Summerhill Rd, Yarra Junction; (03) 5967 1358; open Fri–Sun for lunch and Fri–Sat for dinner; www.bulongestate.com.au

Warragul

THE GRANGE CAFE AND DELI $
CAFE PROVEDORE

The new chef/owner of this bustling country cafe has big plans to add to its current menu of great toasted sandwiches by introducing a small à la carte menu of more substantial dishes, such as risotto, pasta, chicken, steaks and more. The deli side of things promotes the region's fabulous regional produce of olive oils, jams, preserves, chutneys etc. The cafe also boasts being the only eatery outside Melbourne to serve Toby's Estate coffee from New South Wales.

15 Palmerston St; (03) 5623 6698; open Mon–Sat for breakfast and lunch

JACK'S AT JINDIVICK $$$
MODERN AUSTRALIAN

The beautifully restored homestead that houses Jack's is almost reason enough for a visit, whether you're dining in the glassed-in terrace-like room out the back, with its bucolic views, or in one of the more ornate and formal rooms further inside the house. The menu takes flavours from both Asia and the Mediterranean, and there is a lean to the free range, organic and locally sourced in both meat and vegetables. The cooking is skilled, whether you opt for a hefty steak sandwich or a chickpea and vegetable tagine.

1070 Jackson's Track, Jindivick; (03) 5628 5424; open Thurs–Sun for lunch and Thurs–Sat for dinner; www.jacksatjindivick.com

STICCADO CAFE $
CAFE

This small single shopfront cafe opened in 2000 to promote local home-grown beef. Today, while it dispenses good coffee and ready-made focaccia and sandwiches to visitors who want a quick meal, it still sources Gippsland beef for its steak sandwiches, burgers, curries, pies, pasta sauces and lasagne. An upgraded menu also offers daily pastas, salads and soups – perhaps pumpkin, ginger and cheddar, chickpea and parsley, or tomato and red lentil. The owner has also just opened Vittles (Shops 2 and 3, 113 Princes Highway) for pizza, pasta and gelati.

Shop 6, The Village Walk, Yarragon; (03) 5634 2101; open Wed–Mon for lunch

THE OUTPOST RETREAT $$
MODERN AUSTRALIAN

The rustic country styling of the Outpost's restaurant and bar might have you thinking this is some sort of tourist theme park, but once the food starts landing on the table you soon realise this is a place completely committed to the idea of regional produce. Everything from the meat – perhaps Red Angus beef or milk-fed kid – to honey, butter and herbs is sourced from the surrounding region, and the skilled cooking certainly shows it off to its best advantage. The wine list, too, gives you a virtual tour of Gippsland's wineries.

38 Loch Valley Rd, Noojee; (03) 5628 9669; open Fri–Sun for lunch and Thurs–Sun for dinner; www.theoutpostretreat.com

WHERE TO EAT

Warrnambool

DONNELLY'S RESTAURANT $$$

MODERN AUSTRALIAN
Map ref. p. 154

Housed in one of the original heritage-listed buildings in the town's main street, this restaurant serves contemporary regional fare in two rooms with open fires in winter. The local fleet of cray boats ensures the freshest crayfish in season end up in their signature risotto, drizzled with truffle oil. Other local produce includes Hopkins River beef and Western District lamb. Typical entrées are Tasmanian oysters, green-tea noodles with pickled ginger, light soy sauce and wasabi, and a Caesar-style salad of locally smoked ocean trout. Roast duck breast with confit leg is a popular main course, while churros (Spanish doughnuts) with hot chocolate sauce are tops for dessert. There is an interesting list of boutique wines.

78 Liebig St; (03) 5561 3188; open daily for dinner; Tues–Sun in winter

KERMOND'S HAMBURGERS $

CAFE
Map ref. p. 154

For 60 years, five generations of the Kermond family have worked in this bustling genuine retro shop, producing that wonderful old-fashioned variety of hamburger you thought had long gone. What started in a caravan on the foreshore in 1949 is now a Victorian institution, considered among the most popular tourist attractions in the state. On the international scene, a Kermond's cheeseburger is considered the ninth best hamburger in the world. On a busy day, 35 casual and six full-time staff produce 50 dozen burgers, cooking everything to order from scratch. And the secret ingredient: premium Western District steak, minced and blended to a specific recipe from local Lucas'

Butchers, who have been supplying the beef since day one – around 12 000 kilograms a year.

151 Lava St; (03) 5562 4854; open daily for breakfast, lunch and dinner

NONNA CASALINGA $$$

ITALIAN
Map ref. p. 154

This elegant dining room cooks up rustic-style Italian dishes that very nearly could have come out of an Italian grandmother's kitchen – except there is not an Italian in the house. Homemade gnocchi with gorgonzola cream is a popular entrée, along with crisp pork belly or perhaps Venetian-style pan-fried mussels with crab spaghetti. Main courses are also good, with dishes such as seafood stew of white fish, mussels and blue swimmer crab, and oven-braised lamb served with parmesan and sage crust. And to finish: tiramisu, of course, or vanilla-bean panna cotta served with saffron and poached pear.

69 Liebig St; (03) 5562 2051; open Mon–Sat for dinner

PIPPIES BY THE BAY $$$

INTERNATIONAL
Map ref. p. 154

Located within Flagstaff Hill maritime village, this contemporary space overlooks the 'best view in the world' through Norfolk pines to the sea. As its name implies, it does have a good smattering of seafood on its menu – local crayfish being a standout in season (November to April). The fisherman's platter of assorted seafood is enormously popular, featuring oysters, prawns, scallops, calamari, squid and whiting. For carnivores, there is also a good selection of steaks, salads and pastas such as homemade gnocchi and cannelloni.

91 Merri St; (03) 5561 2188; open daily for breakfast, lunch and dinner

---

🍾 BYO AVAILABLE   💳 CREDIT CARDS ACCEPTED   ♿ DISABLED ACCESS   👔 DRESS CODE APPLIES

Wodonga

ZILCH FOOD STORE $
CAFE PROVEDORE

Off a pleasant courtyard on the main road, this friendly modern cafe is open for breakfast, lunch and morning and afternoon teas and coffee. Start the day with a toasted Zilch sandwich: bacon, cheese and alfalfa with poppy seed dressing on wholemeal bread. In summer, choose from a variety of salads; in winter, warming homemade soups and pies. Patrons can choose from ready-made or made-to-order sandwiches and focaccias, and choose their own mix of freshly squeezed juice.

8/1 Stanley St; (02) 6056 2400; open weekdays for breakfast and lunch

SOURCE DINING $$$
MODERN AUSTRALIAN

This contemporary restaurant in the main street of Albury has won many gongs for its innovative contemporary menu including 'best in the region'. At lunch, a casual menu of entrée-size dishes is offered – perhaps order three for two to share – with cheese boards and small portioned sweets. At night, double tablecloths are donned, linen napkins and candles appear and long-stemmed glassware complements the very respectable wine list. Start with crayfish, octopus and potato salad before moving on to wild rabbit sausage, then finish with their imaginative spin on a lamington ice-cream.

664 Dean St, Albury; (02) 6041 1288; open Thurs–Fri for lunch and Tues–Sat for dinner; www.sourcedining.com

Woodend

CAMPASPE COUNTRY HOUSE $$$
MODERN AUSTRALIAN

There is always a warm country welcome at this gracious manor house, where the kitchen philosophy promotes and champions local and regional produce. You will usually find smallgoods from Istra in Musk, trout and lamb from Tuki – even herbs and vegetables from the kitchen garden. Dishes are always well thought out, and might be roasted lamb rump with sautéed artichokes, broad beans from the garden, confit tomatoes with olive and a basil jus. Desserts are simply delicious, such as lemon tart with fresh blueberries and yoghurt sorbet. The wine list features only central Victorian wines.

Goldies La; (03) 5427 2273; open weekends for breakfast, Sun for lunch, and Fri–Sat for dinner; www.campaspehouse.com.au

HOLGATE BREWHOUSE $$$
BREWERY RESTAURANT

This imposing two-storey red brick hotel used to be a coach stop 150 years ago, serving the route from Melbourne to the goldfields of Ballarat and Bendigo. Part of the old stables remain and are today used for storage. Today a thriving brewery, it produces some ten beers and ales that all end up somehow or other on the menu – either actually in the food or as suggested drink matches. Typical dishes are nori-crusted salmon fillet with White Ale, coriander, wasabi and ginger dressing, the Extra Special Bitter–marinated kangaroo fillet, or slow-cooked goat in Holgate's tangy Hopinator. There is also a casual bar menu

WHERE TO EAT

FAMILY FRIENDLY   LICENSED   OUTDOOR DINING   VEGETARIAN OPTIONS

with steak sandwiches, locally made Stella's pasta and their signature Dark Ale and beef pie.

79 High St; (03) 5427 2510; open Tues–Sun for lunch and daily for dinner; www.holgatebrewhouse.com

Yackandandah

STAR HOTEL $$
INTERNATIONAL

Built in 1863, this popular hotel bistro does classic pub food a rung or two above what you might expect. They know their patrons do not always have huge appetites and so offer smaller serves such as half schnitzels and chicken parmigianas, and smaller helpings of bangers and mash, scotch fillet and pasta. Good vegetarian options might be homemade lasagne, spinach and ricotta filo or polenta and mushrooms. In summer, the place to be is under an umbrella in the courtyard or on the covered verandah.

30 High St; (02) 6027 1493; open Wed–Sun for lunch and daily for dinner

PERFECTLY MATCHED FOOD AND BEER, HARGREAVES HILL BREWING COMPANY RESTAURANT, YARRA GLEN

STICKY TARTS CAFE $
CAFE

This charming reproduction shopfront cafe looks every bit as historic as its neighbours, possibly because it was built from recycled timbers and fittings. With seating on the pavement as well as on a rear deck, it offers a warm welcome in any season. Free-range eggs, hydroponic tomatoes and Milawa breads form the basis of many a breakfast dish, and everything is made on the premises, including ice-creams, muffins and cakes for morning and afternoon teas. Light meals such as focaccias and risotto are popular, and they are well known for their lemon meringue cheesecake.

26 High St; (02) 6027 1853; open Wed–Mon for breakfast and lunch, and Fri for dinner

Yarra Glen

HARGREAVES HILL BREWING $$$
COMPANY RESTAURANT
BREWERY RESTAURANT

An old bank building in the main street of Yarra Glen has become the public face of the much-awarded and admired Hargreaves Hill Brewing Company, located in nearby Steel's Creek. The front bar is the scene of both quaffing and tasting the microbrewery's output, which includes a Pale Ale, a Porter and a Hefeweizen. Those looking to match their beer with some food should head into the wooden-floored rooms out the back where simple but deftly handled Mediterranean-style dishes complement the beer, perhaps cumin-dusted squid, freshly shucked oysters or tasting plates of local produce.

25 Bell St; (03) 9730 1905; open weekends for breakfast, Wed–Sun for lunch and Wed–Sat for dinner; www.hargreaveshill.com.au

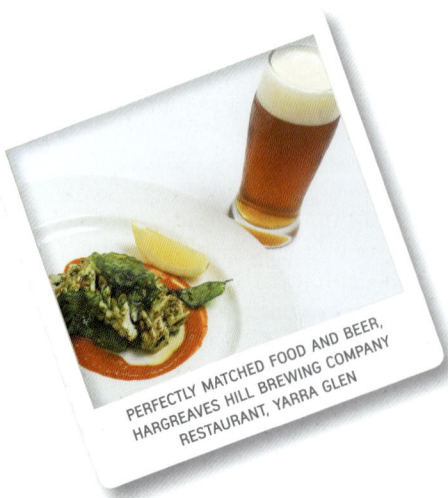

TARRAWARRA ESTATE WINE BAR CAFE $$$

VINEYARD RESTAURANT

The TarraWarra winery has one of the more spectacular cellar door buildings in the Yarra Valley, including a cellar door, a stunning gallery of modern Australian art and an elegant wine bar that takes in the views of this very beautiful property. The clean-lined room with its stone fireplace is minimal without being sterile and is an ideal backdrop to the rustic Italian- and French-influenced menu. Duck terrine is teamed with pumpernickel while pasta is tossed with braised local rabbit. The food has obviously been designed with TarraWarra's deftly crafted wines in mind, making this a very civilised winery pit stop indeed.

311 Healesville–Yarra Glen Rd; (03) 5957 3510; open Tues–Sun for lunch; www.tarrawarra.com.au

ELEONORE'S RESTAURANT AT CHATEAU YERING $$$$

EUROPEAN

Hidden behind cypress pines, historic Chateau Yering is a luxury hotel nestled among established gardens adjacent to the vast Yering Station winery complex. This 1850s homestead boasts one of the most elegant restaurants you will find, offering special occasion dining at its best. Entrées might be a crisp parcel of Yarra Valley feta with shaved beetroot, black truffle salad and beetroot jelly, or roast Yarra Valley quail with foie gras. Main courses are deliciously intricate, with dishes such as roasted suckling pig with date-stewed kohlrabi with miso butterscotch sauce and apple cider foam, or slow-cooked rump of spring lamb with Jerusalem artichoke, pea and mint custard with roast garlic and mascarpone purée.

42 Melba Hwy, Yering; (03) 9237 3333; open weekends for lunch and daily for dinner; www.chateauyering.com.au/dining-restaurant.asp

YERING STATION WINE BAR RESTAURANT $$$

VINEYARD RESTAURANT

With its soaring, curving roof and floor-to-ceiling windows capturing some of the Yarra Valley's best views, this winery restaurant certainly offers diners a dramatic sense of place. The wine list mainly sticks to the house labels – many of them available by the glass – but the modern Australian menu is not afraid to venture beyond the local, and might include Western Australian crab and ocean trout. The food is clever without being tricky, with desserts being a particular highlight. Noise levels can rise when the buses roll in and the place fills up, but the roar is convivial rather than oppressive.

38 Melba Hwy, Yering; (03) 9730 0100; open daily for lunch; www.yering.com

Yarrawonga

LADY MURRAY CRUISES $$$

INTERNATIONAL

Cruise 22 kilometres up and down the mighty Murray River towards Albury on this comfortable 50-seat cruise boat for lunch or dinner. Barbecue lunches are set price and comprise a smorgasbord of barbecued meats, a variety of salads and sweets. Set-price three-course dinners start with finger food served while guests arrive and mingle as the cruise gets under way. There is usually a choice of main course – perhaps porterhouse steak or

FAMILY FRIENDLY   LICENSED   OUTDOOR DINING   VEGETARIAN OPTIONS

chicken breast stuffed with spinach and feta – both served with roast vegetables and fresh garden salad. And for dessert: baked cheesecake or homemade apple strudel. The three-hour cruises with live commentary give guests a good look at river life along this historic waterway.

Yarrawonga foreshore; (03) 5744 2005; open daily for lunch and dinner; members.dodo.com.au/~ladymurray

YARRAWONGA & BORDER GOLF CLUB $$

INTERNATIONAL

Take a seat in this lively bistro overlooking the impressive 45-hole golf course – the largest public-access course in the country. They cater for country appetites here and dishes offer outstanding value. The locally produced northeast Victorian 400-gram Hereford rump is exceptional – cooked to order and served with seasonal vegetables or salad from the bar. Other dishes might be lamb loin, eye fillet, chicken and camembert pie or chicken parmigiana. There is a special children's menu, and also light and healthy options. A carvery is offered on Friday and Saturday nights and throughout holiday periods. Good local wine list.

Gulai Rd, Mulwala; (03) 5744 1911; open Sun for lunch and daily for dinner; www.yarragolf.com.au

Yea

MARMALADES $

CAFE PROVEDORE

This rustic cafe and produce store is housed in a charming 1880s heritage-listed building, which was once a bustling general store in this former goldmining town. High ceilings, original long counter benches and open fires all add to the country ambience. Located about 100 kilometres from Melbourne, it is about halfway to the snowfields of Mount Buller and just perfect for a welcome coffee break, with good homemade pies, cakes, breads, slices and biscuits. Try the beef and mushroom or chicken and leek pies, hearty soups in winter or always warming traditional Indian dishes such as tandoori chicken, beef vindaloo, lamb saag and lentil dahl. Regulars come back for the decadent chocolate brownie, lumberjack-style apple and fig cake, and gluten-free options such as chocolate almond or orange and lemon polenta.

20 High St; (03) 5797 2999; open Wed–Mon for breakfast and lunch; www.marmalades.com.au

BYO AVAILABLE   CREDIT CARDS ACCEPTED   DISABLED ACCESS   DRESS CODE APPLIES

ART AND COMFORT COME TOGETHER AT TOLARNO HOTEL, ST KILDA, MELBOURNE

victoria

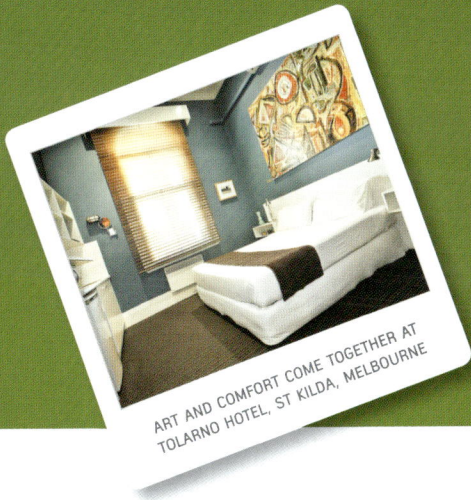

Town entries are ordered alphabetically, with places nearby listed at the end.

LEGEND
$	=	under $100
$$	=	$100–$150
$$$	=	$150–$200
$$$$	=	$200–$300
$$$$$	=	over $300

For low-season rack rate

BREAKFAST INCLUDED	CREDIT CARDS ACCEPTED	FAMILY FRIENDLY
FITNESS CENTRE	ROOM SERVICE	SWIMMING POOL

Melbourne

ADELPHI HOTEL $$$$
Map ref. p. 8

For inner-city luxury, the thoroughly modern Adelphi Hotel is an architectural darling of Melbourne. Adelphi's visionary style has transformed a former warehouse into a cocoon of tranquillity, with exceptional attention to detail. Guests are generously catered for in each of the 34 guest rooms, including babysitting services for parents looking to slip away and explore the surrounding art and business district. Make sure you escape to the rooftop and take a plunge in the spectacular pool perched above the laneway below, or be pampered in the new Spa @ Adelphi.

187 Flinders La; (03) 8080 8888; www.adelphi.com.au

APARTMENT 401 $$$$
Map ref. p. 8

Located right in the heart of Melbourne's cafe scene overlooking Degraves Street, this chic one-bedroom apartment is housed on the fourth floor of the Art Deco–era Majorca House. It boasts a light-filled lounge-dining room with well-equipped kitchen for self-catering, a queen-size bed and a cute Juliet-style balcony overlooking lively Centre Place. Antique and contemporary pieces from the owners' private collection blend well together. There is a minimum booking of two nights.

258 Flinders La; (03) 9428 8104; www.apartment401.com.au

COTTERVILLE $$

Map ref. p. 7 E4

There are just two rooms of accommodation in this gracious art-filled terrace house in leafy Toorak. The owners are great cooks and will provide meals by arrangement, but more than that they'll make you feel part of the family – sharing the elegant front lounge, the music room, home cinema, rear entertaining room and garden with schnauzers Elizabeth and Taylor. Join your hosts for complimentary pre-dinner drinks before trying one of the many restaurants within walking distance – or indeed dining in-house.

204 Williams Rd, Toorak; (03) 9826 9105; www.cotterville.com

CROWN PROMENADE HOTEL $$$$$

Map ref. p. 16

Built in 2003, this multi-award-winning hotel is conveniently located for work and pleasure and features 465 contemporary rooms, including 18 studios and three suites. Functional and stylish, all rooms have spectacular views over the city or Port Phillip Bay. Mesh restaurant is open for all-day meals; Tonic bar is the place to meet friends; and if you need to cool down or work out after a day in the city, check out The Deck – a leisure centre on the third floor with indoor heated pool, cafe and wireless internet.

Crown Entertainment Complex, 8 Whiteman St, Southbank; (03) 9292 6688 or 1800 776 612; www.crownpromenade.com.au

FOUNTAIN TERRACE $$$

Map ref. p. 6 D5

Just off bustling cosmopolitan Fitzroy Street, the heartbeat of colourful St Kilda, this comfortable, restored 1880s Victorian home is in a leafy residential street. It offers B&B accommodation in seven well-appointed rooms – all with ensuites. Rooms are individually furnished, each named and themed after an Australian icon – Dame Nellie Melba, Caroline Chisholm, Henry Lawson, Dorothea Mackellar, Norman Lindsay, Edna Walling and Sidney Nolan. Two one-bedroom apartments suitable for longer stays are available in a lovely Art Deco building nearby.

28 Mary St, St Kilda West; (03) 9593 8123; www.fountainterrace.com.au

GRAND HOTEL MELBOURNE $$$$

Map ref. p. 11

Housed in heritage-listed former railway administrative offices, this hotel is within easy walking distance of Southern Cross Station, perfect for guests who might arrive in Melbourne by train. Many of the 100 spacious suites are loft suites, built over two levels with a comfortable lounge area and workable kitchen downstairs, bedroom and bathroom upstairs. The hotel has an in-house restaurant and bar, and is within easy walking distance of any number of dining options. Check out the building's original imposing central staircase and remember that as state minister for transport, the late Sir Robert Menzies had his office here for six parliamentary terms.

33 Spencer St; (03) 9611 4567; www.grandhotelmelbourne.com.au

GRAND MERCURE FLINDERS LANE APARTMENTS $$$

Map ref. p. 8

This very central, welcoming business or leisure hotel has a peaceful central courtyard for summer enjoyment and has been a city favourite for years. It might belong to a major chain, but the intimate hotel with just 59 rooms has an air of seclusion, away from the city hustle and bustle. The hotel also offers secure parking next door, a corporate health club facility and two suites for the disabled.

BREAKFAST INCLUDED   CREDIT CARDS ACCEPTED   FAMILY FRIENDLY

321 Flinders La; (03) 9629 4088;
www.mercure.com

HOTEL LINDRUM $$$$

Map ref. p.13

Located in the heart of cosmopolitan Melbourne and a stone's throw from the famous MCG, Hotel Lindrum is full of elegant, old-world charm. The former venue where the famous Walter Lindrum demonstrated his mastery of billiards (he won the World Billiards Championship every year from 1933 to 1950), today the premises has 59 beautifully appointed guest rooms glowing with cosy luxury. The hotel's restaurant, Felt, overlooking busy Flinders Street, offers a fine dining experience with the focus on fresh seasonal cuisine. There is also a chic bar and popular spa, contributing to the emphasis on tranquillity and comfort at this award-winning city hotel.

**26 Flinders St; (03) 9668 1111;
www.hotellindrum.com.au**

LANGHAM HOTEL $$$$$

Map ref. p.16

Supreme comfort and style await guests at the Langham Hotel on the famous Southbank promenade. Enjoying spectacular views of the city and the Yarra River, the five-star Langham has 387 guest rooms lavishly decorated with rich fabrics and furnishings, and guests have an enviable choice of suites to choose from. The award-winning Chuan Spa offers a luxurious haven of pampering treatments on the ninth floor. This is the only Melbourne hotel, and one of only five in Australia, to be included on 'The Leading Hotels of the World' listing. The National Gallery of Victoria, Federation Square, the Arts Centre and myriad Melburnian landmarks are located nearby.

**1 Southgate Ave, Southbank; (03) 8696 8888;
www.melbourne.langhamhotels.com.au**

QUAY WEST SUITES MELBOURNE $$$$$

Map ref. p. 16

This riverside complex comprises just 97 suites and is discreetly tucked away alongside Southgate on the bustling Southbank promenade, with spectacular views over the Yarra River and the city lights. With a choice of one-, two- or three-bedroom fully equipped suites, it is a popular choice for families or those enjoying a longer stay in Melbourne. There is a good in-house restaurant, popular bar, superb recreation centre and luxuriously lit swimming pool and spa. Centrally located in the city's renowned cultural heart adjacent to the Concert Hall, the hotel is just a minute's walk over Princes Bridge to Federation Square and the city beyond.

**26 Southgate Ave, Southbank; (03) 9693 6000
or 1800 800 193; www.mirvachotels.com/
quay-west-suites-melbourne**

THE ALBANY $$

Map ref. p. 6 D4

Nestled in one of the city's most desirable residential pockets, this former modest 1960s motel has morphed into a cheeky, colourful boutique hotel with great style and flair. A recent renovation has seen the hotel redecorated in a 'fashion meets music' theme – evident in the black-and-white-striped walls of the cafe, photo-collage headboards in the deluxe rooms and hip artwork throughout. Rooms at The Albany range from simple doubles to deluxe spa rooms and the one-bedroom Millswyn Suite. The cafe offers breakfast and bar food daily, with dinner from Thursday to Saturday.

**Cnr Toorak Rd and Millswyn St, South Yarra;
(03) 9866 4485; www.thealbany.com.au**

WHERE TO STAY

FITNESS CENTRE   ROOM SERVICE   SWIMMING POOL

THE COMO $$$$

Map ref. p. 7 E4

Intimate and discreet, this contemporary hotel is regarded by visiting celebrities as a 'home away from home'. On the corner of Chapel Street and Toorak Road, it is conveniently located in the heart of trendy South Yarra's fashion shopping strip. There are 107 one- and two-bedroom suites, penthouses and spacious studios, most with individual spas and offering individual floor plans. The area abounds with bars and cafes, and many restaurants in the vicinity operate a handy 'charge back' facility in conjunction with Como, so your restaurant bill can be added to your hotel account.

630 Chapel Street, South Yarra;
(03) 9825 2222 or 1800 033 400;
www.mirvachotels.com/como-melbourne

THE CULLEN $$$

Map ref. p. 7 E4

The first in a series of art hotels to grace Melbourne's inner suburbs, this 115-room boutique accommodation is a welcome addition to cosmopolitan Prahran. Filled with more than 450 'grunge' works by artist Adam Cullen, the $48 million development also boasts two life-sized mosaic cows that greet guests in the foyer. Six floors high, it includes 19 lime-green pod balconies with views over Melbourne's skyline, a roof-top gymnasium and two dining venues: HuTong dumpling restaurant, and Mediterranean-inspired The Terrace. Located opposite Prahran Market and in the midst of a thriving retail precinct, it makes an ideal near-city base. The group's flagship hotel, The Olsen, is at 452 Chapel Street, South Yarra.

160–162 Commercial Rd, Prahran;
(03) 9098 1555 or 1800 278 468

THE HATTON $$$$

Map ref. p. 6 D4

This stylish boutique hotel is housed in an elegant 1902-built mansion in a residential pocket of trendy South Yarra. Its 20 rooms are well equipped, each with its own charm and appeal, and there is a rooftop garden with city views. The front reception converts to a bar each evening and continental breakfast is served here each morning. Just minutes from town, the hotel is within easy walking distance of Toorak Road's many restaurants and boutiques, the Botanic Gardens and the Victorian Arts Centre.

65 Park St, South Yarra; (03) 9868 4800;
www.hatton.com.au

THE HOTEL CHARSFIELD $$$$

Map ref. p. 6 D4

Located in one of St Kilda Road's gracious old original mansions, this 41-room boutique hotel with its elegant architecture is classified by the National Trust. It is close enough to the CBD for work, yet far enough away for play, and offers corporate suites, premier and deluxe rooms, apartments and premier spa rooms. The 50-seat Charsfield Restaurant serves French fare, with several other good restaurants in the neighbourhood. There is a snooker room and off-site parking.

478 St Kilda Rd; (03) 9866 5511 or
1300 301 830; www.charsfield.com

THE LYALL HOTEL $$$$$

Map ref. p. 7 E4

With just 40 suites, this is arguably Melbourne's most chic small hotel, located in fashionable South Yarra, just metres from boutique- and restaurant-lined Toorak Road. At the Lyall, it is the little things that count – like a pillow menu, private kitchen facilities for self-catering from a well-stocked fridge, a gym and spa, intimate champagne bar and a shopping privilege card. There is a limousine service available to take you to the CBD if you really have to work. The Lyall is the only hotel in Victoria to be a member of the Small Luxury Hotels of the World group.

14 Murphy St, South Yarra; (03) 9868 8222; www.thelyall.com

THE PRINCE $$$$$
Map ref. p. 6 D5

The Prince, in the bayside suburb of St Kilda, is modern, glamorous and playful, with dazzling shots of hot pink. No two of the 40 rooms are the same, and there is an indoor pool as well as the Aurora Spa Retreat for those who need to be pampered. Enjoy a drink at the atmospheric restaurant bar before dining at the multi-award-winning Circa, The Prince, one of Melbourne's very best dining establishments – utterly romantic and perfect for that special night out.

2 Acland St, St Kilda; (03) 9536 1111; www.theprince.com.au

THE SEBEL MELBOURNE $$$$
Map ref. p. 11

This stylish hotel is housed in a historic and elegant 1876-built former bank in fashionable Collins Street, in the heart of Melbourne's CBD. The heritage sandstone building has been lovingly restored to retain its original character and charm, and offers 115 deluxe studio rooms, one- and two-bedroom suites, and two-storey, one-bedroom loft suites, many of which look out over tree-lined Queen Street to spectacular city rooftop views. The former trading hall on the ground floor is now a fine restaurant, Treasury, and bar.

394 Collins St; (03) 9211 6600 or 1800 500 778; www.mirvachotels.com/sebel-melbourne

THE WESTIN MELBOURNE $$$$$
Map ref. p. 8

Situated on central City Square, the Westin is literally on the doorstep of Melbourne's best boutiques, theatres, galleries and Federation Square. Many of the 262 rooms have terrific views. After a day in the city, have the staff at the chic Martini Bar brew you a blend of pick-me-up tea before relaxing in the Wellness Centre, dining at Allegro or retiring to your Heavenly Bed. The Westin has earned such a reputation for its custom-designed beds, guests end up buying them for their homes. The hotel can ship its exclusive bed collection around the country.

205 Collins St; (03) 9635 2222; www.westin.com.au

TOLARNO HOTEL $$
Map ref. p. 6 D5

Housed in an original Victorian mansion, this boutique hotel offers 36 stylish colour- and art-filled single rooms and two-bedroom apartments. Some have kitchen facilities for self-catering; others boast small balconies onto cosmopolitan Fitzroy Street. Ideally located in St Kilda's heart, the hotel is above the highly acclaimed Mirka at Tolarno restaurant, with a terrific bar alongside. It is also within a minute's walk from dozens of other restaurants, cafes and bars, colourful Acland Street and the St Kilda Esplanade Sunday market. The tram passes the front door, heading to either the city or the seaside.

42 Fitzroy Street, St Kilda; (03) 9537 0200; www.hoteltolarno.com.au

VILLA DONATI $$$
Map ref. p. 7 E3

This lovely Italianate villa has had a chequered life over the years, from being home to a former mayor of Richmond and an Anglican archbishop, to housing a massage parlour. Today, it is run as a small boutique hotel offering four contemporary rooms for accommodation, all with ensuites and furnished with an assortment of Asian and European antiques and original artwork. It is within walking distance of the many restaurants and retail outlets in Swan Street, Bridge Road and Chapel Street.

377 Church St, Richmond; (03) 9428 8104; www.villadonati.com

Alexandra

ATHLONE COUNTRY COTTAGES $$$

Fly-fishermen will be in their element staying in either of these two cottages or studio, as the property's dam has been stocked with rainbow trout. You can also learn fly-fishing techniques from local experts. The cottages are well equipped to sleep four in each; the studio is purely a romantic interlude for two. Owners provide the makings for breakfasts and are also happy to stock the larder with quality foods from the nearby Ruffy Produce Store. If desired, they can also organise a meal on arrival.

266 UT Creek Rd; (03) 5772 2992; www.athlonecountrycottages.com.au

MITTAGONG HOMESTEAD AND COTTAGES $$$

Accommodation on this 400-hectare working cattle farm near Lake Eildon is in three well-appointed cottages: one purpose-built, the other two housed in a converted shearing shed. All are well appointed with king-size beds, large double spas, air-conditioning and log fires, TV, DVD and CD players, and outside private

barbecues. Guests are offered the makings of a hearty country breakfast, which they can cook at their leisure. There is also a sauna, tennis court and swimming pool for guests to use.

462 Spring Creek Rd; (03) 5772 2250; www.countrycottages.biz

STONELEA COUNTRY ESTATE $$$$

This country retreat is in a little slice of picturesque Australian countryside, with lush pastures and tall timbers tucked between the wine-rich Yarra Valley and the ski fields of Mount Buller. The 607-hectare family-owned and run property offers comfortable accommodation in 20 verandah rooms in the main building and 27 free-standing cottages – three are self-contained with two bedrooms, a kitchen and lounge. For the energetic, there is a tennis court, private golf course, spa and sauna, and the ability to fly-fish or go clay pigeon shooting. It boasts a fine in-house restaurant and estate-grown wines.

Connellys Creek Rd, Acheron; (03) 5772 2222; www.stonelea.com.au

Anglesea

AIREYS-ON-AIREYS $$

These three villas are on a property where sea breezes rustle through ironbark trees in the surrounding native gardens. The two- and three-bedroom villas are available for overnight and long-term stays. Spas, wood fires and big balconies might tempt you to take the long-term option. It is only a few minutes' walk from the villas to Sandy Gully beach. Attractive weekend packages are also available.

19 Aireys St, Aireys Inlet; (03) 5289 6844; www.aireysonaireys.com.au

BREAKFAST INCLUDED   CREDIT CARDS ACCEPTED   FAMILY FRIENDLY

Apollo Bay

CAPTAIN'S AT THE BAY $$$$

The name has a ship-ahoy theme but leave the sextant at home for your stay in this traditional B&B. The heart of Apollo Bay is just out the front door; the beach is a mere 150 metres away. There are four types of accommodation with a total of 11 rooms: cottages (two), terrace rooms (four), a two-bedroom loft (one) and the new bridge rooms (four). The bridge rooms were built in October 2008 and are the most modern of the contemporarily furnished rooms.

21 Pascoe St; (03) 5237 6771; www.captains.net.au

CHOCOLATE GANNETS $$$$

This luxury beachfront accommodation includes four villas set on a 40-hectare property. There is plenty of floor-to-ceiling glass to take in the views of Bass Strait. Apart from the extraordinary views there are also wood fires and leather sofas. The sounds of the surf can keep you company while in the double spa and, later, in bed. Chocolate Gannets is 2.5 kilometres from Apollo Bay. But don't even think about driving into town – you can walk along the beach the entire way.

6180 Great Ocean Rd; 1300 500 139; www.chocolategannets.com.au

CHRIS'S BEACON POINT RESTAURANT & VILLAS $$$$$

The option of staying at one of Chris's luxury suites and villas transforms a memorable dining experience at his on-site Mediterranean-style restaurant into a wonderful weekend getaway. The six two-bedroom suites (ideal for families or two couples) are modern, comfortable and fully equipped; the two new luxury studios have king-size beds and ensuites, ideal for a romantic getaway. Both villas and suites have the best views on the coast.

280 Skenes Creek Rd; (03) 5237 6411; www.chriss.com.au

POINT OF VIEW $$$$

These five villas come with views over green fields and trees and, as they are set up on a hill, fabulous views over much of Apollo Bay and Bass Strait. Each villa features a luxurious king-size bed, flat-screen TV with surround sound, large spa and double shower. There are sun decks for when the sky is blue and the days are warm but the wood heaters also make this a perfect winter destination. This just-for-couples place is barely five minutes off the Great Ocean Road. There is a two-night minimum stay.

165 Tuxion Rd; 0427 376 377; www.pointofview.com.au

Avoca

ECO-LUXE @ MOUNT AVOCA $$$$$

These three luxury lodges overlooking vineyards, an olive grove and the Pyrenees mountains and valleys are the new stars at Mount Avoca Wines, and make the perfect base from which to discover this wine-rich region. Architecturally designed using eco-friendly materials, the lodges cater mainly for couples with a king-size bed, travertine bathroom with spa bath, and kitchenette for self-catering. There's also a small bunkroom for extra

WHERE TO STAY

guests. Tariffs include breakfast provisions, a complimentary bottle of the estate's wine and a $30 voucher that is redeemable at the cellar door. The original Barry homestead nearby boasts log fires and can accommodate up to 10 people.

**Mount Avoca Winery, Moates La;
(03) 5465 3282; mountavoca.com**

WARRENMANG VINEYARD & RESORT $$$

In the heart of the Pyrenees wine region near Avoca, Warrenmang Vineyard & Resort is set on 101 hectares, effortlessly blending style and comfort with hospitality and warmth. The resort offers wonderful views of the purple Pyrenees Mountains and the chance to see a variety of native wildlife living on the property, including kangaroos. There are cottage-style chalets and luxury suites available; the most coveted of these are the penthouse suite at the grand Grange Chalet overlooking the vineyards and, for old country charm, Rose Cottage. The award-winning in-house restaurant specialises in regional produce and the cellar door is open for tastings of estate-grown wines, handpicked from 30-year-old vines and basket pressed.

**188 Mountain Creek Rd, Moonambel;
(03) 5467 2233; www.bazzani.com.au**

Bairnsdale

COMFORT INN RIVERSLEIGH $$$

Centrally located off the highway in the heart of town, this National Trust–listed property comprising two 1886 Victorian terrace houses was restored to its original splendour in 1987. With its elegance and historic charm, it is considered an East Gippsland icon. It offers

accommodation in 20 spacious rooms, two with spas, but all with comfortable furnishings, ensuite bathrooms, air-conditioning or ceiling fans, electric blankets, TVs and DVD players. An in-house restaurant serving modern Australian food is open for breakfast, lunch and dinner.

**1 Nicholson St; (03) 5152 6966;
www.riversleigh.info**

TARA HOUSE $$$

This elegant 1880s Victorian country home has been beautifully restored and offers gracious accommodation in three ensuite rooms amid beautiful gardens. With log fires in winter and shady verandahs in summer, guests are well catered for and made to feel at home. Cheese and wine are served late afternoons so guests can mingle and mix, and gourmet meals are served by prior arrangement, featuring quality local produce. There are literally hundreds of videos, DVDs and CDs available, plus a comprehensive library of books.

**37 Day St; (03) 5153 2253;
www.tarahouse.com.au**

WATERHOLES GUEST HOUSE $$$$$

The pristine wilderness lures guests to this remote rural accommodation with no TV, no mobile phone service and no daily papers. The only sounds are those of whipbirds, kookaburras and the occasional generator kicking in when lack of winter sun cuts solar power. Kaye and Bob Munro have lived here for 30 years with wombats, gliders, echidnas and lyrebirds. In 2001 they decided to share their 17-hectare property with guests and had three spacious suites built. Each is individually designed and stylishly furnished with hydroponic heating and windows that offer ever-changing landscapes. Kaye pampers

---

🛏 BREAKFAST INCLUDED   💳 CREDIT CARDS ACCEPTED   👪 FAMILY FRIENDLY

with excellent home-style food. Meals by arrangement are recommended.

**540 Archies Rd; (03) 5157 9330;
www.waterholesguesthouse.com.au**

Ballarat

ABENA'S BOUTIQUE ACCOMMODATION $$$

Map ref. p. 64

Set in one of Ballarat's most historic streets, Abena's is a stylish self-contained house only a few minutes from Sovereign Hill and the CBD. Three bedrooms feature a four-poster bed, a double and two singles, with luxury linens, and there is a comfy lounge and a kitchen with all mod cons where guests can cook the generous welcome hamper (bacon, eggs, muesli, yoghurt etc) at their will. Other creature comforts include a flat-screen TV, DVD library, books and magazines, and toys for kids. A private patio and rear yard are another bonus of this relaxing family-friendly retreat.

**210 Grant St; (03) 5338 7397;
www.ballarat.com/abenas**

CRAIG'S ROYAL HOTEL $$$$

Map ref. p. 64

This beautiful heritage hotel, built from 1862, features 41 elegant suites and rooms bedecked with antiques and featuring luxury bathrooms (suites have spas). The gracious public areas, bars and dining rooms have been restored to their original splendour. The Melba Suite is lavish, with a real mahogany bed; the Tower Suite has sweeping views across Lydiard Street; and the Oriental Suite boasts an elaborately carved 600-year-old wedding bed. The hotel's fine dining venues include a grand Victorian dining room, sun-filled conservatory and rustic bluestone cellar.

**10 Lydiard St South; (03) 5331 1377;
www.craigsroyal.com.au**

CUMBERLAND VILLA $$$

Map ref. p. 64

Built in 1890, this self-contained Victorian villa has been graciously restored to accommodate eight guests in four bedrooms. There are two bathrooms, a well-equipped kitchen, a large lounge room with dining table, central heating and an open fire. Antique furniture and a claw-foot bath add to the Cumberland's heritage charm. It is surrounded by a lovely garden with boxed hedge parterre in the front and a paved area at the back with old-fashioned bikes for childhood fun. Its central location makes it ideal for walking to restaurants, theatre, antique shops, art gallery and even the local railway station.

**332 Lydiard St North; (03) 5331 6216;
www.ballarat.com/cumberland**

MONTROSE OF BALLARAT $$$

Map ref. p. 64

This beautiful 150-year-old bluestone cottage has a National Trust A-classification, which translates as 'to be preserved at all cost'. As the first bluestone residence on the Ballarat goldfields – and the only one remaining today – it operated for 35 years as a tourist attraction showing how people lived in that era. Today it has undergone a massive renovation to offer luxurious private accommodation with great flair and style, with French provincial-style furniture, claw-foot bath and open fires. Guests can relax in the original old cobblestone courtyard and swing in a hammock under a shady century-old Ellison orange apple tree. Pampering and indulgent packages are available. Minimum two-night weekend stay.

**111 Eureka St; 0429 439 448;
www.montroseofballarat.com.au**

WHERE TO STAY

FITNESS CENTRE   ROOM SERVICE   SWIMMING POOL

Beechworth

1860 LUXURY ACCOMMODATION $$$$

This 1860s original timber slab hut has been carefully deconstructed from Taggerty in Victoria's High Country, then beautifully restored and transformed into a private escape oozing warmth and character. Now relocated in the heart of historic Beechworth, it offers peace and luxury with pure old-fashioned charm. Rebuilt from original timbers using traditional methods, the retreat also features recycled furniture, roofing iron, floorboards, pine ceiling and even fence palings from old properties in the area. There is a cosy fire, full-size kitchen, double bath and good selection of DVDs, CDs, board games and books. Minimum two-night stay at weekends; packages are available.

**4 Surrey La; 0408 273 783;
www.1860luxuryaccommodation.com**

BLACK SPRINGS BAKERY $$$$

Escape to Provence in this charming B&B housed in a cosy 19th-century stone barn, simply furnished in a South of France style – just five minutes from Beechworth. Meander through the olive grove or the quince walk, smell the lavender and take a picnic to the top of the hill with views over the countryside (a picnic hamper can be organised). Because the owners also operate the very chic Frances Pilley homewares shop in Beechworth, lovely soaps and French body products are provided. Guests also get ten per cent off shop purchases. Minimum two-nights stay.

**464 Wangaratta Rd; (03) 5728 2565;
www.blackspringsbakery.com**

PROVENANCE RESTAURANT $$$$
& LUXURY SUITES

The former old stables and carriage houses at the rear of Provenance Restaurant – housed in the imposing historic bank building on the corner of the town's main street – have been converted into four luxury suites. They have recently had a major makeover with contemporary design and decor, each boasting a king-size bed fitted with top-quality bed linen, double shower and spa with luxurious L'Occitane toiletries. Guests can opt for a continental or full cooked breakfast in the restaurant. Tariff includes a bottle of sparkling wine.

**86 Ford St; (03) 5728 1786;
www.theprovenance.com.au**

STONE COTTAGE $$$

With Beechworth's town attractions just a short walk away, Stone Cottage offers two self-contained and private accommodation options – The Cottage and The Barn. Just like the town, there is plenty of old-world charm, from the grand stone walls inside and out, to the dignified 100-year-old trees in the gardens. The Cotswold-style Cottage is ideal for couples with a downstairs kitchen, dining area, sitting room with wood fire and double spa, while upstairs is an attic-like room with a queen-size bed. The Barn is a little cosier, but can fit four guests with a separate bedroom with en-suite bathroom and double spa downstairs, and a spiral staircase leading to a queen-size bed upstairs.

**6 Tanswell St; (03) 5728 2857;
www.beechworth.com/stonecottage**

THE STANLEY $$

In the heart of flourishing apple, chestnut and berry farms about 10 kilometres from Beechworth, this gem of a country pub attracts locals and visitors alike with its genuine

BREAKFAST INCLUDED   CREDIT CARDS ACCEPTED   FAMILY FRIENDLY

hospitality, bistro-style restaurant and comfortable boutique accommodation. Its two bedrooms are French Provincial in style, with double doors opening onto a private perfumed garden with outdoor furniture. Both have quality bed linen, pampering spa bath with French toiletries, open fire and a selection of local teas, freshly ground coffee and the makings for a continental breakfast – including Stanley's celebrated fruit and nuts.

1 Wallace St, Stanley; (03) 5728 6502; www.thestanley.com.au

Benalla

MERRIOLLIA $$$

Built in 1904, this elegant Federation home with beautiful stained-glass windows and lovely cornices throughout sits in the middle of a large country garden and offers ample off-street parking. Accommodation is in three rooms. The Rose Room and Magnolia Room both have ensuites, while the more family-friendly Jacaranda Room has a full bathroom and an extra queen-size settee if required. Guests are offered sparkling wine and chocolates on arrival. There are 24-hour tea and coffee facilities in the lounge and complimentary after-dinner port or whisky.

17–19 Cecil St; (03) 5762 3786; www.countryoccasions.com.au

NILLAHCOOTIE ESTATE $$$$

This self-contained guesthouse is part of a winery complex, but is conveniently located on the opposite side of the Midland Highway. It overlooks the vineyards, Broken River Valley and Lake Nillahcootie – a popular spot with the locals who come to sail, waterski and

fish. The guesthouse can accommodate up to eight guests in its three bedrooms. There are two double rooms, one with an ensuite and one with two lots of double bunks, plus a full kitchen, central dining room, spacious living area and wrap-around verandah for taking in the views. Guests receive a complimentary bottle of estate-grown wine and a breakfast basket can be provided on request.

3630 Midland Hwy, Lima South; (03) 5768 2685; www.nillahcootieestate.com.au

Bendigo

ANCHORAGE BY THE LAKE $$$
Map ref. p. 70

These half-dozen one-bedroom serviced apartments are set in landscaped gardens and conveniently located about a 15-minute walk from Bendigo's CBD, restaurants and bars. Front apartments have views over Lake Weeroona and all offer contemporary accommodation with gas log fires, air-conditioning, spa bath or traditional claw-foot bath, kitchen and laundry facilities, wide-screen TVs and CD players. Two feature a French Provincial theme, two are oriental in decor, reflecting the city's early Chinese heritage, and two are modern in natural earth colours.

300–302 Napier St; (03) 5442 4777; www.anchoragebythelake.com

FOUNTAIN VIEW SUITES $$$
Map ref. p. 70

Offering some of the best boutique accommodation in Bendigo, these ten suites have views over leafy Rosalind Park or cosmopolitan View Street and the city's iconic Alexandra fountain. Housed in lovely old 1863 Victorian buildings, the classical-style suites take up several levels, with nine king suites,

WHERE TO STAY

including an elegant bridal suite, and one queen suite. Two have kitchenettes, almost all have corner spas and three have gas log fires. Suite 9 is popular. Three suites also have balconies overlooking View Street and all have broadband internet access.

10–12 View St; (03) 5435 2121; www.fountainview.com.au

THE HOTEL SHAMROCK $$$

Map ref. p. 70

This gracious wrought-iron lace-trimmed hotel has been a part of Bendigo's history and cultural scene since 1854. Although the original hotel was burnt down, the owners replaced the building in 1897 and carried on without missing a beat. Today it offers accommodation in 28 well-appointed, modernised but atmospheric rooms with high ceilings – some with marble floors, tea- and coffee-making facilities and deluxe ensuite bathrooms. Two large spa suites have luxurious bathrooms and views over Pall Mall. The Saloon Bar downstairs is open for breakfast, lunch and dinner, serving casual meals, while the Victorian Wine Room on the first floor offers a more elegant dinner venue. Guests have access to undercover secure parking.

Cnr Pall Mall and Williamson St; (03) 5443 0333; www.shamrockbendigo.com.au

BYRONSVALE VINEYARD B&B $$$

Offering friendly country accommodation, this lovely 140-year-old stone horse stable on a vineyard has been lovingly restored and converted into three one- and two-bedroom apartments. The spacious loft apartment features a welcoming living room, full kitchen and two loft bedrooms to accommodate four people; the two smaller one-bedroom apartments with cooking facilities are downstairs with private entrances. A minimum two-night stay at weekends is preferred.

51 Andrews Rd, Maiden Gully; (03) 5447 2790; www.byronsvale.net.au

Bright

CENTENARY PEAKS $$$$

Map ref. p. 76

The eight luxury two-bedroom town houses have polished wood floors, stone walls, plasma TVs and original artwork. Quality is a specialty here; for example, the full kitchens come with Miele appliances. The apartments are opposite the highly acclaimed Simone's restaurant and adjacent to Bright Brewery, with other restaurants, cafes, shops and the Ovens River nearby. Packages are available and can include facials and massages. Clearly, the owners have hit on an appealing formula and there are grand expansion plans for this family-friendly place, with 32 more town houses being built over the next few years.

1 Delaney Ave; (03) 5750 1433; www.cpbright.com.au

THE ODD FROG $$$

Map ref. p. 76

The heart of Bright might be just a six-minute walk away but The Odd Frog does a fine line in seclusion. This Land for Wildlife property includes several hectares of bushland, and the five arresting north-facing studios are designed to draw heat from the winter sun and yet limit the effects of the harshest summer sun. All the green here doesn't just come from the bush. The contemporary studios have grey-water recycling systems and solar hot water. The property is also connected to walking and bikeriding trails. Breakfast baskets can be arranged.

3 McFadyens La; 0418 362 791; www.theoddfrog.com

THE BUCKLAND STUDIO RETREAT $$$$

Award-winning Buckland Studio Retreat near Bright is nestled in the Buckland Valley, with sweeping views of surrounding vineyards, chestnut groves and Mount Buffalo beyond. This pristine location is the inspiration for the retreat's five stunning architect-designed eco-friendly luxury studios. The studios are for couples and are spaced well apart on 16 hectares of bushland, ensuring total privacy. The contemporary styling offers open living area, private deck, Queensland walnut timber beds and great bathrooms with double showers and dramatic full-length glass walls overlooking the bush. At the Buckland Cafe guests can linger over breakfast on the deck while soaking up the views, tranquillity and delectable fare.

116 McCormacks La, Buckland; 0419 133 318; www.thebuckland.com.au

THE KILNS $$$$

Located in a paddock, about 10 minutes by car from Bright, this three-bedroom house is a modern architectural interpretation of the typical Australian homestead. It has been reconstructed from two 1950s corrugated-iron tobacco kilns that were dismantled and transformed into luxury accommodation with a spacious living area, high ceilings and a real cook's kitchen – all with magnificent views. There's a slow-combustion stove, heated floors and a drying cabinet for damp ski gear, plus a barbecue for summer dining, cowhide rugs and lovely contemporary Italian furniture. Go with friends.

Cavedons La, Porepunkah; 0408 553 332; www.kilnhouse.com.au

VILLA GUSTO $$$$

This purpose-built Tuscan-style retreat is located at the foot of Mount Buffalo, with ringside views over the beautiful Buckland Valley. It offers a range of accommodation: one grande and three deluxe suites luxuriously furnished with Italian tapestries, Venetian porcelain, elegant antiques and artworks from Milan; three external cabina suites ideal for three couples travelling together; and two standard villa rooms with less opulent fittings. All have Bulgari amenities. The small in-house Italian restaurant has been voted one of regional Victoria's best, and serves a set five-course dinner alongside High Country and Italian wines.

630 Buckland Valley Rd, Buckland; (03) 5756 2000; www.villagusto.com.au

Buchan

PARKS VICTORIA WILDERNESS RETREAT BUCHAN CAVES $$

Situated near the town of Buchan, this comfortable bush camp offers a unique camping experience in five spacious elevated permanent tents. Each tent is insect-proof with a large sundeck and can accommodate a family of four in one queen-size bed and two pull-out single beds. Bed linen and bath towels are provided. There is an amenities block with shower facilities and a communal kitchen with gas cook-top, microwave, fridge and coffee- and tea-making facilities for individual catering. All cutlery, crockery and utensils are provided, and continental breakfast can be pre-arranged by request. Run by Parks Victoria, the camp is set in typical East Gippsland bushland, about a kilometre from the magnificent

WHERE TO STAY

limestone Buchan Caves. Minimum two-night booking.

Buchan Caves Reserve; 13 1963; www.parkweb.vic.gov.au

Camperdown

PURRUMBETE HOMESTEAD $$$$$

For an insight into the Western District's wealth in the 1800s, head to Purrumbete Homestead, built in 1842 for the pioneering Manifold family (they lent their name to Camperdown's main street). Art Nouveau interiors radiate grace and charm, while outside the sweeping gardens are perfect for picnics and a stroll around the lake. There are three sumptuous guest rooms, all individually appointed for an indulgent retreat. It is worth pre-arranging to dine in the Grand Dining Room, with the opportunity to select wines from the extensive cellar.

3551 Princes Hwy; (03) 5594 7374

TIMBOON HOUSE & STABLES B&B $$$

This historic bluestone property circa 1855 is a former coaching inn. There are three rooms within the house available to guests – all with private bathrooms and antique furnishings. Breakfast is served in a dining room redolent of squatters and other colonial times. The heritage-listed 1840s stables were converted with assistance from Heritage Victoria into a two-bedroom self-contained studio. Soak up this wonderful room while relaxing in the claw-foot bath. The very English, beautifully maintained gardens include 480 rose bushes.

320 Old Geelong Rd; (03) 5593 1003

Cann River

POINT HICKS LIGHTHOUSE $$$$

Operating since 1890, Point Hicks Lighthouse marks Captain James Cook's first Australian landfall in the *Endeavour* and is named after his first lieutenant, Zachary Hicks. Prominent on a granite headland and surrounded by national park, it is the tallest lighthouse on mainland Australia and is about 50 minutes by car off Princes Highway from Cann River in East Gippsland. The two historic keepers' cottages each sleep six; a bungalow sleeps two. Cottages are well equipped, and bedding and towels can be hired.

Point Hicks Rd; (03) 5158 4268; www.pointhicks.com.au

Castlemaine

THE EMPYRE $$$$

One of the original hotels from the fabulous gold-rush era of the mid-1800s, this two-storeyed hotel offers the most elegant accommodation in the area. There are four luxury suites upstairs in the main hotel building and two adjoining suites in the rear garden. Owner John Ganci has sourced exquisite French furniture, most of it through local antique dealers, to give the building a strong French flavour. Fine bed linen, beautiful soft furnishings and exquisite chandeliers reinforce the feel. Contemporary marble bathrooms are well fitted out with feature walls of Italian glass mosaic tiles. There is an in-house cafe, bar and restaurant. Ask about their local tours.

68 Mostyn St; (03) 5472 5166; www.empyre.com.au

BREAKFAST INCLUDED   CREDIT CARDS ACCEPTED   FAMILY FRIENDLY

THE HERMITAGE B&B $$

Guests at this B&B stay in the second-floor addition of an 1860s sandstone cottage, with a private entrance to the spacious upstairs rooms. If two couples are staying, the ensuite to the rooms is shared. Privacy and the sounds of silence are features as much as the kangaroos, which are regularly found poking about outside the cottage. Other assets are the extensive local walking and cycling tracks. The Hermitage is in a rural setting, a mix of farmland and bush, just 4 kilometres north of Castlemaine.

181 Blakeley Rd; (03) 5472 2008; www.mtalexander.net/Hermitage.htm

TUCKPOINT $$

This historic home takes its name from the distinctive facade, the name an ode to the black lines between the handmade bricks and the blocks of local stone that welcome visitors to this 1907 home, a tasteful blend of heritage and modern style. The original cottage was just three rooms, including the two bedrooms. The modern extension, which includes the kitchen, living room and bathroom, was built to environmental principles. And though the concrete slab floor is a heat bank, you might still be moved to light the wood stove in the kitchen. Local stone walls are a feature of the landscaping in the rear garden. The centre of town and the botanical gardens are only a five-minute walk away.

60 Kennedy St; 0439 035 382; www.tuckpointcottage.com

SAGE COTTAGE $$

This two-bedroom miners cottage is cute enough to want to cuddle it. Brass double beds and the potbelly (gas) heater seem true

to the miner theme, but the electric blankets, microwave and in-house movies are modern comforts that will be no less appreciated. As will the view from the kitchen doors that open right onto the verandah. Castlemaine Diggings National Heritage Park is right by the cottage, and the Dry Diggings Track and ruins of the goldfields are close by too. In spring the wildflowers and old-world garden can be a riot of colour. Castlemaine is just a 10-minute drive away.

25 Castlemaine St, Fryerstown; (03) 5473 4322; www.mtalexander.net/sage.htm

SHACK 14 @ PROSPECT HOUSE $$$

This eco-friendly, low-impact bush cabin outside of Castlemaine has been designed by environmentally attuned architect Ken Latona of Tasmania's Bay of Fires fame. Its clever design incorporates two bedrooms to sleep four, with open-plan living and dining areas so guests can commune with nature. It also features a Bang & Olufsen sound system, stylish furniture and contemporary Australian and Asian artworks. And blissfully, there is no TV, phone or internet and little mobile coverage. Two-night minimum weekend stay.

Hooper Rd, Chewton; (03) 5472 1677; www.shack14.com.au

Chiltern

THE MULBERRY TREE $$$

Housed in an 1879 former Bank of Australasia building, ensuite accommodation is offered in the charming Henry Handel Richardson Suite – honouring the local authoress – and also in the Bank Residence with queen-size bed, separate lounge with open fire,

---

FITNESS CENTRE   ROOM SERVICE   SWIMMING POOL

kitchenette and bathroom. Like much in historic Chiltern, the building is on the National Trust Historic Buildings Register. The building also accommodates tearooms that combined with an established cottage garden can provide delicious morning and afternoon teas, and meals.

28 Conness St; (03) 5726 1277; www.mulberrytreechiltern.com.au

KOENDIDDA COUNTRY HOUSE $$$$

Built in 1855 beside the Indigo Creek at Barnawartha – from the proceeds of a gold-rush fortune – this stately home stands graciously in wonderful landscaped gardens. An elegant family-run B&B at the end of a tree-lined drive, the impressive, old red brick two-storey house has five spacious and individually appointed guest rooms. The guest lounge and dining areas are beautifully furnished with antiques, the perfect setting for formal dinners, which are highly recommended and must be pre-booked. Full country breakfasts make the most of the superior local produce and picnic hampers are available. A very secluded retreat in the heart of rural Victoria.

79 Pooleys Rd, Barnawartha; (02) 6026 7340; www.koendidda.com.au

Cobram

TOKEMATA RETREAT $$$

You do not have to be a golfer to stay at any of the four cottages that comprise this golfers' retreat on the edge of a 250-metre private golf range, complete with bunkers and practice putting green. Two of the cottages have one bedroom; the others two and three respectively. Decor is English country and overlooks natural

bushland and a state forest. There is a solar-heated pool for cooling off in summer and a cubbyhouse and sandpit for children.

100 Cemetery Rd, Cobram East; (03) 5873 5332; www.tokemata.com.au

Colac

ELLIMINOOK HERITAGE B&B $$$

This charming B&B in an 1865 National Trust–classified homestead is set in attractively landscaped gardens. Originally built out of handmade bricks for a local pioneer farmer, it shelters at the end of a sweeping driveway, with a giant bunya pine on the front lawn. The homestead has been lovingly restored, with hosts Jill and Peter Falkiner attending to every detail. There are three B&B ensuite rooms and two queen-size bedrooms in a new self-contained wing. All guest rooms are furnished with period pieces, while being designed for comfort. Explore the manicured gardens and enjoy an evening drink in the courtyard with its riot of iceberg roses. There is also a grass tennis court and a croquet lawn with authentic pavilion. Hearty breakfasts can be enjoyed on the verandah.

585 Warncoort Rd, Birregurra; (03) 5236 2080; www.elliminook.com.au

Cowes

ALL SEASONS ECO RESORT PHILLIP ISLAND $$$

Map ref. p. 82

This holiday resort offers accommodation in 211 villas scattered over hectares of gentle countryside overlooking Phillip Island's beautiful rural farmland. They range from well-appointed spa studios to two- and three-bedroom villas. Decor is pleasantly modern and some villas are air-conditioned. The resort has an on-site kiosk for convenience shopping, but the island's main shopping precinct is only a two-minute drive away by car. The pool is solar-heated for year-round use, barbecue facilities are provided and guests have access to broadband internet.

2128 Phillip Island Rd; (03) 5952 8000; www.theislandecoresort.com.au

HOLMWOOD GUESTHOUSE $$$

Map ref. p. 82

What started life as a modest cottage in 1934 is now a lovely guesthouse offering B&B accommodation in three guest rooms. Guests have access to a welcoming lounge with books, magazines and the daily papers, made even more comfortable in winter with an open fire. Adjoining is the dining room where co-owner Eric van Grondelle prepares dinner by arrangement using local seasonal produce, herbs and vegetables from his garden and free-range island farm eggs. There are also two themed cottages – one with oriental decor, the other with a fresh coastal theme. With Cowes' main beach a mere 300-metre walk away, it is perfectly positioned away from the madding crowd.

37 Chapel St; (03) 5952 3082; www.holmwoodguesthouse.com.au

QUEST PHILLIP ISLAND $$$

Map ref. p. 82

This is one of the most convenient and central accommodation options in the heart of the township of Cowes, one block from the local shopping precinct and restaurants. It offers 31 one-, two- and three-bedroom serviced apartments, ideal for families and couples. All apartments include separate lounge and dining areas along with kitchen and laundry facilities and complimentary car parking. There is a gas-fire spa near the solar-heated pool and also a barbecue. Continental breakfast packs are available. Check for off-peak specials.

Cnr Bass Ave and Chapel St; (03) 5952 2644; www.questphillipisland.com.au

SILVERWATER RESORT $$$

This fully integrated resort is a welcome addition to the island's family-friendly accommodation options. Set on hectares of high undulating land above San Remo, it enjoys spectacular views over the bay and along the Bass Coast. Architect-designed, it offers 150 self-contained apartments and 20 hotel-style rooms with outstanding resort facilities. There are one-, two- and three-bedroom apartments – all with balconies and water views. Facilities include heated indoor and outdoor pools, three tennis courts, a sand volleyball court, multi-use basketball and volleyball court, children's playground and playroom with table tennis, pool and air hockey. The on-site Watermark restaurant is open daily for breakfast, lunch and dinner, serving modern Australian fare, while a bar lounge is open all day from coffee to cocktails.

17 Potters Hill Rd, San Remo; (03) 5671 9300 or 1800 033 403; www.silverwaterresort.com.au

Creswick

NOVOTEL FOREST RESORT CRESWICK $$$

This new luxury resort is part of a $250 million forest resort development, which also includes a boutique day spa, restaurants, residential community and fishing village. All 144 rooms and suites have balconies and terrific views. Most are one-bedroom although 46 executive rooms boast twin king-size beds, plus there are eight two-bedroom suites with twin ensuites. Other facilities include tennis court, gym, year-round swimming pool, petanque, horseriding and an 18-hole golf course designed by Robert Allenby and Tony Cashmore. The property is drought-proof – with Australia's only privately owned water treatment plant.

1500 Midland Hwy; (03) 5345 9600; www.novotel.forestresort.com.au

ROSSMORE COTTAGE $$$

This charming 1860s miners cottage dates from the region's bonanza gold-rush days and, while now restored to offer comfortable accommodation for up to four guests in two bedrooms, still retains its historic ambience. A modern bathroom has spa bath and heated towel rails while the kitchen is well equipped for self-catering. The larder is stocked with essentials and the makings for a continental breakfast; a cooked breakfast is an optional extra. It is within easy walking distance to town, and pets are welcome.

12 Bald Hills Rd; (03) 5345 2759; www.rossmorecottage.com.au

Daylesford

LAKE DAYLESFORD LODGE $$$$$
Map ref. p. 88

This architect-designed accommodation complex on the shores of pretty Lake Daylesford comprises seven luxurious two- and three-bedroom villas with uninterrupted views over the lake and surrounding bushland setting. Downstairs, villas feature an open-

plan living space with welcoming gas log fire and well-equipped kitchen for self-catering. Upstairs, bedrooms have private ensuite facilities – some with a spa bath. Basic provisions for a continental breakfast are supplied and it is within easy walking distance of one of Australia's finest country restaurants – Lake House.

32 King St; (03) 5348 4422; www.lakedaylesford.com.au

LAKE HOUSE $$$$$

Map ref. p. 88

This multi-award-winning country house with outstanding restaurant lures guests locally and internationally with its unique style of hospitality. Located on several hectares of waterfront gardens overlooking Lake Daylesford, Lake House comprises 12 waterfront suites and 12 waterfront rooms, while the original comfortable main lodge contains nine recently refurbished guest rooms near a spacious guest lounge. There is a luxurious Salus Spa on site, and dinner, bed and breakfast packages are available.

King St; (03) 5348 3329; www.lakehouse.com.au

LATTE COTTAGE $$

Map ref. p. 88

Coffee lovers will love contemporary Latte Cottage, which offers stylish self-contained accommodation in the very heart of Daylesford. Accommodation is in two queen-size bedrooms finished in warm coffee-coloured bed linens; one boasts a romantic warming open fireplace – perfect in chilly winters. Located in a tranquil, leafy street, the cottage is a short stroll from Lake Daylesford and just minutes from the town's bustling Vincent Street.

33 Fulcher St; 0416 264 165; www.lattecottage.com.au

BREAKFAST INCLUDED   CREDIT CARDS ACCEPTED   FAMILY FRIENDLY

PEPPERS SPRINGS RETREAT & SPA

$$$$

Map ref. p. 88

This luxury complex, part of the renowned Peppers group, encompasses a 1930s 13-room hotel (nine are spa rooms), the separate Villa Palma, seven Mineral Spa Villas and the acclaimed Deco restaurant. Villa Palma is a Tuscan-style villa built by an Italian vigneron in 1864, and the interior, offering three suites, is simply furnished with authentic pieces. The rooms offer a stunning slice of Tuscan living set in lovingly tended gardens. The seven self-contained and luxurious Mineral Spa Villas are tucked away in the grounds – contemporary, modern and architect designed. Completely private, they each feature an open fireplace and double spa. The restaurant is open daily for breakfast and dinner.

124 Main Rd, Hepburn Springs; (03) 5348 2202; www.peppers.com.au/springs

Drysdale

THE OL' DUKE HOTEL

$$$

The Ol' Duke is a charming 1855-built property that was Portarlington's original hotel, and enjoys a terrific location on the main road with views over Portarlington pier and Port Phillip Bay. Today it is city chic with an 'eat drink sleep' concept that discerning patrons appreciate. There are six bedrooms upstairs with ensuite facilities, minibars and TV. Tea- and coffee-making facilities are available in a common area upstairs. Two self-catering stable apartments at the rear are ideal for families. One sleeps up to four – the other up to six in queen-size bed, bunk beds and singles.

40 Newcomb St, Portarlington; (03) 5259 1250; www.theolduke.com.au

Dunkeld

AQUILA ECO LODGES

$$$$

The four-star self-contained accommodation at Aquila Eco Lodges is testament that eco-living does not mean primitive bark huts. Four sleek, architecturally designed and award-winning eco lodges stand in 40 hectares of Australian bushland, gleaming, tranquil and environmentally friendly. Featuring solar power, massive glass windows, red-gum floors, wood-burning fires and spectacular contemporary furnishings, there is a choice of two types of lodge. The two-level Loft House sleeps six and is ideal for families. The three-level Tree House is a more intimate interior. Aquila is passionate about eco philosophy and has a resource library plus a range of interpretive trails and guided walks for you to choose from. The property is encircled on three sides by the Grampians National Park.

Manns Rd; (03) 5577 2582; www.ecolodges.com.au

GRIFFINS HILL

$$$$

Set in a rambling garden just 2 kilometres from Dunkeld, the rooms – twin share or king deluxe suites – at this stylish yoga retreat open onto a viewing deck that has been positioned so guests can escape for hours observing stunning Mount Sturgeon. Beyond the views and attention to detail – like fine bed linen – some guests might be moved to visit purely for the breakfasts, which can include homemade sourdough bread and omelettes. Guests do not have to take a yoga class to stay here. There are plenty of accommodation packages, including one with a flying option from

WHERE TO STAY

FITNESS CENTRE   ROOM SERVICE   SWIMMING POOL

Melbourne's Essendon airport to Hamilton with local transfers.

Victoria Valley Rd; (03) 5577 2499; www.griffinshill.com.au

ROYAL MAIL HOTEL $$

The Royal Mail Hotel is set against the spectacular backdrop of Mount Sturgeon in the quiet town of Dunkeld. This is regional accommodation at its best, with a range of guest rooms, studio apartments and Mulberry House that sleeps 11 – just perfect for families. There are also eight self-contained rustic bluestone cottages managed by the hotel on blissful pastureland some 3 kilometres away – note that the iron 'water tank' attached to each cottage is the ensuite bathroom. The hotel boasts an award-winning restaurant – with an outstanding wine list – as well as a casual bistro and friendly front bar. Surrounded by mountain views and towering red gums, this is a fantastic getaway for couples, families and friends exploring this beautiful region.

Glenelg Hwy; (03) 5577 2241; www.royalmail.com.au

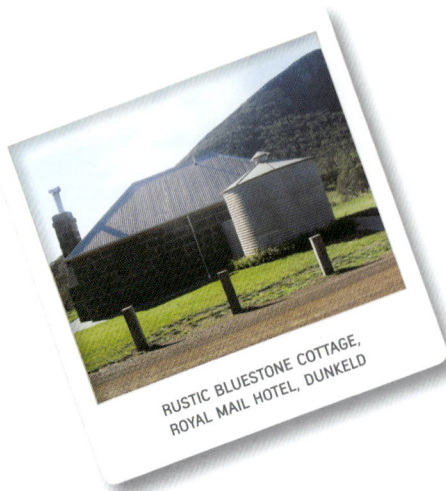

RUSTIC BLUESTONE COTTAGE, ROYAL MAIL HOTEL, DUNKELD

SOUTHERN GRAMPIANS COTTAGES $$

Enjoying gorgeous views of the Grampians, this little cluster of self-contained cottages is on land just a kilometre from Dunkeld or an easy eight-minute stroll – four minutes if you run. Nine log cabins offer four different levels of accommodation with one or two bedrooms that can sleep up to five. Features include open fires as well as wood combustion burners for winter warmth. Four have double spa baths; all have private barbecue facilities. Sporting gear such as golf clubs is available for hire. Breakfast options are available.

33–35 Victoria Valley Rd; (03) 5577 2457; www.grampianscottages.com.au

Echuca

PS EMMYLOU $$$

The *Emmylou* is one of a fleet of three historic paddlesteamers that ply the waters of the great Murray River. Built last century for the purpose of accommodation and dining, she is powered by a completely restored 1906 steam engine. She can accommodate up to 49 passengers for day cruises on the river and 18 guests in eight two-berth cabins and one double cabin. She does overnight cruises from September to June as well as two- and three-night cruises that include all meals prepared by local Coriander catering, including three-course à la carte dinner.

57 Murray Espl; (03) 5482 5244; www.emmylou.com.au

BREAKFAST INCLUDED   CREDIT CARDS ACCEPTED   FAMILY FRIENDLY

QUEST ECHUCA $$$

The first dedicated complex of serviced apartments in town, this new property offers a range of 60 studio, one-, two- and three-bedroom apartments. All are spacious, air-conditioned and fully furnished with smart neutral decor, many with private balconies. Four are wheelchair accessible. Babysitting can be arranged, dry cleaning can be organised and continental breakfast packs are available. Conveniently, a pantry service is offered to stock your larder for self-catering and there are charge-back options at several nearby restaurants. Other facilities include on-site parking, an outdoor heated pool, barbecue facilities and access to high-speed broadband internet. The property is also 'Green Star' listed as being environmentally friendly.

25–29 Heygarth St; (03) 5481 3900; www.questechuca.com.au

BRIGHT ON THE MURRAY $$

This gracious 110-year-old homestead is beautifully sited right on the banks of the Murray River at Moama, about 9 kilometres from Echuca. It offers comfortable B&B accommodation in five in-house rooms, each named after paddlesteamers that ply the river: Emmylou, Pevensey, Pride of the Murray, Perricoota and Adelaide. All have queen-size beds and some have open fires, while both the Emmylou and Pride of the Murray rooms enjoy great river views. You can land your helicopter on the front lawn, and dinners are available on request.

93 Goldsborough Rd, Moama; (03) 5483 6264; www.brightonthemurray.com.au

PERRICOOTA VINES RETREAT $$$

This 4-hectare complex comprises 22 one-, two- and three-bedroom self-contained spa villas built using superb Australian timbers. The prized villas are from numbers 8 to 23, as their balconies edge a private lake. All have reverse-cycle air-conditioning, full kitchens and access to broadband internet. Other facilities include a tennis court, a large solar-heated pool, solar-heated children's wading pool and playground, two barbecues, recreation room with open fire, table tennis and pool tables, and grassed area for safe and general play. There is also a bocce court and a par-three chipping green for golf practice. A minimum two-night stay is preferred and packages are available.

400 Perricoota Rd, Moama; (03) 5482 6655, 1800 826 655; www.perricootavines.com

Eildon

ROBYNS NEST B&B $$

This purpose-built building accommodates two couples in a private retreat upstairs, both with private entries and balconies with views over Eildon Valley, the pondage and Mount Torbreck and the Black Range in the distance. Both have reverse-cycle air-conditioning for year-round comfort; one has a spa bath. Situated on the edge of Eildon township, it is 400 metres from the pondage and less than a kilometre from the famous lake. Guests linger long over the full cooked breakfast with everything from fresh fruits to omelettes and eggs Benedict. The thoughtful owners can cater for special dietary requirements

WHERE TO STAY

such as vegetarian, diabetic, coeliac and gluten-intolerant.

13 High St; (03) 5779 1064; www.robyns-nest.com.au

Emerald

FERNGLADE ON MENZIES $$$

This Federation-style building set in extensive gardens and tall forest has direct access to the Emerald–Kallista walking track. It was purpose built to accommodate up to 14 people in four suites. There are two self-contained suites with limited self-catering: one has two bedrooms and is ideal for families. The two B&B suites have twin corner spas with separate shower and gas log fires. Full cooked breakfasts are served in the rooms at private dining tables – and since the owner/cook is Scottish, porridge is enormously popular. Lunch and dinner can also be arranged as well as picnic hampers.

11 Caroline Cres; (03) 5968 2228; www.ferngladeonmenzies.com.au

FERNHEM COTTAGES $$$

The names of these three self-contained cottages tell you a little about the romantic ambience and privacy the owners have tried to create: Possums' Cottage, Love in the Mist and Teddy Bears Cottage. All very private, they are nestled among rambling country gardens with lovely bushwalks. Each contains a large spa bath, open log fires, ducted heating, air-conditioning, either canopy or four-poster beds and well-equipped kitchens for self-catering. Provisions for a full cooked breakfast are supplied, plus a few other little gourmet treats.

109 Emerald–Monbulk Rd; (03) 5968 5462; www.fernhemcottages.com.au

Euroa

FORLONGE B&B $$$$

Traditional B&B and self-catering accommodation are offered in a private wing of this comfortable country home set in a large rambling garden. The King Garden Suite has a large ensuite and spa, with the bedroom opening onto a furnished private terrace. The Conservatory Suite has two bedrooms – one queen size, the other with two king-size singles – and is ideal for families or two couples travelling together. It has an ensuite bathroom with comfortable sitting room and lovely breakfast room. Both have separate entrances through the garden. Home-cooked breakfasts are served either in-room, on the terrace or in the breakfast room; other meals are available by arrangement. Guests have access to a tennis court, barbecue facilities and a gazebo kitchen for self-catering.

76 Anderson St; (03) 5795 2460

Flinders

FLINDERS B&B $$

Charming accommodation is offered in this self-contained period-style fisherman's cottage that nestles in a lovely garden on the western outskirts of the village of Flinders. Take in the rural views from the double bedroom with ensuite and comfortable sitting room, and cook up a storm in the full timber kitchen. Pack your tennis gear for a hit on the court and be ready to take care of the resident cat and dog. The cottage is an easy 10-minute walk to the golf course and just five minutes from the village shops and casual cafes.

94 Cook St; (03) 5989 0301

BREAKFAST INCLUDED   CREDIT CARDS ACCEPTED   FAMILY FRIENDLY

CAPE SCHANCK LIGHT STATION $$$

Accommodation here is in four old lighthouse buildings, including the original keeper's cottage. Nestled in a fully enclosed compound, the 1939 red cottage sleeps eight, the 1887 museum cottage at the rear sleeps four, while the 1859 limestone keeper's cottage has three large bedrooms to accommodate up to eight. An attached inspector's room sleeps just one couple. All are self-contained. The limestone cottage, for example, comprises a comfortable lounge room with cosy gas heater and high ceilings, a more formal dining room and well-equipped separate kitchen. Breakfast is available at an extra charge.

420 Cape Schanck Rd, Cape Schanck; (03) 5968 6411; www.austpacinns.com.au

LINDENDERRY $$$$$

This five-star luxury country house sits on prime hilltop real estate amid 12 hectares of gardens and estate-owned vineyards. It serves both the leisure and corporate market with its 40 beautifully furnished, spacious rooms, most opening out onto a wide upstairs verandah or the downstairs garden. The Linden Tree restaurant is open daily for breakfast and at weekends for lunch and dinner, serving modern European cuisine featuring regional produce and local seafood. Guests have access to an indoor pool with sauna and spa facilities, two tennis courts, volleyball court and mountain bikes. There is an Endota day spa on the premises and in-room massages can be arranged.

142 Arthurs Seat Rd, Red Hill; (03) 5989 2933; www.lindenderry.com.au

SHOREHAM BEACH HOUSE $$

Located near the quiet coastal village of Shoreham, this Australian beach house overlooks a farm valley and vineyards towards Westernport Bay. With a barbecue on an outside sundeck, private courtyard, stone open fireplace and well-equipped kitchen, the multi-level house is ideal in any season. It sleeps up to 10 guests in five bedrooms, and has two bathrooms. Enquire about their other property Le Pavillon nearby.

20 Myers Dr, Shoreham; (03) 5989 8433; www.lepav.com.au

Foster

BASIA MILLE LUXURY APARTMENTS $$$$

Translating as 'one thousand passionate kisses', Basia Mille is the home of Geraldine and Tony Conabere, and is situated along the South Gippsland wine trail. Located on undulating farmland overlooking Wilsons Promontory and the Bass Strait, the 5-hectare property encompasses a vineyard, olive grove, nine-hole golf course and three luxurious apartments called Waratah, Oliv and Luscious. This Tuscan-inspired accommodation has under-floor heating in the marble bathrooms, digital flat-screen TVs and complimentary bottles of estate-pressed olive oil for guests' use. A barbecue is available for self-catering in the under-house cellar, and guests are invited to choose wines from the cellar on an honour system. There is a minimum two-nights stay.

1 Taylor Court, Fish Creek; (03) 5687 1453 or 0414 295 048; basiamille.com.au

FITNESS CENTRE   ROOM SERVICE   SWIMMING POOL

Geelong

CHIFLEY ON THE ESPLANADE $$$

Map ref. p. 98

This hotel right on Corio Bay has been refurbished in recent years to offer 67 hotel rooms and apartments. All have air-conditioning and heating, tea- and coffee-making facilities, minibar, iron and ironing board and hair dryer. There is a licensed in-house restaurant that serves breakfast and dinner for guests. Corio Sands Bar is where guests can relax for pre- or post-dinner drinks.

13 The Esplanade; (03) 5244 7700; www.chifleyhotels.com.au

FOUR POINTS BY SHERATON GEELONG $$$

Map ref. p. 98

This is considered the plushest hotel along the vibrant Geelong waterfront, with all 109 rooms, studios and one luxurious suite enjoying uninterrupted views of Corio Bay. Staff here like to think it is the little things that count, with complimentary internet access and bottled water provided in all rooms. For a special occasion, perhaps check into the stylish Point Henry Suite on the top floor, with corner spa bath, king-size bed, two balconies overlooking the bay, Bose surround-sound, two LCD TVs, separate lounge and dining rooms, and the best views to wake up to in the morning.

10–14 Eastern Beach Rd; (03) 5223 1377; www.fourpoints.com

HAYMARKET BOUTIQUE HOTEL $$$$

Map ref. p. 98

This multi-award-winning boutique hotel is centrally located in the heart of Geelong's CBD. Built in 1855 as The Haymarket Hotel,

the historic building has undergone extensive renovations in recent years to re-open for personalised accommodation in 2003. Today its six guest suites are individually designed and furnished with beautiful antique furniture. Each is air-conditioned and has tea- and coffee-making facilities, gourmet minibar, LCD TV, complimentary wireless internet access and interesting international magazines to read.

244 Moorabool St; (03) 5221 1174; www.haymarkethotel.com.au

MERCURE HOTEL GEELONG $$$

Map ref. p. 98

This hotel has 137 rooms in several categories including standard, family, bay view and privilege, as well as apartments and luxury suites – all in the heart of the 'city by the bay'. Privilege rooms offer extras such as bathrobe and slippers, complimentary internet, chocolates, mineral water, newspapers and a selection of magazines. For longer stays, self-contained apartments have king-size bed and well-equipped kitchenette with microwave and full-size fridge. Luxury suites are on the top floor and are fitted with double spa baths with gorgeous bay views.

Cnr Gheringhap and Myers Sts; (03) 5223 6200; www.mercuregeelong.com.au

WERRIBEE OPEN RANGE ZOO SLUMBER SAFARI $$$$

Running between September and May, an overnight stay at Werribee Zoo is the closest thing to an African safari without the flying miles. Guests are treated to four up-close animal encounters, including a tour through the open savannah where giraffes, rhinoceros and zebras can be found, and a night-time adventure. The other up-close encounters may be handfeeding giraffes or watching the lionkeepers train their 'pupils'. The accommodation area is cleverly situated on a hill over the savannah, to really make you feel as if you are part of the environment. The eight tents include a queen-size bed with a mosquito net, and some with two single beds for families. Blankets and hot water bottles are available during the cooler months. A barbecue dinner and cooked breakfast are served in the communal mess tent, and guests are invited to enjoy marshmallows around the campfire, with a free lesson in African drumming.

K Rd, Werribee; 1300 9667 842; www.zoo.org.au/Werribee/Slumber_Safari

Halls Gap

BOROKA DOWNS $$$$$

Boroka Downs, a self-catering luxury retreat for couples that spares no expense, is located in the Grampian ranges. The five large, self-contained apartments are open plan with soaring ceilings, windows offering spectacular mountain views, wood fires and double spas. Features include king-size beds, TV, DVD, iPod dock and wireless broadband internet. Set on a 120-hectare property that is home to kangaroos, emus and a range of native birds, Boroka Downs promises tranquillity and seclusion.

Birdswing Rd; (03) 5356 6243; www.borokadowns.com.au

DULC CABINS $$$$
Map ref. p. 104

Tucked away in the seclusion of Grampians National Park, these three environmentally friendly and modern cabins have an enviable bush backdrop. Each cabin is an architectural masterpiece of rough-sawn timber with an interior that gleams with contemporary

luxury; all have spa baths, with one cabin boasting a spa resting beneath a starlit roof. The Treehouse features an attic bedroom in the treetops and all showers have glass-top ceilings. This is the best of modern living and opulent comfort, with the proximity of the Australian bush as a bonus.

9 Thryptomene Crt; (03) 5356 4711; www.dulc.com.au

LAKUNA RETREAT $$$$
Map ref. p. 104

Entry to this architect-designed retreat is via an impressive red-gum front door. Here, accommodation is offered in three beautifully appointed bedrooms that can sleep up to eight guests. Features include warm polished timber floors, soft-carpeted bedrooms, well-equipped kitchen and two bathrooms – the one upstairs with a spa so big it could nearly cope with the whole family. These features aside, its biggest appeal is the wall opening that reveals the full outdoors – a 180-degree panoramic view of the Serra Ranges. About five minutes from Halls Gap, it is tucked away in a quiet spot that invites the outdoors in. There are outdoor barbecue facilities for casual summer dining.

81 High Rd; (03) 5221 1606; www.ellimata.com.au

KANGAROOS IN THE $$$
TOP PADDOCK

This adults-only retreat is named after a mob of friendly visiting kangaroos and nestles on 9 hectares of natural bushland with magnificent views of Mount Difficult and the Wartook Valley. Built of rammed earth, accommodation is in two ensuite queen bedrooms – one of which can be converted into twin beds – with a spacious living area in the middle. There is a well-equipped kitchen

WHERE TO STAY

FITNESS CENTRE   ROOM SERVICE   SWIMMING POOL

for self-catering; a cold or hot breakfast hamper can be provided by arrangement.

Northern Grampians Rd, Wartook; (03) 9497 2020; www.kangaroosinthetoppaddock.com

Hamilton

GARLAND COTTAGE $$

This cosy cottage started life as a spacious garage at the side of the owners' house on the edge of town. Today it has been redesigned to accommodate just one couple with queen-size bedroom, ensuite, kitchen and comfy sofa – ideal for short-term stays. Overlooking Grange Burn River, it is a comfortable 10-minute walk into town and offers off-street parking. It has heating in winter, ceiling fans in summer, and the makings of a continental breakfast provided.

18 Skene St; (03) 5572 1054

SEVEN PALMER STREET $$$

This ultra-chic, architect-designed, self-contained, two-bedroom house is minimalist, offering a contemporary environment that is almost Zen. Each bedroom has its own private courtyard, while the bathroom features an in-ground Japanese-style concrete bath with glass ceiling. Floor-to-ceiling sliding glass panels are in all rooms and the floors are polished concrete. It is equipped with modern fittings, European appliances, gas flame heater and extra cosy beds. Located overlooking the Grange Burn River and oval, it is an easy stroll to the local heritage-listed botanic gardens and a five-minute drive to town.

7 Palmer St; 0408 212 100; www.sevenpalmerstreet.com.au

Healesville

HEALESVILLE HOTEL $$

Built in 1910, the two-storey hotel has been rendered and painted white with green detailing – entry being between two established oak trees and an imposing triple archway. Although the hotel's restaurant has won numerous awards for its outstanding food, the upstairs accommodation is modest but stylish, with high pressed-metal ceilings, queen-size beds, coffee- and tea-making facilities and decor in fun colours. There are no ensuites, but rather three bathrooms down the hallway, so remember to bring your own bathrobe. Dinner, bed and breakfast packages are available.

256 Maroondah Hwy; (03) 5962 4002; www.healesvillehotel.com.au

MT RAEL RETREAT $$$

High on a hill near Healesville, this luxury gourmet escape has unsurpassed views of the entire Yarra Valley. There are six suites featuring contemporary designs, all individually furnished and varying in price according to size and fixtures. Four suites along the balcony have panoramic views, while two in garden settings enjoy treetop scenes. The indulgent Sharman corner suite boasts a luxurious spa and king-size bed with possibly the best views of the valley, and comes with sparkling wine and chocolates. Breakfast is served in the in-house restaurant, 3777, and is worth lingering over. The retreat has a friendly relaxed atmosphere and is well placed for exploring the region's wineries.

140 Healesville–Yarra Glen Rd; (03) 5962 1977; www.mtrael.com.au

---

BREAKFAST INCLUDED   CREDIT CARDS ACCEPTED   FAMILY FRIENDLY

RACV HEALESVILLE COUNTRY CLUB $$$$

You don't have to be a golfer to check into this redeveloped country club in the Yarra Valley, but you do have to be a club member. While its 80 luxurious rooms are all nicely furnished with a large ensuite, flat-screen TV and wireless internet access, guests can also indulge in a game of tennis or a swim in the indoor pool. The in-house restaurant features regional produce, but the best place to relax with a coffee is the lounge area filled with comfortable leather couches and sweeping views of the Healesville surrounds.

Healesville–Yarra Glen Rd; (03) 5962 4899; www.racv.com.au

MODERN LUXURY AT MT RAEL RETREAT, HEALESVILLE

THE SEBEL HERITAGE YARRA VALLEY $$$$

Surrounded by the celebrated natural beauty of the Yarra Valley countryside, the Sebel Heritage is an oasis of elegant luxury and an ideal retreat for relaxation and golfing. In fact, Heritage is home to the only private Jack Nicklaus Signature Golf Course in Australia. Many other leisure activities are available, including a heated indoor swimming pool, two floodlit tennis courts and a day spa. There are 96 spacious guest rooms and six suites offering a choice between golf course or garden views, providing all the comfort and style that will ensure your tranquil break doubles your expectations. The famous Yarra Valley vineyards are within easy reach.

2 Heritage Ave, Chirnside Park; (03) 9760 3333 or 1800 002 105; www.mirvachotels.com/sebel-heritage-yarra-valley

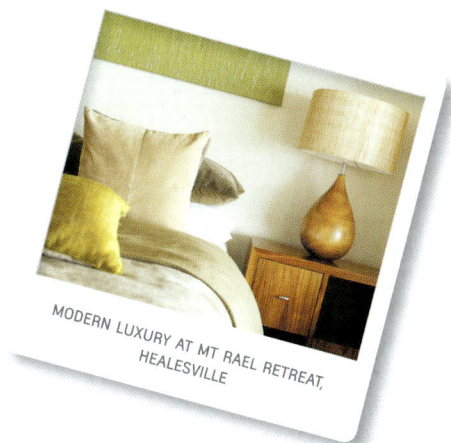

Heathcote

EMEU INN $$$

Accommodation at Emeu Inn comprises six comfortable suites – some with open fires, some with double spas and some with both – and one self-contained cottage that can sleep four and is accessed through a cottage garden. All guest rooms have been lovingly restored and appointed with antique furniture and period furnishings. All have TV, DVD players and wireless internet, and some are dog-friendly. Some of the accommodation and the adjacent Emeu Inn restaurant is housed in one of the town's oldest buildings, dating from 1857.

187 High St; (03) 5433 2668; www.emeuinn.com.au

HUT ON THE HILL $$$$

This country 'hut' is really a well-equipped two-bedroom luxury cottage with private solar-heated outdoor pool and Endless

Swimspa that massages travel-weary bodies as you relax in it – perhaps while watching the sun set or kangaroos grazing in the distance. The open-plan living area has soaring cathedral ceiling, comfy leather lounges, split-system air-conditioning, full kitchen and outdoor barbecue facilities for alfresco dining. Guests can choose between fluffy duvets and woollen blankets, and breakfast on farm-fresh eggs and bacon. Stay two nights and receive a complimentary bottle of local wine.

720 Dairy Flat Rd; (03) 5433 2329; www.hutonthehill.com.au

OLIVE GROVE RETREAT $$$$$

This retreat is a luxurious boutique establishment offering tranquil Mediterranean living from its secluded location in the Australian bush. The guesthouse sleeps two and guests have a chef, housekeeper and masseuse at their disposal. Drenched in European style and sumptuous comfort, the decor is white and light, with bed linen from Italy. There is a beautiful swimming pool overlooking bushland and views from the house justify the lack of TV. Olive Grove Retreat is a true retreat: an escape into luxury.

Travers La; 0403 876 988; www.olivegroveretreat.com

Horsham

ORANGE GROVE B&B $$

Historic Orange Grove homestead offers peaceful country accommodation in its original three-bedroom mud-brick cottage or a more modern two-bedroom unit nearby. The fully restored 1905 cottage is well appointed with open fire, private courtyard and gardens, plus the makings for a full country-style breakfast.

While the unit does not have cooking facilities, provisions are supplied for a continental breakfast. A five-minute drive from town, the 10-hectare property is also home to some 20 friendly alpacas. This is a pet-friendly zone.

123 Keatings Rd; (03) 5382 0583; www.orangegrovebandb.com.au

SYLVANIA PARK MOHAIR FARM $$

Accommodation on this historic 200-hectare property (home of the Mulgowrie Mohair Goat Stud) is in two self-contained houses – Mill End and Riversleigh. Mill End lodge is the original mud-brick homestead, comprising four bedrooms – one queen-size, one double and two twin rooms – lounge, dining room, kitchen and laundry. Two-storey Riversleigh can accommodate up to 10 guests in five bedrooms. Both are comfortably furnished and fitted with all modern conveniences. Take a farm tour, join in farm activities or simply enjoy the rural environment.

Lubeck–Horsham Rd; (03) 5382 2811; www.sylvaniapark.com.au

Inverloch

RACV INVERLOCH RESORT $$$$

The modern architecture of this resort makes excellent use of its natural surrounds, with 26 rooms overlooking the Bass Coast and Anderson's Inlet. All resort rooms are extremely comfortable with contemporary furnishings, a private balcony, microwave and tea- and coffee-making facilities. The resort itself is also worth exploring: the on-site bistro is a bright space with floor-to-ceiling glass windows, serving tasty modern Australian fare; while the kids will be happy on the tennis court or in the large, heated swimming pool. There are also self-contained villas for those after more privacy, and a well-equipped caravan park with 32 sites. RACV members (club members, not roadside assist) receive a discount on accommodation, but even at the non-member rate this is a real value-for-money option in southern Gippsland.

70 Cape Paterson–Inverloch Rd; (03) 5674 0000; www.racv.com.au

Kilmore

BINDLEY HOUSE B&B $$$

Just two blocks from Kilmore's collection of antique shops and smart eateries is historic Bindley House. Built around 1862, it offers accommodation in two suites – the elegant Victorian Suite or the rustic Elm Tree Cottage. Each has a queen-size bed with duvet and electric blanket, and a sofa bed for extra accommodation. Both have double spas, open fires and a larder stocked with provisions for a full country breakfast. A complimentary cheese platter greets guests on arrival, with port and chocolate to help guests relax after dinner.

20–22 Powlett St; (03) 5781 1142

LAUREL HILL COTTAGE $$

The stables of Melrose Farm, one of the region's most historic properties, have been converted to become Laurel Hill Cottage. Surrounded by its own private garden, it has been beautifully refurbished to accommodate couples or small families in two bedrooms – one double and the other with twin beds. The cottage is fitted with a well-equipped kitchen, comfortable lounge and bathroom with double spa bath. Catered meals can be arranged.

12 Melrose Dr; (03) 5782 1630; www.laurelhillcottage.com.au

WOODBURY ESTATE B&B $$$

Located in gardens on a 5-hectare rural property with magnificent mountain views, this 30-year-old English-style home offers two in-house rooms for B&B accommodation. Both have private entrances, private lounges, kitchenettes and pampering indoor mineral spa baths. In winter, join other guests or friends by the open fire in Fergusson's on-site licensed Scottish Bar; in summer, cool off in the adjacent swimming pool. The estate is only a few minutes by car from restaurants, a golf course and the popular Kilmore country racecourse.

110A Butlers Rd; (03) 5782 0307

Korumburra

CYPRESS HILL B&B $$$

This Mediterranean-style guesthouse offers three suites – two with queen-size beds, the other with a king-size that can be converted into two singles. All suites have private entrances with French doors leading to a verandah and outside dining area, and are fitted with ceiling fans, heaters, electric blankets, fridge and tea- and coffee-making facilities. Guests can relax by the log fire in a communal lounge with TV, video and CD player, daily newspapers, books, magazines and games. Complimentary port and chocolates are offered, and barbecue facilities are available.

75 Korumburra–Bena Rd, Whitelaw; (03) 5657 2240; www.cypresshillbnb.com.au

WHERE TO STAY

FITNESS CENTRE   ROOM SERVICE   SWIMMING POOL

Kyneton

ROCKVILLE $$$$

Don't be misled by this bungalow's very plain exterior. Inside, it is a chic, spacious, centrally heated house that sleeps six in two king-size rooms and one queen-size. It has a well-equipped kitchen for those who might want to show off their cooking skills, a double shower, open-plan living area, outdoor barbecue area and all mod cons. Breakfast vouchers are provided to some of the terrific little cafes just a few metres away in trendy Piper Street.

59 Ebden St; (03) 5422 2617

ST AGNES HOMESTEAD $$$

This historic property nestles in a charming woodland garden, with thriving vineyard, tennis court and tranquil pond. There are several very private accommodation options. Guests can choose to stay in one of two in-house gallery rooms, in the beautifully appointed freestanding groom's retreat or in the self-catering French-style Flynn apartment – complete with cosy Aga stove. Commune with nature under the old mulberry tree, relax in the garden or walk into Piper Street for some retail therapy (Burton Avenue is the continuation of Piper Street). Minimum two-night stay.

**30 Burton Ave; (03) 5422 2639;
www.saintagnes.com.au**

THE RECTORY $$$$

This long-established B&B is housed in a lovely 1850s National Trust–listed bluestone rectory. On the corner of busy Piper Street, it is secluded behind a stately pittosporum hedge in gardens designed by renowned landscape designer Paul Bangay. Accommodation is in three rooms: the Drawing Room, the Minister's Room – both queen size – or the Old Library, which is a double room. The gardens are usually part of the Open Garden Scheme and the local Kyneton Daffodil Festival, when the gardens are a sea of yellow. Complimentary local wine is offered on arrival and regional winery tours can be arranged.

**61 Ebden St; (03) 5422 6738;
www.macedonranges.org.au/user/rectory**

TILWINDA B&B AND $$$
WOOLSHED BARN

Enjoy country hospitality in this 120-year-old homestead on a former sheep property on the outskirts of town. Guests can choose between two luxurious B&B in-house bedrooms with ensuites and a full country cooked breakfast, or opt for the more romantic self-contained wool shed that has been converted into self-catering studio-style accommodation. Situated on a couple of hectares, it is just five minutes from Piper Street with its range of terrific eateries and shops.

**1793 Kyneton–Trentham Rd; (03) 5422 2772;
www.tilwinda.com**

Lakes Entrance

GOLDSMITH'S IN THE FOREST $$$

Enjoy the sights and smells of one of the last remaining pockets of warm temperate rainforest in Victoria with a stay at this four-room private retreat. Located on 24 hectares of covenanted natural forest, guests are invited to join owners on guided walks checking out sugar gliders, looking for up to 115 species of birds and plucking available native foods to flavour dinner – perhaps lemon myrtle, native pepper or native mint. This unique destination makes the most of its situation – with a claw-foot bath and sauna in the fernery, and a spa house in the forest where guests can commune with nature and listen to forest sounds. A full cooked breakfast and afternoon tea are included; dinner packages are available.

191 Harrisons Track; (03) 5155 2518;
www.goldsmithsintheforest.com.au

THE LAKES APARTMENTS $$$

Map ref. p. 112

This architect-designed accommodation complex comprises 15 contemporary apartments in the heart of Lakes Entrance. These one-, two- and three-bedroom self-contained apartments are individually designed and adjoining – built town-house style. Some have balconies, but all have private courtyards, spa baths and well-equipped kitchens. There are three pet-friendly apartments with basic behavioural rules. There is off-street boat parking, barbecue facilities, a spa and games recreation room. Breakfast is provided at a nearby cafe.

35 Church St; (03) 5155 6100;
www.thelakesapartments.com.au

WAVERLEY HOUSE COTTAGES $$$

Located in private landscaped native gardens with ocean views, this relatively new property offers accommodation in six secluded one- and two-bedroom cottages. Shaded by established gum trees, each cottage is spacious, thoughtfully designed and fitted with excellent facilities – either king- or queen-size beds, quality bed linen, leather couches, well-equipped kitchen, laundry and private spa room. After a day touring, jump into the communal hydrotherapy spa in the garden

gazebo with open fire, spacious lounge area and overhead plasma TV. Barbecue facilities are also available.

205 Palmers Rd; (03) 5155 1257;
www.waverleyhousecottages.com.au

5 KNOTS $$$$

Built on the old boating slipway in nearby Metung, if this stunning new accommodation complex was any closer to the water, guests would have to wear wetsuits. It comprises eight one-, two- and three-bedroom luxury apartments, possibly the most high-tech in the region. Everything is press button – sun blinds, lights – plus there's a kitchen full of European appliances, under-floor bathroom heating, spa baths, built-in coffee machines, stylish leather and contemporary furniture, huge flat-screen TV and cable TV. Some apartments have hot tubs, barbecue facilities and furnished outside decks.

42 Metung Rd, Metung; (03) 5156 2462 ;
www.5knots.com.au

Leongatha

LAMONT HOUSE $$

This three-bedroom historic cottage might date back to the early 1900s, but it has all the comforts of home with reverse-cycle air-conditioning, period furniture with modern fittings, full kitchen for self-catering and barbecue facilities for alfresco dining. Provisions for a continental breakfast are provided.

19 Long St; (03) 5662 4510;
www.lamonthouse.com

WHERE TO STAY

FITNESS CENTRE   ROOM SERVICE   SWIMMING POOL

LYRE BIRD HILL WINERY $$$

The owners of this family-operated winery offer two accommodation options: three in-house B&B rooms in a purpose-built guesthouse that is ideal for couples; and one self-catering three-bedroom cottage expressly furnished for young families. Set in beautiful gardens near the vineyard, the guesthouse is air-conditioned and each room has a private entrance. There is also a guests' lounge/dining room with open fire, sitting room with TV and tea-making facilities, and a garden terrace with a beautiful rose garden and thriving fruit orchard. Dinners are by arrangement, with special winemaker's dinner menus also available – usually on Saturday nights, with matching wines.

370 Inverloch Rd, Koonwarra; (03) 5664 3204; www.lyrebirdhill.com.au

Lorne

ACACIA VILLAS $$$

You will not want for much at these villas, something of an oasis in thriving Lorne. Each of the four villas has its own deck, polished wood floors, a spa, dishwasher, oven, DVD and queen-size beds. Other equally valued accoutrements are the ever-present locals including koalas, willy-wagtails, rosellas and kookaburras. The beach is just a 15-minute walk away. There are no sea views but the vistas over the valley of Lorne more than compensate. There are electric barbecues on each balcony. The location is quiet and serene.

9 Fletcher St; (03) 5289 2066

CUMBERLAND LORNE RESORT $$$$

The 99 one- and two-bedroom self-contained apartments have private balconies and corner spas. The 12 two-storey penthouses are suitable for two couples. Pay TV and in-house movies are complimentary, as are loads of extras like the gym, indoor heated pool, tennis and squash courts. The Cumberland was once pilloried for its shade of pink but these days the garish has gone and the resort seems part of Lorne's heartbeat. You are close to everything here, including the beach.

150 Mountjoy Pde; (03) 5289 4444; www.cumberland.com.au

GRAND PACIFIC HOTEL $$

On the headland by the Lorne pier, this grand heritage building has been transported into the 21st century in fine style. The facade, the ornate balconies, the sandstone interior walls and the ocean views may have changed little from the building's earliest days (c. 1870), but the 19 hotel rooms, from the doubles to the spa suites, have had fashionable makeovers. All rooms have queen- or king-size beds, TV and video. There is an open fire in a bar with enough groove to be at home in an inner-Melbourne laneway. There are also 15 one- to three-bedroom apartments available for overnight and week-long visits.

268 Mountjoy Pde; (03) 5289 1609; www.grandpacific.com.au

MANTRA ERSKINE BEACH RESORT $$$

The resort is indicative of Lorne's popularity and has been built around the heritage-listed Erskine House and sprawling lawns and gardens. Thirty-two of the rooms are heritage hotel rooms. All 271 apartments (studios and one- and two-bedrooms) have pay TV and internet access. Some of the apartments have dedicated parking at the base of the building. Other amenities include a brasserie, bar, heated indoor swimming pool and day spa. This is the only absolute beachfront property in Lorne and reception is open 24 hours.

1–35 Mountjoy Pde; (03) 5228 9777; www.mantraerskinebeachresort.com.au

Maldon

CLARE HOUSE $$$

Built in 1875, this comfortable home offers traditional B&B with loads of country charm. There are three bedrooms, all individually decorated. The front Garden Room overlooks the rose garden; the Renoir Room is decorated in French Provincial style; while the rear Carriage Room features smart black-and-white decor. All have ensuites with L'Occitane toiletries, reverse-cycle air-conditioning and ceiling fans. A three-course breakfast is included, and private massages and facials can be arranged.

99 High St; (03) 5475 2229; www.clarehouse.com.au

HEATHERLIE $$$$

This lovely 1880 house comprises a main house to accommodate up to three couples and an intimate pool house perfect for a romantic tryst in historic Maldon. Magnificently presented, owners Robyn and Ian Slattery have furnished it with chic country furniture collected from local and overseas markets to create a warm European villa ambience. French doors open onto the pool for outdoor relaxing; open fires beckon you to snuggle up in front of them. A complimentary breakfast hamper is chock-full of goodies for self-catering. Two-night minimum stay at weekends.

High St; 0413 123 650; www.heatherlie.com.au

MOUNT HAWKE OF MALDON $$$

This 1860s home has been beautifully restored to provide traditional B&B accommodation in three rooms in Australia's first 'Notable Town' as designated by the National Trust. Typical of other historic homes in the area, the rooms are large and high-ceilinged – with even a ballroom where guests are invited to relax by the open fire, listen to music or enjoy a glass of wine. A full cooked breakfast is served on the lawns, on the verandah or indeed in that beautiful ballroom.

24 Adair St; (03) 5475 1192

WYWURRI B&B $$

This Federation home offers private accommodation for one couple or two singles travelling together, with exclusive use of the front verandah and pretty garden. The main queen-size bedroom features beautiful linen and lace, and has its own private lounge area and bathroom, appropriately decorated with period furniture. A second double bedroom is also available by arrangement. It is literally around the corner from the town's shops and restaurants.

3 Templeton St; (03) 5475 2794; www.wywurri.com

FITNESS CENTRE   ROOM SERVICE   SWIMMING POOL

Mallacoota

KARBEETHONG LODGE $$

Only 5 kilometres from Mallacoota township, this classic green-and-white-painted historic guesthouse has been renovated to accommodate guests in 10 single, double and family bedrooms – most with ensuite facilities. Guests mingle in the communal lounge and dining room, and can self-cater in the spacious well-equipped country kitchen. With no phone and no TV, you just might have to relax on the big wooden outside deck and enjoy the great views over Mallacoota Inlet.

16 Schnapper Point Dr; (03) 5158 0411; www.karbeethonglodge.com.au

GIPSY POINT LODGE $$$$$

Adjoining Croajingolong National Park in the state's far east, this wonderful wilderness escape is located some 20 kilometres north-west of Mallacoota, perched above Mallacoota Inlet. The beautiful guesthouse has walls of glass affording wonderful views over the Genoa River. The lodge has seven rooms, tastefully furnished, as well as three self-contained cottages. Tariff includes full gourmet breakfast and dinner prepared by the in-house chef, featuring great local produce. You can hire kayaks, rowboats and canoes for outdoor exploring.

35 Macdonald St, Gipsy Point; (03) 5158 8205, 1800 063 556; www.gipsypoint.com

Mansfield

BURNT CREEK COTTAGES $$$$

Located on 16 hectares of farmland just 10 minutes by car from Mansfield, these six one- and two-bedroom cottages are comfortably furnished with all mod cons for a comfortable short- or long-term stay. All have king-size beds with duvets and electric blankets, fully self-contained kitchens for self-catering and private elevated balconies with magnificent views over the surrounding countryside. There is a communal barbecue area around the pool, and a tennis court. The location makes a good base from which to explore the spectacular region.

68 O'Hanlons Rd; (03) 5775 3067; www.burntcreekcottages.com.au

HIGHTON MANOR $$$$

One of the earliest buildings in the High Country, this imposing Italianate manor house was built by the Highett family from Dorset in England. It took 20 years to complete and was finished in 1896, with uninterrupted views across to Mount Buller, Mount Timbertop, Mount Sterling and the Bluff. Dame Nellie Melba used to sing duets in the ballroom, which is now a formal dining room. Today there are six queen bedrooms with ensuites and reverse-cycle air-conditioning for year-round comfort, one party room that is ideal for a large family or group, and five motel-style units. The pick is the Tower Suite with four-poster bed, sitting room and spa bath.

140 Highton Lane; (03) 5775 2700; www.hightonmanor.com.au

⬮ BREAKFAST INCLUDED   ▭ CREDIT CARDS ACCEPTED   👪 FAMILY FRIENDLY

MAGNOLIA GOURMET COUNTRY HOUSE
$$

This gracious century-old cottage offers simple comfortable accommodation upstairs in two attic rooms, with views from front balconies over the established garden and 110-year-old magnolia tree. Both rooms have TV, electric blankets and tea- and coffee-making facilities. A full cooked breakfast is available. Strategically located en route to the ski fields, ski hire can be arranged at a discount, while an in-room massage can also be organised to restore weary après-ski bodies.

190 Mount Buller Rd; (03) 5779 1444; www.magnoliamansfield.com.au

WOMBAT HILLS COTTAGES
$$$$

About 20 kilometres from Mansfield – but 300 metres above it, between Barwite and Tolmie – this country accommodation enjoys stunning mountain views behind Lake Eildon. It comprises three romantic stone cottages. Fern and Snowgum cottages each have one bedroom and are designed for a couple, while three-bedroom Rose Cottage is ideal for a family or friends travelling together. All have corner spa baths, full kitchens, reverse-cycle air-conditioning and open fires as well as cosy heaters. There are private barbecue facilities and a wireless internet hotspot. A breakfast hamper can be provided, as well as other meal options: a barbecue hamper in summer or slow-cooked dinners in winter.

55 Lochiel Rd, Barwite; (03) 5776 9507; www.wombathills.com.au

Marysville

WOODLANDS RAINFOREST RETREAT
$$$$$

This award-winning retreat offers a beautiful and secluded nature escape, located between Healesville and Marysville. Sprawled across 16 hectares of rainforest, stringy-bark, peppermint and blackwood trees, it comprises four luxurious architect-designed bungalows. Each private and spacious unit is made entirely of timber, with plenty of handcrafted elements. Comforts include an open fireplace, heated ceramic-tiled floors, a double spa room opening up to a view of the rainforest, CD and DVD facilities, and a sprawling deck visited by morning sunlight, perfect for spotting local wombats, platypus and wallabies. You can self-cater if you choose, or order meals catered by a local gourmet chef. In-house massages are available, making it easy to unwind at your woodland cabin. The private setting in a rainforest glade seems almost magical.

Manby Rd, Narbethong; (03) 5963 7150; www.woodlandscottages.com.au

Milawa

LINDENWARRAH COUNTRY HOUSE HOTEL
$$$$$

Set among the rich vineyards of Milawa's famed gourmet region, this stylish boutique hotel offers 40 spacious rooms – two of them suites, all with vineyard views. Modern art and exotic artefacts add colour to this slick architect-designed building. All rooms are individually decorated with king-size beds, minibar and tea- and coffee-making facilities.

FITNESS CENTRE   ROOM SERVICE   SWIMMING POOL

Massages and beauty treatments are available in special poolside spa rooms. The in-house cafe and restaurant champion regional and seasonal produce.

Milawa–Bobinawarrah Rd; (03) 5720 5777; www.lindenwarrah.com.au

CASA LUNA GOURMET ACCOMMODATION $$$

About 30 kilometres from Milawa, this purpose-built modern home offers luxury accommodation. Two stylish Asian-inspired bedrooms with ensuites occupy one wing; the other has an open-style dining area and lounge in a light-filled central space. Rooms have separate entrances and both open out onto a sun-drenched rear courtyard with views over the Myrrhee Valley. Co-owner Gwenda Canty is a former Melbourne caterer, and cooks exceptional food with great breakfasts and regional Italian-style dinners by arrangement. There's plenty of wildlife on the property and, if lucky, guests might spy the odd wombat and echidna.

Boggy Creek Rd, Myrrhee; (03) 5729 7650; www.casaluna.com.au

WILLOAKS BOUTIQUE ACCOMMODATION $$$

A class act, this simply beautiful property has two guest rooms (the Spa and Garden Rooms) built around a worker's hut, part of the original homestead complex that dates back to 1920. The wisteria draping the balconies in no way interrupts the views to Mount Buffalo or of the surrounding farm's Angus cattle and small vineyard. The breakfast of homemade muesli, fresh fruit compote and eggs Benedict is an indication of the attention to detail.

31 Tetleys La, Oxley; (03) 5727 3292; www.willoaks.com.au

Mildura

MURRAY HAVEN $$$

Map ref. p. 120

This beautifully renovated four-bedroom house caters for everyone: couples – with master ensuite bedroom; families – with terrific outdoor entertaining area with barbecue facilities; friends travelling together – TVs in all double bedrooms; and those on business – there is a work station with printer, stationery, complimentary broadband internet and free local calls. And to make guests really welcome, local wines, beer and fresh fruit are offered on arrival.

118A Thirteenth St; 0408 213 404; www.murrayhaven.com.au

PIED-À-TERRE $$$

Map ref. p. 120

Centrally located, this five-bedroom home caters for up to 10 guests in stylish accommodation on two levels. Ducted air-conditioning and ceiling fans assure summer comfort, and a glass-doored sunroom and large outdoor entertaining area allow for comfortable down time. Complimentary wireless internet is a bonus, likewise hearty provisions for breakfast and a range of teas and fresh coffee. There is private parking for four vehicles and boats.

97 Chaffey Ave; (03) 5022 9883; www.piedaterre.com.au

QUALITY HOTEL MILDURA GRAND

$$$

Map ref. p. 120

Originally opened in 1891 as a coffee palace, this huge two-storey hotel with its iconic arches is a Mildura landmark. Occupying a large slab of real estate between two streets, it also houses the Mildura Brewery Pub, drive-in bottle shop, sports bar with gaming facilities and six restaurants, including celebrated Stefano's of *Gondola on the Murray* TV fame, which is housed in the hotel's old cellar. There are six levels of accommodation, from the luxurious presidential and grand suites with spa baths to lower-cost standard rooms in the older section of the hotel. Gradually, all 92 rooms are being refurbished. Guests have access to the in-house gym with sauna and spa. Two- and three-night packages are available.

Seventh St; (03) 5023 0511; www.qualityhotelmilduragrand.com.au

ADVENTURE HOUSEBOATS

$$$$$
Map ref. p. 120

Located just over the border in Buronga, this small fleet of houseboats is growing and boasts the only solar-powered vessel on the Murray River. Sister boats *Advantage 1* and *All Class* might look the same – both have four bedrooms, two ensuites, open-plan lounge, dining and kitchen area, spacious upper deck with barbecue facilities and spa tub for eight. However, the former has a few discerning differences that make it the slickest houseboat on the river: it offers outside access from each bedroom, it has dual upstairs and downstairs driving ability, and its bank of solar panels halves the average fuel bill. Guests are given a lesson before they set off for what is simply the best way to appreciate this mighty waterway.

16 Sturt Hwy, Buronga; (03) 5023 4787; www.adventurehouseboats.com.au

Mornington

GEORGE'S BOUTIQUE B&B & CULINARY RETREAT

$$$$$

You don't have to be a budding chef to stay at this Mornington Peninsula retreat; nor do you have to book into one of their gourmet cooking classes – but indeed cooking packages are available. Accommodation is in three spacious and luxurious units on an upper level with terrific views from private balconies, with a smaller comfortable unit downstairs, close to Cafe George. Breakfast is the full deal, from hot semolina porridge and bircher muesli to thick baked pancakes and French omelettes.

776 Arthurs Seat Rd, Arthurs Seat; (03) 5981 8700; www.georgesonarthurs.com.au

GLYNT MANOR

$$$$$

This gracious manor house was originally built as a family holiday home overlooking Port Phillip Bay. Over the years it changed hands and for more than 25 years now it has been a boutique hotel nestled in its English- and French-inspired gardens. New owners have elevated it to a luxury retreat for the discerning traveller. Each of the six suites has a different theme and is decorated with a wonderful mix of beautiful fabrics and furniture, with European or Asian influences and indulgent chandeliers. Breakfast is a sumptuous spread of anything that is local, regional and seasonal, and dinner is available by prior arrangement. Two-night minimum stay.

10 Greenslade Crt, Mount Martha; (03) 5974 8400; www.glyntmanor.com.au

WHERE TO STAY

FITNESS CENTRE   ROOM SERVICE   SWIMMING POOL

MORNING STAR ESTATE $$$$

This gracious century-old mansion overlooks hectares of vines and beautiful gardens that are amassed with 50,000 rose bushes in bloom in summer. Built originally as a holiday retreat, it more recently was a boys' home before a major conversion in 2002 transformed it into a 20-room boutique hotel. There are 15 standard double rooms, four standard queen bedrooms and one executive suite with a spa bath.

2 Sunnyside Rd, Mount Eliza; (03) 9787 7760; www.morningstarestate.com.au

WOODMAN ESTATE $$$$$

This 20-hectare estate comprises a boutique hotel and spa retreat located halfway between Mount Martha and Hastings at Moorooduc. The two-storey gracious manor house would look at home in the pages of the English *Country Life* magazine yet it is only 20 years old, but was indeed built by an Englishman as his family home. Accommodation is in three lakeside chalets with four-poster bed, large marble bathroom, spacious lounge room and an outside deck; there are also five bedrooms in the manor house and two other suites in the spa retreat building. There are two dining options: the formal dining room and a casual brasserie that opens onto a lakeside terrace with market umbrellas.

136 Graydens Rd, Moorooduc; (03) 5978 8455; www.woodmanestate.com

Myrtleford

MOTEL ON ALPINE $$

This traditional 17-room motel has four levels of accommodation, from corporate, garden and family to the up-market premium. Outdoor facilities include a pool, spa and communal barbecue area. Guests who might like more salubrious surroundings can opt to stay at Ferndale – a private, comfortably furnished two-bedroom home some 600 metres down the road. The motel has an on-site restaurant, Range, and can also prepare barbecue hampers and tasting plates.

258 Great Alpine Rd; (03) 5752 1438; www.motelonalpine.com

Nagambie

BLACKWOOD PARK COUNTRY HOUSE $$$$

Nestled in the heart of the well-established Mitchelton vineyards, on the banks of the meandering Goulburn River, is the former estate manager's home in what was originally the Blackwood Park Grazing Estate. Nowadays it is a comfortable self-contained family home with three bedrooms (two queen and one double) and two bathrooms (one ensuite and the main bathroom with spa). Designed for three couples sharing, it has full kitchen and barbecue facilities for self-catering, as well as heating and air-conditioning. It is usually offered only at weekends for a two-night stay.

Mitchelton Wines, Mitchells Town Rd; (03) 5736 2222; www.mitchelton.com.au

NAGAMBIE LAKES LEISURE PARK $$

This new concept leisure park is designed to encourage guests to stay and enjoy its country location and family-based facilities. With Lake Nagambie on one side and the lovely Goulburn River on the other, it offers 33 modern, self-contained cabins clad in corrugated iron and all with reverse-cycle air-conditioning. There is also a selection of ensuite and powered caravan sites and a camping area. Two recreation halls house a billiard table and other games. There is also a tennis court and terrific on-site cafe/restaurant that is open most days for breakfast, lunch and dinner.

69 Loddings La; (03) 5794 2373; www.nagambielakespark.com.au

Olinda

FOLLY FARM RURAL RETREAT $$$$

Light and bright, this stand-alone cottage is located on 4 hectares of gardens that include a commercial blueberry farm, a chestnut plantation, lovely dry-stone walls and one of just ten remaining intact Edna Walling gardens, according to Heritage Victoria. The property is one of the original hill station properties where wealthy Melburnians fled to escape the rat-race of the early 1900s. Tastefully decorated, it offers a romantic hideaway for just one couple.

192 Falls Rd; (03) 9751 2544; www.follyfarm.com.au

LOCHIEL LUXURY ACCOMMODATION $$$$

Squirrel yourself away in one of the contemporary treetop cottages or the larger 1920s-built family-style cottage. Set amid 2 hectares of rainforest, Lochiel has three one-bedroom treetop cottages built over three levels, with king-size bedrooms on the top that seem to sit out among the trees. These ultra-chic cottages feature peaked ski-lodge-style gables and treetop balconies. All have large spas in luxuriously equipped bathrooms and are warmed with central heating and

open fires. The larger, charmingly refurbished original Lochiel cottage offers generous family accommodation for up to six guests in three bedrooms, with a large outdoor spa. Guests breakfast at nearby Ranges Cafe, which is also part of the Lochiel stable.

1590–1594 Mt Dandenong Tourist Rd; (03) 9751 2300 ; www.lochielaccommodation.com

WOOLRICH RETREAT $$$$

This Art Deco–style executive retreat is set among historic gardens on the top of Mount Dandenong. Ideal for just one couple, or indeed two couples travelling together, it is self-contained with two bedrooms, two bathrooms, open fire, reverse-cycle air-conditioning and huge four-person Jacuzzi spa bath. A large deck with barbecue facilities has views over the established garden, hills and the beautiful Cloudehill gardens next door. The owner also has three other cottages available throughout the Dandenongs.

7–9 Monash Ave; (03) 9751 2464; www.woolrichretreat.com.au

JAPANESE MOUNTAIN RETREAT $$$$$

Set on 2 hectares of ravishing bushland, this retreat is the pinnacle of luxury and relaxation, perfect for slowing down and restoring yourself. Two serene Japanese guest suites balance tradition with plush contemporary comfort. From the translucent screens to the deep spa tub with a beautiful view of your private Japanese garden – including a traditional water feature – you are enfolded in peace and privacy. Each suite also has its own moon-viewing dais overlooking a lake. The spa offers blissful treatments and a traditional tea ceremony performed on request.

14 Mountain Cres, Montrose; (03) 9737 0086; www.japanesemountainretreat.com.au

WHERE TO STAY

FITNESS CENTRE   ROOM SERVICE   SWIMMING POOL

Paynesville

CAPTAIN'S COVE $$

Like a string of grown-up bathing boxes, these two-storey architect-designed apartments edge one of the attractive artificial waterways on Victoria's Gippsland Lakes. Comprising 18 units, the stylish complex has a distinct nautical theme with steel yachting-cable stair rails, industrial-style mesh balcony safety surrounds, double viewing decks over the canal, and a blue-and-white colour scheme. Self-contained units are well equipped with three bedrooms to sleep six, two bathrooms, practical kitchen and spacious family room opening on to a downstairs deck, complete with barbecue and outdoor furniture for casual meals and entertaining. Upstairs there is a quiet deck off the main bedroom, and right at the back door there is your very own private boat jetty. Skippered yacht charters are available.

13 Mitchell St; (03) 5156 7223; www.captainscove.com.au

Port Campbell

DAYSY HILL COUNTRY COTTAGES $$

Just out of the village of Port Campbell, this 1.8-hectare property's sandstone and cedar cottages have pitched ceilings and polished wood floors, and come in a variety of configurations. Some of the two-bedroom cottages and cabins are perfect for families, with a queen-size bed in one bedroom, and a bunk and a single bed in the second. There are four studio-style suites with views of Port Campbell to the south and Newfield Valley to the north, plus spas and wood heaters. The self-contained cottages with full laundry facilities also have beautiful leadlight windows crafted by the property's owner.

2585 Cobden–Port Campbell Rd; (03) 5598 6226 ; www.daysyhillcottages.com.au

LOCH ARD MOTOR INN $$

Sixteen of the 17 bright and clean motel rooms have views of Port Campbell's pocket-size bay. Eight apartments – some at the front, the side and the rear of the property – are almost the size of a small house. They are great for families and groups as they sleep up to six people. There are complimentary DVDs and, at additional cost, wireless internet. This is perhaps the best positioned motel in Port Campbell.

18–24 Lord St; (03) 5598 6328

SEA FOAM VILLAS $$

On Port Campbell's main thoroughfare, these apartments are only some 50 metres from the beach. The complex is built on a corner; some of the beachside apartments have balconies overlooking the horseshoe bay, others face back up the main street. They really do cater for a range of needs here. There are one-, two- and three-bedroom configurations, and half of the apartments have spas. All but four are fully self-contained, and these have the cheapest tariff as they don't have kitchens. Some of these modern apartments were only completed at the end of 2008. All of Port Campbell, including the pub and cafes, is barely the length of a fishing rod from all rooms.

14 Lord St; (03) 5598 6413; www.seafoamvillas.com

BREAKFAST INCLUDED   CREDIT CARDS ACCEPTED   FAMILY FRIENDLY

Port Fairy

HEARN'S BEACHSIDE VILLAS $$$$

The waterfront location affords ocean views so proximate they could be considered furnishings. But all that blue, no matter how gloriously wild, is not the only feature. The polished wood floors, stainless-steel kitchen and mod cons including king-size beds make this a very desirable seaside address. Six of the seven apartments have either one or two bedrooms. The other villa has three bedrooms, so bring your friends. There is a cafe for breakfast right next door.

13–17 Thistle Pl; (03) 5568 3150

MERRIJIG INN $$

Historically and architecturally, the Merrijig Inn is a very significant building; in fact, it is one of the oldest surviving hotels in the state. Originally constructed in 1845–47, it has survived fire, closure and use as a police barracks and government offices. Its simplicity of form is more in keeping with early colonial buildings in New South Wales and Tasmania. Nestled on a grassy rise overlooking the Moyne River and the historic working dock, the heritage inn offers comfortable B&B accommodation in four large rooms with ensuites, and in four cosy attic rooms. The conservatory is a light-filled sunny spot to savour the lavish breakfast menu. An in-house restaurant is open Monday to Saturday for dinner.

1 Campbell St; (03) 5568 2324; www.merrijiginn.com

MOYNE MILL TOWNHOUSE $$$

This three-bedroom riverside accommodation was once a flour mill and the (part) bluestone facade right by the Moyne River has aged gracefully and spreads over four floors. The two main bedrooms have river views, though the Loft Room is the better choice, and the reading den has a sofa bed, which means it can morph easily into a third sleeping option. Port Fairy's best features, the cafes, restaurants and the beach, are within easy walking distance. A selection of complimentary teas and coffees are provided, along with Moyne Mill port or sherry and homemade shortbreads.

Unit 4, 25 Gipps St; (03) 5568 2229

OSCARS WATERFRONT BOUTIQUE HOTEL $$$$

Guests could almost change a yacht's spinnaker from the verandah of this hotel, as it is right by a marina on the Moyne River. There is a French Provincial style here, which comes in part from the courtyard and the timber shutters on the building. Some of the seven rooms include a spa room opening onto the courtyard. The drawing room is suitably grand and the open fires will be roaring in winter. Oscars does not cater for children aged under 16.

41B Gipps St; (03) 5568 3022; www.oscarswaterfront.com

Portland

CLIFFTOP ACCOMMODATION PORTLAND $$$

These three studio apartments are built right on the edge of a cliff, and the views can

FITNESS CENTRE   ROOM SERVICE   SWIMMING POOL

resemble what a captain might have from the bridge of his ship. The views over the ocean are almost 180 degrees. Guests, like that captain, can hear the ocean lapping from the comfort of their bed. The island visible from the rooms is not Tasmania but Lady Julia Percy Island, 35 kilometres off the coast. Watch for whales in the winter months from these lovely modern rooms.

13 Clifton Crt; (03) 5523 1126; www.portlandaccommodation.com.au

SHEOAK TINNTEAN $$

From the comfort of your own private balcony, early rousers can watch the sun rise over Bass Straight and see the local fleet leave for the nearby bountiful fishing grounds. These two second-floor studio apartments are beautifully located above Portland Bay, with magnificent ocean views. Both have queen-size beds with electric blankets, ensuites – with views – and a double sofa bed for children. A kitchenette allows for moderate self-catering with provisions for breakfast included. Complimentary internet is a bonus, and off-street parking is provided.

22 Cavendish St; (03) 5523 2296; www.sheoaktinntean.com.au

Queenscliff

ATHELSTANE HOUSE $$$

This 'small hotel by the sea' is Queenscliff's oldest operating guesthouse – dating from 1860. However, extensive renovations have recently brought it right up to date, with all mod cons and then some. All eight queen-size rooms and the one apartment have ensuites,

most with corner spa baths, heating, ceiling fans and broadband wireless internet access. Decor is fresh and modern throughout, and some rooms have private balconies; all guests can enjoy the wide communal second-floor balcony. The on-site restaurant is one of the best in the region, with outdoor dining areas in summer.

4 Hobson St; (03) 5258 1024; www.athelstane.com.au

LATHAMSTOWE $$$

Memories of Marnie Riddell's stewed stone fruit and berries followed by her baked scrambled eggs wrapped in smoked salmon and served on a muffin linger long after you have departed her beautiful historic accommodation in Queenscliff. The two-storey French Renaissance–style building dates from the 1880s, with spectacular views from the rooftop tower. There are seven chic bedrooms, all individually furnished with lashings of good taste, Asian-style furniture alongside antiques, objets d'art that have been collected over 30 years and modern artwork by Marnie herself. Next door is a 100-year-old three-bedroom cottage set in a beautiful garden full of century-old fruit trees, ideal for families.

44 Gellibrand St; (03) 5258 4110

THE QUEENSCLIFF HOTEL $$$$

With its lavish interiors and intricate latticework, The Queenscliff Hotel harks back to a time when this seaside town was a resort for wealthy 19th-century Victorians. Built in 1887 in red brick, with enclosed tower, two-storey bay windows and Flemish gables, it has been elegantly restored and furnished to capture the late-Victorian era. Visitors can dine opulently here and stay in one of the 15 heritage ensuite bedrooms.

BREAKFAST INCLUDED   CREDIT CARDS ACCEPTED   FAMILY FRIENDLY

16 Gellibrand St; (03) 5258 1066;
www.queenscliffhotel.com.au

VUE GRAND HOTEL $$$$

Located in the heart of Queenscliff, the Vue Grand is a multi-award-winning and beautifully restored boutique hotel. The hotel is grand indeed, built in 1881 to replace a wooden hotel on the site. Originally a three-storey Victorian building known as The Grand Hotel, the central section was gutted by fire in 1927 and was partly rebuilt, emerging with a more solid, 1920s-style tower and detailing. There are 33 sumptuous guest rooms, including a selection of indulgent suites. Dining is taken to a grand scale in the impressive dining room.

46 Hesse St; (03) 5258 1544;
www.vuegrand.com.au

Rutherglen

BANK ON MAIN $$$

Centrally located on the town's main street, this former 1899 two-storey Bank of Australasia has been tastefully converted to offer luxury B&B in two king-size ensuite rooms. Entry is via a side gate, the original private entrance to the manager's house. The former banking chamber, with lofty ceiling, log fire, ornate ceiling roses and walk-in vault, has been converted into a guests' lounge and dining room. The two bedrooms are upstairs and furnished with modern period-style furniture. Guests can enjoy a cooked breakfast in the downstairs dining room or outside under the shade of a century-old tree.

80 Main St; (02) 6032 7000;
www.bankonmain.com.au

READY COTTAGE B&B $$$

This most comfortable family home has been thoughtfully renovated to host traditional B&B accommodation in three queen-size bedrooms, all with ensuites. Named after the original owners of the property, Ready Cottage dates from the 1890s and today is a lovely blend of old and new furniture and fittings. Appropriately, guests are offered a nightcap of terrific local Rutherglen fortified wine and yummy chocolates. It is an easy walk to good local restaurants, cosy cafes and country pubs in the town's main street.

92 High St; (02) 6032 7407;
www.readycottage.com.au

THE HOUSE AT MOUNT PRIOR $$$

Offering the only accommodation with restaurant on a working winery in the historic wine-rich region of Rutherglen, The House at Mount Prior is a magnificent home overlooking vines that produce some of the region's finest tipples. Built in the 1880s, the heritage home is full of old-world charm and warm country hospitality. Its five elegant queen-size guest rooms are individually furnished – some have open fires, others have ducted heating. A full cooked breakfast is served in the dining room.

1194 Gooramedda Rd; (02) 6026 5256;
www.houseatmountprior.com

VINEYARDS AT TUILERIES $$$

Over the years the Tuileries has evolved into perhaps the region's most exciting accommodation option. Once simply a fine restaurant, it has gradually added a cafe and in more recent years great accommodation. It

WHERE TO STAY

now has 12 rooms overlooking vineyards and four two-bedroom units overlooking the olive grove. All rooms have king-size beds with spa baths, reverse-cycle air-conditioning, TVs and DVDs, with themes including Moroccan, Zen, African, contemporary and romantic. There is complimentary wireless internet in the business centre, and dinner, bed and breakfast packages are available.

13–35 Drummond St; (02) 6032 9033; www.tuileriesrutherglen.com.au

Sale

MINNIES B&B $$$

This country gem wouldn't look out of place overlooking a beach, though its farmland setting is pretty hard to beat. Made of mini-orb, the stand-alone contemporary house thrills with its unique original artworks and colourful furniture and fittings, designed and made by co-owner Mandy Rowe. The building is simplicity itself, with a central open-plan lounge, dining and kitchen area with external deck that links two queen bedrooms with ensuites at either end. A fabulous course-by-course dinner can be arranged with local wines, and a great country breakfast will send you on your way.

202 Gibsons Rd; (03) 5144 3344; www.minnies.com.au

QUEST SALE $$$

This new accommodation complex offers 53 studios and one-, two- and three-bedroom serviced apartments that are ideal for business or leisure, for singles, couples or families. Fully serviced, all the apartments are also self-contained with well-equipped kitchen, laundry, lounge and dining areas, reverse-cycle air-

conditioning, DVD player and stereos. Smaller studios have a kitchenette and communal laundry. High-speed internet access is available and there is on-site carparking.

180–184 York St; (03) 5142 0900; www.questsale.com.au

FROG GULLY COTTAGES $$$

Only ten minutes from Sale on a sheep and cattle property, these two self-contained contemporary cottages enjoy an elevated position overlooking tranquil wetlands that abound with wildlife – and those eponymous frogs that provide constant background 'music' through late winter, spring and early summer. Both cottages have a king and queen bedroom with ensuites, central living area with kitchen, and barbecue facilities on north-facing decks where guests can sit back, relax and enjoy beautiful sunsets. Both cottages are fitted for disabled access, with peace and quiet guaranteed.

Lot 2419 Rosedale Rd, Longford; (03) 5149 7242; www.froggully.com.au

Seymour

ROSEHILL COTTAGES $$$

Lucky the guests who stay at these two self-contained cottages, for they are part of The Shed at Trawool complex in the heart of the historic Trawool Valley – and breakfast is served in the outstanding adjacent restaurant. The surroundings don't get much better than this, as the spectacular valley is classified by the National Trust for its scenic beauty. The cottages are designed for one couple with queen bedroom – and double sofa if there are extras – kitchenette, cosy wood burner, reverse-cycle

---

BREAKFAST INCLUDED   CREDIT CARDS ACCEPTED   FAMILY FRIENDLY

air-conditioning and private barbecue facilities. The cottages are surrounded by gardens and are a leisurely stroll to the Goulburn River.

8447 Goulburn Valley Hwy, Trawool; (03) 5799 1595; www.rosehillcottages.com.au

TRAWOOL VALLEY RESORT $$$

Located in the picturesque Trawool Valley en route to Yea, this Tudor-style resort is beautifully sited overlooking the valley itself. Family-run, it offers 27 comfortable suites with all mod cons – reverse-cycle air-conditioning, TV, tea- and coffee-making facilities and complimentary broadband internet. Rooms range from country standard to four-poster luxurious grand master. Tariff includes use of all facilities, including tennis and squash courts, spa and pools (indoor and outdoor). Massages and accommodation packages are available. The Bistro and Erica's Restaurant offer dining options, with high tea served on the first Sunday of the month.

8150 Goulburn Valley Hwy, Trawool; (03) 5792 1444; www.trawoolresort.com.au

Shepparton

CENTRAL SHEPPARTON APARTMENTS $$$

This new complex of 15 two-bedroom serviced apartments has five different categories of accommodation: spa, lake view, deluxe, deluxe spa and deluxe lake view spa – the ones with 'the lot'. Contemporary in design and decor, all are equipped with a full kitchen and laundry, two bathrooms, three toilets, clothes dryer, reverse-cycle air-conditioning, large-screen TV and a DVD player. There is also off-street parking and complimentary high-speed internet.

507 Wyndham St; (03) 5821 4482; www.sheppapartments.com.au

THE CARRINGTON $$$$

Originally built as a private mansion after the grand style of Graceland, Carrington Manor was bought by the motel operators next door to offer additional accommodation in two large suites and four smaller rooms. Its grand sweeping staircase impresses romantics, the boutique accommodation proving popular for honeymoons. The Carrington Motel itself offers more-traditional accommodation in 19 standard rooms, 18 executive suites and one self-contained two-bedroom apartment to sleep four.

505 Wyndham St; (03) 5821 3355; www.thecarrington.net.au

THE CHURCHES $$$

You might wonder why two churches stand together on the outskirts of Shepparton. It is not to catch the overflow of parishioners from one to the other. Rather, one has been converted into appealing self-contained accommodation with three bedrooms. The main bedroom and ensuite are on a mezzanine level; the other two are on the ground floor with a second bathroom. There is a full kitchen, laundry and two comfortable lounges. The second church, originally located 5 kilometres away, has morphed into an appealing lavender-produce shop selling skincare creams and potions made from oil from the lavender farm. Minimum two-night stay is preferred.

Woodlands Estate Lavender, 325 Poplar Ave, Orrvale; (03) 5829 1019; www.thechurches.com.au

WHERE TO STAY

Sorrento

OCEANIC SORRENTO $$$$

Map ref. p. 144

Opposite the lovely century-old Whitehall guesthouse, these 18 new architect-designed apartments spread over two levels, with elegant loft bedroom and spacious living area downstairs opening onto private front and rear courtyards. Partly self-contained, they are equipped with fridge, dishwasher, microwave, TV and reverse-cycle air-conditioning. The more budget-conscious should check out the original old guesthouse that is gradually being restored and refurbished for better comfort, and where a full cooked breakfast is included in the tariff.

231 Ocean Beach Rd; (03) 5984 4166; www.oceanicgroup.com.au

SORRENTO BEACH MOTEL $$$

Map ref. p. 144

In keeping with the casual beach atmosphere, these 19 ground-floor studios resemble the strings of colourful bathing boxes that line the beach at Sorrento. There are three different types of rooms to cater for all requirements. All are equipped with limited self-catering, with ensuites, reverse-cycle air-conditioning, electric blankets, tea-, coffee- and toast-making facilities and casual outdoor furniture. Around the corner from the main shopping street and a few hundred metres from the beach, there is ample carparking and room enough to park your boat.

780 Melbourne Rd; (03) 5984 1356; www.sorrentobeachmotel.com.au

AQUABELLE APARTMENTS $$$

Placed strategically above the string of shops that lines the main road at Rye, these three architect-designed apartments are spacious and beautifully furnished, with great views across the bay. There are two two-bedroom suites – both with main queen bedroom with ensuite and two king-size singles – and one three-bedroom suite with two queen beds (one with ensuite) and two king-size singles. Polished concrete floors, private balconies, gourmet kitchen and full laundry facilities mean guests have everything at hand for a carefree holiday. Each apartment has secure parking for two vehicles.

Level 1, 2331–2335 Point Nepean Rd, Rye; 1300 880 319; www.aquabelle.com.au

LAKESIDE VILLAS AT CRITTENDEN ESTATE $$$$

These three contemporary one-bedroom villas offer luxury accommodation on one of the peninsula's longest established vineyards at nearby Dromana. Designed with open-plan living, each has its own private north-facing balcony that juts out over the tranquil lake and is equipped with king-size bed, walk-in robe, double spa bath, full laundry facilities, split-system heating and cooling, and authentic wood heater for extra winter cosiness. Bring your runners for a game of tennis (racquets and balls are supplied), enjoy a complimentary bottle of estate-grown wine and be sure to dine in the on-site restaurant, Stillwater at Crittenden.

Crittenden Estate, Harrisons Rd, Dromana; (03) 5987 3275; www.crittendenwines.com.au

PEPPERS MOONAH LINKS RESORT

$$$$$

This golf resort offers great facilities for guests and golfers alike. Located behind the popular bathing beaches of Port Phillip Bay, it has 93 deluxe rooms and suites, all with balconies overlooking the two 18-hole championship golf courses or putting greens. Some 44 suites are self-catering, 12 are standard hotel-style accommodation, while the others are luxury studio-style rooms. There is an in-house restaurant and bar, and a pampering Endota day spa. Golf and relaxation packages are available.

55 Peter Thomson Dr, Fingal; (03) 5988 2000; www.peppers.com.au/moonah

Swan Hill

BIG 4 SWAN HILL

$$

This award-winning family-focused holiday park is on 4 hectares of landscaped grounds, a two-minute drive from Swan Hill. Accommodation is in one-, two- and three-bedroom cabins – all with reverse-cycle air-conditioning. Spa cabins are ideal for couples, while the most popular with families are the new two- and three-bedroom superior cabins. Some of these have spas and all have lounge rooms and furnished decks. The park has exceptional facilities for children, including a racetrack for bikes, go-karts and a jumping pillow.

186 Murray Valley Hwy; (03) 5032 4372; www.swanhill.vic.big4.com.au

BEST'S RIVERBED AND BREAKFAST

$$

This traditional B&B offers guests the chance to stay in what was originally part of the shearers' quarters of historic Murray Downs homestead. Built in 1917, the building has been converted to accommodate eight guests in five rooms. Choose the main bedroom with ensuite, corner spa and terrific river views, and make good use of the two private guest lounges with open fire. The other rooms – a queen, double and two king singles – all have shared bathrooms. Breakfast can be served in the dining room on the verandah – or indeed down by the river.

7 Kidman Reid Dr, Murray Downs; (03) 5032 2126; www.bestbnb.com.au

BURRABLISS B&B

$$$

Situated on the shore of Lake Boga about 10 minutes by car from Swan Hill, this traditional B&B property has three accommodation options. Suite Bliss is ideal for a secluded romantic getaway with king-size bed, double spa bath and private amenities. Villa Bliss is perfect for a young family or two couples travelling together, as it has two bedrooms and self-catering facilities – one room has disabled access. Traditional Bliss offers two in-house rooms with shared bathroom facilities.

169 Lakeside Dr, Lake Boga; (03) 5037 2527; www.burrabliss.com.au

MURRAY DOWNS RESORT

$$$

You don't have to be a golfer to stay at this golf resort, but since the course is considered one of the best along the Murray River, it could tempt you to take up the sport – or to at least

WHERE TO STAY

book a lesson. Situated on part of Kidman Reid's historic Murray Downs Station, this resort has 50 hotel rooms and 14 self-contained apartments surrounded by manicured lawns and gardens. Outstanding guest facilities include a basketball court, tennis court, playground and a supervised children's room at night. Golf packages are available.

Lot 5, Murray Downs Dr, Murray Downs; (03) 5033 1966 or 1800 807 574; www.murraydownsresort.com.au

Torquay

CROWNE PLAZA TORQUAY $$$

Enjoying an absolute beachfront location, this new low-rise 164-room hotel includes 82 one-bedroom apartments and is only a short drive to the famous surfing beaches of Bells and Jan Juc. Contemporary in style, it is beautifully fitted and furnished, with all rooms looking out onto the sweeping outdoor swimming pool and over to Zeally Bay itself. There is a heated indoor lap pool for all-year use, a pampering day spa for massage and a tennis court, as well as a restaurant, cafe lounge and convivial bar.

100 The Esplanade; (03) 5261 1500; www.ichotelsgroup.com

PEPPERS THE SANDS RESORT $$$$

About five minutes from the main beach, this 112-room golf resort appeals with its contemporary style and abundant leisure facilities. All rooms are spacious and tastefully furnished, with minibars, flat-screen TVs, internet access and private balconies – some with views over the Stuart Appleby–designed 18-hole championship golf course. Larger suites have separate lounge and dining rooms,

and are suitable for longer stays. As this is a private course, resort guests have the bonus opportunity to play the course and also use the health club facilities. There is also a tennis court and an on-site restaurant.

2 Sands Blv; (03) 5264 3333; www.peppers.com.au/sands

Walhalla

WALHALLA'S STAR HOTEL $$$

This country hotel is a property with great style. Rebuilt in 1999 with a facade replicating the original gold-rush-era Star Hotel, the exterior of the building remains true to the town's 19th-century character, while the interior has been designed to suit latter-day travellers. It offers 12 large modern suites, all with ensuite facilities. Decor is country chic, with atmospheric touches such as galvanised iron bedside tables.

Main Rd; (03) 5165 6262; www.starhotel.com.au

Wangaratta

KING RIVER STABLES $$

Just 2 kilometres from town, these converted horse stables overlook a tranquil billabong on the King River frequented by myriad waterbirds. Accommodation on the 16-hectare farm is stylish, catering for up to eight in two double rooms and a bunk room that sleeps four. Ideal for a family or group of friends, there's a full kitchen for self-catering, laundry, barbecue facilities and secure playground for children. Enjoy beautiful views, cosy fires and a breakfast basket of local goodies.

170 Oxley Flats Rd; (03) 5721 8195

QUALITY HOTEL WANGARATTA GATEWAY $$

This award-winning hotel is simply the best of its kind in town. After a recent major refurbishment and extension, accommodation is now offered in 76 suites and apartments, including 12 new luxury king-bedroom suites, an executive spa suite and a three-bedroom town house. Popular with corporate types and for weddings, it also has a state-of-the-art conference centre, functions area, well-regarded restaurant, lounge and wine bar, heated pool, sauna, spa and gym.

29–37 Ryley St; (03) 5721 8399; www.wangarattagateway.com.au

Warburton

CHARNWOOD COTTAGES $$$$

There are two country cottages designed for a romantic escape: Ella's Cottage has a four-poster queen-size bed, while Savannah's Cottage is furnished with a decorative wrought-iron queen-size bed. Both are fitted with a large double spa, kitchenette, gas log fire and spacious private balcony overlooking the upper Yarra River. Three-bedroom 100-year-old Jessica's Cottage is ideal for a family or group of friends. There's a tennis court on the property, pets are welcome, and the local restaurants and cafes are just over the 'suspension bridge' in front.

2 Wellington Rd; (03) 5966 2526

FORGET ME NOT COTTAGES $$$$

Set amid peaceful gardens with a meandering creek and waterfalls, these three themed stone cottages are designed indulgently for just one couple, with colourful decor and private outdoor hot spa. A self-contained water garden apartment has an indoor corner spa bath for two. Indoor log fires are cosy in winter, while barbecues offer casual dining in private courtyards. Slippers, towelling robes and toiletries all add to a feeling of wellbeing. Plus you can bring your dog – the cottages are pet-friendly.

18 Brett Rd; (03) 5966 5805; www.forgetmenotcottages.com.au

3 KINGS B&B $$$$$

These three apartments' weatherboard, country-style exterior belies the sleek, contemporary design and luxury fittings inside. You can relax in the spa bath, or in the comfortable lounge while warming yourself by the open fire and watching movies on the huge plasma TV. Double doors open into the spacious master bedroom and also out onto a private deck with views to Mount Donna Buang and Mount Ben Cairn. The kitchen is well equipped (including a coffee machine) for self-catering, with private barbecue facilities on each deck and a free-standing barbecue in the garden if entertaining guests. The apartments are a short stroll from the village of Yarra Junction.

2482 Warburton Hwy, Yarra Junction; 0409 678 046; www.3kingsbnb.com.au

Warrnambool

104 ON MERRI APARTMENTS $$$$

Map ref. p. 154

These six elegant and deluxe open-plan apartments are right by the Flagstaff Hill Maritime Village. Some of the apartments

WHERE TO STAY

sleep six, and they all have different colour schemes and furnishings. The luxury theme is a constant, and extends to bed linen and towels, and the granite or quartz benchtops. There are coffee machines, stainless-steel cooking appliances and wireless broadband. The main bathrooms have large spas and, if you plan on soaking a while, you might be glad of the spa-side TV. It is about a three-minute walk to the beach and the same distance to Warrnambool's CBD.

104 Merri St; 0448 668 738; www.104onmerri.com.au

AQUA OCEAN VILLAS $$$$

Map ref. p. 154

Ocean views, polished wood floors and tiles, plasma TVs, barbecues, decks, sleek lines, spas and even a double lock-up garage are part of this refined package. Park the car and you might never have to unlock the garage during your stay, as you can walk to the restaurants and the beach. All these self-contained apartments have three bedrooms and two bathrooms. The front two have courtyards as well as balconies; the two rear apartments have three storeys. Wireless internet is included in the tariff. If you're too transfixed by the view to leave your apartment for dinner, the owners have made arrangements with some Warrnambool eateries to deliver meals.

72 Merri St; (03) 5562 5600; www.aquaoceanvillas.com.au

FLAGSTAFF HILL LIGHTHOUSE LODGE $$$

Map ref. p. 154

After a day exploring the historic Flagstaff Hill Maritime Village, why not stay overnight in the original harbour master's house and continue the adventure? Painted in heritage cream and white, the 1909 Federation home is in a landscaped garden and overlooks the heritage-listed Lady Bay Lighthouses. Converted into three double bedrooms with ensuites, there is a communal kitchen for self-catering, a barbecue area, private courtyard, laundry facilities and a comfortable lounge where guests can mingle. Each room has a plasma-screen TV and wireless internet facility. Breakfast is available at the on-site Pippies by the Bay restaurant; the town's main restaurant precinct is a short stroll away. Various entertainment packages are available.

Merri St; (03) 5559 4600 or 1800 556 111; www.flagstaffhill.com

LOGANS BEACH SPA AND FITNESS $$$

Map ref. p. 154

The waters off Logans Beach are a nursery for whales and their calves, and watching their antics is a favourite pastime of winter visitors here, as the beach is just 400 metres from these comfortable and homely self-contained apartments. The loft, with a one-bedroom mezzanine suite, has an oval spa and barbecue facilities. The downstairs retreat is also self-contained but has two bedrooms. Both places are part of the Logans Beach Spa and Fitness complex, and guests have free use of the bath house, which includes a heated indoor swimming pool, saunas and hydrotherapy spa.

7 Logans Beach Rd; (03) 5561 3750; www.logansbeach.com.au

THE SEBEL DEEP BLUE WARRNAMBOOL $$$$

Map ref. p. 154

This couples retreat of 73 hotel rooms and six penthouse apartments, a couple of kilometres from the centre of Warrnambool, is sited on top of mineral-rich hot water. The naturally heated water is used for bathing in the day spa and is reticulated through the resort for heating. The rooms, some self-contained, come with generous balconies and views of either

Lady Bay or Stingray Bay, and all have a deluxe holiday house feel. They come with cable TV, broadband connections and tea- and coffee-making facilities, and guests get 50 per cent off treatments in the day spa. The Water Table restaurant is another of the resort's stars, where local regional produce is featured on the menu.

16 Pertobe Rd; (03) 5559 2000; www.mirvachotels.com/sebel-deep-blue-warrnambool

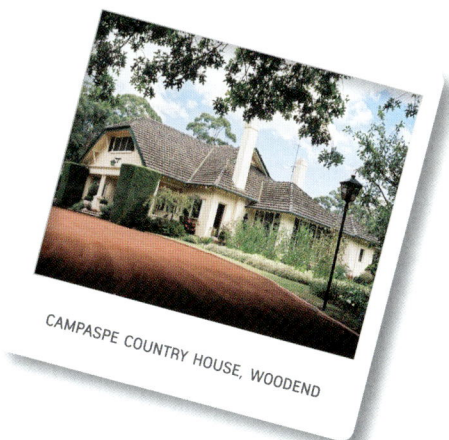

CAMPASPE COUNTRY HOUSE, WOODEND

Woodend

CAMPASPE COUNTRY HOUSE $$$$

Staying at this award-winning country retreat in the Macedon Ranges is like being a guest at a friend's country manor house. The welcome is warm, the ambience country perfect, with enough polish and style to know this is something special. Accommodation is upstairs in two bedrooms in the 1927-built Art Deco manor house, in a two-bedroom cottage or in 16 modern courtyard rooms overlooking a central heated swimming pool and natural bush beyond. The kitchen serves arguably the finest regional cuisine in the area, and has won many accolades for its innovative menus that champion the exceptional local produce. To linger over their indulgent buffet or à la carte breakfast is an absolute treat. Oh, and take a wander in the beautiful Edna Walling garden before leaving or stay on for high tea.

Goldies Lane; (03) 5427 2273; www.campaspehouse.com.au

HOLGATE BREWHOUSE $$$

Originally a Cobb & Co stopover between Melbourne and the goldfields of Bendigo, this imposing solid brick building has been refurbished by the current owners to offer stylish accommodation in 10 queen-size bedrooms, each with ensuites and views over the appealing township of Woodend or over to nearby Mount Macedon. Since this is primarily a brewery with a restaurant, there are dinner, bed and beer-tasting packages available, as well as a spa package linked with a day spa nearby.

79 High St; (03) 5427 2510; www.holgatebrewhouse.com

WOODBURY COTTAGE B&B $$

As cute as it gets, these converted stables make a charming country cottage. Self-contained, it nestles quietly on rambling country gardens in the foothills of beautiful Mount Macedon. Decorated in simple but fetching country style, it has a queen-size bedroom and an open fire, and is perfect for a couple wanting to escape the city. Woodbury was originally a dairy farm and horse stud, and today still offers scenes of bucolic bliss with wild ducks, grazing Suffolk sheep and beautiful views.

18 Jason Dr; (03) 5427 1876; www.woodburycottage.com.au

WHERE TO STAY

FITNESS CENTRE   ROOM SERVICE   SWIMMING POOL

Yackandandah

CREEK HAVEN COTTAGE $$

Surrounded by a beautiful garden on a 12-hectare property with creek frontage a few kilometres from Yackandandah, this self-contained cottage is set well away from the main homestead and offers accommodation for up to seven people in three bedrooms. It is air-conditioned for summer comfort, with an open fire for winter warmth, and front and back verandahs to take in the country landscapes all year round. It has its own laundry and barbecue facilities and pets are welcome by arrangement.

281 Osbornes Flat Rd; (02) 6027 1389; www.creekhaven.com.au

KARALILLA B&B $$$

Located just 5 kilometres from town, this traditional B&B is housed in a beautifully restored 1911 homestead surrounded by a beautiful cottage garden on 16 hectares in the tranquil Ben Valley. There are four in-house rooms: three have queen beds and one has twin beds. Two of the rooms have ensuites with private entrances, while the others have access off a central hallway. All have access to a lovely lounge with open fire and elegant dining room, where a hearty breakfast is served each morning.

271 Ben Valley La; (02) 6027 1788

Yarra Glen

ART AT LINDEN GATE $$$

Art lovers will especially relish the little touches that make a stay at these mud-brick and timber suites so special. After all, the property is the home of noted steel and stone sculptor Ernst Fries, who welcomes guests to his world. There are two suites overlooking a small home vineyard and a third gallery suite below – often earmarked for visiting artists. Earth-coloured walls with flashes of blue and yellow make a lovely background for original artworks. Each suite has a separate lounge, dining room and well-equipped kitchen, as well as a spa bath and cosy wood heater.

899 Healesville–Yarra Glen Rd; (03) 9730 1861

VALLEY GUEST HOUSE $$$

They are not even an hour from Melbourne, yet these six secluded suites could be hundreds of miles away. Situated in peaceful Steels Creek Valley, two hillside suites boast king-size beds with private balconies overlooking the garden that in spring is filled with tulips and daffodils. Each has a heated double spa, open fire, tea- and coffee-making facilities and bar fridge. The other four suites are in the main building: two are queen-size, two are king-size. All are beautifully furnished and perfect for short or long stays.

319 Steels Creek Rd; (03) 9730 1822; www.valleyguesthouse.com.au

CHATEAU YERING $$$$$

Hidden behind roadside cypress pines, this historic luxury hotel lies adjacent to the vast Yering Station winery complex. A graceful chateau built in the early 1850s, its entrance is framed by a picturesque garden, landscaped with tall established trees and beds of annuals and ornamental statuary. The interior combines opulence with comfort and tasteful furnishings and antiques. Rooms are beautifully appointed, with views over the Yarra Valley hills or the courtyard rose garden. Dining options include the sumptuously appointed Eleonore's Restaurant, and the light-filled, more casual Sweetwater Cafe. There is also a small bar and library, complete with leather lounge chairs and sofa.

42 Melba Hwy, Yering; (03) 9237 3333;
www.chateauyering.com.au

Yarrawonga

CLUB MULWALA $$$

Located on the edge of Lake Mulwala, this club offers accommodation in 60 motel-style rooms surrounded by hectares of landscaped gardens. There are four categories, from economy to executive. The best are the very private bank-side executive rooms, positioned to appreciate the beautiful sunrises and sunsets, and conveniently located adjacent to the resort's essenza spa. All rooms are air-conditioned, with flat-screen TVs, tea- and coffee-making facilities and minibars, and many have spas or spa baths. There is a guest laundry and communal barbecue facilities.

271 Melbourne St, Mulwala; (03) 5744 2331;
www.clubmulwala.com.au

YARRAWONGA & BORDER GOLF CLUB $$$

Claiming to have the largest public access of any golfing complex in Australia, this golf club does indeed offer a whopping 45 holes to master. Self-contained accommodation is available in 65 suites, apartments, villas or cabins – many with views over the golf course or bush setting. Suites are designed to sleep two, apartments sleep four, villas sleep six and standard cabins sleep three. A good option is one of the 42 suites with small lounge, bathroom and kitchenette for self-catering.

Gulai Rd, Mulwala; (03) 5744 1911;
www.yarragolf.com.au

Yea

CHEVIOT GLEN COTTAGES $$$

Located on a 170-hectare beef and sheep property in the Cheviot Hills near Yea, these two country cottages enjoy a peaceful aspect over the lovely countryside, with cattle and sheep grazing as far as the eye can see. Each has a queen-size bed, full kitchen, twin spa, futon couch, wood heater, TV, CD and DVD player, and they share laundry facilities. Breakfast facilities are provided so guests can dictate their own program.

175 Limestone Rd; (03) 5797 2617;
www.cheviotglencottages.com.au

291

Mildura
A20
Robinvale
A79
Ouyen
Swan Hill
Kerang
Nhill
A8
Warracknabeal
Charlton
Dimboola
Horsham
St Arnaud
Stawell
Maryborough
Bendigo
A200
Castlemaine
Ararat
Casterton
Coleraine
Ballarat
283
Hamilton
Heywood
A1
278
Terang
Geelong
Portland
Warrnambool
A1
Port Fairy
Colac
Tor
Lorne
286

280

288

Legend

Freeway, with toll	MELBOURNE ○ State capital city	✈ Airport
M31 23 Highway, sealed, with National Highway Route Marker	GEELONG ○ Major city/town	★ Lighthouse
M1 18 Highway, sealed, with National Route Marker	Cowes ○ Town	▲ Hill, mountain
A300 Highway, sealed, with State Route Marker	Hepburn Springs ○ Other population centres/localities	● Gorge, gap, pass, cave or saddle
Highway, unsealed	Karoonda Roadhouse Roadhouse	
3 Main road, sealed, with State Route Marker	GREAT OCEAN ROAD Place of interest	Maps are in a Lamberts Conformal Conic Projection
Main road, unsealed	Text entry in A to Z listing	
Other road	Lake, reservoir	Geocentric Datum Australia 1994 (GDA94)
Walking track	Intermittent lake	
Railway	National park	
45 Kilometres between points	Other reserve	
State border	Prohibited area	
Fruit fly exclusion zone boundary	Aboriginal/Torres Strait Islander land	

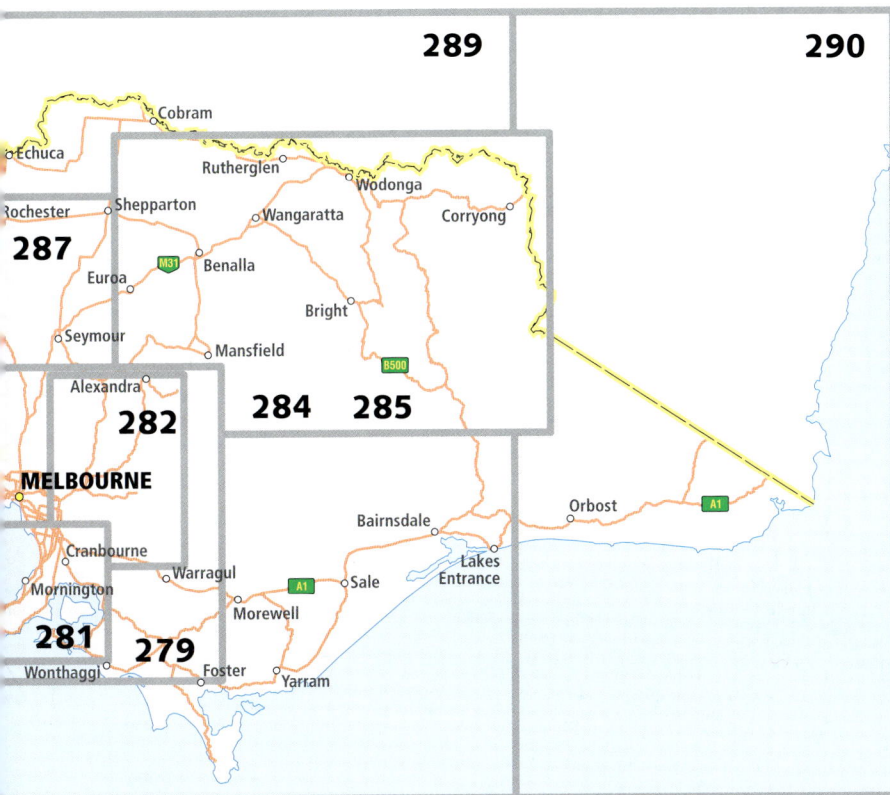

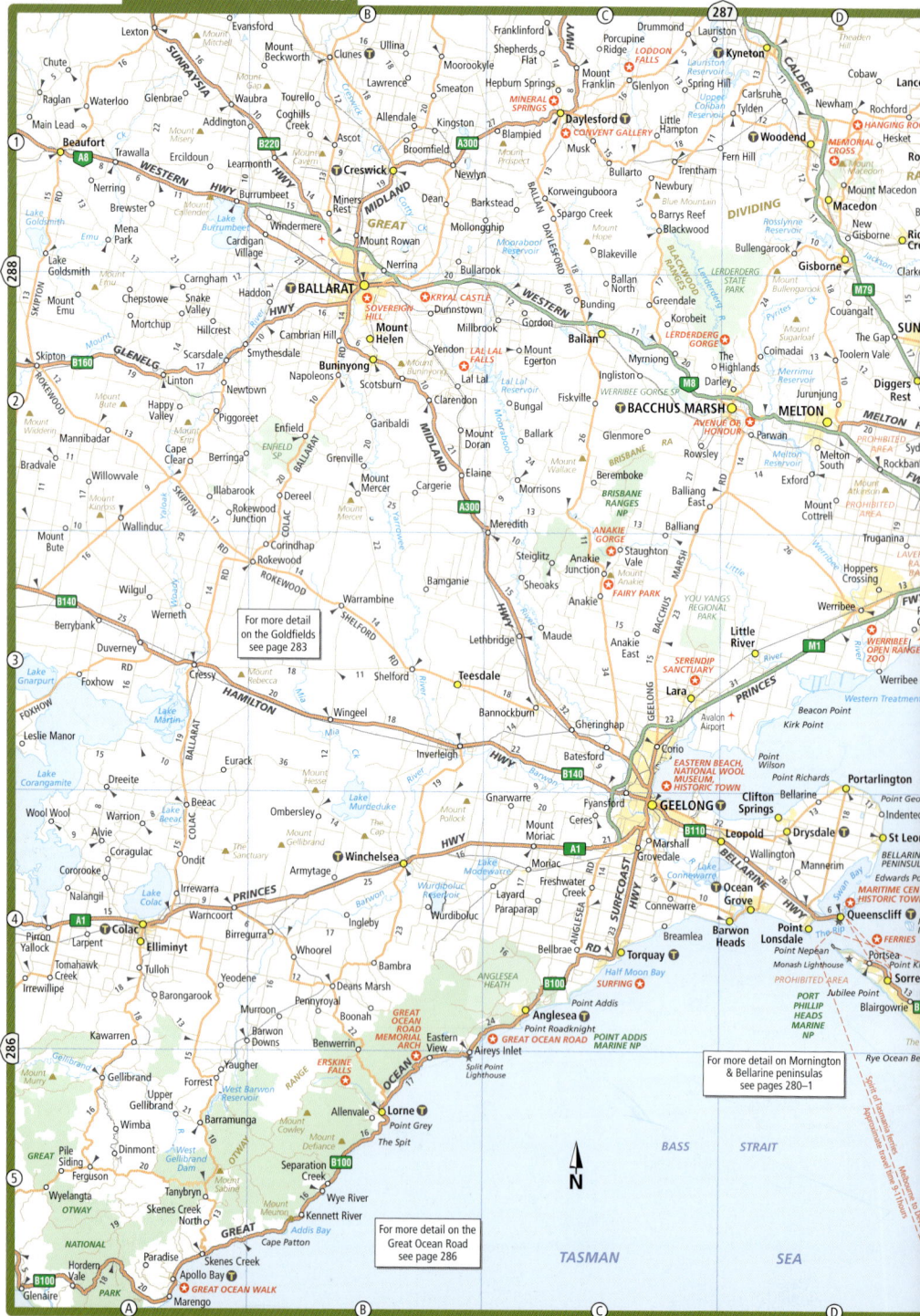

For more detail on the Goldfields see page 283

For more detail on Mornington & Bellarine peninsulas see pages 280–1

For more detail on the Great Ocean Road see page 286

N

BASS   STRAIT

TASMAN   SEA

Towns and localities (selected):

Lexton, Evansford, Franklinford, Porcupine Ridge, Drummond, Lauriston, Kyneton, Cobaw, Lance, Mount Mitchell, Mount Beckworth, Clunes, Ullina, Mooroolbark, Shepherds Flat, Hepburn Springs, Loddon Falls, Glenlyon, Spring Hill, Carlsruhe, Tylden, Newham, Rochford, Raglan, Waterloo, Glenbrae, Waubra, Tourello, Coghills Creek, Ascot, Lawrence, Smeaton, Kingston, Allendale, Mount Franklin, Daylesford, Convent Gallery, Musk, Little Hampton, Trentham, Fern Hill, Woodend, Hanging Rock, Hesket, Main Lead, Beaufort, Trawalla, Ercildoun, Learmonth, Creswick, Newlyn, Blampied, Mount Prospect, Bullarto, Newbury, Mount Macedon, Memorial Cross, Macedon, Gisborne

Chute, Addington, Mount Misery, Broomfield, Korweinguboora, Barrys Reef, Blackwood, Rosslynne Reservoir, New Gisborne, Ric Cre, Nerring, Brewster, Burrumbeet, Windermere, Nerrina, Bullarook, Dean, Barkstead, Millbrook, Spargo Creek, Greendale, Korobeit, Bullengarook, SUN

Ballarat, Sovereign Hill, Kryal Castle, Mount Helen, Buninyong, Dunnstown, Gordon, Ballan, Myrniong, The Highlands, Darley, Coimadai, Toolern Vale, Diggers Rest, Melton, Bacchus Marsh, Avenue of Honour, Parwan, Rowsley, Balliang, Exford, Mount Cottrell, Rockbank

Ballan North, Bunding, Ballan, Greenrake, Glenmore, Beremboke, Balliang East, Brisbane Ranges NP, Anakie Gorge, Staughton Vale, Anakie Junction, Fairy Park, Anakie, Sheoaks, Maude, Lethbridge, Teesdale, Shelford, Bannockburn, Gheringhap, Lara, Serendip Sanctuary, You Yangs Regional Park, Little River, Werribee, Werribee Open Range Zoo

Skipton, Linton, Scarsdale, Smythesdale, Napoleons, Scotsburn, Clarendon, Lal Lal, Yendon, Mount Egerton, Morrisons, Meredith, Steiglitz, Batesford, Fyansford, GEELONG, Corio, Eastern Beach National Wool Museum, Marshall, Grovedale, Portarlington, Clifton Springs, Drysdale, Leopold, Wallington, Mannerim, St Leon, Bellarine, Point Richards, Indented

Winchelsea, Moriac, Mount Moriac, Ceres, Freshwater Creek, Connewarre, Barwon Heads, Ocean Grove, Queenscliff, Point Lonsdale, Point Nepean, Portsea, Sorrento, Sorre, Blairgowrie, Port Phillip Heads Marine NP

Colac, Elliminyt, Irrewarra, Warncoort, Birregurra, Whoorel, Yeodene, Deans Marsh, Bambra, Bellbrae, Torquay, Jan Juc, Anglesea, Aireys Inlet, Eastern View, Point Addis, Point Roadknight, Great Ocean Road, Point Addis Marine NP, Half Moon Bay, Surfing

Gellibrand, Barwon Downs, Murroon, Pennyroyal, Benwerrin, Erskine Falls, Lorne, Point Grey, The Spit, Great Otway National Park, Forrest, Barramunga, Wimba, Dinmont, Tanybryn, Wye River, Kennett River, Separation Creek

Wyelangta, Ferguson, Skenes Creek North, Skenes Creek, Apollo Bay, Marengo, Cape Patton, Addis Bay, Great Ocean Walk, Paradise, Hordern Vale, Glenaire, Marengo

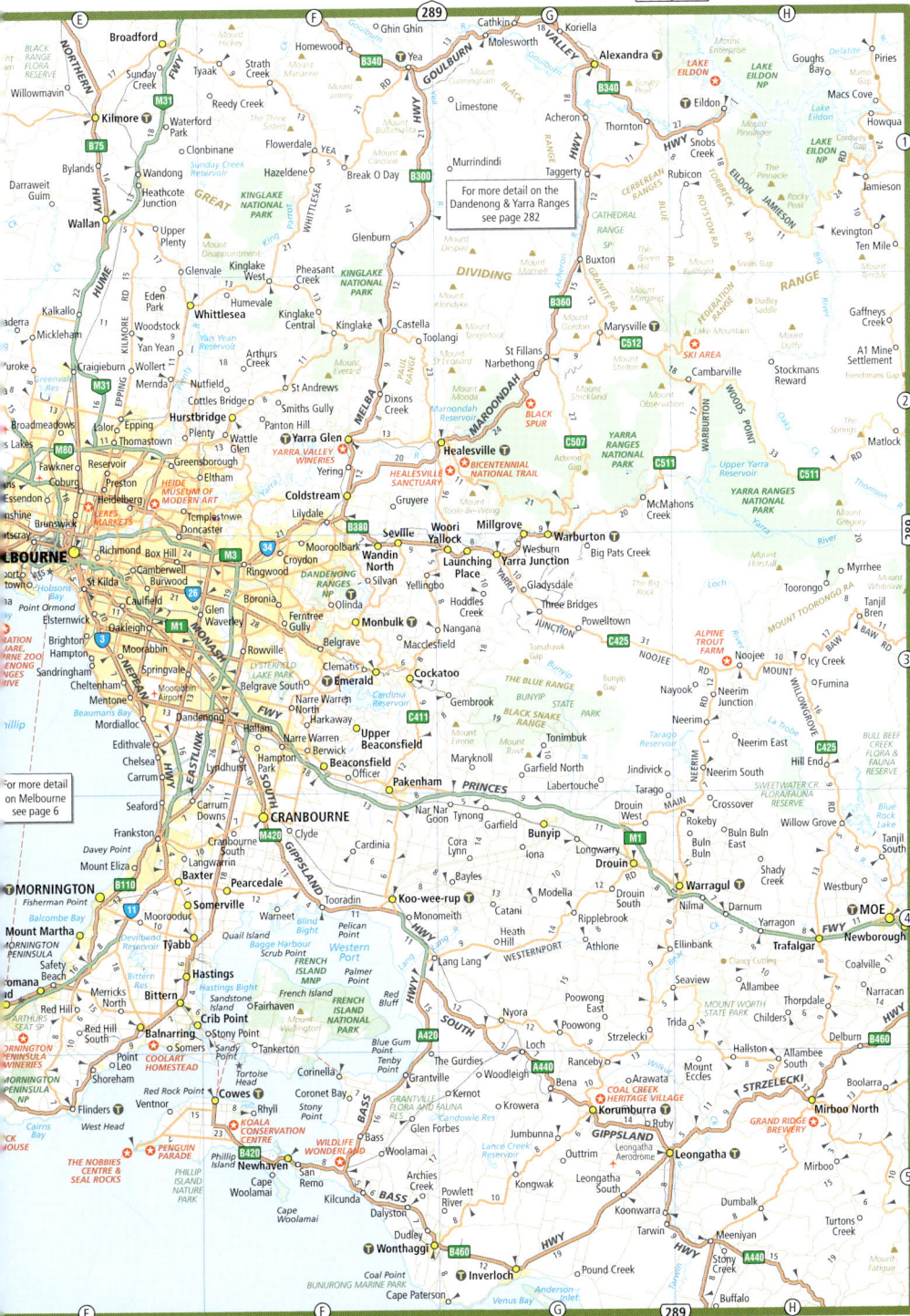

0 5 10 km

Grid references (top): E F 289 G H

Broadford
Ghin Ghin
Homewood
Yea
Cathkin
Molesworth
Koriella
GOULBURN VALLEY
Alexandra
Goughs
Piries
LAKE EILDON NP
LAKE EILDON
Macs Cove
Mount Hickey
Strath Creek
B340
B340
Limestone
Acheron
Eildon
Snobs Creek
LAKE EILDON NP
Howqua
Tyaak
Willowmavin
Sunday Creek
Kilmore
M31
Waterford Park
Reedy Creek
Murrindindi
Thornton
Rubicon
Jamieson
Clonbinane
Flowerdale
YEA
Break O Day
Taggerty
The Pinnacle
Rocky Peak
B75
Hazeldene
Kevington
Bylands
Wandong
Heathcote Junction
Sunday Creek Reservoir
B300
CERBERUS RANGES
Ten Mile
Darraweit Guim
Kalkallo
Upper Plenty
Glenburn
Marysville
C512
Gaffneys Creek
A1 Mine Settlement
Wallan
HUME
GREAT
KINGLAKE NATIONAL PARK
DIVIDING
Buxton
B360
SKI AREA
Cambarville
Stockmans Reward
Glenvale
Kinglake West
Humevale
Pheasant Creek
Kinglake
Castella
Toolangi
St Fillans
Narbethong
Matlock
Whittlesea
Kinglake Central
CATHEDRAL RANGE
RANGE
Eden Park
Woodstock
Yan Yean
Arthurs Creek
St Andrews
Dixons Creek
BLACK SPUR
YARRA RANGES NATIONAL PARK
Craigieburn
Wollert
Nutfield
Smiths Gully
MAROONDAH
C507
C511
Mernda
Cottles Bridge
Panton Hill
Yarra Glen
Healesville
BICENTENNIAL NATIONAL TRAIL
McMahons Creek
Upper Yarra Reservoir
C511
Hurstbridge
YARRA VALLEY WINERIES
Yering
HEALESVILLE SANCTUARY
Gruyere
YARRA RANGES NATIONAL PARK
Thomson
Epping
Plenty
Wattle Glen
Eltham
Coldstream
HEIDE MUSEUM OF MODERN ART
Greensborough
Lilydale
Warburton
Big Pats Creek
289
Reservoir
Preston
Heidelberg
Templestowe
Mooroolbark
Seville
Woori Yallock
Millgrove
Wesburn
Myrrhee
Richmond
Box Hill
Doncaster
Croydon
Launching Place
Yarra Junction
Toorongo
MELBOURNE
St Kilda
Camberwell
Burwood
M3
Ringwood
Wandin North
Silvan
Yellingbo
Gladysdale
Three Bridges
Point Ormond
Caulfield
Oakleigh
Boronia
DANDENONG RANGES NP
Ferntree Gully
Olinda
Hoddles Creek
Powelltown
ALPINE TROUT FARM
Noojee
Icy Creek
Glen Waverley
Monbulk
Nangana
C425
Fumina
Brighton
Moorabbin
Belgrave
Macclesfield
NOOJEE
Nayook
Neerim Junction
Sandringham
Springvale
Clematis
Emerald
Cockatoo
Gembrook
THE BLUE RANGE STATE PARK
Neerim
Mentone
Narre Warren North
Harkaway
Cardinia
BLACK SNAKE RANGE
BUNYIP STATE PARK
Neerim East
C425
Mordialloc
Dandenong
Hallam
Narre Warren
Berwick
Upper Beaconsfield
Maryknoll
Garfield North
Jindivick
Neerim South
BULL BEEF CREEK FLORA & FAUNA RESERVE
Chelsea
Hampton Park
Beaconsfield
Officer
Pakenham
PRINCES
Labertouche
Tarago
Carrum
EASTLINK
Lyndhurst
Nar Nar Goon
Tynong
Garfield
Drouin West
Rokeby
Willow Grove
Blue Rock Lake
Seaford
Carrum Downs
Clyde
Cardinia
Cora Lynn
Iona
Bunyip
Longwarry
M1
Drouin
Tanjil South
Frankston
Cranbourne South
Langwarrin
CRANBOURNE
M420
Bayles
Modella
Drouin South
Warragul
Darnum
Shady Creek
Westbury
MORNINGTON
Baxter
Pearcedale
Koo-wee-rup
Catani
Heath Hill
Ripplebrook
Nilma
Yarragon
MOE
Mount Eliza
Mooroduc
Somerville
Warneet
Tooradin
Monomeith
Athlone
Ellinbank
Trafalgar
Newborough
Davey Point
B110
Tyabb
Blind Bight
Pang Lang
WESTERNPORT
Poowong East
Seaview
Coalville
Mount Martha
Hastings
Quail Island
Bagge Harbour
FRENCH ISLAND MNP
Palmer Point
Nyora
Poowong
Trida
Thorpdale
Childers
Narracan
Merricks North
Bittern
FRENCH ISLAND NATIONAL PARK
Red Bluff
Loch
Strzelecki
MOUNT WORTH STATE PARK
Delburn
B460
Balnarring
Crib Point
Stony Point
Fairhaven
Blue Gum Tenby Point
The Gurdies
Woodleigh
Ranceby
Mount Eccles
Allambee South
Boolarra
Red Hill
Somers
Shoreham
Sandy Point
Tankerton
Corinella
Grantville
Kernot
Krowera
Bena
Arawata
COAL CREEK HERITAGE VILLAGE
Korumburra
STRZELECKI
Mirboo North
Cowes
Rhyll
Stony Point
Coronet Bay
GRANTVILLE FLORA AND FAUNA RES
Glen Forbes
Jumbunna
Ruby
GIPPSLAND
GRAND RIDGE BREWERY
Mirboo
KOALA CONSERVATION CENTRE
Bass
WILDLIFE WONDERLAND
Woolamai
Outtrim
Leongatha South
Leongatha
Newhaven
San Remo
Kilcunda
Anderson
Archies Creek
Powlett River
Kongwak
Koonwarra
Dumbalk
Turtons Creek
Wonthaggi
B460
BASS
Dalyston
Dudley
HWY
Koonwarra
Meeniyan
Stony Creek
A440
Inverloch
Pound Creek
Tarwin
Buffalo
Cape Paterson
BUNURONG MARINE PARK
Venus Bay

Grid references (bottom): E F 289 G H

278

C

D

Rothwell

SERENDIP SANCTUARY

Werribee South

M1 FWY

AVALON RACEWAY

Lara

Lara Lake

PRINCES

Avalon Airport

Lake Borrie

Western Treatment Plant

Beacon Point

Port Phillip

1

C141

Moorabool

RD

C704

Rosewall

Hovell Park

GEELONG BACCHUS MARSH

Kirk Point

LIMEBURNERS LAGOON NATURE RESERVE

WILDLIFE RESERVE

For more detail on Geelong see page 98

BALLAN

Corio

M1

Norlane

Bell Park

North Shore

Avalon

Point Lillias

Point Wilson

A10

MIDLAND

Geelong North

Drumcondra

Corio Bay

Outer   Harbour

Point Henry

Point Richards

Port Bellarine

Portarlington

A300

Fyansford

Stingaree Bay

EASTERN BEACH, NATIONAL WOOL MUSEUM, HISTORIC TOWN

Bellarine

RD

Point George

GEELONG

HAMILTON HWY

BUCKLEY FALLS

Geelong East

CLIFTON SPRINGS GOLF COURSE

C123

PORTARLINGTON GOLF COURSE

Indented Head

Indented Head

2

Highton

Belmont

Geelong South

Thomson

Breakwater

C123

Clifton Springs

CHANNEL

Drysdale

Murradoc

C125

St Leonards

B110

Moolap

GEELONG

PORTARLINGTON

BELLARINE PENINSULA RAILWAY

QUEENSCLIFF RD

Marshall

St Albans Park

Leopold

Curlewis

C126

LOWER BLUFF WILDLIFE RESERVE

Grovedale

WILDLIFE RESERVE

Lake Connewarre

ADVENTURE PARK

BELLARINE

PENINSULA

C121

Wallington

OCEAN GROVE RD

Mannerim

Edwards Point

Mount Dunned

BARWON HEADS

DRYSDALE

A MAZE 'N GAMES

Marcus

Swan

Duck Island

PORT PHILLIP HEADS MARINE NP

286

B100

Connewarre

C129

Fenwick

HWY

Marcus Hill

B110

Bay

MARITIME CENTRE, HISTORIC TOWN, BELLARINE PENINSULA RAILWAY

SURFCOAST

WILDLIFE RESERVE

JIRRAHLINGA KOALA & WILDLIFE RESERVE

Collendina

Lake Victoria

Queenscliff

SYMONDS CHANNEL

PORT PHILLP HEADS MARINE NP

Mud Islands

CHANNEL

Breamlea

Barwon Heads

BARWON HEADS GOLF CLUB

Ocean Grove

Barwon Head

Lonsdale Bay

BLACK LIGHTHOUSE, FORT QUEENSCLIFF, WHITE LIGHTHOUSE

PINNACE

3

SURFWORLD AUSTRALIA

Point Impossible

Point Lonsdale

Point Nepean

FERRIES

SOUTH

South Channel Island

Torquay

PORT PHILLIP HEADS MARINE NP

FORT NEPEAN

Observatory Point

CHANNEL

Point Danger MARINE SANCTUARY

Point Lonsdale

PORT PHILLIP HEADS MARINE NP

Monash Lighthouse

Portsea

Point King

SURFING

PROHIBITED AREA

LONDON BRIDGE

Sorrento

COLLINS SETTLEMENT HISTORIC SITE

Capel Sound

MCCRAE HOMES EASTERN LIGHTH

MORNINGTON

PENINSULA

Jubilee Point

B110

Blairgowrie

Rosebud

NATIONAL

For more detail on Sorrento see page 144

NEPEAN

Rye

Tootgarook

11

ROSEBUD COUNTRY CLUB

PARK

ROSEBUD FLINDERS RD

MORNIN PENIN.

4

N

POINT

Rye Ocean Beach

Saint Andrews Beach

MORNINGTON

Boneo

Fingal

MORN PENI

NEPEAN

PENINSULA

C777

Gunnamatta Beach

NATIONAL

Cape S

Spirit of Tasmania ferries
Approximate travel time 9-11 hours

PARK

CAPE SCHANCK LIGHTHOUSE

Cape Schanck

5

BASS

STRAIT

A

B

C

D

0   2   4 km

CRANBOURNE

MORNINGTON

PAKENHAM

Beaconsfield

Emerald · Lakeside

Cockatoo

Avonsleigh

Clematis

Belgrave South

Narre Warren North

Narre Warren East

Upper Beaconsfield

Officer

Fountain Gate

Harkaway

Berwick

Hampton Park

Narre Warren

Cranbourne North

Cranbourne West

Clyde North

Clyde

Cranbourne South

Cardinia

Fiveways

Dalmore

Koo-wee-rup

Koo-wee-rup North

Pakenham South

Monomeith

Caldermeade

Lang Lang

Lang Lang Beach

Red Bluff
Jam Jerrup

Grantville

Queensferry

Coronet Bay

Tenby Point

Corinella

Almurta

Glen Forbes

Bass

Bass Landing

Woolamai

Kilcunda

Dalyston

Ryanston

Archies Creek

Anderson

San Remo

Newhaven

Woolamai Waters

Cape Woolamai

Smiths Beach Estate

Surf Beach Estate

Cowes

Silverleaves

Rhyll

Ventnor

Summerland

Point Leo

Shoreham

Flinders

Balnarring

Somers

Red Hill

Merricks

Hastings

Bittern

Crib Point

Stony Point

Tankerton

Fairhaven

FRENCH ISLAND NATIONAL PARK

Tyabb

Somerville

Pearcedale

Tooradin

Baxter

Langwarrin

Devon Meadows

Frankston

Seaford

Carrum Downs

Mornington

Mount Martha

Balcombe

Mooroolbark

Mornington

Dromana

Rosebud

Cheltenham

Mentone

Beaumaris

Mordialloc

Aspendale

Edithvale

Chelsea

Bonbeach

Carrum

Parkdale

Braeside

Noble Park

Dingley Village

Springvale

Heatherton

Dandenong

Dandenong South

Doveton

Endeavour Hills

Eumemmerring

Hallam

Lyndhurst

PHILLIP ISLAND

WESTERN PORT

For more detail on Cowes see page 82

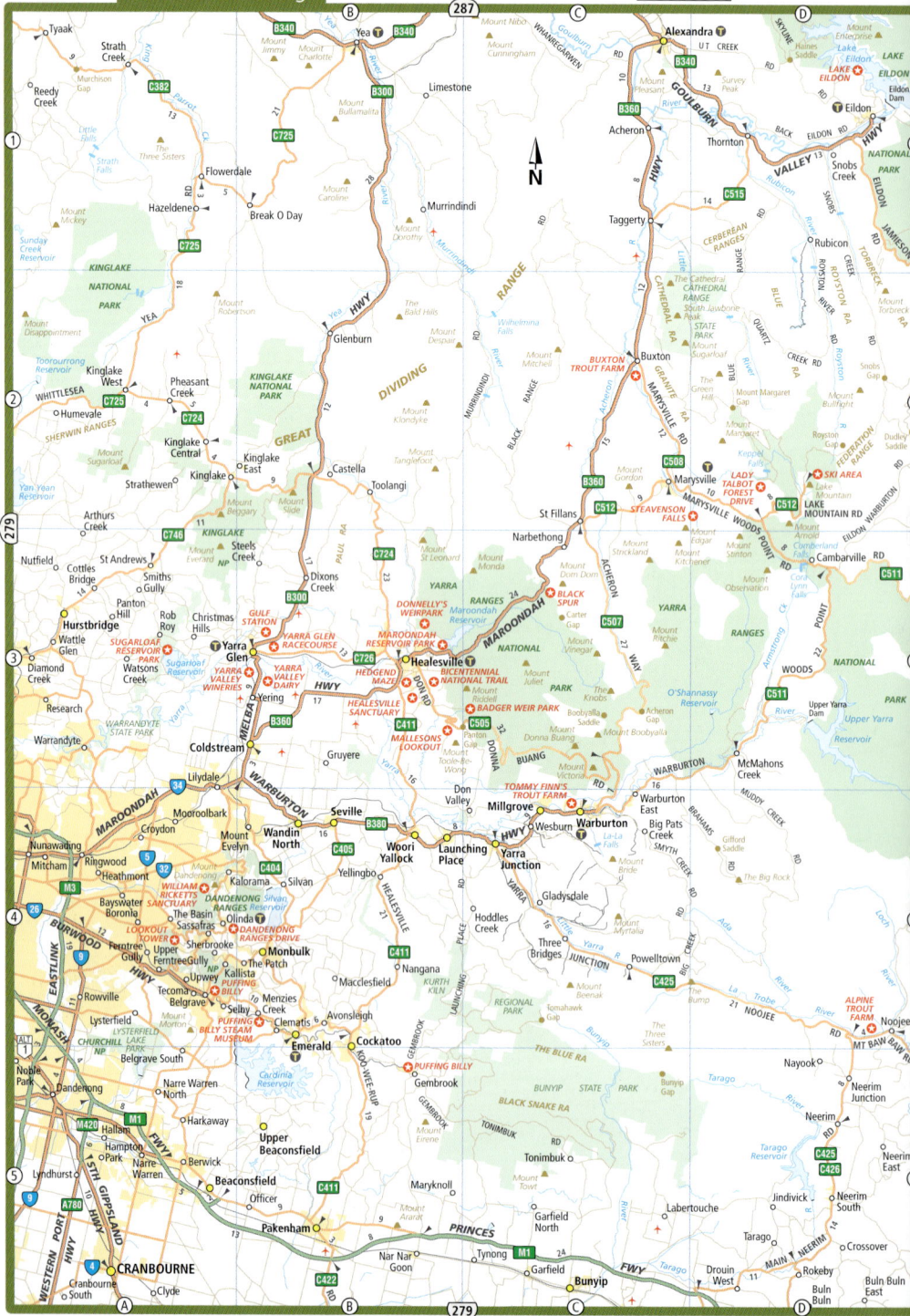

0   4   8 km

N

Tyaak
Strath Creek
Reedy Creek
Murchison Gap
C382
Little Falls
Strath Falls
The Three Sisters
Flowerdale
Hazeldene
Break O Day
Mount Mickey
Sunday Creek Reservoir
KINGLAKE NATIONAL PARK
C725
C725
Mount Roberton
Mount Disappointment
Mount Sugarloaf
Toorourrong Reservoir
Yan Yean Reservoir
WHITTLESEA
Humevale
SHERWIN RANGES
Kinglake West
Pheasant Creek
Kinglake Central
Kinglake
Strathewen
Kinglake East
C725
C724
C724
KINGLAKE NATIONAL PARK
Mount Beggary
Mount Slide
GREAT
Castella
Toolangi
Arthurs Creek
Nutfield
Cottles Bridge
St Andrews
Smiths Gully
Panton Hill
Rob Roy
Christmas Hills
C746
Steels Creek
Dixons Creek
Mount Everard
PAUL RA
NP
Hurstbridge
Wattle Glen
Diamond Creek
Research
Warrandyte
Nunawading
Mitcham
Ringwood
Heathmont
Bayswater
Boronia
M3
BURWOOD
EASTLINK
Ferntree Gully
Rowville
Lysterfield
Noble Park
Dandenong
Hallam
Hampton Park
Narre Warren
Lyndhurst
CRANBOURNE
Cranbourne South
Clyde
Mount Jimmy
Mount Charlotte
Yea
B340
B340
287
B300
Limestone
Mount Bullamalita
Mount Caroline
Murrindindi
Mount Dorothy
Mount Despair
YEA HWY
Glenburn
The Bald Hills
DIVIDING
RANGE
Mount Klandyte
Mount Tanglefoot
St Fillans
Narbethong
Mount St Leonard
Mount Monda
YARRA
RANGES
Donnelly's Weirpark
Maroondah Reservoir
BLACK SPUR
MAROONDAH NATIONAL
Gulf Station
Yarra Glen Racecourse
C726
C724
B300
Yarra Glen
Yering
Healesville
Hedgend Maze
Healesville Sanctuary
Badger Weir Park
C411
Mallesons Lookout
C505
C507
Coldstream
Lilydale
Mooroolbark
Croydon
Mount Evelyn
Wandin North
Seville
Woori Yallock
Launching Place
Gruyere
Don Valley
Millgrove
Warburton
Warburton East
C405
C404
Kalorama
Silvan
Yellingbo
Yarra Junction
Gladysdale
WILLIAM RICKETTS SANCTUARY
DANDENONG RANGES NP
DANDENONG RANGES DRIVE
The Basin
Sassafras
Olinda
Sherbrooke
Monbulk
Nangana
Macclesfield
Hoddles Creek
Three Bridges
Powelltown
C425
Upper Ferntree Gully
The Patch
Kallista
Tecoma
Belgrave
Selby
Menzies Creek
Avonsleigh
Puffing Billy Steam Museum
Emerald
Cockatoo
Clematis
Gembrook
C411
NOOJEE
ALPINE TROUT FARM
Noojee
MT BAW BAW RD
Nayook
Belgrave South
Narre Warren North
Harkaway
Berwick
Upper Beaconsfield
Maryknoll
Gembrook
REGIONAL PARK
KURTH KILN
BLACK SNAKE RA
BUNYIP STATE PARK
TONIMBUK
Tonimbuk
Neerim
Neerim Junction
Neerim South
Neerim East
C425
C426
Beaconsfield
Officer
Pakenham
C411
C422
Nar Nar Goon
Tynong
M1
Garfield North
Garfield
Bunyip
Mount Ararat
PRINCES FWY
Labertouche
Jindivick
Tarago
Drouin West
Rokeby
Crossover
Buln Buln
Buln Buln East
Alexandra
B340
B360
GOULBURN VALLEY HWY
Acheron
Thornton
Eildon
LAKE EILDON NATIONAL PARK
Snobs Creek
Taggerty
Buxton
BUXTON TROUT FARM
C515
CERBEREAN RANGES
Rubicon
Cambarville
C511
Marysville
C508
C512
STEAVENSON FALLS
LADY TALBOT FOREST DRIVE
SKI AREA
MOUNT LAKE MOUNTAIN RD
C512
FEDERATION RANGE
YARRA RANGES NATIONAL PARK
WOODS POINT RD
O'Shannassy Reservoir
Upper Yarra Reservoir
McMahons Creek
C511
Big Pats Creek
WARBURTON
The Big Rock
Mount Bride
Mount Boobyalla
Mount Donna Buang
MONASH FWY
M1
5TH GIPPSLAND HWY

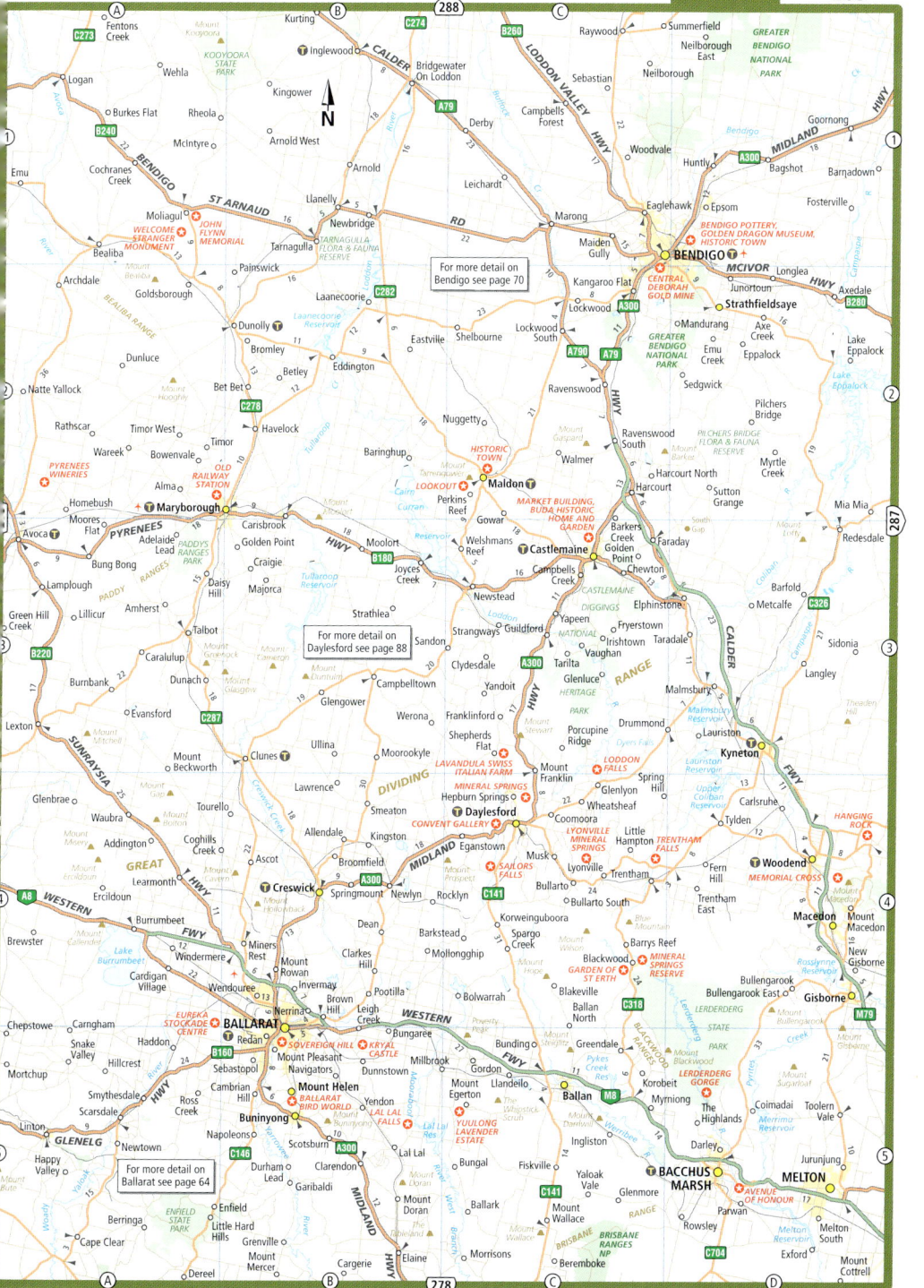

For more detail on Bendigo see page 70

For more detail on Daylesford see page 88

For more detail on Ballarat see page 64

0 5 10 km

N

BENDIGO

BALLARAT

BACCHUS MARSH

MELTON

GISBORNE

KYNETON

WOODEND

MACEDON

CASTLEMAINE

MARYBOROUGH

DAYLESFORD

CRESWICK

BALLAN

STRATHFIELDSAYE

MALDON

EUREKA STOCKADE CENTRE

SOVEREIGN HILL

KRYAL CASTLE

BALLARAT BIRD WORLD

LAL LAL FALLS

YUULONG LAVENDER ESTATE

CONVENT GALLERY

LAVANDULA SWISS ITALIAN FARM

HEPBURN SPRINGS

SAILORS FALLS

LYONVILLE MINERAL SPRINGS

TRENTHAM FALLS

HANGING ROCK

AVENUE OF HONOUR

MEMORIAL CROSS

GARDEN OF ST ERTH

MINERAL SPRINGS RESERVE

HISTORIC TOWN

LOOKOUT

MARKET BUILDING, BUDA HISTORIC HOME AND GARDEN

OLD RAILWAY STATION

WELCOME STRANGER MONUMENT

JOHN FLYNN MEMORIAL

CENTRAL DEBORAH GOLD MINE

BENDIGO POTTERY, GOLDEN DRAGON MUSEUM, HISTORIC TOWN

GREATER BENDIGO NATIONAL PARK

CASTLEMAINE DIGGINGS NATIONAL HERITAGE PARK

PYRENEES WINERIES

GREAT DIVIDING RANGE

KOOYOORA STATE PARK

TARNAGULLA FLORA & FAUNA RESERVE

ENFIELD STATE PARK

BRISBANE RANGES NP

PILCHERS BRIDGE FLORA & FAUNA RESERVE

PADDYS RANGES PARK

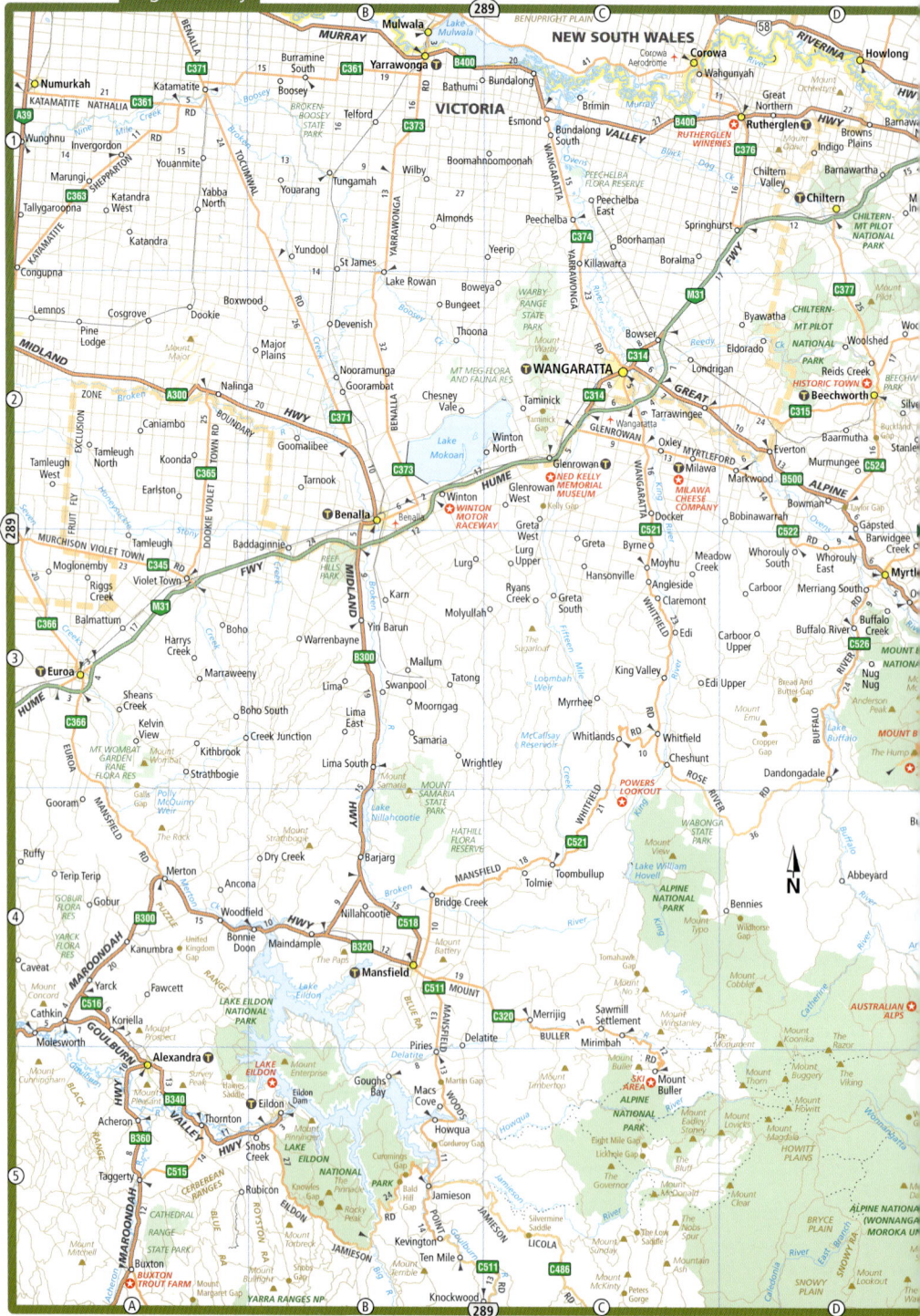

NEW SOUTH WALES

VICTORIA

RIVERINA

MURRAY

Lake Mulwala

Mulwala Yarrawonga Corowa Howlong Wahgunyah

Rutherglen RUTHERGLEN WINERIES Chiltern CHILTERN–MT PILOT NATIONAL PARK

WANGARATTA NED KELLY MEMORIAL MUSEUM Beechworth HISTORIC TOWN

Glenrowan Milawa MILAWA CHEESE COMPANY

Benalla WINTON MOTOR RACEWAY

Euroa

Hume Midland Hwy

Mansfield Merrijig Mt Buller SKI AREA

LAKE EILDON NATIONAL PARK Lake Eildon

Alexandra Eildon BUXTON TROUT FARM

ALPINE NATIONAL PARK

AUSTRALIAN ALPS

POWERS LOOKOUT

SNOWY PLAIN

N

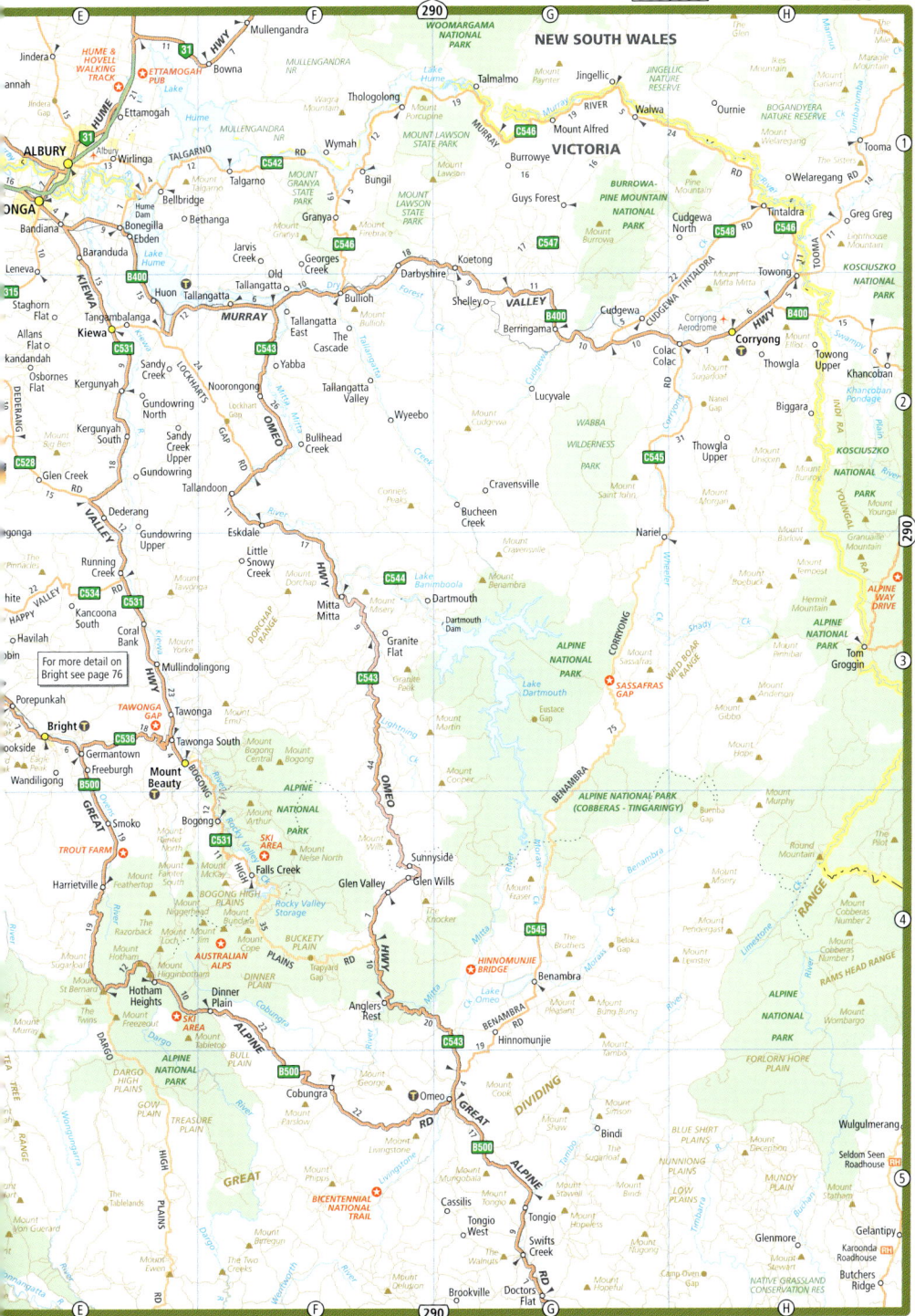

NEW SOUTH WALES

VICTORIA

ALBURY

Bright

Mount Beauty

Falls Creek

Hotham Heights

Dinner Plain

Omeo

Corryong

Dartmouth

MURRAY VALLEY

OMEO HWY

GREAT ALPINE RD

ALPINE NATIONAL PARK

KOSCIUSZKO NATIONAL PARK

Tallangatta

Cudgewa

Nariel

Bogong High Plains

BENAMBRA

For more detail on Bright see page 76

5   10 km

0 5 10 km

Map — Great Ocean Road region (Victoria)

Pomborneit North, Wool Wool, Lake Corangamite, Lake Beeac, Ombersley, The Cap, Mount Gellibrand, Mount Pleasant, Ceres, Belmont, Thomson, Moolap, ADVENTURE PARK

Pomborneit, Alvie, Warrion, C146, Ondit, The Sanctuary, Armytage, C145, HWY, Mount Moriac, Mount Moriac, Waurn Ponds, Marshall, Grovedale, Leopold

RED ROCK LOOKOUT, Vaughan Island, Herring Point, Coragulac, Salt Lake, Winchelsea, Buckley, Moriac, A1, B100, Wallington

Pomborneit East, Cororooke, Balintore, Irrewarra, Lake Modewarre, Freshwater Creek, C121, Conneware, Ocean Grove

Stoneyford, Nalangil, Warncoort, Ingleby, Layard, Modewarre, Paraparap, Bellbrae, Breamlea, Barwon Heads

PRINCES, Colac, Birregurra, Wurdiboluc, C134, JIRRALINGA KOALA & WILDLIFE RESERVE, Barwon Head

A1, Pirron Yallock, Larpent, Elliminyt, C152, Whoorel, Bambra, SURFWORLD AUSTRALIA, Half Moon Bay, SURFING

Bungador, Swan Marsh, Tulloh, Yeodene, Deans Marsh, Boonah, ANGLESEA HEATH, Bells Beach

Irrewillipe, Barongarook West, Coram, C155, Pennyroyal, Point Addis, Ingoldsby Reefs

C163, Tomahawk Creek, Barongarook, Murroon, Anglesea, Soapy Rock, Point Roadknight, POINT ADDIS MARINE NATIONAL PARK

BURTONS LOOKOUT, Kawarren, C154, Barwon Downs, Gerangamete, Memorial Arch, Eastern View, Eagle Nest Reef, Split Point Lighthouse

Kincaid, Gellibrand, Yaugher, Forrest, ERSKINE FALLS, Benwerrin, Aireys Inlet, Loutit Bay

Carlisle River, Upper Gellibrand, Barramunga, West Barwon Reservoir, Mount Cowley, Allenvale, Lorne, Point Grey, GREAT OCEAN ROAD

Mount Mackenzie, Wimba, Dinmont, GREAT OTWAY, Mount Sabine, Mount Saint George, The Spit, The Brothers

Chapple Vale, Weeaproinah, Pile Siding, Ferguson, West Gellibrand Dam, NATIONAL, Separation Creek, Wye River

C156, Wyelangta, Beech Forest, PARK, Wye River, Point Sturt

C155, Lavers Hill, C119, Tanybryn, Kennett River, Point Hawdon

Wangerrip, B100, CROWS NEST LOOKOUT, MARRINERS LOOKOUT, Skenes Creek North, Cape Patton, Addis Bay

Johanna, GREAT, Hordern Vale, Paradise, Skenes Creek, Apollo Bay, GREAT OCEAN WALK

Johanna Beach, Glenaire, MAITS REST, Marengo, The Blowhole, Mounts Bay

Rotten Point, NATIONAL, C157, PARK, Point Lewis, Blanket Bay

Point Flinders, CAPE OTWAY LIGHTHOUSE, Cape Otway, Point Franklin

BASS STRAIT

TASMAN SEA

For more detail on Geelong see page 280

Joins map below

Lower map

288, Kirkstall, SPENCER, RD, Koroit, Southern Cross, C174, Grassmere, Framlingham, Terang, C156, Naroghid, Lake Bullen Merri, Camperdown, Weerite

Yambuk, C184, Toolong, Tower Hill, Mailors Flat, HOPKINS, Purnim, PRINCES, Garvoc, Dixie, Cobrico, C164, Bostock Creek, Tesbury, HWY

Rosebrook, Killarney, Tower Hill, Woodford, Wangoom, Bushfield, Cudgee, Panmure, Mount, Laang, Mumblin, Cobden, C149, Tandarook

Cape Reamur, Port Fairy, Sisters Point, Dennington, B120, Allansford, Naringal, WARRNAMBOOL, Ecklin South, Elingamite, Jancourt, Jancourt East, Carpendeit

PORT FAIRY BEACH, WHALES, Middle Island, Lady Bay, HWY, COBDEN, Mepunga East, Ayrford, Glenfyne, Scotts Creek, CARPENDEIT FLORA & FAUNA RESERVE

For more detail on Warrnambool see page 154, Middle Island, BAY OF, Mepunga West, GREAT, Nullawarre, Brucknell, Timboon, Cowleys Creek, C163

ISLANDS, Childers Cove, The Cove, C163, Nirranda, Curdies, Lower Heytesbury, Newfield, Simpson

Buttress Point, Springvale, Nirranda South, Curdie Vale, Paaratte, C164, COORIEMUNGLE CREEK FLORA RESERVE

COASTAL, Bay of Islands, OCEAN, Bay of Martyrs, Peterborough, Port Campbell, Waarre, Newfield, Kennedys Creek, C156

PARK, Newfield Bay, LONDON BRIDGE, THE ARCH, Sentinel Rock, Broken Head, GREAT OCEAN WALK, PORT CAMPBELL NATIONAL PARK, Devondale

SOUTHERN, Mutton Bird Island, LOCH ARD GORGE, THE TWELVE APOSTLES, GIBSON STEPS, Princetown, Point Ronald, GREAT OTWAY NP, Yuulong, Mount Alcand

OCEAN, TWELVE APOSTLES MARINE NATIONAL PARK, Pebble Point, Lower Gellibrand, RD, Wattle Hill

Moonlight Beach, The Gable, Moonlight Head, Point Reginald

N

0 10 20 km

289
B75
A300
A39
A300
HWY

MIDLAND

SHEPPARTON
Mooroopna
Merrigum
Dookie
Cosgrove
Nalinga
Caniambo
Gowangardie

Serpentine
Glenalbyn
Salisbury West
Kurting
Inglewood
Kingower
Arnold
Llanelly
Newbridge
Tarnagulla
Dunolly
Bromley
Eddington
Bet Bet
Havelock
Baringhup

Tandarra
Drummartin
Kamarooka
Summerfield
Neilborough
Campbells Forest
Goornong
Elmore
Raywood

FRUIT FLY EXCLUSION ZONE
Corop
Byrneset
Stanhope
Colbinabbin West
Colbinabbin
Wanalta
Rushworth
Murchison East
Murchison
Moorilim

Girgarre
Tatura
Kialla
Kialla West
Toolamba
Arcadia
Mooroopna

BENDIGO
HISTORIC TOWN
Epsom
Eaglehawk
Maiden Gully
Strathfieldsaye

B260
B240
A79
CALDER HWY
LODDON VALLEY HWY
MCIVOR HWY

Euroa
Harston
Wahring
Nagambie
Graytown
Tabilk
Locksley
Monea
Avenel
Mangalore

Maryborough
HISTORIC TOWN
Maldon
Castlemaine
Carisbrook
Craigie
Majorca
Strathlea

Seymour
Whiteheads Creek
Trawool
Kerrisdale
Tallarook

BALLARAT
Mount Helen
Buninyong
Scotsburn

BACCHUS MARSH
MELTON
SUNBURY
Diggers Rest
Gisborne

MELBOURNE
GEELONG
HISTORIC TOWN

Werribee
Little River
Lara
Corio

PORT PHILLIP

MORNINGTON
Mount Martha
Dromana
Rosebud
Rye
Sorrento
Portsea
Blairgowrie
Balnarring
Flinders

CRANBOURNE
Pakenham
Berwick
Koo-wee-rup
Warragul
Drouin
Leongatha
Wonthaggi
Inverloch

PHILLIP ISLAND
PENGUIN PARADE
Cowes
Newhaven
San Remo
Cape Woolamai

BASS STRAIT

N

For more detail on the Melbourne & surrounds see pages 278–279

SOUTH AUSTRALIA | VICTORIA

BIG DESERT WILDERNESS PARK
WYPERFELD NATIONAL PARK

Major towns and places:

Bordertown, Nhill, Dimboola, Horsham, Natimuk, Stawell, Ararat, Beaufort, Ballarat, Mount Helen, Buninyong, Geelong, Winchelsea, Colac, Camperdown, Cobden, Warrnambool, Port Fairy, Portland, Heywood, Casterton, Coleraine, Hamilton, Dunkeld, Halls Gap, Maryborough, Castlemaine, Maldon, Bendigo, Charlton, Donald, St Arnaud, Birchip, Warracknabeal, Hopetoun, Lascelles, Boigbeat, Berriwillock, Kerang, Koondrook, Cohuna

THE GRAMPIANS
GRAMPIANS NATIONAL PARK
LITTLE DESERT NATIONAL PARK
WIMMERA
MALLEE
MOUNT ECCLES NP
LOWER GLENELG NATIONAL PARK
DISCOVERY BAY
GREAT SOUTH WEST WALK
CAPE NELSON LIGHTHOUSE
GREAT OTWAY NATIONAL PARK
CAPE OTWAY LIGHTHOUSE
THE TWELVE APOSTLES
PORT CAMPBELL NP
GREAT OCEAN ROAD
GREAT OCEAN WALK

CALDER HWY
SUNRAYSIA HWY
BORUNG HWY
WESTERN HWY
HENTY HWY
GLENELG HWY
HAMILTON HWY
PRINCES HWY
GREAT OCEAN RD
PYRENEES HWY

SOUTHERN OCEAN

BASS STRAIT

For more detail on Great Ocean Road see page 286

10 20 km

E   F   G   H

NEW SOUTH WALES

VICTORIA

MELBOURNE

GIPPSLAND

Deniliquin · Mayrung · Logie Brae · Blighty · Finley · Berrigan · Oaklands · Daysdale · Rand · Five Ways · Urangeline East · Yerong Creek · Mangoplah · Burrandana · Tarcutta

Caldwell · Bunnaloo · Mathoura · Womboota · Moira · Picola · Barmah · Katunga · Tocumwal · Koonoomoo · Barooga · Savernake · Coreen · Walbundrie · Lowesdale · Brocklesby · Burrumbuttock · Rennie · Gerogery · Culcairn · Morven · Cookardinia · Little Billabong · Kyeamba · Humula · Carabost

Moama · Kanyapella · Nathalia · Numurkah · Yarrawonga · Mulwala · Corowa · Howlong · Jindera · Table Top · Bowna · Talmalmo · Jingellic · Walwa

ECHUCA · Rochester · Kyabram · Mooroopna · **SHEPPARTON** · Rutherglen · **WODONGA** · **ALBURY** · Bandiana · Bonegilla · Kiewa · Tangambalanga · **CORRYONG** · Colac Colac

Elmore · Tongala · Tatura · Benalla · Chiltern · Springhurst · Barnawartha · Baranduda · Tallangatta · Berringama

Heathcote · Nagambie · Euroa · **WANGARATTA** · Beechworth · Yackandandah · Kergunyah · Nooroongong · Lucyvale

Puckapunyal · Seymour · Longwood · Violet Town · Winton · Milawa · Myrtleford · Dederang · Eskdale · Mitta Mitta · Dartmouth · Nariel

Broadford · Avenel · Strathbogie · Whitfield · Cheshunt · **Bright** · Wandiligong · **Mount Beauty** · Bogong · Falls Creek · Glen Wills · Glen Valley · Benambra

Kilmore · Romsey · Wallan · Alexandra · Eildon · Mansfield · Merrijig · Mirimbah · Mt Buller · Howqua · Hotham Heights · Dinner Plain · Anglers Rest · Cobungra · Omeo · Hinnomunjie · Bindi

SUNBURY · Whittlesea · Healesville · Marysville · Matlock · Woods Point · Licola · Dargo · Cassilis · Tongio · Swifts Creek · Ensay North · Ensay

MELBOURNE · Coburg · Ringwood · Warburton · Aberfeldy · Cobbannah · Castleburn · Deptford · Tambo Crossing · Bruthen

Werribee · Lilydale · Coldstream · Woori Yallock · Millgrove · Toorongo · Beardmore · Glenmaggie · Valencia Creek · Bullumwaal

Portarlington · Emerald · Cockatoo · Upper Beaconsfield · Neerim · Erica · Walhalla · Boisdale · Maffra · Briagolong · **BAIRNSDALE** · Metung · Lakes Entrance

CRANBOURNE · Pakenham · Bunyip · Drouin · Warragul · Yallourn North · Toongabbie · Heyfield · Stratford · Perry Bridge · Meerlieu · Paynesville

MORNINGTON · Baxter · Pearcedale · Somerville · Koo-wee-rup · **MOE** · Trafalgar · **MORWELL** · **TRARALGON** · Rosedale · Longford · Kilmany · Fulham · **SALE** · Dutson · Seacombe · Golden Beach · Paradise Beach

Sorrento · Dromana · Hastings · Lang Lang · Poowong · Allambee South · Churchill · Gormandale · Willung · Le Roy · Stradbroke · Ninety Mile Beach · Seaspray · Flamingo Beach

Rye · Rosebud · Cowes · Newhaven · **Korumburra** · Ranceby · Mirboo North · Boolarra · Carrajung · Balook · Won Wron · Giffard · Woodside Beach

PHILLIP ISLAND · San Remo · Kongwak · **Leongatha** · Meeniyan · Dumbalk · Madalya · Devon North · Yarram · Alberton · Darriman · Woodside

Wonthaggi · Inverloch · Fish Creek · **Foster** · Toora · Welshpool · Port Albert · Manns Beach · McLoughlins Beach

Cape Woolamai · Cape Paterson · Venus Bay · Tarwin Lower · Waratah North · Port Welshpool · **NOORAMUNGA MARINE & COASTAL PARK**

Walkerville · Cape Liptrap · Waratah Bay · Grinder Point · Yanakie · Townsend Point

WILSONS PROMONTORY NATIONAL PARK · Tidal River · Oberon Point · South East Point

TASMAN SEA

BASS STRAIT

N

0   10   20 km

Boxed notes

For more detail on Bright see page 76

For more detail on Lakes Entrance see pages 112–3

Water bodies

TASMAN SEA

BASS STRAIT

N

Major towns and places

CANBERRA, QUEANBEYAN, ACT, ALBURY, WODONGA, BAIRNSDALE, SALE, Cooma, Holbrook, Culcairn, Tumbarumba, Corryong, Bright, Mount Beauty, Omeo, Orbost, Eden, Merimbula, Bega, Bombala, Batemans Bay, Moruya, Narooma, Dalmeny, Tathra, Tura Beach, Pambula Beach, Bermagui, Tilba Tilba, Tuross Head, Bodalla, Braidwood, Bungendore, Michelago, Adaminaby, Berridale, Jindabyne, Thredbo, Perisher, Charlotte Pass, Khancoban, Cabramurra, Tumut, Batlow, Gundagai, Wagga, Tarcutta, Holbrook

Selected labels

Yerong Creek, Mangoplah, Five Ways, Henty, Walla Walla, Morven, Gerogery, Jindera, Bandiana, Leneva, Kiewa, Kergunyah, Tangambalanga, Tallangatta, Bullioh, Granya, Koetong, Berringama, Lucyvale, Nariel, Biggara, Geehi, Tom Groggin, Thredbo, Dead Horse Gap, Falls Creek, Hotham Heights, Dinner Plain, Cobungra, Dargo, Tongio, Swifts Creek, Ensay, Doctors Flat, Cassilis, Bindi, Benambra, Hinnomunjie, Anglers Rest, Glen Wills, Glen Valley, Mitta Mitta, Eskdale, Dederang, Tallandoon, Running Creek, Coral Bank, Tawonga, Bogong, Harrietville, Smoko, Bright, Mount Hope, Wandiligong, Porepunkah, Myrtleford, Gapsted, Whorouly, Everton, Tarrawingee, Milawa, Oxley, Moyhu, Whitfield, Cheshunt

GREAT DIVIDING RANGE

SNOWY MOUNTAINS

KOSCIUSZKO NATIONAL PARK

ALPINE NATIONAL PARK

NEW SOUTH WALES

VICTORIA

GIPPSLAND

MONARO

PRINCES HWY

HUME HWY

MURRAY VALLEY HWY

GREAT ALPINE RD

SNOWY RIVER NATIONAL PARK

ERRINUNDRA NATIONAL PARK

CROAJINGOLONG NATIONAL PARK

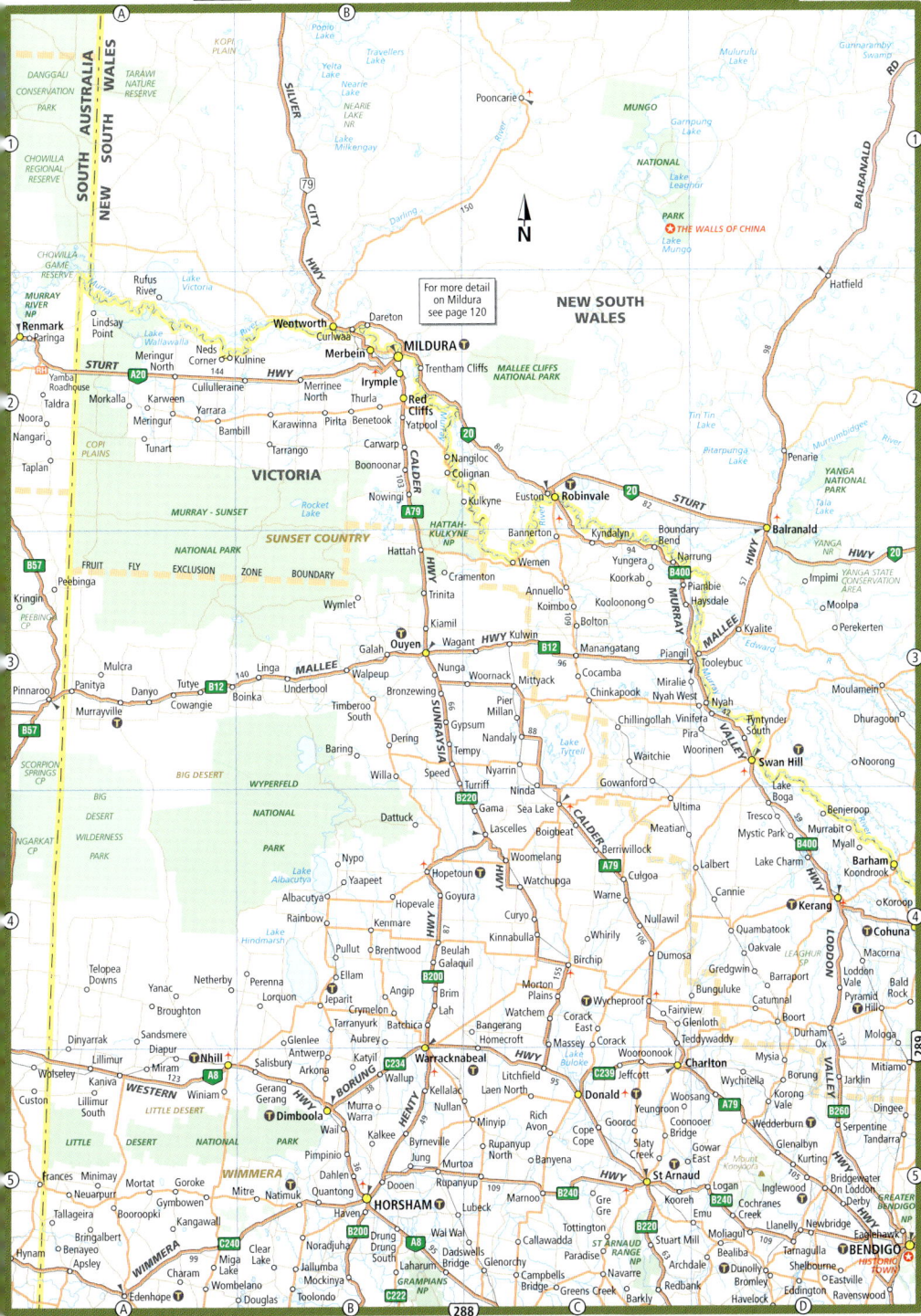

0 10 20 km

SOUTH AUSTRALIA
NEW SOUTH WALES
VICTORIA
NEW SOUTH WALES

For more detail on Mildura see page 120

N

THE WALLS OF CHINA

DANGGALI CONSERVATION PARK
CHOWILLA REGIONAL RESERVE
CHOWILLA GAME RESERVE
MURRAY RIVER NP

KOPI PLAIN
TARAWI NATURE RESERVE
Popio Lake
Yelta Lake
Nearie Lake
NEARIE LAKE NR
Lake Milkengay
Travellers Lake
Mulurulu Lake
Gunnaramby Swamp
MUNGO NATIONAL PARK
Lake Leaghur
Gampung Lake
Lake Mungo
Pooncarie
Hatfield

SILVER CITY HWY
BALRANALD RD

Renmark
Paringa
Rufus River
Lake Victoria
Lindsay Point
Wentworth
Curlwaa
Dareton
Neds Corner
Kulnine
MILDURA
Merbein
Irymple
Red Cliffs
Yatpool
Trentham Cliffs
MALLEE CLIFFS NATIONAL PARK

Yamba Roadhouse
Taldra
Morkalla
Meringur North
Meringur
Cullulleraine
Karween
Yarrara
Bambill
Karawinna
Pirlta
Benetook
Thurla
Merrinee North
Boonoonar
Nowingie
Carwarp
Nangiloc
Colignan
Kulkyne

Noora
Nangari
Taplan
COPI PLAINS
Tunart
Tarrango

CALDER HWY
SUNSET COUNTRY
MURRAY - SUNSET NATIONAL PARK
Rocket Lake

Euston
Robinvale
STURT HWY
Balranald
Bannerton
Kyndalyn
Boundary Bend
Narrung
YANGA NATIONAL PARK
YANGA NR
YANGA STATE CONSERVATION AREA
Penarie

Kringin
Peebinga
PEEBINGA CP
FRUIT FLY EXCLUSION ZONE BOUNDARY
Hattah
HATTAH-KULKYNE NP
Wemen
Yungera
Koorkab
Kooloonong
Impimi
Moolpa
Perekerten

Mulcra
Panitya
Linga
Danyo
Tutye
Boinka
Cowangie
Murrayville
B57
B12
MALLEE HWY
Underbool
Walpeup
Ouyen
Galah
Wagant
Nunga
Kulwin
Woornack
Mittyack
B12
Manangatang
Cocamba
Chinkapook
Miralie
Nyah West
Piangil
Tooleybuc
Moulamein
Dhuragoon

Cramenton
Trinita
Kiamil
Bronzewing
Timberoo South
Gypsum
Pier Millan
Nandaly
Chillingollah
Vinifera
Pira
Woorinen
Nyah
Tyntynder South
Noorong

Baring
Dering
Tempy
Speed
Willa
Turriff
Nyarrin
Lake Tyrrell
Waitchie
Gowanford
Swan Hill
Lake Boga
Benjeroop
Murrabit
Myall
Barham
Koondrook
Koroop
Cohuna

SCORPION SPRINGS CP
BIG DESERT
WYPERFELD NATIONAL PARK
BIG DESERT WILDERNESS PARK

Dattuck
Ninda
Gama
Sea Lake
Lascelles
Boigbeat
Ultima
Meatian
Tresco
Mystic Park
Lake Charm
Kerang
Quambatook
Oakvale
Macorna
Bald Rock

Nypo
Yaapeet
Hopetoun
Woomelang
Watchupga
Berriwillock
Lalbert
Cannie
Koorong
LODDON VALLEY

Albacutya
Lake Albacutya
Hopevale
Goyura
Warne
Culgoa
Nullawil
Gredgwin
Barraport
Loddon Vale
Pyramid Hill
Boort

Rainbow
Lake Hindmarsh
Kenmare
Curyo
Whirily
Dumosa
Buloke
Bunguluke
Catumnal
Durham Ox
Mologa

Pullut
Brentwood
Beulah
Galaquil
Kinnabulla
Birchip
Morton Plains
Fairview
Glenloth
Teddywaddy
Mysia
Mitiamo

Netherby
Perenna
Lorquon
Ellam
Jeparit
Angip
Brim
Watchem
Corack East
Wooroonook
Charlton
Wychitella
Borung
Korong Vale
Jarklin
Dingee

Telopea Downs
Yanac
Broughton
Sandsmere
Diapur
Miram
Crymelon
Tarranyurk
Batchica
Lah
Bangerang
Homecroft
Massey
Corack
Donald
Jeffcott
Woosang
Coonooer Bridge
Wedderburn
Glenalbyn
Kurting
Serpentine
Tandarra

Dinyarrak
Lillimur
Wolseley
Kaniva
Custon
Lillimur South
Nhill
Salisbury
Antwerp
Aubrey
Litchfield
Laen North
Yeungroon
Goorambat
Gowar East
Inglewood
On Loddon
Derby
Mitre

WESTERN
LITTLE DESERT
Gerang Gerang
Murra Warra
Katyil
Wallup
Kellalac
Nullan
Minyip
Rich Avon
Rupanyup North
Banyena
Slaty Creek
St Arnaud
Logan
Koreen
Emu
Moliagul
Dunolly
Tarnagulla
Eaglehawk
BENDIGO

Dimboola
Arkona
Kalkee
Dooen
Marnoo
Paradise
Navarre
Redbank
Bealiba
Llanelly
Newbridge
GREATER BENDIGO NP

Frances
Minimay
Mortat
Goroke
Gymbowen
Natimuk
Quantong
Dahlen
Lubeck
Gre Gre
Cochranes Creek
Shelbourne
Eastville

Neuarpur
Tallageira
Booroopki
Kangawall
Clear Lake
Noradjuha
Drung
Drung South
Wal Wal
Dadswells Bridge
Callawadda
ST ARNAUD RANGE NP
Tottington
Stuart Mill
B220
Bromley
Eddington
Ravenswood

Hynam
Bringalbert
Benayeo
Apsley
Charam
Miga Lake
Jallumba
Mockinya
Laharum
GRAMPIANS NP
Glenorchy
Campbells Bridge
Greens Creek
Barkly
Havelock

WIMMERA
Edenhope
Douglas
Toolondo
Wombelano

HORSHAM
Haven
Pimpinio
Jung
Murtoa
Rupanyup
Lubeck

WIMMERA HWY
HENTY HWY
BORUNG HWY
SUNRAYSIA HWY
CALDER HWY
MURRAY VALLEY HWY
MALLEE HWY
STURT HWY

INDEX

B

H

ACKNOWLEDGEMENTS

Much of the material in this book originally appeared in *Explore Australia 2010*, published by Explore Australia Publishing in 2009, where full acknowledgements for individual contributions appear.

The publisher would also like to acknowledge the help of the following people in the production of this edition:

Publications manager
Astrid Browne

Project manager
Melissa Krafchek

Design
Erika Budiman

Layout
Megan Ellis

Cartographers
Bruce McGurty, Emily Maffei, Jason Sankovic

Editor
Stephanie Pearson

Indexer
Fay Donlevy

Photo selection
Melissa Krafchek

Pre-press
PageSet Digital Print & Pre-press

Writers
Introduction by Rachel Pitts, Melissa Krafchek; Melbourne by Rachel Pitts, Melissa Krafchek, Michelle Bennett; Towns by Karina Biggs, Antonia Semler; Where to Eat and Where to Stay by Tricia Welsh

Photography credits
Cover
Twelve Apostles, Port Campbell National Park (David Sainty)

Back cover
Puffing Billy railway, near Belgrave (Tourism Victoria)

Polaroid image
Tolarno Hotel, St Kilda, Melbourne (Courtesy of Tolarno Hotel)

Full cover background
©iStockphoto.com/saffiresblue

Title page
Rochford Wines cellar door, Coldstream (Tourism Victoria)

Contents
Bathing Boxes, Mornington Peninsula (Peter Dunphy/ Tourism Victoria)

Other images (left to right where more than one image appears on a page):
Pages iv–1 JB; 3 AC; 4–5 JD; 9 JB; 12 Tim Webster/TV; 15 David Hannah/TV; 17 & 19 BB/LT; 22 Courtesy of St Kilda Pier Kiosk; 31 (a) Geoff Murray (b) BP; 33 BP; 35 Courtesy of Mornington Peninsula Tourism Inc.; 37 BP; 39 Mike Leonard/ AUS; 41 AS; 43 BB/LT; 45 AusGeo; 47 & 49 AC; 51 Dallas & John Heaton/AUS; 53 Hans & Judy Beste/LT; 55 AS; 56 JD; 66 TV; 71 AC; 77 JLR/AUS; 84 JB/EAP; 89 Simon Griffiths; 100 Jon Barter/AUS; 105 AusGeo; 113 Hans & Judy Beste/ LT; 121 AC; 144 & 156 AS; 163 Tim James; 193 Zoe Geshen; 201 MK; 202 Mark Chew/TV; 209 Courtesy of Plunkett Fowles; 220 Courtesy of Hargreaves Hill Brewing Company; 223 Courtesy of Tolarno Hotel; 242 MK; 249 Courtesy of Mt Rael Retreat; 273 Courtesy of Campaspe Country House.

Abbreviations
AC Andrew Chapman
AUS Auscape International
AusGeo Australian Geographic
AS Australian Scenics
BB Bill Belson
BP Bruce Postle
EAP Explore Australia Publishing
JD Jeff Drewitz
JB John Baker
JLR Jean-Marc La Roque
LS Len Stewart
LT Lochman Transparencies
MK Melissa Krafchek
TV Tourism Victoria

Explore Australia Publishing Pty Ltd
85 High Street,
Prahran, VIC 3181

This ninth edition published by Explore Australia
Publishing Pty Ltd, 2010

First published by Penguin Books Australia Ltd 1997
Second edition published 1999
Third edition published 2001
Fourth edition published by Explore Australia Publishing
    2002
Fifth edition published 2004
Sixth edition published 2005
Seventh edition published as *Holiday in Victoria* 2007
Eighth edition published 2009

10 9 8 7 6 5 4 3 2 1

ISBN 978 1 74117 283 6

Printed and bound in China by C & C Offset Printing Co. Ltd

Publisher's Note: Every effort has been made to ensure
that the information in this book is accurate at the time
of going to press. The publisher welcomes information
and suggestions for correction or improvement.
Email: info@exploreaustralia.net.au

Publisher's Disclaimers: The publisher cannot accept
responsibility for any errors or omissions. The
representation on the maps of any road or track is not
necessarily evidence of public right of way.

TRAVELLING TIMES & DISTANCE CHART

Victoria

	Ararat	Bairnsdale	Ballarat	Bendigo	Bright	Cowes	Daylesford	Geelong	Halls Gap	Hamilton	Hopetoun	Horsham	Lakes Entrance
Ararat		6:00	1:15	2:15	5:40	4:30	1:45	2:35	0:40	1:35	2:55	1:25	6:
Bairnsdale	484		5:00	5:40	4:00	4:20	5:05	4:45	6:45	7:35	8:45	7:20	0:
Ballarat	93	388		1:50	4:40	3:30	0:40	1:25	2:00	2:30	4:00	2:35	4:
Bendigo	158	423	124		3:45	4:10	1:10	2:45	3:00	3:50	3:30	3:10	6:
Bright	502	227	412	310		5:50	4:25	4:30	6:20	7:10	7:10	6:55	4:
Cowes	343	273	252	296	469		3:30	3:10	5:10	6:00	7:10	5:50	4:
Daylesford	133	391	43	76	353	251		1:35	2:20	3:10	4:10	3:05	5:
Geelong	182	349	86	210	386	212	101		3:15	3:15	5:15	3:55	5:
Halls Gap	48	532	142	206	551	391	175	242		1:20	2:45	1:10	7:
Hamilton	106	596	180	264	615	455	240	234	96		3:25	1:45	8:
Hopetoun	194	679	289	257	520	538	294	389	183	248		1:45	9:
Horsham	95	577	192	218	524	440	225	278	76	132	119		7:
Lakes Entrance	520	36	429	473	234	308	428	389	568	633	709	615	
Mallacoota	718	234	627	671	411	506	626	587	766	830	907	815	20
Mansfield	393	257	302	213	177	278	250	277	441	505	461	430	29
Melbourne	206	277	111	146	326	142	113	72	253	318	389	300	3
Mildura	413	825	460	402	616	688	462	546	378	443	195	305	8
Moe	338	149	247	291	377	131	246	207	386	450	527	433	18
Portland	192	639	265	350	672	498	325	289	182	85	333	215	6
Sale	416	69	325	369	296	204	324	285	464	528	605	513	10
Shepparton	279	380	276	121	175	332	193	251	327	387	337	336	4
Sorrento	306	334	222	262	434	145	217	178	357	281	494	400	3
Swan Hill	251	622	284	187	400	481	255	357	250	356	135	227	6
Traralgon	367	118	276	320	386	155	275	236	415	479	556	464	1
Wangaratta	389	359	338	237	77	394	274	313	477	541	437	452	3
Warrnambool	145	534	174	298	579	405	215	185	169	109	352	234	5
Wodonga	498	303	407	306	96	463	343	382	512	610	492	523	3
Wonthaggi	337	232	246	290	463	41	245	206	385	449	526	432	2
Yarrawonga	461	391	370	202	133	426	306	345	509	573	413	433	4

Distances between towns are shown below the white line (km). Travel times between towns a
Distances/travel times on this chart have been calculated over main roads and do not necessar